Microsoft® Excel VBA Programming for the Absolute Beginner

Second Edition

DUANE BIRNBAUM

THOMSON
COURSE TECHNOLOGY
Professional ■ Technical ■ Reference

ISBN: 1-59200-729-5

Library of Congress Catalog Card Number: 2004114911

Printed in the United States of America

05 06 07 08 09 BH 10 9 8 7 6 5 4 3 2

THOMSON
COURSE TECHNOLOGY™
Professional ■ Technical ■ Reference

Thomson Course Technology PTR,
a division of Thomson Course Technology
25 Thomson Place
Boston, MA 02210
http://www.courseptr.com

Publisher and General Manager of Course Technology PTR:
Stacy L. Hiquet

Associate Director of Marketing:
Sarah O'Donnell

Marketing Manager:
Heather Hurley

Manager of Editorial Services:
Heather Talbot

Acquisitions Editor:
Mitzi Koontz

Senior Editor:
Mark Garvey

Marketing Coordinator:
Jordan Casey

Project Editor:
Scott Harris/Argosy Publishing

Technical Reviewer:
Arlie Hartman

PTR Editorial Services Coordinator:
Elizabeth Furbish

Copy Editor:
D. A. de la Mora

Interior Layout Tech:
Shawn Morningstar

Cover Designer:
Mike Tanamachi

CD-ROM Producer:
Keith Davenport

Indexer:
Nancy Fulton

Proofreader:
Jan Cocker

ACKNOWLEDGMENTS

First, a special thank you goes out to my family:

- My wife Jill, for putting up with the late nights and weekends I spent writing
- My 8-year old son Aaron, who thinks it's cool that his Dad writes such long books with so many words, but wishes it included chapters on dragons or wizards
- My 5-year old son Joshua, who wished his Dad would have played more games with him instead of working on this book. Don't worry, Josh; because of the guilt trip you sent me on, I'll more than make it up to you.

I would also like to thank Scott Harris at Argosy Publishing, Mitzi Koontz, and all of the other contributors associated with Course Technology for their invaluable help in putting this book together.

About the Author

Duane Birnbaum began programming in graduate school, where he wrote custom software for interfacing the electronic equipment required for his experiments and analyzing the data obtained from them. Since completing his Ph.D. in physical chemistry in 1991, he has worked as a post-doctoral and research scientist in academia and industry while continuing to teach on a part-time basis. He has been teaching courses in introductory programming, database design, and data analysis in the Computer Science department at Indiana University/Purdue University at Indianapolis for the past 8 years.

Contents

INTRODUCTION

Visual Basic for Applications (VBA for short) is a programming environment designed to work with Microsoft's Office applications (Word, Excel, Access, and PowerPoint). Components in each application (for example, worksheets or documents) are exposed as objects to the programmer to use and manipulate to a desired end. Almost anything you can do through the normal use of the Office application can also be automated through programming.

VBA is a complete programming language, but you can't use it outside the application in which it is integrated. This does not mean VBA can be integrated only with Office programs. Any software vendor that decides to implement VBA can include it with their application.

VBA is relatively easy to learn, but to use it in a new application, you must first become familiar with the *object model* of the application. For example, the `Document` and `Dictionary` objects are specific to the Word object model, whereas the `Workbook`, `Worksheet`, and `Range` objects are specific to the Excel object model. As you proceed through this book, you will see that the Excel object model is fairly extensive; however, if you are familiar with Excel, you will find that using these objects is generally straightforward.

WHY VBA?

As a beginning language, VBA will suit your needs well. VBA is not as vast as many popular languages because such extensiveness is simply unnecessary. VBA was built to work with and extend the abilities of Office applications, so it doesn't need the substance of a programming language used to build full-blown applications from scratch. The relative simplicity of VBA makes it less intimidating and easier for you to learn. VBA, however, does share many of the programming constructs common to all languages, so it also serves as a great introduction to programming. For these reasons, and the fact that Excel is the most popular spreadsheet application available, I am writing this book.

As a scientist, I never really gave business-orientated Excel a chance. The earliest versions of Excel didn't even have graphical capabilities; even after they were added, Excel still couldn't match other spreadsheet applications geared toward the scientist. After ignoring Excel for several years, I started a new job where Excel was the only spreadsheet application available; it was then that I discovered that it uses a macro language based on the already very popular Visual Basic. I started writing programs to handle some of the routine data analyses required around the lab, and the time I have saved using these programs has sold me on Excel as a valuable component in any lab or business.

Who Should Read This Book?

The goal of this book is to help you learn VBA programming with Excel. No prior programming experience is required or expected. Although you do not have to be an Excel user, you must have a good understanding of the basic tools involved in using any spreadsheet application. This includes a basic understanding of **ranges** and **cell references**, **formulas**, **built-in functions**, and **charts**. I ask my students at the start of every semester if they know how to use Excel. At least 90 percent of them say they are very comfortable with the application. Within two weeks of the start of the semester it is clear that no more than 10 percent of the class can write a proper formula—one that takes advantage of absolute and relative references, and built-in functions. Furthermore, fewer than 5 percent know anything about chart types and the kind of analyses they should be used in. If you're not comfortable with spreadsheet applications or it's been a while since you have used a spreadsheet, then I recommend you consider purchasing another introductory book on how to use the Excel application prior to learning how to program in VBA for Excel. In addition to spreadsheets, I also expect you to have a basic understanding of the Windows operating system.

What's in This Book and What Is Required?

I developed the programs in this book using Excel 2003 for Windows. Although Excel and VBA don't change much from one version to the next, I can't guarantee that the programs in this book will execute without error in earlier versions of Excel. With each new version of Excel, VBA is updated with new objects, and existing objects are expanded with new properties and methods. If I use even one new object, property, or method specific to VBA-Excel 2003 in a program, then it will generate an error if executed in a previous version of Excel; therefore, you need Excel 2003—with VBA installed and activated—to use this book.

The chapter projects in this book feature the development of games using VBA with Excel. This is somewhat unusual in the sense that prior to writing this book, I had never seen an Excel application that runs any kind of a game; however, it does serve to make programming more fun. After all, what's the first thing anybody does when a new computer is purchased?

The answer: find the games that are installed and start playing. With this book, you get to write the program and then play the game. It actually works quite well. The games developed in this book illustrate the use of basic programming techniques and structures found in all programming languages as well as all of the common (and some less common) components in Excel.

What's on the CD-ROM?

The CD that accompanies this book includes the following:

- The source code for the longer sample programs and the chapter projects discussed in the book, including all supporting image and sound files
- Audacity, an open-source audio editor
- The GIMP for Windows, a photo retouching and image composition program
- POV-Ray, a tool for creating high-quality three-dimensional graphics
- SawCutter, a tool for designing sounds
- cEdit Professional, an advanced, alternative text editor and IDE

Visual Basic for Applications with Excel

In this first chapter, I introduce you to the programming tools available in Excel. These tools include the VBA IDE (Integrated Development Environment), controls and functions available through the main Excel application, and VBA on-line help. After your introduction to the VBA programming environment, I take you through a very short and simple program that calculates some basic statistics from a sample data set. The program displays the statistics in a worksheet formatted with a large font, bright colors, and a border to complete the *Colorful Stats* project.

Specifically this chapter will cover:

- Installing and enabling VBA
- The VBA IDE and components within
- Programming tools within Excel
- Using VBA on-line help

Project: Colorful Stats

The project in this chapter is short and simple, but will serve as your first introduction to the VBA programming environment, ActiveX controls, event-driven programming, and using VBA to interact with your spreadsheet. A view of the *Colorful Stats* spreadsheet is shown in Figure 1.1.

In the Real World

Event-driven programming **refers to the creation of a program that is designed to run when the user generates a stimulus. For example, a keystroke or a mouse click may trigger specific pieces of a program to execute. The event-driven programming model has been popular for years (since the first graphical-based operating systems such as Windows and Macintosh were introduced) and is now commonplace. It is vastly superior to older programs that did not allow for much user interaction because the programmers dictated the flow of the program. In event-driven programming, the user dictates the flow of the program and it is up to programmers to anticipate the user's needs.**

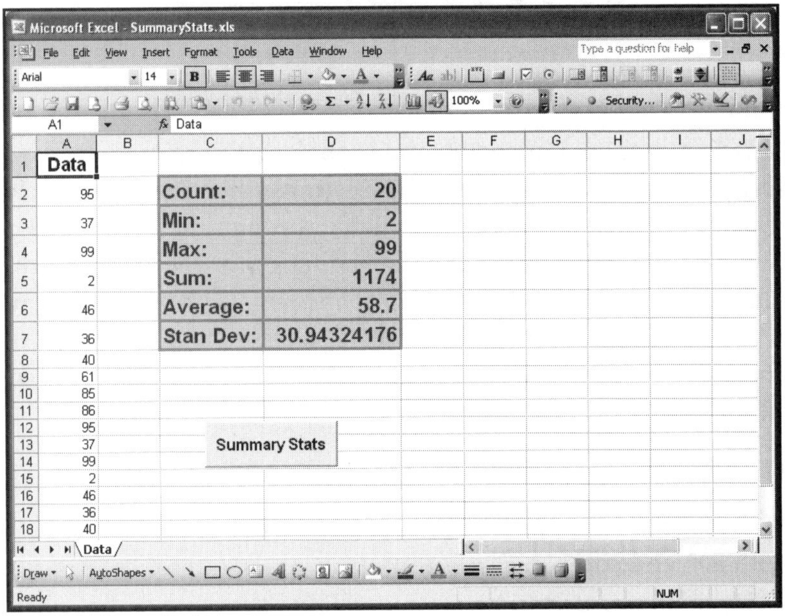

FIGURE 1.1

The *Colorful Stats* project.

Don't concern yourself with syntax (the rules of the VBA language) at this time. In subsequent chapters, I will show you the tools needed to build VBA projects. For right now, I just want you to see how easy it is to make something work and recognize that many of the keywords we use in VBA programming projects in this book are already familiar to you as an Excel user.

Keywords are words used by the programming language for a special purpose and therefore are reserved. This means you cannot use a keyword in your program for anything other than what was designed into the language.

Installing and Enabling VBA

Unfortunately, there are enough unscrupulous programmers out in the world that security is of paramount importance for your computer. Computer viruses are common and, like technology in general, are becoming increasingly more complex. Macro language viruses such as those written in VBA are relatively easy to write—even for a beginning programmer. As a result, Microsoft has added several levels of security to its Office programs in order to protect against macro viruses. The first level of security Microsoft has implemented is simply to disable macro language support for its Office programs. Disabling macro language support is now the standard for the normal installation of Office or any of its component programs.

If items such as add-ins, wizards, and the VBA project files on this book's accompanying CD do not function, then your Excel program was either installed without VBA or with VBA disabled. You must install VBA and enable macro language support before you can access the VBA IDE and create your own projects or use any of the aforementioned tools.

To install or enable VBA, you must insert the CD that contains the Excel program into your computer and run the Office/Excel setup program by doing the following:

1. Double-click the Add/Remove Programs icon in the Microsoft Windows Control Panel (found on the Start menu).
2. If you installed Excel as part of Microsoft Office, click Microsoft Office (edition and version) in the currently installed programs box, and then click the Change button. If you installed Excel individually, click Excel (edition and version) in the currently installed programs box, and then click the Change button.
3. On the features to install screen in the Setup program, click the plus sign (+) next to Office Shared Features.
4. Select Visual Basic for Applications, click the arrow next to your selection, and then click Run from My Computer.
5. In addition, you should install the VBA help files by selecting Visual Basic Help and Run from My Computer.

After the installation is complete, you may also need to change the macro security setting in Excel before you can run any VBA programs. To change the macro security setting in Excel, do the following:

1. Select Tools, Macro, Security from the Excel application window (see Figure 1.2).
2. Set the security level to Medium or Low to enable macros.

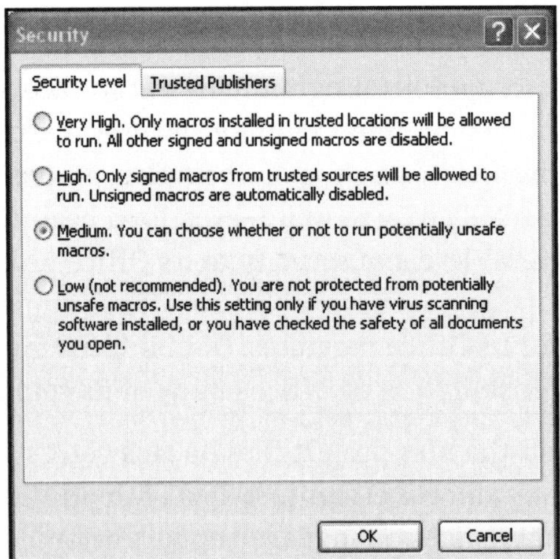

FIGURE 1.2

Macro security level settings in Excel.

I recommend setting the macro security level to Medium so that you will be able to run (and therefore test) your VBA programs, yet still receive a warning message that macros are present in the file. With the macro security level set to Medium, you will always know if a macro is present in an Excel file, and then you can decide if it's safe. Never enable macros attached to an Excel file from an untrustworthy source! Note that setting the security level to High will disable any macro attached to an Excel file that has not been digitally signed.

IN THE REAL WORLD

To ensure that third-party software written for Excel 2003 is from a trustworthy source, Microsoft allows programmers to digitally sign a file or a VBA project by using a digital signature. A digital signature is an electronic authentication mechanism for a program or document. A digital signature confirms that the program originated from the signer and has not been altered. To digitally sign macro projects, you must install a digital certificate. A digital certificate attached to a program vouches for its authenticity. Digital certificates are obtained from commercial vendors such as Verisign who act as a trusted third party in the transaction. When you set the macro security level to High, you can run macros written by programmers if they are digitally signed and have been added to your list of trusted sources.

The VBA Integrated Development Environment (IDE)

Before learning how to program in VBA, you have to learn how to use the software required for creating your projects. The VBA development software is included with each component of the Microsoft Office suite of programs, including Excel. Starting the VBA development software places you in the VBA programming environment IDE, which provides you with a number of tools for use in the development of your project.

In the Real World

An IDE is software used by programmers for rapid application development (RAD). IDE's are available for numerous programming languages and are often quite expensive to purchase (several hundred dollars or more for a single license). The price is worth it because IDE's provide tools that enable programmers to develop applications quickly, saving them considerable time and money. Yet, the most important component of any development software is the compiler, which for many languages can be obtained at no cost. The compiler converts your program into the binary code your computer understands. If you have the compiler, all you really need to create an application—albeit with considerably more effort—is a text editor. Excel comes with its own IDE and VBA compiler, thus making it more of a value than you may realize.

Getting to the IDE from Excel

Before you begin creating projects with VBA you must know your way around the IDE. You can access the IDE from Excel in a couple of different ways. In Excel: select Tools, Macro, Visual Basic Editor (as shown in Figure 1.3); or use the keystroke Alt + F11.

Alternatively, select the Visual Basic toolbar from the View/Toolbars menu item in Excel. When the toolbar is displayed, select the Visual Basic Editor icon found in the middle of the toolbar (see Figure 1.4).

Components of the IDE

After opening the VBA IDE you may find yourself looking at a window similar to what is shown in Figure 1.5. This figure shows the VBA IDE and some of the tools that can be used to create projects.

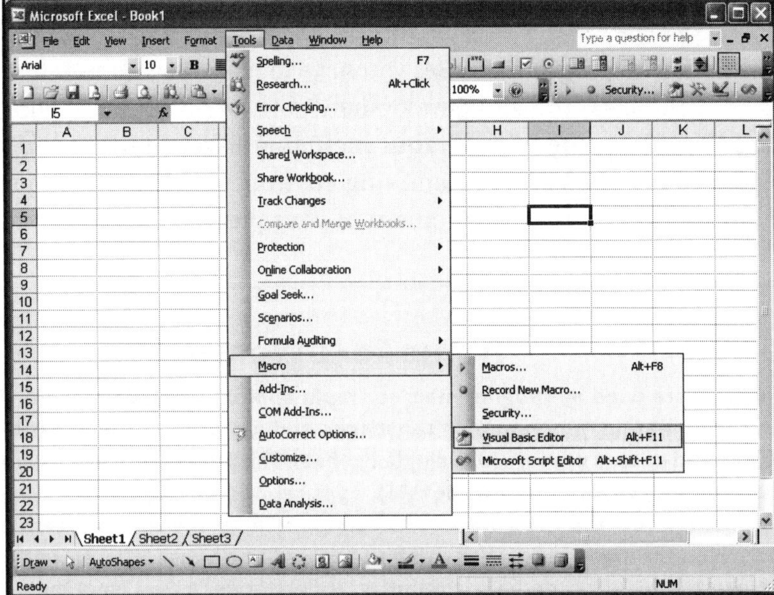

FIGURE 1.3

Accessing the VBA IDE from the Tools menu in Excel.

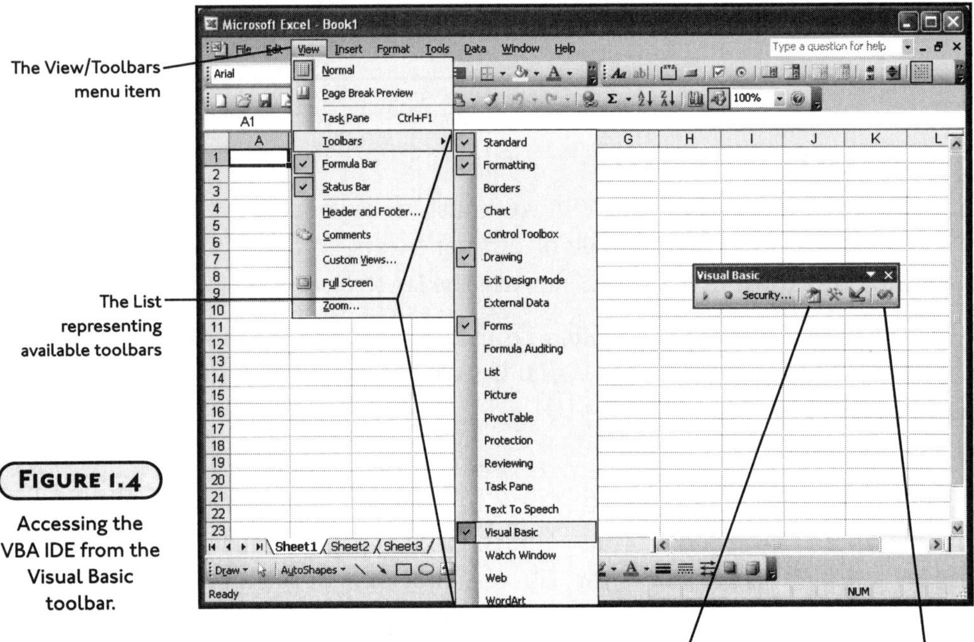

FIGURE 1.4

Accessing the VBA IDE from the Visual Basic toolbar.

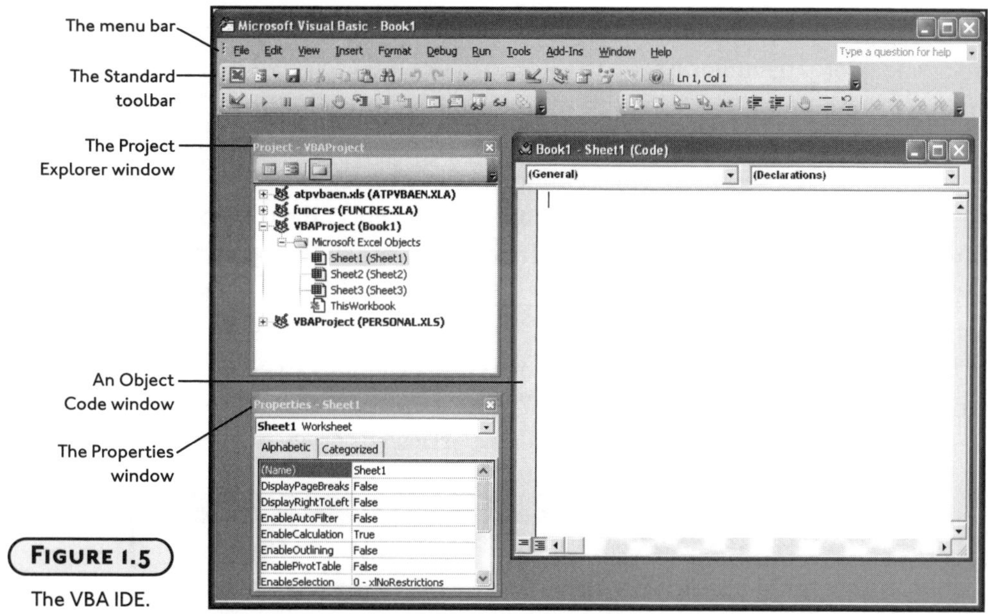

FIGURE 1.5

The VBA IDE.

Like in most applications, there is a menu bar across the top of the window. You may only recognize a few items that exist within this menu, but don't worry. I'll show you the function of most of these items as we proceed through the book.

The Standard toolbar is one of four toolbars available from the IDE. Like any toolbar, its function is to give the user fast access to common tools available within the application. Again, I will explain the use of many of these functions, as well as the use of other toolbars, as we proceed through the book.

Of particular importance is the Project Explorer window, shown in the upper left corner of the IDE window in Figure 1.5. The Project Explorer lists all projects currently open, including those opened by Excel upon startup. The Project Explorer also lists the components of any opened projects. For example, Figure 1.5 shows that there is currently one project, called `Book1`, open, and that this project contains four Excel objects: `Sheet1`, `Sheet2`, `Sheet3`, and `ThisWorkbook`. I will discuss Excel objects in detail in Chapter 5. For right now, recognize that these objects represent familiar components from Excel (the workbook and worksheets it contains).

If I open more workbooks in Excel, or add more worksheets to a currently open workbook in Excel, then their names will appear on the object list in the Project Explorer window.

Just below the Project Explorer window in Figure 1.5 is the Properties window. The Properties window displays a list of attributes or properties of the currently selected object in the Project Explorer window. These properties are used to manipulate the behavior and appearance of the object to which they belong. The properties of `Sheet1` are displayed in Figure 1.5 because it has been selected in the Project Explorer. Choosing a different object will result in a different properties list in the Properties window, as not all objects have the same properties. As a simple example in manipulating the properties of a worksheet, open a new workbook in Excel, note the name of your workbook and any worksheets it contains (do not change any names), then open the VBA IDE. Once in the IDE, display the Project Explorer and Properties windows. If the Project Explorer and Properties windows are not already displayed you can access them through the View menu item (see Figure 1.6). You can also use the keystrokes Ctrl+R and F4 to access the Project Explorer and Properties windows, respectively.

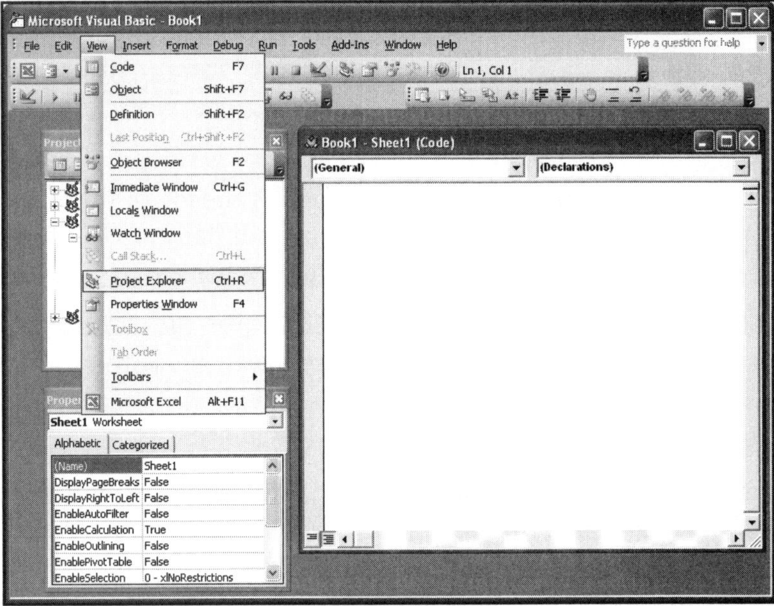

FIGURE 1.6

Accessing the Project Explorer and Properties windows.

Once the Project Explorer window is displayed, find the project that represents the workbook you opened while in Excel (probably `Book1` or `Book2`). If the components of the workbook you opened in Excel are not displayed, click the + sign next to the Microsoft Excel Objects folder directly underneath the project name. Next, find the object labeled `Sheet1`, select it with your mouse and then turn your attention to the Properties window. Scroll down the Properties window until you come to the `Name` property (the one without the parentheses around it). Delete the text entered to the right of the `Name` property and enter `MySheet`. Figure 1.7 illustrates how to find the `Name` property.

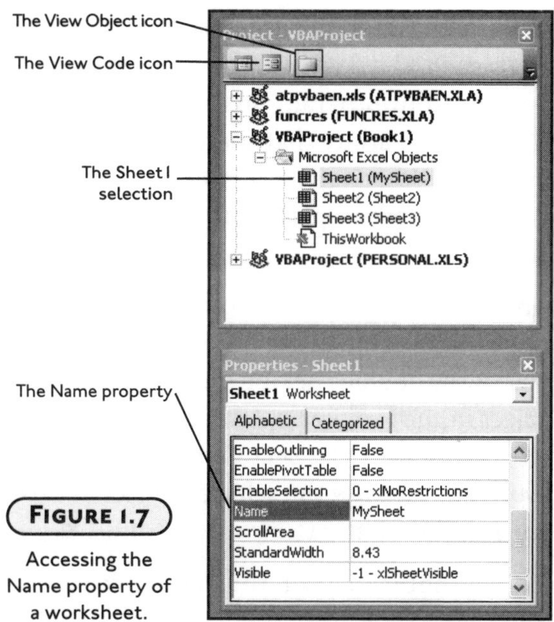

FIGURE 1.7

Accessing the Name property of a worksheet.

Toggle back to Excel by pressing Alt+F11, or select it from the taskbar in Windows. You will note that the name of `Sheet1` has now been replaced with `MySheet` in your Excel workbook, as shown in Figure 1.8.

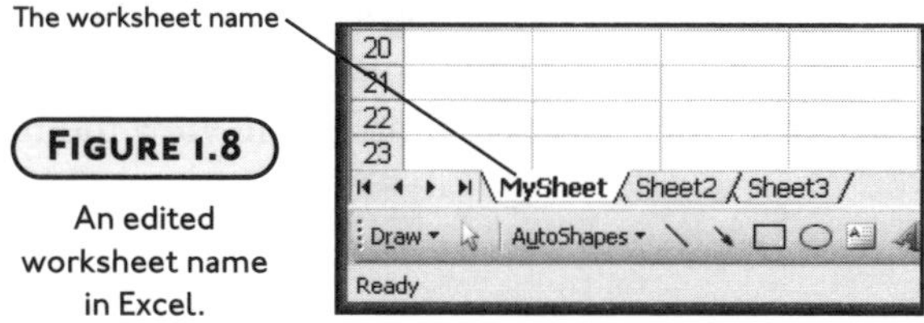

FIGURE 1.8

An edited worksheet name in Excel.

See how easy it is to alter the properties of a worksheet in Excel using VBA? As VBA developers, however, we will seldom, if ever, alter the properties of a workbook or worksheet at design time. The bulk of the work affecting workbooks and worksheets will occur at run time; however, we will alter properties of ActiveX controls at design time.

Design time refers to project development and the manipulation of object properties using the VBA IDE prior to running any code. Conversely *run time* will refer to the manipulation of object properties using a program; thus, the properties of the object do not change until the code is executed.

Finally, I will show you one more component of the VBA IDE. If you look back at Figure 1.5 you will also see a standard code window. Windows such as these are used as containers for your program(s). This is where you type in the code for your program, so these windows are essentially text editors very similar to Notepad. You must be aware that there are pre-defined code windows for specific Excel objects, namely the workbook (for example, `ThisWorkbook`) and the worksheets (for example, `Sheet1`). The code window displayed in Figure 1.5 represents `Sheet1` contained within the workbook `Book1`.

You will also be able to add components to your project and they will have their own code windows. I will explain how to use code windows more thoroughly as we proceed through this book. For now, know that you can open a code window by double clicking on any object listed in the Project Explorer. You can also select the object in the Project Explorer and click on the View Code icon at the top left of the window (refer to Figure 1.7), select Code from the tools menu, or press F7 (refer to Figure 1.6). Note that you can also view the selected object in Excel by selecting the appropriate item from these same locations (refer to Figures 1.7 and 1.8).

There are, of course, more components to the VBA IDE, but I've shown you enough to get you started for now. As the need arises, I will introduce more tools from the IDE that will aid in the development of various projects.

Programming Components within Excel

Not everything of interest to the VBA programmer can be found in the VBA IDE. There are a few programming-related components that you can access from the Excel application. The components I am referring to are the Macro items found under the Tools menu, and three of the available toolbars—Visual Basic, Control Toolbox, and Forms—found in the View menu in Excel.

Macro Selection

Now that you've had an introduction to the VBA IDE, it's time to look at development tools accessed directly from Excel. To begin, take a closer look at the Macro selection from the Tools menu, shown in Figure 1.3. Notice two other items displayed in Figure 1.3 that I have not yet discussed: Macros and Record New Macro. Essentially the Record Macro tool will allow you to create a VBA program by simply selecting various tasks in Excel through the normal interface. The Record Macro tool is quite helpful, as you will see in Chapter 4 when I discuss it in detail. The Macros menu item will simply display a dialog box with a list of some or all of the currently loaded VBA programs. Again I will explain the Macro menu item in more detail later in the book, but for now, remember that it is one way to access and run desired VBA programs. Figure 1.9 shows the Macro dialog box.

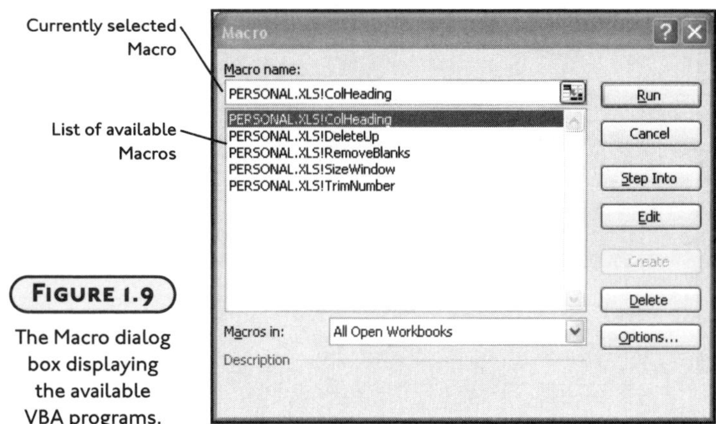

FIGURE 1.9

The Macro dialog box displaying the available VBA programs.

Macros typically refer to programs that are recorded as the user executes a series of tasks from the normal application interface. They are useful when a user repeatedly performs the same tasks in Excel. Instead of having to repeat tasks, the user can simply record his/her actions once, then "play back" the macro when he/she needs to repeat the same series of tasks. However, it is possible to access programs that were not recorded through the Macro menu item, thus I will use the term *macro* to refer to both recorded programs and those programs written from scratch.

The Visual Basic Toolbar

The Visual Basic toolbar shown in Figure 1.4 provides another set of tools for the VBA developer. You have already seen how selecting the Visual Basic Editor icon from this toolbar gives you access to the VBA IDE. There are several other useful items on the Visual Basic toolbar, including Run Macro, Record Macro, and Design Mode, that I will discuss later. Also included on the Visual Basic toolbar is an icon for the Control Toolbox, denoted by the crossed hammer and wrench. The Control Toolbox can also be accessed via the Toolbars item on the View menu.

The Control Toolbox (refer to Figure 1.10) provides you with ActiveX controls which are graphical tools, such as a Check Box or Command Button, that may be associated with a macro. The Text Box, Command Button, Label, and Image Control are just some of the ActiveX controls available and are specifically labeled in Figure 1.10. You place controls on a worksheet by first clicking on the desired control and then drawing it onto the worksheet. Start by selecting the Command Button control and drawing it on a worksheet as shown in Figure 1.11.

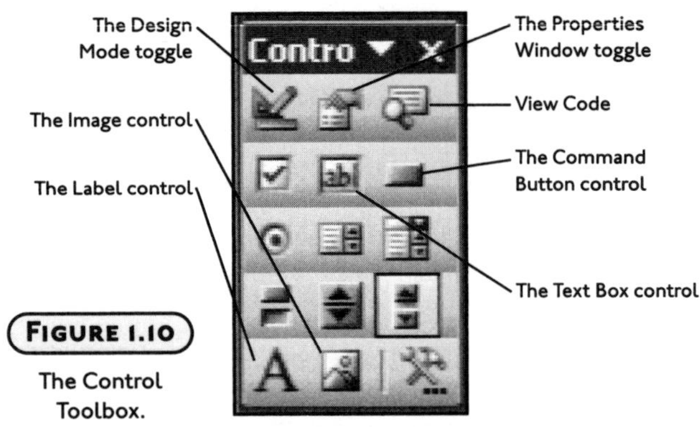

FIGURE 1.10

The Control Toolbox.

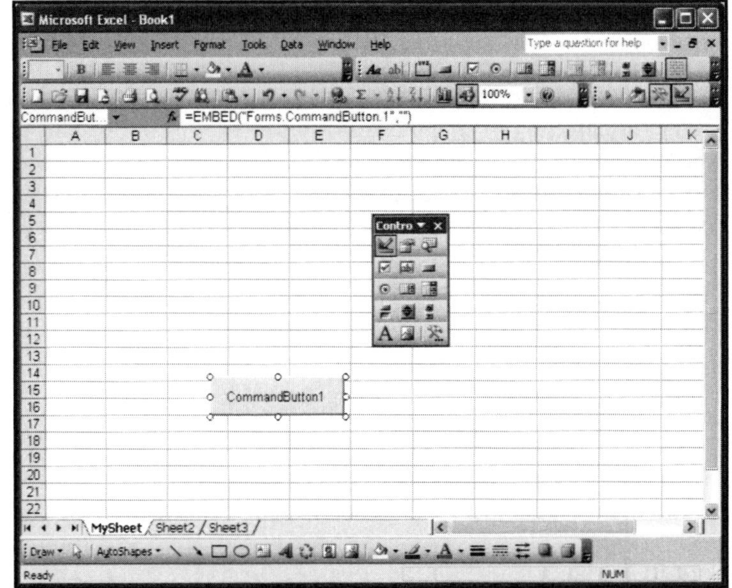

FIGURE 1.11

The Command Button control placed on a worksheet.

After the Command Button is placed on the worksheet, you will notice that it is selected and the application is currently in Design Mode (check that the Design Mode icon in the upper left corner of the Control Toolbox appears "pressed in"). You can access the properties of the Command Button control while in Design Mode. With the Command Button control selected while in Design Mode, select the Properties icon from the Control Toolbox. A window much like the Properties window in the VBA IDE will appear. The Properties window lists all the attributes or properties used to describe the Command Button control. Figure 1.12 shows the Properties window.

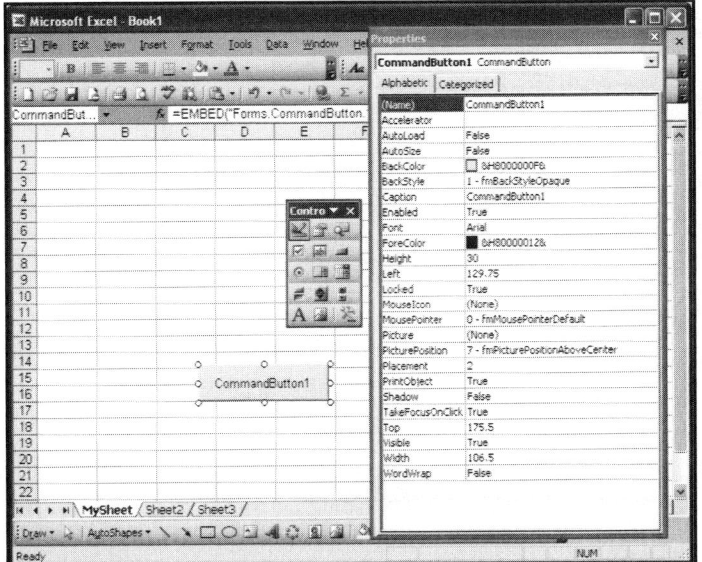

FIGURE 1.12

The Properties window of the Command Button control.

In the Properties window of the Command Button control change the `Caption` property to `Click Me` and then notice how the new caption is displayed on the control. You should also change the `Name` property to something like `cmdColorChange`. The prefix `cmd` references the type of control (Command Button) and the rest of the name refers to the function of the program that is triggered when the button is pressed. You can also play with some of the other properties such as `Font`, `ForeColor`, `BackColor`, `Width`, and `Height` to change the appearance of the control. You can even display a picture within the Command Button control through the `Picture` property, and then select an image file from your computer.

The `Name` property is an important property of any ActiveX control. The value of the `Name` property should be changed to something meaningful as soon as the control is added to the worksheet. Typically, an abbreviated word telling us the type of control (the `cmd` at the beginning of the name above denotes a Command Button) and its function in the program will work well. The `Name` property of an ActiveX control should be changed if you refer to it in your program. A meaningful name will help you remember it, as well as make the code more readable.

Once the appearance of your Command Button control is to your liking, select the View Code icon from the Control Toolbox, or double click on the Command Button control to access the code window. You will be taken immediately to the VBA IDE. Now it's time to make the Command Button control functional, and you can only do that by adding code to its code window. Figure 1.13 shows the code window for the Command Button control.

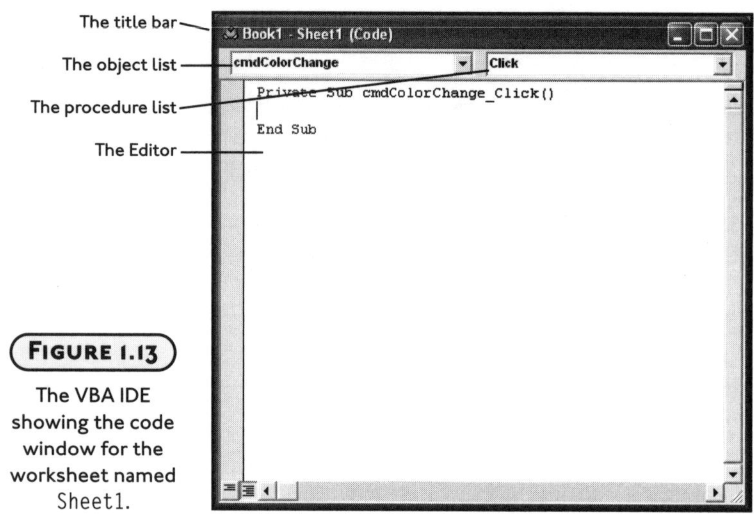

FIGURE 1.13

The VBA IDE showing the code window for the worksheet named `Sheet1`.

The title bar tells us the object to which this code window belongs. In this case, the code window belongs to the worksheet named `Sheet1` in the workbook named `Book1`. This is because I placed the Command Button control on `Sheet1` of `Book1` in the Excel application. You may recall that I changed the name of the worksheet in Excel to `MySheet`, but the name of the worksheet as it will have to be referenced in code is still `Sheet1`. In the upper left corner of the code window is a dropdown list box containing the names of all objects contained within the selected worksheet. The name of the Command Button control is displayed because the cursor in the editor is within an event procedure of this Command Button control.

Event procedures are self-contained blocks of code that require some type of stimulus in order to run. The stimulus often comes directly from the user (for example, a mouse click), but may also result from another piece of code.

Event procedures are predefined for ActiveX controls and other Excel objects, such as workbooks and worksheets. All event procedures for the selected object are listed in the upper right corner of the code window in a dropdown list box. I will discuss event procedures in more depth in Chapter 3. For now, just take a look at the `Click()` event. The `Click()` event is a very common event procedure that is built into most ActiveX controls. Any code placed within the predefined procedure will trigger when the user clicks once on the object—in this case, the Command Button control named `cmdColorChange`. The procedure is defined as listed in Figure 1.13 with the following two lines of code:

```
Private Sub cmdColorChange_Click()
End Sub
```

The name of the procedure will always be the name of the object with an underscore followed by the name of the event. You cannot change the name of a predefined event procedure without changing the Name property of the object. If you do change the name of the event procedure, the code within the procedure will not run when you want it to. The keyword Sub is required and is used as the defining opening of any procedure—event-type or programmer-defined. Private is an optional keyword; I'll discuss it in Chapter 3. The second line End Sub is always used to close a procedure. Now type the following lines of code within the Click() event procedure of the Command Button control named cmdColorChange.

```
Range("A1").Select
Cells.Interior.ColorIndex = Int(Rnd * 56) + 1
```

These two lines will select cell A1 on the worksheet and set the fill color of all cells in the worksheet to one of fifty-six possible colors. This is the equivalent of a user first selecting all the cells in a worksheet and then changing the fill color from the formatting toolbar in the Excel application. The color of the cells is chosen randomly and will change with each click of the Command Button control because the above code will run once with each click event. So the entire procedure now looks like the following.

```
Private Sub cmdColorChange_Click()
    Range("A1").Select
    Cells.Interior.ColorIndex = Int(Rnd * 56) + 1
End Sub
```

Return to the Excel application and exit Design Mode by toggling the icon on the Control Toolbox (refer to Figure 1.10). Now test the program by clicking on the Command Button control. The color of all cells in the worksheet will change color with each click. Figure 1.14 shows an example of my worksheet after one click on the Command Button control.

You can save the workbook as you would an Excel workbook. The Command Button control and event procedure code will be saved with the workbook.

Getting Help with VBA

I can't emphasize enough how important it is that you become comfortable with the on-line help in the VBA IDE (not to mention in the Excel application). The on-line help provides fast access to solutions for any programming problems you have with your project. Books make good resources and are much better at teaching you how to program, but they can't cover everything. Often, all you need to see is a simple example of how to use a particular function or other keyword; the on-line help does contain documentation on every keyword, programming construct, and object you might use in your project. The bottom line is this: there is always something helpful on-line, it's just a matter of finding the right document.

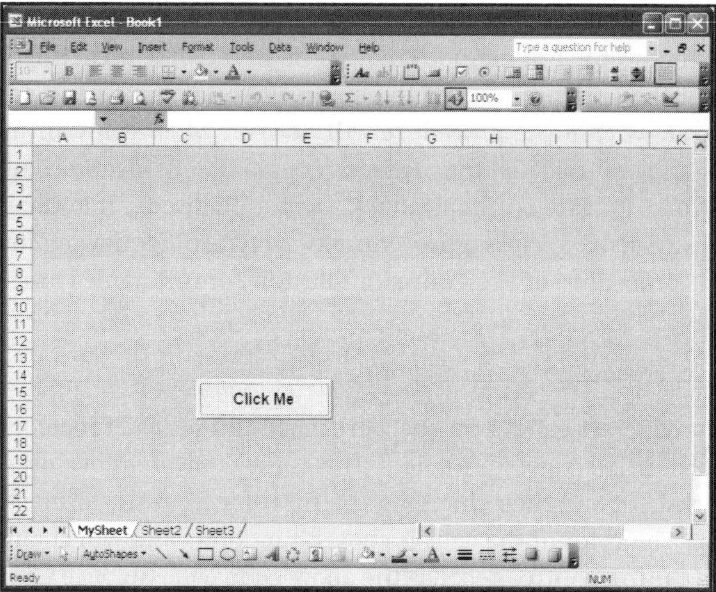

FIGURE 1.14

The Color Changer program.

VBA Help

Using the on-line help with VBA subject matter is identical to using the on-line help in Excel. To access the VBA help, you must have the IDE open and active; otherwise, everything is the same, from the Help menu to the help window and even the office assistant (if you choose to use it). Select Help, Microsoft Visual Basic Help to activate the Visual Basic Help dialog box shown in Figure 1.15. With the Visual Basic Help dialog you can browse a table of contents or enter keywords to search for on-line documentation. After you select a topic, documentation related to that topic appears in another Visual Basic Help window (for example, refer to Figure 1.16).

To look up documentation concerning a known keyword in VBA (for example, the syntax requirements for a particular VBA keyword), first select that keyword in the code, press F1, and the document that describes that keyword will immediately appear in the Help window.

You will not have on-line help with your VBA projects until you install these VBA help files with a custom installation. Refer to the Installing and Enabling VBA section earlier in this chapter to learn how to install the VBA help files.

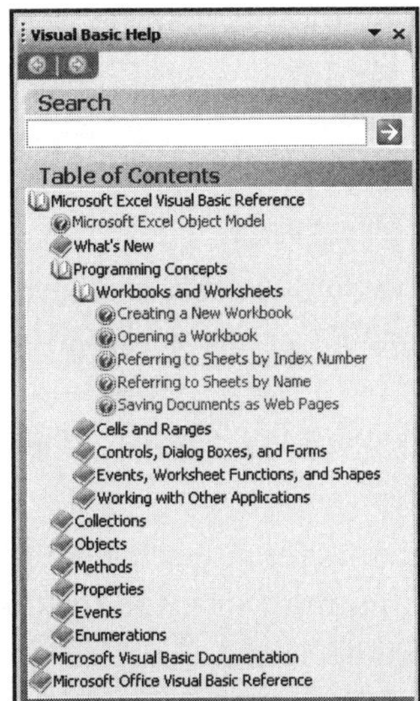

FIGURE 1.15

The Visual Basic Help dialog box.

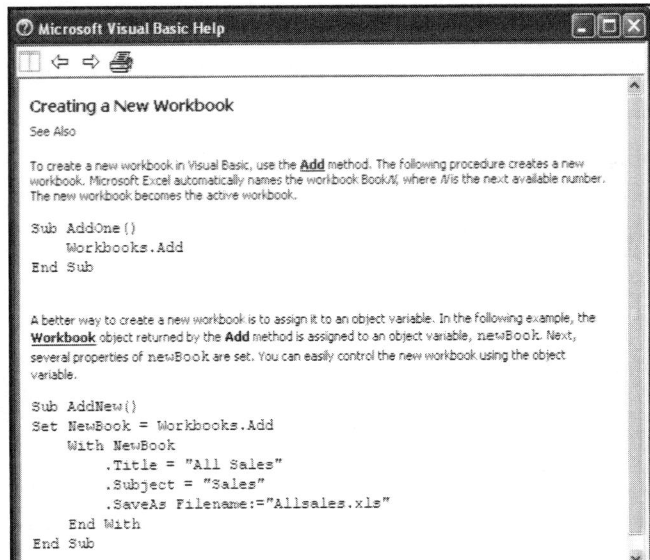

FIGURE 1.16

The Visual Basic Help dialog window showing a help document.

CONSTRUCTING THE COLORFUL STATS PROGRAM

When starting a project, programmers often compile a list of specific requirements, then refer to this list while designing the algorithm(s) that will be followed when writing the program.

The advantage you have when compiling a requirement list is that the source document can be used to build a protocol for testing the program. I will follow this procedure for the chapter projects including the *Colorful Stats* project that follows.

Requirements of the Colorful Stats Program

The purpose for the *Colorful Stats* program (as it relates to this book) is to give you a demonstration of ActiveX controls, event procedures, and using VBA to interact with an Excel worksheet. The practical purpose of the *Colorful Stats* program is to allow a user to immediately calculate basic statistics for a selected set of data. I've defined a few specific requirements for the *Colorful Stats* program and they are listed as follows:

1. The program shall calculate the following statistics for a selected data set—the number of data elements selected by the user, the minimum value, the maximum value, the sum total, the average value, and the standard deviation.
2. The program shall use Excel worksheet formulas to calculate the statistical parameters listed in Requirement 1.
3. The program shall write the formulas for the statistical parameters to the worksheet cells D2 through D7. Corresponding labels shall be written to cells C2 through C7.
4. The program shall change the interior color of cells C2 through D7 to green.
5. The program shall change the border color of cells C2 through D7 to red.
6. The program shall format the font of cells C2 through D7 to Arial, 16 pt, bold, and blue.
7. The program shall be initiated from a mouse click of a Command Button control placed on the worksheet.

Designing the Colorful Stats Program

When designing a program, I consider the user interface, program inputs and outputs, the location of the code (for example, event procedures of ActiveX controls), and the use and configuration of other programming components that I have not yet discussed. Since this is the first chapter project, I have kept it short and simple to make it easier to follow the design procedure.

I start by making the very simple user interface for the *Colorful Stats* program. The interface will use a single Command Button control placed on a worksheet to activate the program. I'm assuming that the data will be entered in column A of the worksheet (although this is not required) so I will place the Command Button control in columns C and D, close enough to the top of the worksheet so it is likely to be seen by the user when opened, but below row 7 to avoid masking the statistical values (refer to Figure 1.17). Note that I have altered the `Name`, `Caption`, and `Font` properties of the Command Button control.

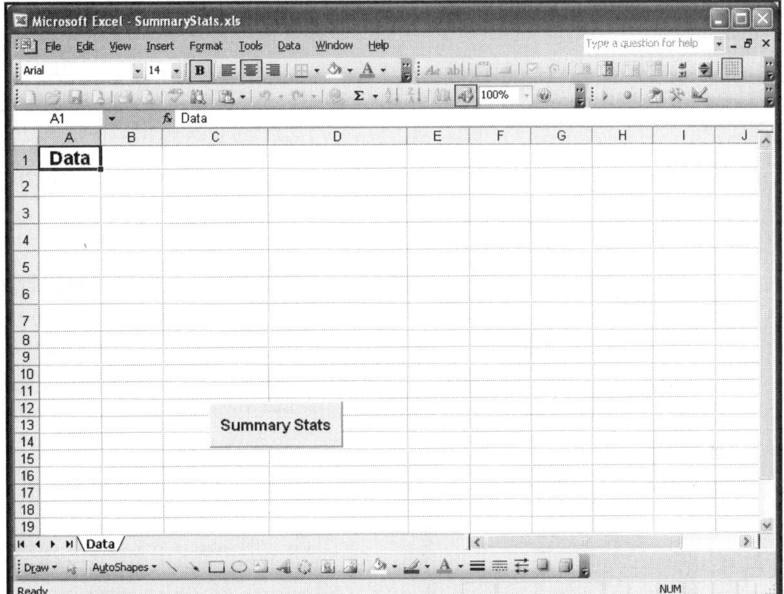

FIGURE 1.17

The user interface for the *Colorful Stats* program.

All program inputs and outputs are from, and to, the current active worksheet. The data used in the calculation of the statistical values must come from the cells that are selected by the user. I will write the program to output cell formulas to the desired worksheet cells so that Excel calculates the statistical values. I must also output labels to the cells adjacent to the statistical values for clarity. I will also format all output as described in the requirements. Finally, the program is to be initiated from a user's click of the Command Button control, so I will enter all programming statements in the `Click()` event procedure of the Command Button control.

Ideally, the *Colorful Stats* program would be activated from an interface independent of the worksheet that contains the data (i.e., using an ActiveX control on the worksheet containing the data is not the best solution). The program should also write the statistics to a new worksheet rather than risk overwriting data in the active worksheet. However, this requires a little more programming than I should show you right now.

At this point in the book, the only tool I've shown you for running a loaded macro that may be independent of the selected worksheet is the Macro dialog box (refer to Figure 1.9). As you proceed through this book you will learn other methods for initiating macros and how to create new worksheets.

Coding the Colorful Stats Program

As stated in the previous section, all of the code is to be placed in the `Click()` event procedure of the Command Button control. The code window can be accessed via the VBA IDE by double clicking on the Command Button control while in Design Mode. You can also select the appropriate object (`cmdCalculate`) from the object dropdown list in the code window for the worksheet on which the ActiveX control was placed (refer to Figure 1.18).

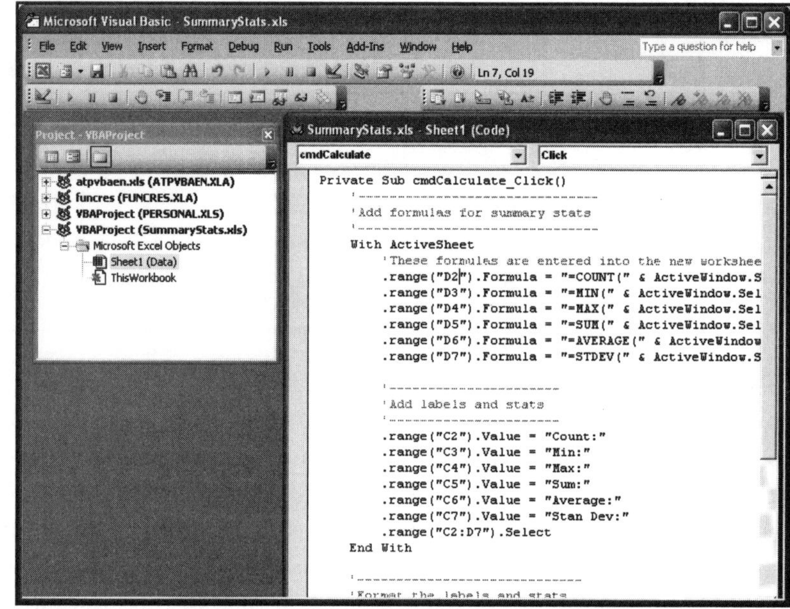

FIGURE 1.18

VBA IDE showing the code window for the worksheet containing the ActiveX Controls of the *Colorful Stats* project.

As you can see, the following code was placed in the `Click()` event procedure of the `cmdCalculate` Command Button control. Now let's take a closer look at each line of code.

The very first and last lines define the type of procedure as a `Click()` event, as described earlier in this chapter. Immediately following the opening line of code is a comment.

Comments (or remarks) are notes left in the code by the programmer to help describe the function of the program. Comments make it easier to find problems with the code, or add different features to the code at a later time. Enter comments (also known as remarks) into the code by beginning the line with an apostrophe (or Rem). You must enter another apostrophe for each new line; the VBA text editor will color each comment line green (default color; change by selecting Tools, Options, Editor Format, and Comment Text from the list of Code colors). Comments are not part of the program, and are ignored when the program runs; thus, comments do not decrease the execution speed of a program.

```
Private Sub cmdCalculate_Click()
    '-----------------
    'Add formulas for summary stats
    '-----------------
    With ActiveSheet
        'These formulas are entered into the new worksheet.
        .Range("D2").Formula = "=COUNT(" & ActiveWindow.Selection.Address & ")"
        .Range("D3").Formula = "=MIN(" & ActiveWindow.Selection.Address & ")"
        .Range("D4").Formula = "=MAX(" & ActiveWindow.Selection.Address & ")"
        .Range("D5").Formula = "=SUM(" & ActiveWindow.Selection.Address & ")"
        .Range("D6").Formula = "=AVERAGE(" & ActiveWindow.Selection.Address & ")"
        .Range("D7").Formula = "=STDEV(" & ActiveWindow.Selection.Address & ")"

        '------------
        'Add labels and stats
        '------------
        .Range("C2").Value = "Count:"
        .Range("C3").Value = "Min:"
        .Range("C4").Value = "Max:"
        .Range("C5").Value = "Sum:"
        .Range("C6").Value = "Average:"
        .Range("C7").Value = "Stan Dev:"
        .Range("C2:D7").Select
    End With

    '----------------
    'Format the labels and stats.
    '----------------
    With Selection
        .Font.Size = 16
        .Font.Bold = True
        .Font.Color = vbBlue
        .Font.Name = "Arial"
        .Columns.AutoFit
        .Interior.Color = vbGreen
        .Borders.Weight = xlThick
        .Borders.Color = vbRed
    End With
    Range("A1").Select
End Sub
```

I will discuss code structures, Excel objects, and object syntax in subsequent chapters. If you are even somewhat familiar with Excel, however, you probably have a pretty good idea as to what's happening in the above code. First, the cell formulas are written to the indicated cells (D2 through D7) using the range selected by the user as the parameter for each worksheet function. Next, the statistical labels are written to the corresponding cells in the adjacent columns (C2 through C7). The last part of the program formats the font, border, and color of cells C2 through D7 before selecting cell A1. Another example of the worksheet after some arbitrary data has been entered in column A and the program run is shown in Figure 1.19.

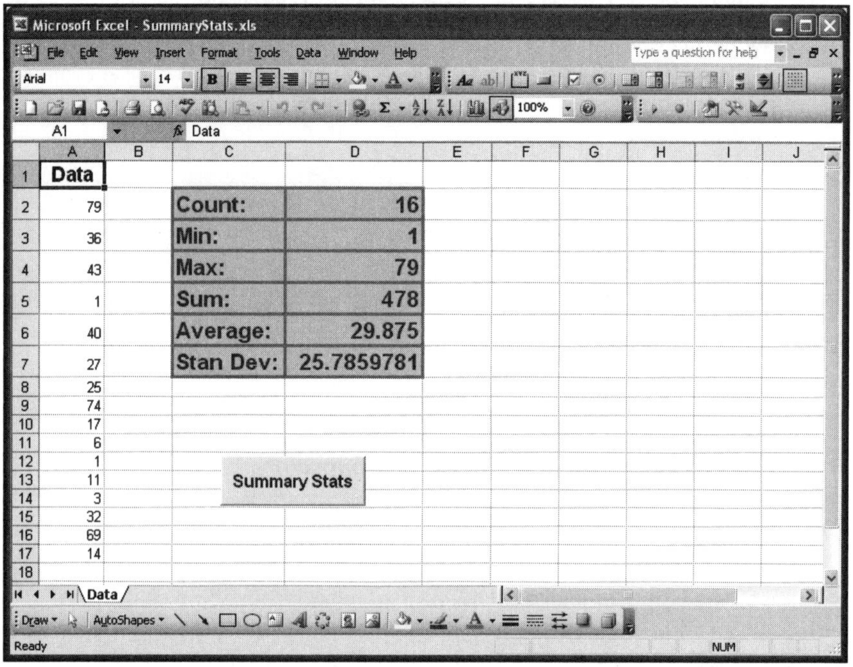

FIGURE 1.19

The Colorful Stats program after running.

That's all there is to it! This code will run once each time the Command Button control is clicked (don't forget to exit Design Mode and select some data first).

CHAPTER SUMMARY

Well, I didn't show you very much program code in this chapter, but you did get a solid introduction to the VBA programming environment. You did learn how to access the VBA IDE and how to view and use some of its major components. You also learned how to add ActiveX controls to a worksheet, change their properties, and add code to their event procedures.

After a brief look at using the on-line help and installing the VBA help files, you developed a small project that used a Command Button control on a worksheet to initiate a program that calculated statistical values from user-selected data. Your program then formatted the output with color, a new font, and a border.

In Chapter 2 you learn about some basic programming concepts and tools, variables and data types. I focus particularly on the string data type.

CHALLENGES

1. **Open a new workbook in Excel, then access the VBA IDE to find the names of the different event procedures for a worksheet. In particular note the `SelectionChange()` event procedure of any worksheet.**
2. **While in the Excel application, add a Label control to a worksheet. Change the `Name` property of the Label control to `lblCellAddress`. Change the `Caption` and other appearance properties (`Font`, `BackColor`, `ForeColor`, and so on) as desired.**
3. **Add the following line of code to the `SelectionChange()` event procedure of the worksheet to which you added the Label control.**

   ```
   lblCellAddress.Caption = "You selected cell " & Target.Address
   ```

4. **Return to the worksheet, exit Design Mode, and click on any cell in the worksheet containing the Label control. What happens?**
5. **Return to the VBA IDE and the line of code above. Place the cursor within the word `Caption` and press F1. Repeat with the `Address` keyword.**

Beginning Programs with VBA

Now that you know your way around the VBA IDE for Excel, it's time to introduce some basic programming concepts common to all languages. The next three chapters are devoted to these basic programming structures that, although they may not be that exciting, are essential for developing VBA projects.

Specifically, in this chapter we look at:

- Variables and data types
- Constants
- Simple input and output
- String functions

Project: Biorhythms and the Time of Your Life

The *Biorhythms and the Time of Your Life* program (see Figure 2.1) begins by asking for the user's name and birth date. The program then calculates the length of the user's life in years, months, days, hours, minutes, and seconds. Following the user input, the user's name, birth date, and age (in the aforementioned units) are displayed in the worksheet. The worksheet also contains an embedded chart that displays the current state of the user's three biorhythm cycles (physical, emotional, and intellectual).

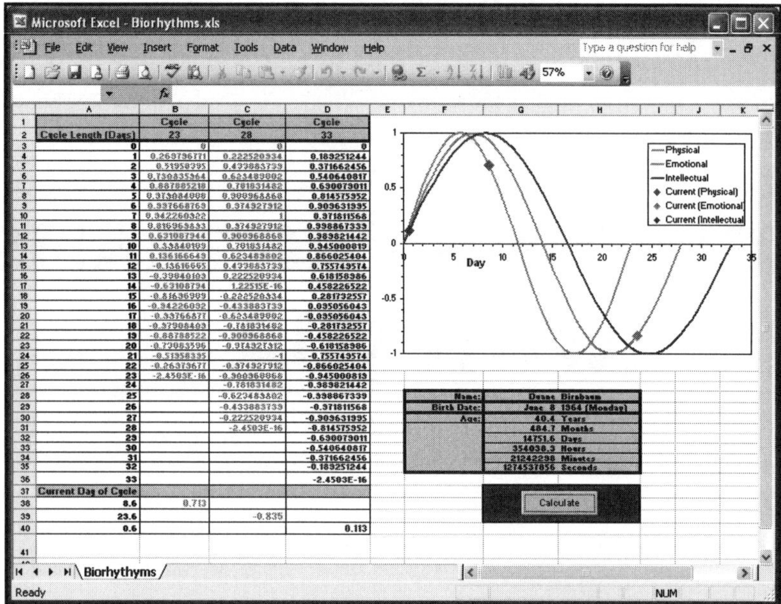

FIGURE 2.1

The Biorhythms and the Time of Your Life spreadsheet.

This program demonstrates the use of several variable types; including numbers, text, and dates. The program also demonstrates the use of some of VBA's built-in functions—primarily those functions used to manipulate text and dates.

Variables, Data Types, and Constants

Since this book focuses on a spreadsheet application, it's only natural that I introduce variables by asking you to think about the following: what types of values can be entered into a spreadsheet cell and how you might use them? You know that you can enter numbers and text in any spreadsheet cell in Excel. Also, you may or may not know that the format of a spreadsheet cell can be changed to one of several possibilities. For example, a number can be formatted such that the value is displayed with or without digits to the right of the decimal point. Numbers can also be formatted as currency or as a percentage (along with a few other options). Text can be displayed as entered or be automatically converted to a date or time. The content or value of a spreadsheet cell can be changed or deleted at any time.

From this point forward, the contents of a spreadsheet cell (text or numbers) in Excel will be referred to as its value. You have already seen in the Chapter 1 project and will continue to see throughout this book, the use of the `Value` property to access or change the contents of a spreadsheet cell.

In essence, spreadsheet cells are temporary storage containers for numbers and text that can be displayed and used in a number of different formats. This also describes a variable in any programming language. You can use variables in programs for temporary storage of data. For example, any data input by a user (possibly from a Text Box Control), can be stored in a variable and used later in the program. In the *Colorful Stats* project from Chapter 1, the following line of code acts a lot like a variable.

```
.Range("C6").Value = "Average:"
```

Here the text `"Average"` is copied to spreadsheet cell C6. I could have just as easily copied the text into a program variable first and then copied the contents of the variable to the cell C6. I didn't use an additional program variable because I wanted to save a couple of steps and because, as discussed earlier, spreadsheet cells already act a lot like variables. To accomplish this same task using a program variable, use the following:

```
Dim myString as String
myString = "Average:"
.Range("C6").Value = myString
```

The variable `myString` is first declared (declaration is discussed in the next section) and then assigned the string literal `"Average:"`. The value of spreadsheet cell C6 is then assigned the value stored in the variable `myString`.

Declaring Variables

To declare a variable is to tell the computer to reserve space in memory for later use. To declare a variable use a `Dim` (short for Dimension) statement.

```
Dim myVar As Integer
```

The name of the variable is `myVar`. The name must begin with an alphabetic character and cannot exceed 255 characters or contain any spaces. You should avoid the use of punctuation marks or other unusual characters in the variable name, as many of them are not allowed; however, the underscore character *is* allowed and works well for separating multiple words contained within a single variable name (for example, `First_Name`). Avoid using reserved VBA keywords and don't repeat variable names within the same scope (discussed later in this chapter). As a convention, the variable name should be descriptive of the value it will hold. For example, if you use a variable to hold someone's first name, then a good name for that variable might be `firstName` or `FirstName`. My preference is to begin a variable name with a lowercase letter and then capitalize the first letter of any subsequent words appearing in the name. I try to keep the length to a minimum (fewer than 12 characters) only because I don't like typing long names. Of course, you can adopt your own conventions as long as they don't contradict rules established by VBA.

Use `Option Explicit` in the general declarations section of a module window to force explicit variable declarations (see Figures 2.2 and 2.3). Otherwise variables can be dimensioned implicitly (without a `Dim` statement) as they are required in code. In other words, you can begin using a new variable without ever declaring it with a `Dim` statement if you don't use the `Option Explicit` statement. This is not good programming practice as it makes your code harder to interpret, and subsequently more difficult to debug. You can automatically have `Option Explicit` typed into each module window by checking the Require Variable Declaration option in the Tools/Options menu item of the VBA IDE.

Following the variable name, the data type is specified for the variable. In the example above, the variable is declared as an integer data type. This tells VBA what kind of data can be stored in this variable and how much memory must be reserved for the variable. I will discuss data types in detail later in this chapter.

Object and Standard Modules

Modules refer to a related set of declarations and procedures. Each module will have a separate window in the VBA IDE and, depending on the origination of the module, it will have different behavior with regard to variable declarations. I will refer to the module window shown in Figure 2.2 as an *object* module because it is associated with an object (the `Worksheet` object in this example).

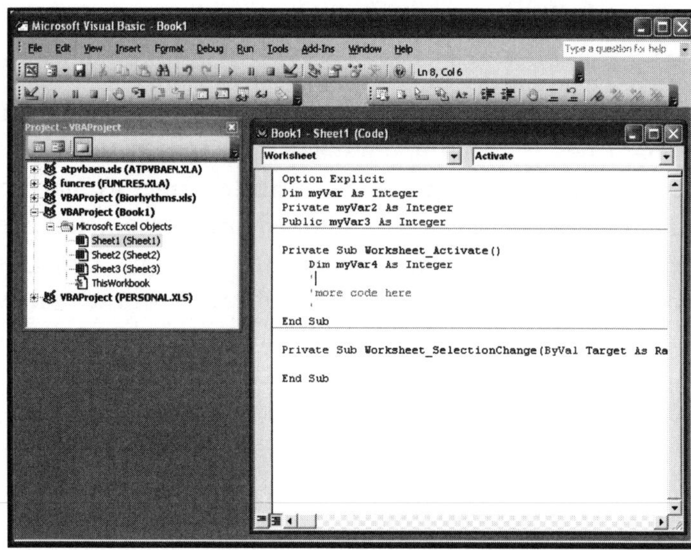

FIGURE 2.2

The object module for an Excel worksheet.

This module will automatically contain all event procedures associated with the worksheet `Sheet1`, and any ActiveX controls added to this worksheet. Object modules may also contain programmer-defined procedures (I will cover procedures in Chapter 3, "Procedures and Conditions"). Each worksheet will have a separate code window as will the workbook.

A standard module must be added to the project via the Insert menu of the VBA IDE, as shown in Figure 2.3.

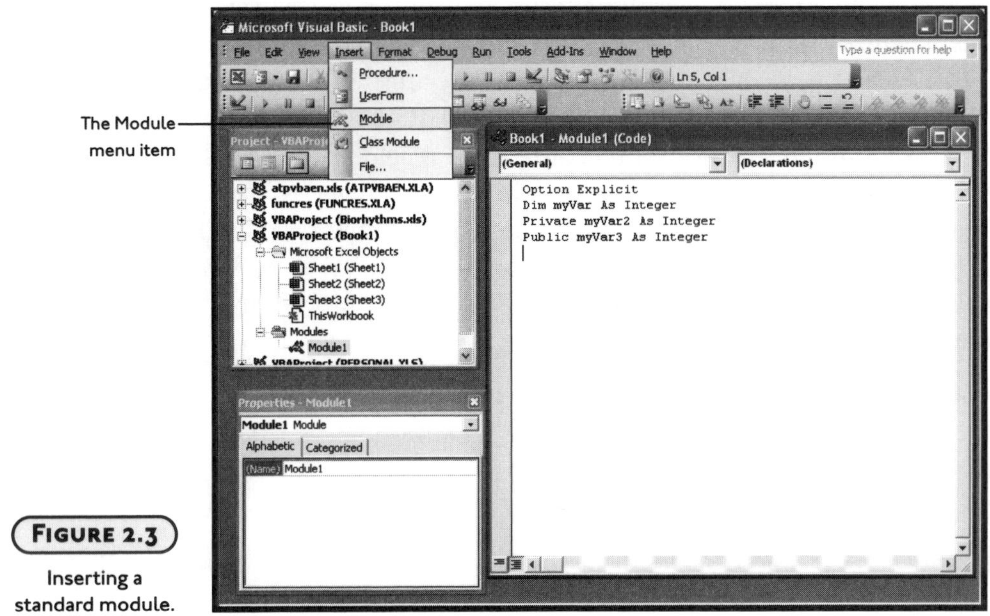

FIGURE 2.3

Inserting a standard module.

Standard modules are contained within a separate folder in the Project Explorer and may be renamed in the Properties window (see Figure 2.3). Standard modules contain variable declarations and programmer-defined procedures.

IN THE REAL WORLD

Modularized code aids in the compartmentalization of program code. *Compartmentalization* is the process of breaking a large programming problem into several smaller problems and then solving each of these smaller problems separately. Compartmentalization is vital in the development of software applications.

Variable Scope

Scope, in the context of variables, refers to the time when a variable is visible or available to the program. When a variable is in its scope, it can be accessed and/or manipulated. When a variable is out of scope, it is unavailable—essentially invisible to the program.

A variable declared within the code block of a procedure (such as the `Click()` event procedure of the Command Button control), is a *procedural level* variable. Procedural level variables are only available while program execution occurs within the procedure that the variable was declared. In Figure 2.2, the variable `myVar4` is only visible to the program while the code in the `Activate()` event procedure of the worksheet executes. When program execution is triggered by the `Activate()` event, the variable `myVar4` is dimensioned in memory. Program execution proceeds through the event procedure until reaching the `End Sub` line of code, after which the variable is released from memory and is no longer available. Each time the procedure executes, the variable is created and destroyed. Thus, `myVar4` will not retain its value between calls to the procedure. If necessary, the `Static` keyword can be used to tell VBA to remember the value of the variable between calls to a procedure. Consider the following example:

```
Private Sub Worksheet_Activate()
    Static myVar4 As Integer
    myVar4 = myVar4 + 1
End Sub
```

In this procedure the variable `myVar4` will increment its value by one with each call to the procedure. If you replace the `Static` keyword with `Dim`, `myVar4` will never exceed a value of 1.

Integer variables are initialized to a value of 0 at declaration.

Declaring a variable outside of a procedure with a `Dim` statement makes it a *module level* variable. The scope of a module level variable depends on the keyword used in the declaration. For example in Figure 2.2 the variables `myVar`, `myVar2`, and `myVar3` are declared outside all procedures.

The area outside of any defined procedure is known as the *general declarations* section of a module (object or standard). This area can only be used for declarations.

These three variables are declared with the `Dim`, `Private`, and `Public` keywords. The `Private` and `Public` keywords are only allowed for variable declaration in the general declarations section of a module. Each of the three variables, `myVar`, `myVar2`, and `myVar3` are visible to any procedure within this module. In addition, the variable `myVar3` is visible to any procedure in any module of this project. Variables declared in the general declarations section of a module (object or standard) with the `Public` keyword are commonly referred to as *global*.

When declaring a variable with the `Public` keyword in the general declarations section of an object module, it must be referenced in other modules of the project by first identifying the name of the object module. For example, to reference and assign a value to the variable `myVar3` in Figure 2.2 in any other module in that project, you must use code similar to the following:

```
Sheet1.myVar3  = 5
```

You do not have to reference the name of the module for variables declared with the Public keyword in the general declarations section of a standard module.

To summarize: the keywords `Dim` and `Private` have the same function in variable declarations when used in the general declarations section of any module; the `Public` keyword can be used to declare global variables in a standard or object module.

Data Types

Data types define the kind of value that may be stored within the memory allocated for a variable. As with spreadsheet cells, there are numerous data types; the most common are defined in Table 2.1.

Numerical Data Types

The numerical data types listed in Table 2.1 are integer, long, single, and double. A variable declared as an integer or long data type can hold whole numbers or non-fractional values within the specified ranges. If you need a variable to hold fractional or "floating point" values, then use a single or double data type. Pay attention to the value of the number that might have to be stored within the variable. If the value gets too large for the data type, your program will crash. For example, the following code will generate an overflow error because the value `50000` is outside the allowed range for an integer data type:

```
Dim myNum As Integer
myNum=50000
```

Table 2.1 Common VBA Data Types

Data type	Storage size	Range
Boolean	2 bytes	True or False
Integer	2 bytes	-32,768 to 32,767
Long	4 bytes	-2,147,483,648 to 2,147,483,647
Single (floating-point)	4 bytes	-3.402823E38 to -1.401298E-45 for negative values; 1.401298E-45 to 3.402823E38 for positive values
Double (floating-point)	8 bytes	-1.79769313486231E308 to -4.94065645841247E-324 for negative values; 4.94065645841247E-324 to 1.79769313486232E308 for positive values
Date	8 bytes	January 1, 100 to December 31, 9999
Object	4 bytes	Any Object reference
String (variable-length)	10 bytes + string length	0 to approximately 2 billion
String (fixed-length)	Length of string	1 to approximately 65,400
Variant (with numbers)	16 bytes	Any numeric value up to the range of a Double
Variant (with characters)	22 bytes + string length	Same range as for variable-length String
User-defined (using Type)	Number required by elements	The range of each element is the same as the range of its data type.

You must also be careful about mixing numerical data types because you may not get the desired result. The following code will execute without errors, but the variable `answer` will hold the value 32 after execution of this block, not 31.8 as you might want.

```
Dim answer As Integer
Dim num1 As Single
Dim num2 As Integer
num1 = 5.3
num2 = 6
answer = num1 * num2
```

Changing the variable `answer` to a single data type will correct the problem. Using the code as shown above is a good way to ensure an integer is stored within a variable that receives its value from a computation involving floating point numbers. Notice that the value stored in `answer` is rounded to the nearest whole integer.

By using variables with numerical data types, you can carry out mathematical operations as you normally would using just the numbers the variables contained. You can add, subtract, multiply, and divide variables; you can square and cube numerical variables or raise them to any desired power. See Table 2.2 for a list of the operators used for common mathematical operations in VBA.

TABLE 2.2 COMMON MATHEMATICAL OPERATORS USED IN VBA

Operation	Operator
Addition	+
Subtraction	-
Multiplication	*
Division	/
Exponential	^

Basically, any mathematical operation that can be performed on a number can be performed on a numerical variable. The following are a few examples:

```
Dim num1 As Integer
Dim num2 As Integer
Dim answer As Integer
num1 = 10
num2 = 5
answer = num1 + num2    ' answer Holds 15
answer = num1 - num2    ' answer Holds 5
answer = num1 * num2    ' answer Holds 50
answer = num1 / num2    ' answer Holds 2
answer = num1 ^ 2       ' answer Holds 100
answer = 2 ^ num2       ' answer Holds 32
```

After declaring the variables `num1`, `num2`, and `answer`, a few mathematical operations are carried out over several lines of code. The result of each line is given as a comment within the same line of code. In the code above, the equal sign (=) does not designate equality; instead it works as an assignment operator. For example, the variable `answer` gets the result of adding the two variables `num1` and `num2`.

Next, I will look at a fairly simple spreadsheet that uses integer variables and some simple math.

Although it is not required, it is a good idea to place all variable declarations for a procedure at the start of your code. With variable declarations at the beginning of your code, you will be able to find them quickly when you need to debug.

Magic Squares

I believe I was first introduced to magic squares in sixth or seventh grade math. The idea is to fill a square grid with numbers such that the sum of all rows, columns, and diagonals add up to the same value. The number of columns/rows in the grid is an odd number and you can only use each value once. For example, a 3 × 3 grid must be filled with the numbers 1 through 9 so that everything sums up to 15. A 5 × 5 grid uses 1 through 25 and all rows, columns, and diagonals add up to 65. The 3 × 3 is pretty easy even if you don't know or see the pattern.

Figure 2.4 shows the spreadsheet containing the 3 × 3 grid. The *Magic Squares* spreadsheet is available on the CD-ROM that accompanies this book.

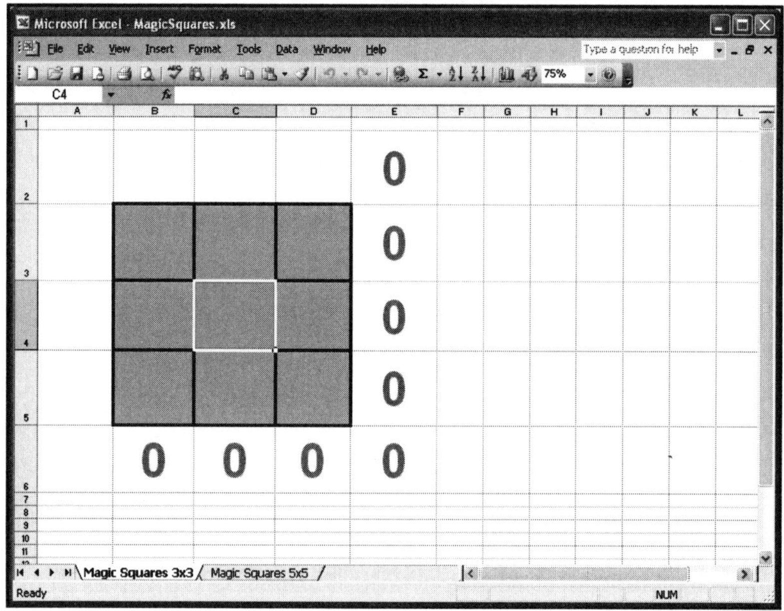

FIGURE 2.4

A 3 × 3 Magic Square.

The *Magic Squares* spreadsheet is preformatted for colors, borders, and font size. The program will be contained entirely within the `SelectionChange()` event procedure of the worksheet. To get to the `SelectionChange()` event procedure, double click the worksheet name in the VBA

Project Explorer window to open its code module. Select Worksheet from the object's dropdown list, then select `SelectionChange` from the procedure dropdown list. The program will simply calculate the sum of all rows, columns, and diagonals in the magic square and display the result in adjacent cells. The program code is listed below. The `SelectionChange()` event procedure triggers every time the user selects a new cell in the worksheet.

```
Private Sub Worksheet_SelectionChange(ByVal Target As Range)
    '--------------------
    'Dimension variables to hold sums
    '--------------------
    Dim row1 As Integer
    Dim row2 As Integer, row3 As Integer
    Dim col1 As Integer, col2 As Integer, col3 As Integer
    Dim diagonal1 As Integer, diagonal2 As Integer

    '-----------------------------------
    'Sum the rows, cols, and diagonals and store result in variables.
    '-----------------------------------
    row1 = Range("B3").Value + Range("C3").Value + Range("D3").Value
    row2 = Range("B4").Value + Range("C4").Value + Range("D4").Value
    row3 = Range("B5").Value + Range("C5").Value + Range("D5").Value

    col1 = Range("B3").Value + Range("B4").Value + Range("B5").Value
    col2 = Range("C3").Value + Range("C4").Value + Range("C5").Value
    col3 = Range("D3").Value + Range("D4").Value + Range("D5").Value

    diagonal1 = Range("B3").Value + Range("C4").Value + Range("D5").Value
    diagonal2 = Range("B5").Value + Range("C4").Value + Range("D3").Value

    '----------------
    'Copy results to the worksheet.
    '----------------
    Range("B6").Value = col1
    Range("C6").Value = col2
    Range("D6").Value = col3

    Range("E3").Value = row1
    Range("E4").Value = row2
    Range("E5").Value = row3

    Range("E6").Value = diagonal1
    Range("E2").Value = diagonal2
End Sub
```

First, variables are declared for holding the summations of the rows, columns, and diagonals in the magic square. I am using integer data types because I know that I will not be working with floating point values, and the numbers used will be small.

Next, the values of three cells are added and stored in the previously dimensioned variables. The values of the individual spreadsheet cells are obtained in what should now be a familiar way. Notice that within a row, the row index does not change in the sum of the three values. Similarly, the column index does not change in the sum of the three values within a column. Finally, both row and column indices change in the sum over the diagonals.

Next the contents of these summations are copied to the spreadsheet cells in the corresponding row or column.

As the user enters in the numbers to the cells in the *Magic Squares* worksheet, the procedure above is triggered and the values of the summations are updated as shown in Figure 2.5.

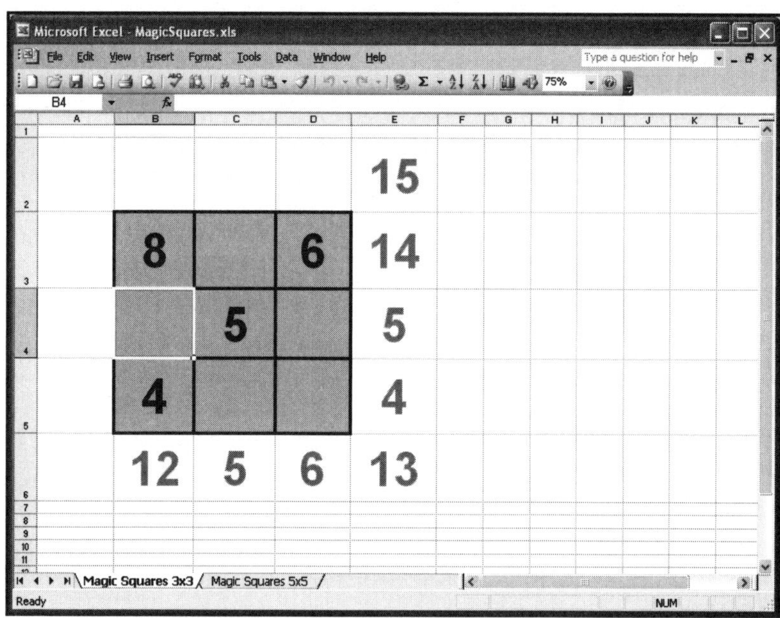

FIGURE 2.5

Magic Squares in action.

I could have bypassed using variables and simply copied the summation of the three cells directly to the appropriate spreadsheet cell, but using variables with descriptive names makes it a little easier to understand the function of the program.

You have probably recognized that the *Magic Squares* worksheet isn't anything you couldn't do with formatting and formulas directly in the Excel application; however, with a program, you can show the spreadsheet to a friend or colleague who knows Excel. He or she will wonder how you did it, as there aren't any formulas in the spreadsheet cells that hold the summations of the rows and columns. Your friend might even be impressed. You can also try a 5 × 5, or any size grid as long as the number of rows and columns is odd and equal. The median value of the number set multiplied by the grid dimension will tell you the sum that the values in all rows, columns, and diagonals should equal (for example, a 5 × 5 grid uses the numbers 1 to 25 with a median of 13. So the rows, columns, and diagonals should sum to 5 × 13 = 65).

As you may have realized by now, VBA is not case sensitive; that is, it does not matter if you type your code with upper or lower case letters. However, VBA does preserve capitalization wherever it's used. This is helpful with variable definitions. If you use uppercase letters when declaring a variable, any additional references to that variable within the same scope will automatically follow the same capitalization scheme. So after a variable is defined with a `Dim` statement, you can type additional references to that variable using all lowercase letters and VBA will automatically convert the capitalization for you. This is a handy feature to ensure you are spelling your variable names correctly as you type them in your code.

String Data Types

Variables with string data types are used to hold characters as text. The characters can be numbers, letters, or special symbols (for example, punctuation marks). Basically, just about anything you can type on your keyboard can be held within a string variable. To declare a variable with the string data type, use the `String` keyword. To initialize a string variable, place the string value within double quotation marks.

```
Dim myText As String
myText = "VBA is fun"
```

There are two types of string variables, variable length and fixed length. The example above is that of a variable length string because `myText` can hold just about any length of text (see Table 2.1). Following is an example of a declaration for a fixed length string:

```
Dim myString As String * 8
myString = "ABCDEFGHIJKL"
```

In the example above, the string variable `myString` can hold a maximum of eight characters. You can try to initialize the variable with more characters (as was done above), but only the first eight characters in this example will be stored in the variable. The value of `myString` is then `"ABCDEFGH"`. Fixed length strings are more commonly used as a part of a user-defined data type discussed in a later chapter. In most cases, you will not know the length of the string to be stored in a variable so you should use the variable length type.

IN THE REAL WORLD

A lot of what programmers do with strings revolves around extracting desirable information out of them. For example, a search engine on the Internet will look for certain keywords on a Web page and store them in a database. The search engine may load the entire textual content of a Web page into a string variable and then extract various keywords from that variable. Then, when a user searches that database by entering in various keywords, the user's keywords are stored in string variables and compared to database content.

I will discuss string manipulation a little later in this chapter. Next, I will finish my discussion on data types by looking at variants and a few less common data types.

Variant Data Types

Variant data types are analogous to the General category in the number format of a spreadsheet cell in the Excel application. Variables are declared as variants by using the keyword `Variant`, or by not specifying a data type.

```
Dim myVar
Dim myVar2 As Variant
```

Variant type variables can hold any type of data except a fixed length string. Variant data types relax the restrictions on the value a particular variable can hold and thus give the programmer more flexibility; however, variant data types can also be dangerous if overused—they can slow down program execution—and programs with a large number of variant data types can be very difficult to debug. So while I don't recommend using them, I do recognize that many programmers do use variants, and the on-line help is filled with examples using variants, so I will offer a brief example here:

```
Dim myVar As Integer
myVar = 10
myVar = "Testing"
```

The example above will generate a type mismatch error because an attempt is made to enter the string `"Testing"` into an integer variable; however, if you change the variable `myVar` to a variant, the code will execute and `myVar` will hold the string value `"Testing"` when all is complete. The following code will run without error.

```
Dim myVar
myVar = 10
myVar = "Testing"
```

Using variants allows you to use the same variable to hold multiple data types (one at a time). The variable `myVar` holds the integer value 10 (albeit briefly) before being assigned the string value `"Testing"`.

You are probably starting to see the danger of using variant data types. Imagine a large program with numerous procedures and variables. Within this program are two variables of type variant that initially hold numerical values and will need to be used within the same mathematical operation before the program is finished executing. If one variable is mistakenly reinitialized with a string before the mathematical operation, an error will result and may crash the program (or at least taint the result). Debugging this program may present problems that depend on how hard it is to find the string initialization of the variant variable, and additional problems associated with the string variant. So even though it may be tempting to use variants as a way to prevent errors that crash your program (as in the example above), in actuality the use of variants make your code "loose," and may result in logic errors that are difficult to find.

Logic errors are the result of a mistake in a programming algorithm. They may or may not cause your program to crash, depending on the specific nature of the error. Trying to multiply variables of a string and integer data type would crash program execution, making the error relatively easy to find. Adding when you should have multiplied is a type of logic error that will not crash a program, but will certainly taint the result. Logic errors can be very serious because you may never find them or even know they exist.

Other Data Types

There are just a couple more data types that need to be mentioned. You will see them in action in subsequent chapters.

The Boolean data type holds the value true or false. You can also represent true as a 1 and false as a 0. Boolean variables will be very useful when dealing with programming structures that use conditions, as you will see in the next chapter. Declare and initialize a Boolean variable as follows:

```
Dim rollDice As Boolean
rollDice = False
```

You can also specify variables of type date. Variables of type date are actually stored as floating point numbers with the integer portion representing a date between 1 January, 100 and 31 December 9999, and the decimal portion representing a time between 0:00:00 to 23:59:59. The date data type is mostly a convenience when you need to work with dates or times.

There are a handful of VBA functions that use variables of type date that add to this convenience. You will see a couple of examples of date functions in the chapter project.

Constants

Constants allow you to assign a meaningful name to a number or string that will make your code easier to read. This is analogous to using named ranges in your spreadsheet formulas. There are numerous mathematical constants for which it makes sense to use constant data types. A constant string might be used when you need frequent use of a particular spreadsheet label. Constants are declared using the `Const` keyword as shown below.

```
Const PI = 3.14159
Dim circumference As Single
Dim diameter As Single
diameter = 10.32
circumference = PI* diameter
```

The declaration and initialization of a constant occur in the same line of code. The value of a constant can never change, so it is a good idea to use constants when you need the same value throughout the life of your program. Constant names are uppercase as a convention only; it is not required by VBA.

Simple Input and Output with VBA

You have already seen how to get input from the user through the use of the `Value` property of a spreadsheet cell. Conversely, you can generate output for the user through the spreadsheet. Yet there may be times when you want something more dynamic and dramatic than a spreadsheet cell. The easiest method for gathering input from the user and sending output back is the `InputBox()` and `MsgBox()` functions.

Just as Excel comes with a large number of functions for the user to use in spreadsheet formulas (for example, the `SUM()` function), VBA contains numerous functions for the programmer. VBA programming functions, just like Excel functions, typically require one or more values (called parameters or arguments) to be passed to them, and then return one or more values (most commonly one) back to the program.

Collecting User Input with InputBox()

When you need to prompt the user for input and want to force a response before program execution continues, then the `InputBox()` function is the tool to use. The `InputBox()` function sends to the screen a dialog box that must be addressed by the user before program execution proceeds. Figure 2.6 shows the dialog box.

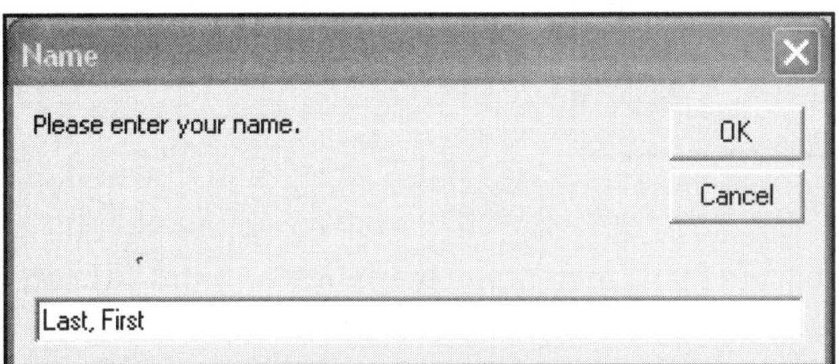

FIGURE 2.6

The `InputBox()` dialog box.

The `InputBox()` function returns the data entered by the user as a string if the OK button is clicked or the Enter key is pressed on the keyboard. If the user clicks the Cancel button, then a zero-length string is returned (`""`). Here is the syntax required for creating an `InputBox()` (parameters in brackets are optional).

```
InputBox(prompt [,title] [,default] [,xpos] [,ypos] [,helpfile, context])
```

The prompt is the only required parameter that must be passed to the function. Typically, the prompt, title, and sometimes the default are used. You must assign the return value of the function to a variable of type string.

```
Dim name As String
name = InputBox("Please enter your name.", "Name", "Last, First")
```

The prompt and title must be strings, which is why they are enclosed in double quotation marks. Alternatively, you can use string variables for these parameters. The title parameter is displayed in the title bar of the dialog box. The default parameter is displayed in the text box of the dialog box. Including a little help in the prompt or default parameter will increase the chances of getting the correct input. In the example above, I included a default parameter that serves to tell the user what format I want the name entered.

Output with MsgBox()

The `MsgBox()` function outputs a message to the user in the form of a message box like the one shown in Figure 2.7.

The `MsgBox()` function is a good way to alert the user about some type of problem, or ask a question that requires a yes/no answer. Here is the syntax for the `MsgBox()` function:

```
MsgBox(prompt[, buttons] [, title] [, helpfile, context])
```

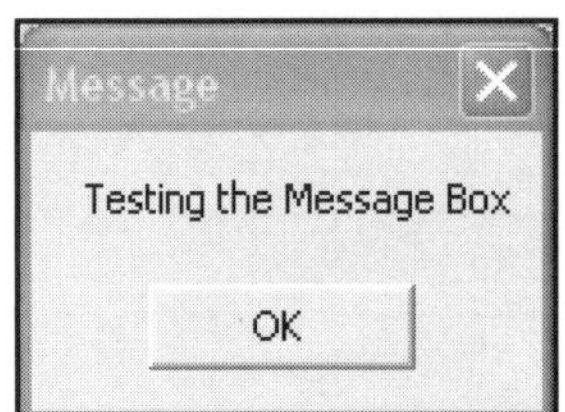

FIGURE 2.7

The message box.

The prompt is the only required parameter, although buttons and title are usually included. The example below was used to generate the message box in Figure 2.7:

```
userResponse = MsgBox("Testing the Message Box",  vbOKOnly, "Message")
```

The prompt must be a string or string variable and is used as the message you want the user to read. The buttons parameter requires a numeric expression (either an integer or constant) and tells VBA what buttons and/or icons are to be placed on the message box. There are several choices for buttons, including OK, OK/Cancel, Abort/Retry/Ignore, and Yes/No. You can also display an icon (warnings or information type), a help button, and add some additional formatting with your choice of buttons. For a complete list of button choices, look up the `MsgBox()` function in the on-line help by typing **msgbox** in the keyword field of the help window (see Figure 2.8). The reference `vbOKOnly`, in the above expression is actually a named constant associated with this function. For example, the value of `vbOKOnly` is zero. I used the constant expressions because it's easier to interpret the code and I know exactly what I am asking for in the appearance of the message box. Finally, the title can be included as a string or string variable.

The `MsgBox()` function returns an integer between 1 and 7 depending on the button selected. Obviously this is only useful when there is more than one button. The return value should then be used to select a course of action in your program.

Finally, you should take care not to use too many message boxes in your program. Always ask yourself: are there other ways to get input or display the message besides including a message box? Most users (including myself) find it extremely annoying to have to answer a message box when it's not really necessary.

MANIPULATING STRINGS WITH VBA FUNCTIONS

Now it's time to get back to strings and have a little fun. Strings are more of an unknown to the programmer in the sense that you seldom know how long they are, or how much of the

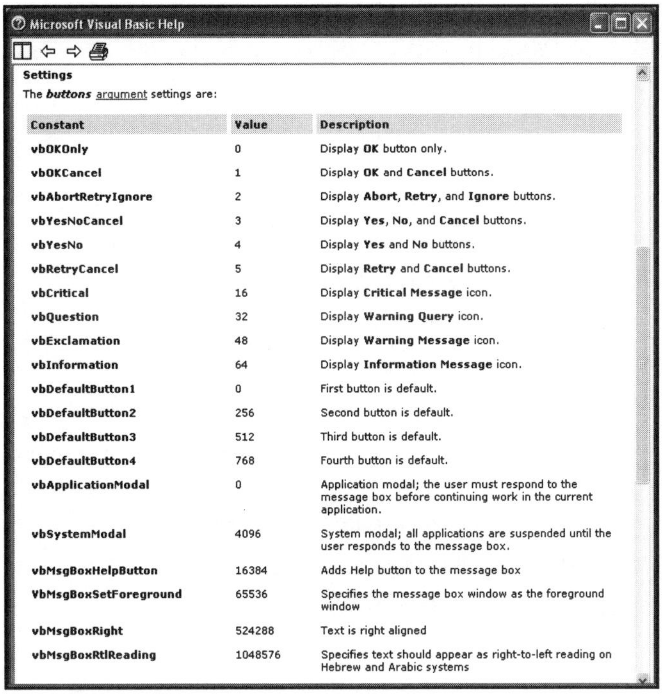

Microsoft Visual Basic Help

Settings

The ***buttons*** argument settings are:

Constant	Value	Description
vbOKOnly	0	Display **OK** button only.
vbOKCancel	1	Display **OK** and **Cancel** buttons.
vbAbortRetryIgnore	2	Display **Abort**, **Retry**, and **Ignore** buttons.
vbYesNoCancel	3	Display **Yes**, **No**, and **Cancel** buttons.
vbYesNo	4	Display **Yes** and **No** buttons.
vbRetryCancel	5	Display **Retry** and **Cancel** buttons.
vbCritical	16	Display **Critical Message** icon.
vbQuestion	32	Display **Warning Query** icon.
vbExclamation	48	Display **Warning Message** icon.
vbInformation	64	Display **Information Message** icon.
vbDefaultButton1	0	First button is default.
vbDefaultButton2	256	Second button is default.
vbDefaultButton3	512	Third button is default.
vbDefaultButton4	768	Fourth button is default.
vbApplicationModal	0	Application modal; the user must respond to the message box before continuing work in the current application.
vbSystemModal	4096	System modal; all applications are suspended until the user responds to the message box.
vbMsgBoxHelpButton	16384	Adds Help button to the message box
VbMsgBoxSetForeground	65536	Specifies the message box window as the foreground window
vbMsgBoxRight	524288	Text is right aligned
vbMsgBoxRtlReading	1048576	Specifies text should appear as right-to-left reading on Hebrew and Arabic systems

FIGURE 2.8

Settings for the buttons argument with the `MsgBox()` function.

string actually represents useful information. Thankfully, there is a plethora of functions designed to work on string variables that you can use to extract the information you need. Table 2.3 summarizes many of these functions.

As with most functions, the string functions require one or more parameters be passed. All functions must return a value so the syntax will look something like this:

```
myVar = FunctionName(parameter list)
```

where `myVar` is a variable of the proper type for the return value of the function, `FunctionName` is the name of the VBA function, and `parameter list` is a list of one or more values to be passed to the function. Parameters can be literals (for example, `5.2` or `"Hello"`), but are usually in the form of variables.

Fun with Strings

The best way to learn these functions is to use them, so let's create a program that asks for the user's name and then outputs components of the name to a worksheet. I call it *Fun with Strings*, and Figure 2.9 shows the spreadsheet, which can also be found on the CD_ROM.

Table 2.3 VBA String Functions

Function Name	Returns
Str()	A string representation of a number
Val()	A numerical representation of a string
Trim()	A string with leading and trailing spaces removed
Left()	A portion of a string beginning from the left side
Right()	A portion of a string beginning from the right side
Mid()	Any portion of a string
InStr()	A number representing the place value of a particular character within a string
InStrRev()	The position of an occurrence of one string within another, from the end of string
StrReverse()	A string with its character order reversed
Len()	A number of characters in a string
LCase()	A string with all characters lowercase
UCase()	A string will all characters uppercase
StrConv()	A string converted to one of several possible formats
StrComp()	A number indicating the result of a string comparison
Asc()	Number representing the ANSI code of a character
Chr()	One character string representing the ANSI code of a number

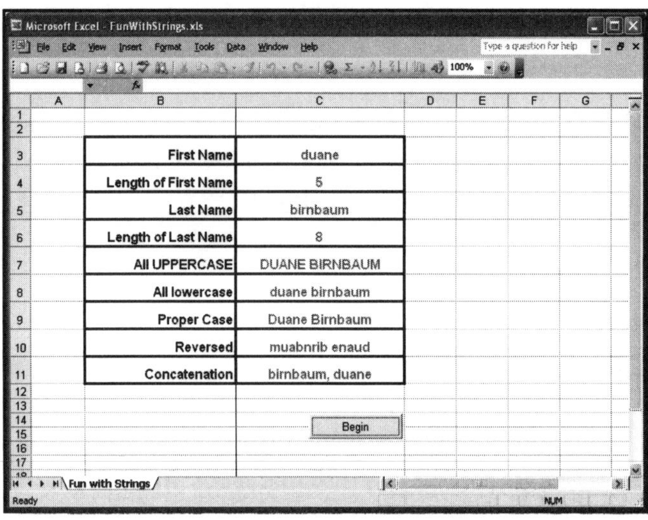

FIGURE 2.9

Fun with Strings.

Specifically, the program will output the user's first name and last name along with the number of characters in each name to separate cells in the spreadsheet. The program will also convert the user's name to both all uppercase and all lowercase characters as well as reverse the order of the first and last name. The code is placed in the `Click()` event procedure of a Command Button control placed on the worksheet. The `Name` property of the Command Button control was changed to `cmdBegin` and the `Caption` property to `"Begin"`. When the user clicks on the command button, code execution begins. After some variable declarations, the `InputBox()` function is used to prompt the user for his/her first and last name. You will notice that I am assuming the user enters his/her first name followed by one space and then the last name.

Input validation is an important component in any program that requires user input. I have not yet covered enough programming constructs to discuss input validation; I will wait until Chapter 4 to discuss it.

Everything entered by the user is stored in the string variable `userName`.

```
Private Sub cmdBegin_Click()
    Dim userName As String
    Dim firstName As String
    Dim lastName As String
    Dim strLength As Integer
    Dim spaceLoc As Integer

    '--------------------------
    'Collect user name, find the space between
    'first and last names, and separate the names.
    '--------------------------
    userName = InputBox("Enter your first and last name.", "Name")
    spaceLoc = InStr(1, userName, " ")
    firstName = Left(userName, spaceLoc - 1)

    '---------------
    'Output to the worksheet
    '---------------
    Range("C3").Value = firstName
    strLength = Len(firstName)
    Range("C4").Value = strLength   'length of first name
    strLength = Len(userName)
```

```
    lastName = Mid(userName, spaceLoc + 1, strLength - spaceLoc)
    Range("C5").Value = lastName
    strLength = Len(lastName)
    Range("C6").Value = strLength
    Range("C7").Value = UCase(userName)
    Range("C8").Value = LCase(userName)
    Range("C9").Value = StrConv(userName, vbProperCase)
    Range("C10").Value = StrReverse(userName)
    Range("C11").Value = lastName & ", " & firstName
End Sub
```

To help picture what will happen in the program, let's assume the variable `userName` contains the string `"Fred Flintstone"`. This string is 15 characters long; Table 2.4 shows the locations of each character.

TABLE 2.4 CHARACTER LOCATIONS IN A STRING

Character	F	r	e	d		F	l	i	n	t	s	t	o	n	e
Location	1	2	3	4	5	6	7	8	9	10	11	12	13	14	15

The program determines the location of the space by using the `InStr()` function. The `InStr()` function is passed three parameters, the number `1`, the string variable `userName`, and a single character string containing a space. The parameter `1` represents the location to start searching within the string passed in the next parameter, in this case, `userName`. The last string is a space and this represents the character the `InStr()` function is searching for within the value of `userName`. The `InStr()` function then returns an integer value representing the location of the space within the `userName` string. This integer value is the location of the space between the first and last name of the user—in this example, location 5 (see Table 2.4)—and is stored in the integer variable `spaceLoc`. The `Left()` function is then passed two parameters, the `userName` string, and the length of the portion of the `userName` string to return. The variable `spaceLoc` is holding the location of the space (5 in our example), so using `spaceLoc - 1` for the length parameter in the `Left()` function returns just the first name (`"Fred"`). The `Len()` function is used to return the length of the `firstName` string as an integer and this value is stored in the variable `strLength`. The values of the `firstName` string and `strLength` variables are then copied to the worksheet.

The `Mid()` function is used to return the last name of the user to the string variable `lastName`. The `Mid()` function takes three parameters: the original string `userName` (`"Fred Flintstone"`), the starting location of the new string (`spaceLoc - 1`), and the length of the string to return (`strLength - spaceLoc`). The variable `strLength` was reinitialized to the length of `userName` prior to using the `Mid()` function. Again, the variables holding the last name and the number of characters in the last name are copied to the worksheet.

The `UCase()` and `LCase()` functions convert the `userName` string to all uppercase and all lowercase letters, respectively; and the `StrConv()` function converts the `userName` string to proper case. Finally, the `StrReverse()` function reverses the order of the characters in the `userName` string and the `&` (ampersand) character is used to concatenate strings and rearrange the user's name such that the last name is first, followed by a comma and the first name.

String concatenation is the process of combining one or more strings together to form a new string. The strings are combined from left to right using either the ampersand (&) or addition (+) operators. To avoid ambiguity with the mathematical addition operator, I recommend that you always use the ampersand (&) operator for string concatenation.

You did not see all the string functions in action in the *Fun with Strings* program. You will see more in the next project and throughout this book. I will explain their use in detail as they appear in various code snippets and programming projects. In the meantime, I recommend you play with the string functions I have already discussed in order to get comfortable using them.

Constructing the Biorhythms and the Time of Your Life Program

This project will utilize several of the VBA programming components discussed in this chapter. The project contains several different examples of data types including integer, floating point, string, and date types. I introduce some new functions designed to work with the date and string data types. The project also demonstrates nesting functions, the use of constants, and some simple mathematical operations.

The majority of the work for this project will be handled by the Excel application via formulas and a chart. The requirements handled by the VBA program will be limited to collecting the user's name and birth date, and outputting the result of some date calculations. As was the case for the *Colorful Stats* project in Chapter 1, there is nothing in this project that could not be accomplished in the Excel application without the aid of a VBA program.

Nonetheless, I will show you how to build a fun little project that you can use daily to track the status of your biorhythms.

Your biorhythms (if you believe in them) are on sinusoidal cycles that vary in length for the three types. The lengths of the cycles are 23, 28, and 33 days for your physical, emotional, and intellectual cycles, respectively; with each cycle type starting on your birth date. Your best days are supposedly in the first half of a cycle when the sinusoidal curve is positive. Likewise, your worst days are in the second half of a cycle when the curve is negative. Critical days are said to be when you cross the boundary between positive and negative days.

I don't have a lot of faith in biorhythms, but they are fun to calculate and examine; and if you are having a bad day when your biorhythms are negative or critical, it gives you something to blame it on.

Requirements for Biorhythms and the Time of Your Life

As mentioned earlier, I've left most of the work to the Excel application by using formulas to calculate the sinusoidal curves for the three cycles, and a chart to display the curves. The specific requirements of the project follow:

1. The biorhythm spreadsheet shall use formulas to calculate a sinusoidal curve for each of the three cycle types. Note that these three curves are static.
2. The spreadsheet shall contain an embedded chart that displays the static curves described in requirement 1.
3. The VBA program shall be initiated from a Command Button control added to the spreadsheet.
4. The program shall ask the user for his or her name and birth date.
5. The program shall output the user's name (formatted in proper case) and birth date (formatted as Month, Day, Year, Weekday) to the spreadsheet.
6. The program shall calculate the user's age in years, months, days, hours, minutes, and seconds and output the results to the spreadsheet.
7. The program shall calculate the current position of the user's biorhythms in each of the three cycles (day and magnitude) and output the results to the spreadsheet.
8. The embedded chart on the spreadsheet shall contain a data series for each of the values calculated in the previous requirement.

Designing Biorhythms and the Time of Your Life

The user interface for the project consists of a single Excel worksheet containing the data for the static sinusoidal curves, an embedded chart, and a Command Button control for initiating the program. The worksheet is preformatted to make the data presentable. The scatter chart contains six different data series that include the three static curves (column A has the *x*-values and columns B through D the *y*-values) and the values for the current status of the user's biorhythms (not visible until the program has been run). I will enter the VBA program within the `Click()` event procedure of the Command Button control on the worksheet so the user can initiate it with a simple mouse click. Figure 2.10 shows the *Biorhythms and the Time of Your Life* spreadsheet prior to executing the program.

The program requires the user to input his or her name and birth date. I will use an `InputBox()` function to collect this input and store it in a program variable. Next, the program will calculate the user's age in the different units (specified in the requirement list) and output the results to cells G30 through G35. Other outputs include the user's birth date to cells G29 and H29 formatted in a long form (month, day, year, weekday) and the current day and magnitude for each of the user's biorhythm cycles (cells A38 through A40 for the days, cells B38, C39, and D40 for the magnitudes). The calculation of the user's current biorhythms is based on his/her birth date and the number of 23, 28, or 33 day periods that have passed since he or she was born. Once the program has output the results to the worksheet, the chart is automatically updated by Excel.

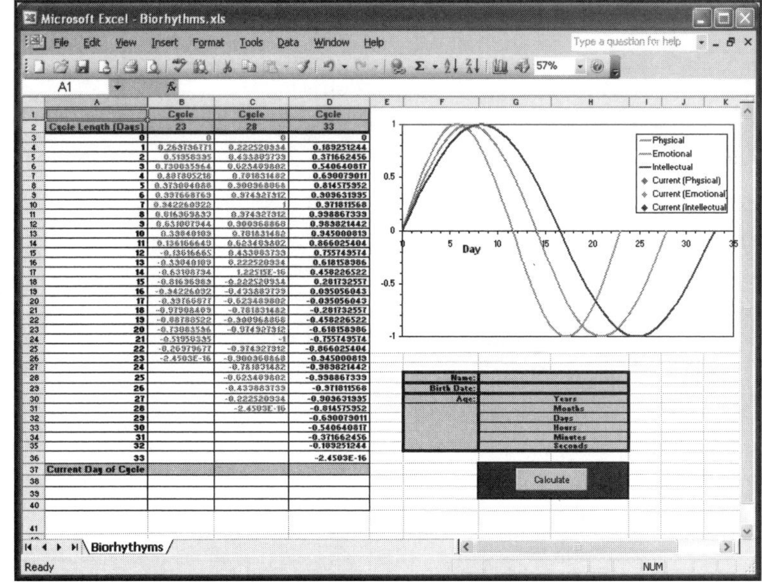

FIGURE 2.10

The Biorhythms and the Time of Your Life spreadsheet.

Coding Biorhythms and the Time of Your Life

I have entered the following code to the object module for the *Biorhythms and the Time of Your Life* worksheet shown in Figure 2.10.

```
Option Explicit
Private Sub cmdCalculate_Click()
    Dim userName As String
    Dim yrPassed As Single, moPassed As Single, dayPassed As Single
    Dim hrPassed As Single, minPassed As Single, secPassed As Single
    Dim userBday As Date, curDate As Date
    Dim bDate As String, bMonth As String
    Dim bDay As Integer, bYear As Integer
    Const SECSPERMIN = 60, MINSPERHOUR = 60
    Const HOURSPERDAY = 24, DAYSPERYEAR = 365.25
    Const PHYSICAL = 23, EMOTIONAL = 28, INTELLECTUAL = 33
    Const PI = 3.14159265358979

    '-------------------
    'Get the user's name and birth date.
    '-------------------
    userName = LCase(InputBox("What is your name?", "Name"))
    userBday = DateValue(InputBox("When is your birthday? (month/day/year)", "Birth Date"))

    '------------------------
    'Calculate length of life in different units.
    '------------------------
    curDate = Now   'Gets current time and date.
    secPassed = DateDiff("s", userBday, curDate)
    minPassed = secPassed / SECSPERMIN
    hrPassed = minPassed / MINSPERHOUR
    dayPassed = hrPassed / HOURSPERDAY
    yrPassed = dayPassed / DAYSPERYEAR
    moPassed = yrPassed * 12

    '--------------------
    'Get user's birthday in proper format.
    '--------------------
    bDate = Format(userBday, "dddd")
    bMonth = Format(userBday, "mmmm")
    bDay = Day(userBday)
    bYear = Year(userBday)
```

```
'-----------
'Format user's name.
'-----------
userName = StrConv(userName, vbProperCase)

'-------------------------------
'Enter time values into appropriate cells in worksheet.
'-------------------------------
Range("G28").Value = Trim(Left(userName, InStr(1, userName, " ")))
Range("H28").Value = Trim(Right(userName, Len(userName) - Len(Range("G28").Value)))
Range("G29").Value = bMonth & " " & Str(bDay)
Range("H29").Value = bYear & " (" & bDate & ")"
Range("G30").Value = yrPassed
Range("G31").Value = moPassed
Range("G32").Value = dayPassed
Range("G33").Value = hrPassed
Range("G34").Value = minPassed
Range("G35").Value = secPassed

'--------------
'Formula for day of cycle.
'--------------
Range("A38").Value = (Range("G32").Value / PHYSICAL - _
                     Int(Range("G32").Value / PHYSICAL)) * PHYSICAL
Range("A39").Value = (Range("G32").Value / EMOTIONAL - _
                     Int(Range("G32").Value / EMOTIONAL)) * EMOTIONAL
Range("A40").Value = (Range("G32").Value / INTELLECTUAL - _
                     Int(Range("G32").Value / INTELLECTUAL)) * INTELLECTUAL

'--------------------
'Formula for magnitude of biorhythym.
'--------------------
Range("B38").Value = Sin((Range("G32").Value / PHYSICAL - _
                    Int(Range("G32").Value / PHYSICAL)) * _
                    PHYSICAL * 2 * PI / PHYSICAL)
Range("C39").Value = Sin((Range("G32").Value / EMOTIONAL - _
                    Int(Range("G32").Value / EMOTIONAL)) * _
                    EMOTIONAL * 2 * PI / EMOTIONAL)
```

```
    Range("D40").Value = Sin((Range("G32").Value / INTELLECTUAL - _
                          Int(Range("G32").Value / INTELLECTUAL)) * _
                          INTELLECTUAL * 2 * PI / INTELLECTUAL)
End Sub
```

Variable declaration is required by adding `Option Explicit` to the general declarations section of the object module for the worksheet. All other code is added to the `Click()` event procedure of the Command Button control named `cmdCalculate`. Variables and constant declarations are placed at the top of the procedure. Date and string variables are used to hold and manipulate the name and birth date obtained from the user. Numerical variables are used to hold the various lengths of time the user has been alive and the numerical components of the user's birthday.

Input is gathered from the user with the `InputBox()` function. Notice that I placed the `InputBox()` function inside the parameter list of the `LCase()` function. This is called *nesting functions*. In nested functions, the innermost function runs first; in this case, `InputBox()`, then whatever the user enters in the input box is passed to the next function, `LCase()`. The string entered by the user is then stored in the `userName` variable with all characters lower case. Another `InputBox()` function is used to retrieve the user's birthday. Again the `InputBox()` is nested in another function. The `DateValue()` function is passed a string parameter representing a date and is used to convert the string to a value of type date. The date is then store in the variable `userBday`.

Now you must process the information obtained from the user. First, I get the current date and time from the operating system by using the `Now` function and store it in the date variable `curDate`. The `Now` function is somewhat unusual in that it does not take any parameters. The `curDate` and `userBday` variables are passed to the `DateDiff()` function along with the single character string "`s`". The `DateDiff()` function calculates the difference between two dates in the interval specified, in this case "`s`" for seconds. Once the user's life in seconds is known, it's a simple matter to convert this number to minutes, hours, days, months, and years using the constants defined earlier.

The `DateDiff()` function returns a value of type variant (long). This means that the function will return a long integer unless the value exceeds its range (2,147,483,647), in which case it will promote the return value to the next largest data type with integer values. In the *Biorhythms and the Time of Your Life* program, the range of the long data type will be exceeded by anyone more than 68 years old. Thus, to avoid a possible data-type error, the variable `secPassed` was declared as a single data type. This ensures the value from `DateDiff()` will be within the variable's allowed range of values. I did not want a floating-point number for the value of `secPassed`, but I don't need to be concerned because I know the `DateDiff()` function will only return a whole number.

The Format() function can be used with numerical, string, and date data. Here Format() is used to return the weekday the user was born, and the month as text rather than the numerical representation. The dates are passed as variables along with format strings ("dddd" and "mmmm"). These strings tell the function what format to use on the return value. For example, "dd" would return the numerical value for the day of the month, and "ddd" would return the three-letter abbreviation.

Next, the Day() and Year() functions are used to return the day of the month and year as integers and the StrConv() function converts the user's name to proper case (first letter of each name is capitalized).

Now that the time of life values have been calculated and the user's name and birth date formatted as desired, they are output to the appropriate cells in the worksheet. The only new element here is the Str() function which converts a numerical value to a string data type. The Str() function is not really needed for the conversion in this case. Since the & is used as the string concatenation operator, VBA assumes I want the variable bDay treated as if it were a string when the Str() function is omitted. If + is used as the string concatenation operator, then the Str() function must be used to avoid a type mismatch error. For clarity, I recommend using Str() in examples like this even when using the &.

The converse of the Str() function is the Val() function. The Val() function is used to convert string data to numerical data.

The last part of the program calculates and outputs the user's current day and magnitude for each of his/her biorhythm cycles. The current status of the user's cycle is calculated using the number of days he or she has been alive (from cell G32) and the length of each cycle. The Int() function is used to return the integer portion of a floating point number and the sin() function calculates the sine of the value passed to it. Note the use of the line continuation characters in the code.

That concludes this chapter's project. Although it's not exactly a long program, you may be feeling a bit overwhelmed by the number of functions used. Don't worry about learning all the functions available in VBA and how to use them—you can't! There are way too many, so it's a waste of time to try to memorize them all. I am familiar with the string functions, because I use them quite often, although I still had to look up syntax and parameter lists a couple of times while writing this project. The date functions are another matter. I didn't know any of the date functions before writing this program. What I did know is the essence of how a function works. I also realized that VBA was very likely to have a number of functions that worked on the date data type. Then it was a simple matter of searching the on-line help and looking at my choices.

Chapter Summary

This chapter introduced you to some important basics of programming; including variables, data types, and constants. I placed particular emphasis on the most common data types: numbers and strings. I also took a look at programming modules in VBA and their effect on the scope of a variable. Finally, I discussed several functions used to manipulate values of type string and date.

In Chapter 3, I will take a more in-depth look at VBA modules and procedures. Then, I will examine some more basic programming constructs with conditional operators and decision structures.

Challenges

1. **Write a program that will add two numbers input by the user and display the result in a spreadsheet. Use an input box and the `Val()` function to convert the user input to a numerical data type.**
2. **Place a Command Button control on a worksheet and write a program in the `Click()` event procedure that increments a variable by 5 with every click of the mouse. Output the value of this variable in a message box.**
3. **Write a program that extracts the time from the string returned by the `Now` function and outputs it in a message box.**
4. **Insert a new standard module and define a procedure that, when executed, prompts the user for his/her name and phone number. The form of the phone number entered by the user should include two dashes; one after the area code and one after the 3-digit prefix. Your program should use string functions to remove the dashes and then output the user's name and dash-less phone number to a worksheet.**
5. **Write a program that automatically sums the rows, columns, and diagonals of a 5 × 5 magic square.**

Procedures and Conditions

Although the two topics in this chapter title don't necessarily go hand in hand, they do represent basic constructs essential for any program. In this chapter, you closely observe both procedures and conditions in order to establish some basic tools with which to work in VBA.

Specifically, in this chapter I will discuss:

- Sub Procedures
- Function Procedures
- Event Procedures
- Conditional Logic
- Conditional Statements and the `If/Then/Else` and `Select/Case` Code Structures

Project: Poker Dice

Poker Dice is a variation of five-card draw using dice instead of cards. This is the first functional program that can't be created in the Excel application alone. The Poker Dice spreadsheet is shown in Figure 3.1.

The program introduces two new controls (Check Box and Image controls), sub procedures, and a conditional programming structure (`If/Then/Else`).

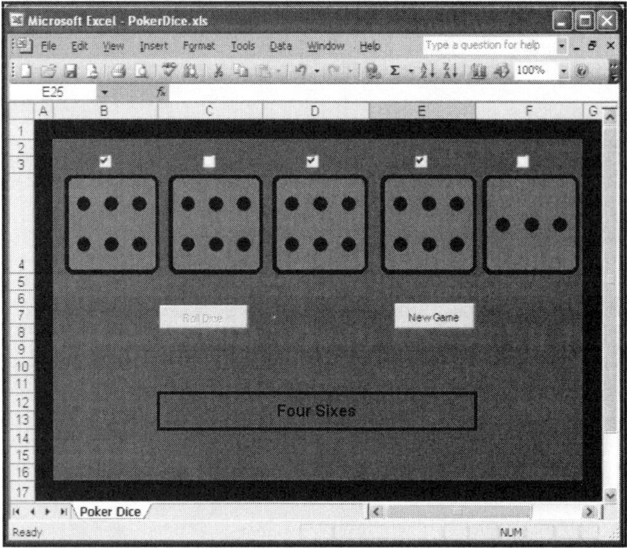

FIGURE 3.1

The *Poker Dice* program.

VBA Procedures

I briefly discussed programming modules in Chapter 2. You may remember that a module is a segment of your project that contains a related set of declarations and procedures. You may also remember that every module has its own window within the VBA IDE and, depending on whether or not it is an object module or a standard module, slightly different behavior regarding variables. Programming procedures can be constructed within each of these module windows if they are not already defined. Let's take a look at the different type of procedures that can be used and/or built using VBA.

Event Procedures

You have already seen a few examples of event procedures; such as the `Click()` event procedure of a Command Button control, and the `SelectionChange()` event procedure of a worksheet. VBA predefines these procedures in the sense that you cannot change the name of the procedure, nor the object within Excel to which the procedure belongs, nor the conditions under which the procedure is triggered. For the most part, all you can do with these procedures is add the code to be executed when the event is triggered. Typically, several events are associated with each Excel object; whether it is a worksheet, workbook, chart, or ActiveX control. Figure 3.2 shows the object module for a worksheet and displays all of the events associated with a worksheet in Excel.

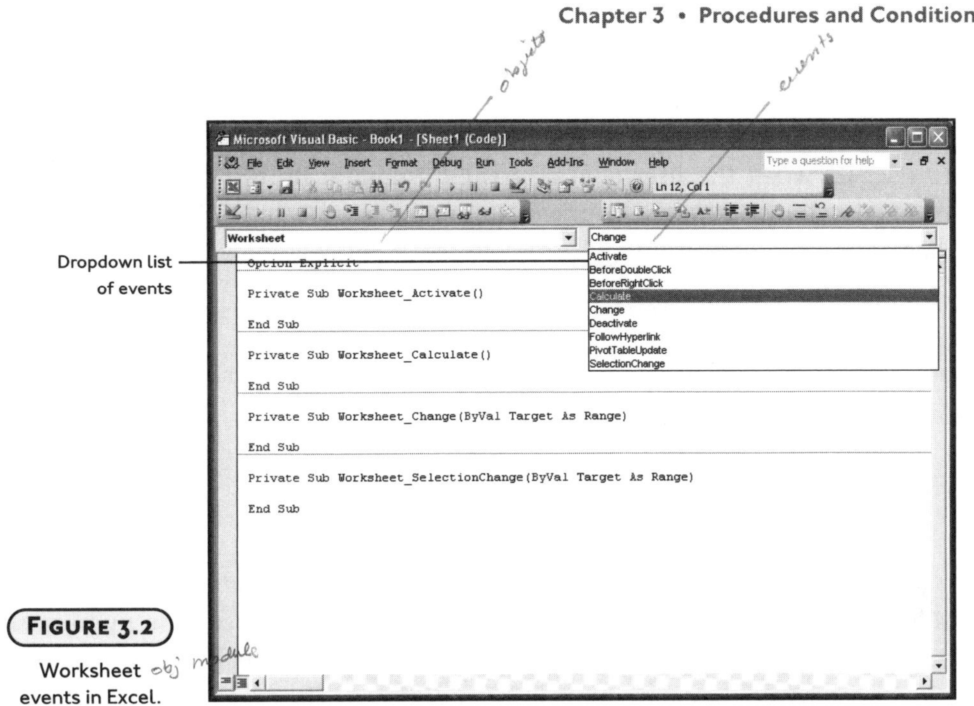

FIGURE 3.2

Worksheet events in Excel.

Event procedures are defined with the `Sub` keyword followed by the name of the procedure.

```
Private Sub Worksheet_Activate()
    'Event procedure code is listed here.
End Sub
```

The name of the procedure listed above is `Worksheet_Activate()`, although it will be more commonly referred to as the `Activate()` event. No parameters are passed to this procedure because the parentheses are empty. This procedure is triggered when the worksheet to which it is associated is activated; that is, when you switch between two different windows or worksheets, the `Activate()` event of the currently selected worksheet is triggered. The procedure ends with the line `End Sub`, unless the statement `Exit Sub` is used within the procedure code.

Parameters with Event Procedures

Parameters are the list of one or more variables passed to the event procedure when it is triggered. The values of the parameters passed to the event procedure contain information related to the event. A comma separates multiple variables, and the variable data type is also declared. VBA defines everything about the parameters passed to the event procedure; including the number of parameters, the name of each parameter and their data types, and the method in which they are passed. Although it is possible to change the name of the variables in the parameter list under certain circumstances, I do not recommend editing the event procedure definition in any way.

The following example shows the `MouseDown()` event procedure of a Command Button control. This procedure triggers when the user clicks on the Command Button control with the mouse. The first and last lines of the procedure are automatically created by VBA. I added the four lines of code within the procedure.

```
Private Sub CommandButton1_MouseDown(ByVal Button As Integer, ByVal Shift As Integer, _
ByVal X As Single, ByVal Y As Single)
    Range("A2").Value = Button
    Range("B2").Value = Shift
    Range("C2").Value = X
    Range("D2").Value = Y
End Sub
```

There are four parameters passed to the `MouseDown()` event procedure: `Button`, `Shift`, `X`, and `Y`; they have all been declared as numerical data types. These parameters contain numerical information describing the event that just occurred, and they can be used as variables within the procedure because they have already been declared. The `ByVal` keyword will be discussed later in this chapter, so just ignore it for now. The previous code was added to the `MouseDown()` event procedure of a Command Button control placed on a worksheet with a few column headers as shown in Figure 3.3.

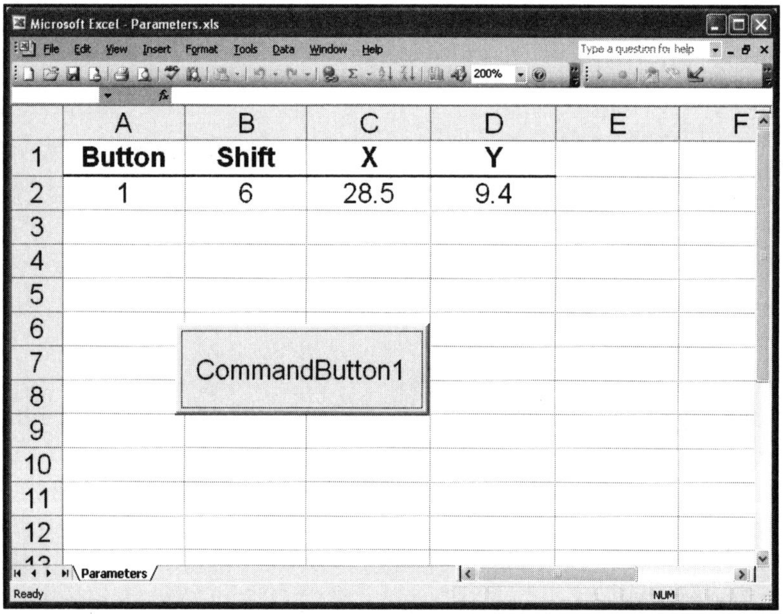

FIGURE 3.3

Parameter values of the `MouseDown()` event procedure.

The values of the parameter variables are copied to the appropriate cells in this worksheet when the user clicks on the Command Button control. The variable `Button` represents the mouse button that was clicked—a value of `1` for the left mouse button, `2` for the right mouse button, and `3` for the middle mouse button (if it exists). The variable `Shift` represents the combination of Shift, Ctrl, and Alt keys held down while the mouse button was clicked. Since there are eight possible combinations of these three keys, the variable `Shift` can hold an integer value between zero and seven. The variables `X` and `Y` represent the location of the mouse cursor within the Command Button control when the mouse button was clicked. The values of `X` and `Y` fall within zero to the value of the `Width` property of the Command Button control for `X`, and zero to the value of the `Height` property for `Y`. The upper left corner of the Command Button control is `X` = 0, `Y` = 0.

You now see how helpful the information within these parameters can be. For example, a programmer might use the `MouseDown()` and `MouseUp()` event procedures of an ActiveX control to catch a right click of the mouse button on the control. The `MouseDown()` event procedure might be used to display a menu with various options, and the `MouseUp()` event procedure would then be used to hide the menu. Does this sound familiar?

It is both impractical and unnecessary to discuss all of the event procedures of all Excel objects and ActiveX controls in this book. The examples you have seen so far are a good representation of how to use event procedures in VBA. In order to establish which event procedures (if any) should be used in your program, do the following:

- Ask yourself, "When should something happen?"
- Search for the event procedure(s) that will be triggered by the answer to the question, "When should something happen?" The event procedures have sensible names related to the action that triggers them; however, it may be useful to look up the description of the event procedure in the online help.
- If you cannot find an event procedure that triggers when desired, redesign your program with ActiveX controls that do contain a useful event procedure. If you still can't find anything, then there are probably errors in the logic of your algorithm.
- Test possible procedures by writing simple programs such as the one for the `MouseDown()` event procedure listed earlier.
- Insert the code that carries out the tasks you want once you recognize the proper event procedure.

Private, Public, and Procedure Scope

The `Private` and `Public` keywords used with procedure definitions have a similar function to that used with variable declarations. `Private` and `Public` are used to define the procedure's scope. The `Public` keyword makes the procedure visible to all other procedures in all modules in the project. The `Private` keyword ensures that the procedure is visible to other procedures within the same module, but keeps it inaccessible to all other procedures outside the module in which it is defined. The `Private` and `Public` keywords are optional, but VBA includes them in predefined event procedures. If `Private` or `Public` is omitted, then the procedure is public by default.

Use the `Option Private` statement in the general declarations section of a module to keep public modules visible only within the project. Omit `Option Private` if you wish to create reusable procedures that will be available for any project.

Sub Procedures

Although all procedures are really sub (short for *subroutine*) procedures, I will use the term to refer to those procedures created entirely by the programmer. The basic syntax and operation of a sub procedure is the same as for an event procedure. You define the procedure with the scope using the `Public` or `Private` keywords, followed by the keyword `Sub`, the procedure name, and the parameter list (if any). Sub procedures end with the `End Sub` statement. You can either type in the procedure definition or use the Insert/Procedure menu item to bring up the Add Procedure dialog box, as shown in Figure 3.4.

```
Private Sub myProcedure(parameter list)
     'Sub procedure code is listed here.
End Sub
```

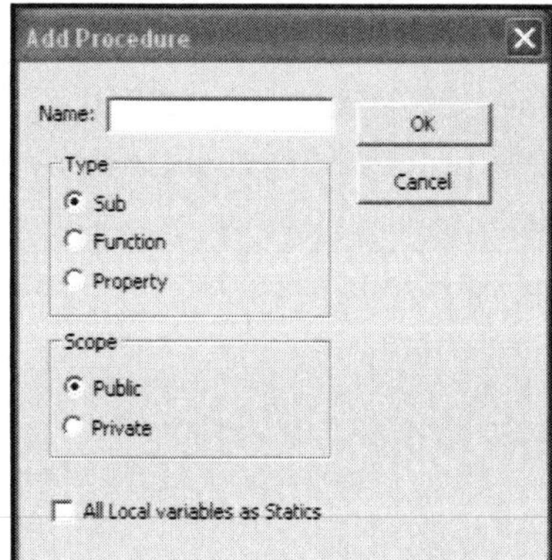

FIGURE 3.4

The Add Procedure dialog box.

Sub procedures differ from event procedures in that:

- the programmer defines the procedure name and any variable names in the parameter list.
- the programmer decides how many (if any) variables are in the parameter list.
- they can be placed in both object and standard modules.
- execution begins when they are "called" using code from other parts of the program and cannot be automatically triggered.

The following program collects two numbers from the user, adds them, and outputs the result. This program can reside in any module. For simplicity, I tested this program by running it directly from the VBA IDE. To begin program execution from the VBA IDE, first insert the mouse cursor within the procedure to be executed, and then press F5 or select the appropriate icon from the Standard toolbar or Run menu, as shown in Figure 3.5.

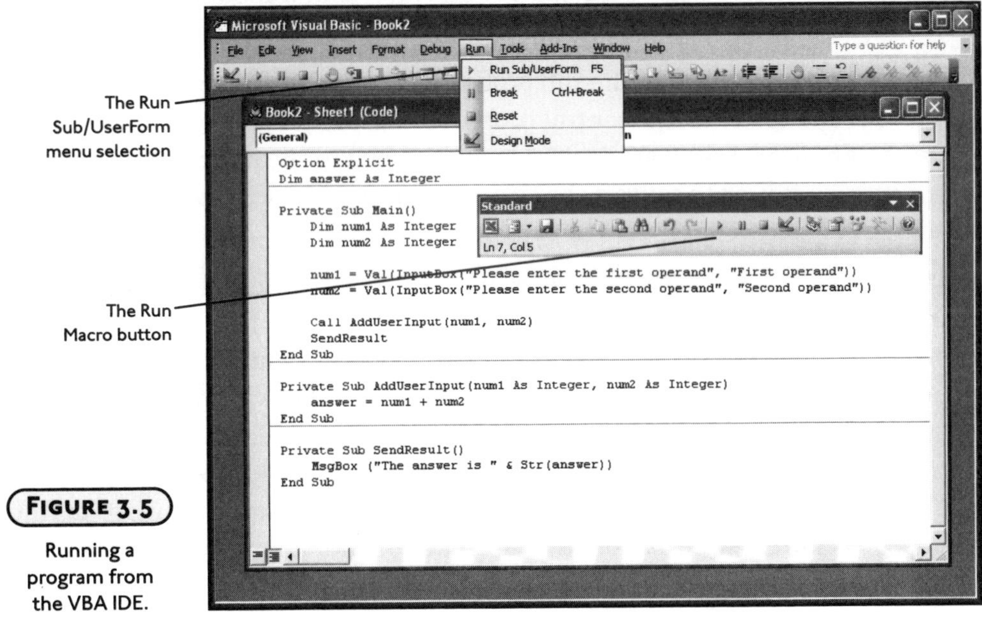

FIGURE 3.5

Running a program from the VBA IDE.

```
Option Explicit
Dim answer As Integer

Private Sub Main()
    Dim num1 As Integer
    Dim num2 As Integer
```

```
    num1 = Val(InputBox("Please enter the first operand", "First operand"))
    num2 = Val(InputBox("Please enter the second operand", "Second operand"))

    Call AddUserInput(num1, num2)
    SendResult
End Sub

Private Sub AddUserInput(num1 As Integer, num2 As Integer)
    answer = num1 + num2
End Sub

Private Sub SendResult()
    MsgBox ("The answer is " & Str(answer))
End Sub
```

First, variable declaration is required with `Option Explicit` and a module level variable (`answer`) is declared.

The majority of the program is listed in the sub procedure `Main()`. The sub procedure `Main()` is declared as `Private` and serves as the central procedure for the program. Two procedure-level integer variables (`num1` and `num2`) are declared and assigned to the return value of input boxes. The `Val()` function is used to convert the string type return value from the `InputBox()` function to a numerical value.

After two values are input by the user, the program makes the calls to the sub procedures `AddUserInput()` and `SendResult()`. The `Call` keyword is used to send program execution to `AddUserInput()` and the variables `num1` and `num2` are passed to this procedure. The `Call` keyword is required when passing parameters enclosed in parentheses; otherwise it is unnecessary (for example, `AddUserInput num1, num2` is an identical statement). After the `AddUserInput()` procedure executes, program execution resumes in the `Main()` procedure where it left off. The line `SendResult` is another procedure call and sends program execution to the `SendResult()` sub procedure. As no parameters are passed, the `Call` keyword is omitted (although you may include it if you like). The `Main()` procedure, and consequently the program, terminates after program execution returns from the `SendResult()` procedure. The `AddUserInput()` procedure's only purpose is to accept the two addends from the `Main()` procedure, add them together, and store the result in the module level variable `answer`. Note that I used the same variable names for the two addends when defining the `AddUserInput()` procedure. This is perfectly legitimate, as this is outside the scope of the original `num1` and `num2` variables. Finally, the `SendResult()` procedure is used to output the answer using a basic message box. A `Str()` function is used to convert the numerical variable `answer` to a string before it is concatenated to the rest of the message.

Keep your procedures as short as possible. You will find that as your procedures get longer, they get harder to read and debug. As a general rule I try to keep my procedures to a length such that all of the code is visible on my monitor. If your procedure gets much longer than one screen, break the procedure into two or more procedures.

ByVal and ByRef

You should have noticed the `ByVal` keyword in the parameter list of the `MouseDown()` event procedure shown earlier in the chapter. The `ByVal` keyword tells VBA to make a copy of the value stored in the accompanying variable. Thus, any manipulation of the copied value within the procedure does not affect the original variable.

The alternative to passing a variable by value is to pass a variable to another procedure by reference; the `ByRef` keyword is used to do so. When you pass by reference you are essentially passing the original variable to the procedure. Any manipulation of the variable in the new procedure is permanent, so the variable does not retain its original value when program execution proceeds back to the calling procedure. This is true even if you use a new variable name in the procedure that accepts the variable passed by reference. Passing by reference is the default behavior, so you can omit the `ByRef` keyword if you wish.

The following short program will make the behavior of `ByVal` and `ByRef` clear. I suggest inserting a new module into a project, adding the code below, and running the program from the procedure `Main()`.

```
Private Sub Main()
    Dim num1 As Integer
    Dim num2 As Integer
    num1 = 10
    num2 = 15
    Call PassByRef(num1)
    Call PassByVal(num2)
    MsgBox (num1 & "  " & num2)
End Sub
Private Sub PassByRef(ByRef num3 As Integer)
    num3 = 20
End Sub
Private Sub PassByVal(ByVal num2 As Integer)
    num2 = 20
End Sub
```

Figure 3.6 shows the message box output by this program.

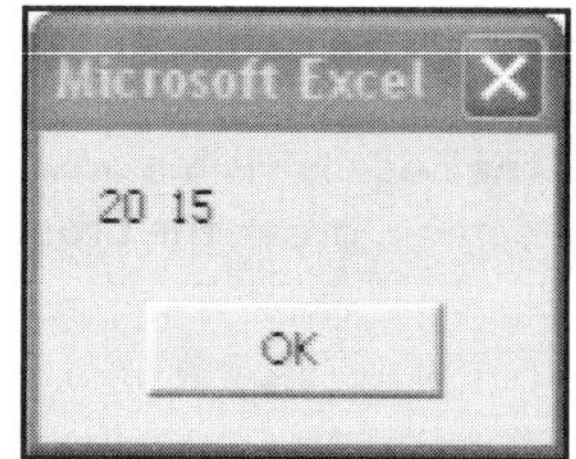

FIGURE 3.6

Message Box output from sub procedure `Main()`.

First two integer variables are declared and initialized to the values `10` and `15`. The first variable, `num1`, is passed by reference to the procedure `PassByRef()` in a variable called `num3`. The value `20` is assigned to the `num3` variable inside the `PassByRef()` procedure. Next the variable `num2` is passed by value to the `PassByVal()` procedure, where it is copied to another variable called `num2`. The `num2` variable in the `PassByVal()` procedure is then assigned the value `20`. The program ends with the output of the original `num1` and `num2` variables in a message box.

Now ask yourself: "What values output in the message box?" The answer is `20` for the `num1` variable, and `15` for the `num2` variable. The variable `num1` holds the value `20` at the end of the `Main()` procedure because it was changed in the `PassByRef()` procedure. Even though a different variable name was used in the `PassByRef()` procedure, the `num3` variable still refers to the same memory location holding the value assigned to the `num1` variable. Essentially, we have one variable with two names, each with its own scope. The `num2` variable retains its value of `15` at the end of `Main()` procedure because it had been passed by value to the `PassByVal()` procedure. Passing by value makes a copy of the variable's value to a new variable, even if the variable in the accepting procedure (`PassByVal`) has the same name. In this case, there are two variables with the same name.

You pass a variable by reference to a procedure in order to change the value of the original variable; or when the variable is needed in the procedure, but its value does not have to be changed. If the variable needs to be altered for another purpose but must retain its original value; then pass the variable by value using the `ByVal` keyword.

Function Procedures

Function procedures are very much like other procedures with one significant difference: they return a value to the calling procedure. Now you might be concerned or confused by the fact that I used the term *functions* back in Chapter 2 in reference to Excel's spreadsheet functions and VBA's string and date functions. So, what's the difference between these two terminologies? There is no difference. Everything I have, or will call a function is essentially the same thing. A *function* is a small program built with a specific purpose that, when used, will return a value to the calling procedure or spreadsheet cell(s).

In the Real World

At the most basic level, you can think of a memory location in your computer as a sequence of electrical switches that can be on or off. With these two possible conditions we have the basis for the binary language a computer understands (0 for off and 1 for on). The values stored by a programming variable are then just a patterned sequence of switches that are either on or off.

Some languages, such as C or C++, allow the programmer to directly access memory locations of variables. This extends the power of a programming language dramatically, but is not without dangers. For example, if you change the state of the wrong memory location you can easily cause the computer to crash. VBA handles memory management for you, so it is inherently safer than these other languages; however, with this safety you sacrifice some powerful capabilities.

If you are familiar with the built-in functions available in the Excel application, such as `SUM()`, `AVERAGE()`, `STDEV()`, then you already have a basic understanding of how they work. Functions are often (but not always) passed one or more values and they always return at least one value. For example, if I enter the formula `=AVERAGE(A2:A10)` into cell `A11` on a worksheet in the Excel application, I know that the average of the nine values given in the range `A2:A10` will be calculated and returned to cell `A11`. Excel recognizes the `AVERAGE` keyword in the formula as one of its built-in functions. Excel then calls the function procedure `AVERAGE()` and passes the range of values specified in parentheses—in this case, 9 values. The function procedure `AVERAGE()` then calculates the average of the values passed in as parameters and returns the result to the spreadsheet cell containing the formula. In VBA, you can also call function procedures such as `Left()`, `Mid()`, and `DateDiff()`, as you have seen in previous examples. You can even use the built-in functions of the Excel application. Finally, you can create your own function procedures in VBA.

Creating Your Own VBA Functions

The basic syntax for creating a function procedure in VBA is as follows:

```
Private/Public Function FunctionName(paramter list) as type
    'Function procedure code is listed here
    FunctionName = Return value
End Function
```

This is similar to the syntax for any procedure with the procedure name, parameter list, and an `End` statement. You can, and should include a `Private` or `Public` keyword to define the scope of the function. One obvious difference is the `Function` keyword replaces `Sub`. Also, you should define a return type to the function. The return data type is used for the value that the function sends back to the calling procedure. If you do not specify the data type, then the function's return value will be of type variant. The function returns a value by assigning the desired value to the name of the function, although the return value is usually stored in a variable.

Use `Exit Sub` or `Exit Function` if you need to return program execution to the calling procedure before the rest of the code in the procedure executes.

Functions are called from expressions where you would normally insert a variable or literal. For example, instead of assigning a literal to a variable, a function call can be used to assign the function's return value to the variable.

```
myVar = MyFunction(param1)
```

Here, the variable `myVar` is assigned the return value of the function named `MyFunction()` that is passed one parameter in the form of a variable named `param1`.

Now let's consider an example of a function that mimics one of Excel's built-in functions. The following function calculates the result of raising a number to a specified power. I named the function `PowerDB()` and set its return value as type double. The `PowerDB()` function accepts two numerical values for input, the number to which the exponent will be applied (`number`), and the value of the exponent (`n`). The function has been given public scope.

The code is really very simple. The value of the variable `number` is raised to the power of the value of the variable `n`, and then the result is restored in the variable `number`. The value of the variable `number` is assigned to the function so that it may be returned to the calling procedure.

```
Public Function PowerDB(ByVal number As Double, n As Single) As Double
    number = number ^ n
    PowerDB = number
End Function
```

A procedure that utilizes the `PowerDB()` function can be written as follows:

```
Private Sub TestPower()
    Dim number As Double
    Dim n As Single
    Dim result As Double
```

```
    number = Val(InputBox("Enter a number.", "Number"))
    n = Val(InputBox("Enter the value of the exponent.", "Exponent"))
    result = PowerDB(number, n)
    MsgBox (number & "^" & n & " = " & result)
End Sub
```

The only new idea here is the line that calls the `PowerDB()` function, `result = PowerDB(number, n)`. The variable `result` is assigned the return value of the function and output in a message box. Note that the data types for the `PowerDB()` function and variable `result` match (double). The variable `number` was passed to the `PowerDB()` function by value because if I passed it by reference its value would be changed by the function. Since I want to use the original value of `number` in the final output, I must pass it by value. The variable `n` was passed by reference because I did not change its value in the function procedure and VBA is more efficient when passing values by reference.

A public scope for the function `PowerDB()` makes it visible to all procedures in the project and the Excel application provided the function is contained in a standard module. Thus, this function can now be used like any other function in Excel. Returning to the Excel application and entering the formula `=PowerDB(2,8)` into any worksheet cell will return the value `256` to that cell. The `PowerDB()` function is even listed in Excel's insert function tool as shown in Figure 3.7 and 3.8.

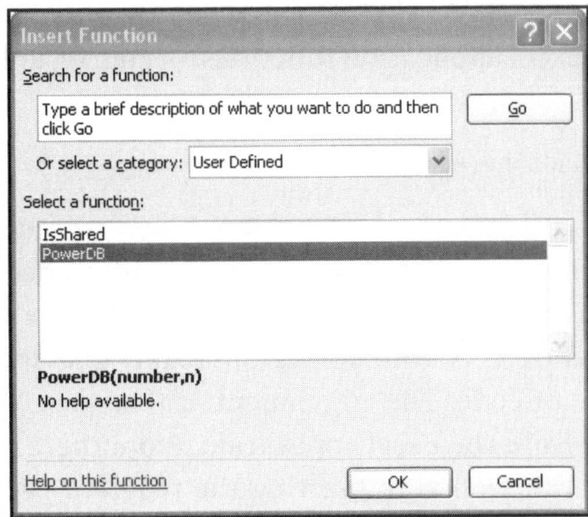

FIGURE 3.7

Step 1 of the Insert Function tool in the Excel application.

You now see that I named the function `PowerDB()` in order to avoid a conflict with Excel's `POWER()` function. You can create your own library of VBA functions to use in your spreadsheet applications. Keeping a library of VBA functions saves you valuable time as you do not have to re-write these functions to use them in another project.

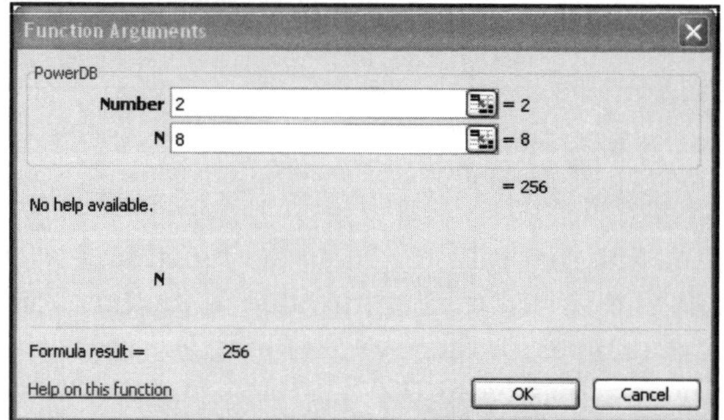

FIGURE 3.8

Step 2 of the Insert Function tool in the Excel application.

Using Excel Application Functions in VBA

Now that you know how to write functions in VBA and make them available to your spreadsheets, you are also aware that you can re-create any function already available in the Excel application. Although recreating Excel's functions would be a good way to improve your VBA programming skills, it's certainly not a practical use of your time. Why reinvent what's already been created for you? It would be nice if you could use Excel's application functions in your VBA code, as they are mostly complimentary, not repetitive, to VBA's set of functions. That way, if you need a specific function performed in your program that is not already included with VBA, you don't have to write it yourself.

Well, there *is* a method to use the Excel application functions, of course, and it is really quite simple.

```
result = Application.WorksheetFunction.Power(number, n)
```

Replacing the call to the `PowerDB()` function in the `TestPower()` sub procedure shown earlier with the line of code above will give the exact same result. The difference is that this code uses Excel's `POWER()` function and not the `PowerDB()` function. The syntax will be explained in detail in Chapter 5, "Basic Excel Objects," but you can probably guess what's happening from the names used in this line of code. The component `Application.WorksheetFunction` will return all functions available from the Excel application. From there it is a simple matter of adding on the name of the function and inserting the required parameters into the parentheses. Two more examples illustrate the use of the `AVERAGE()` and `STDEV()` functions from the Excel application.

```
myVar = Application.WorksheetFunction.Average(5, 7, 9)
myVar2 = Application.WorksheetFunction.StDev(3, 7, 11)
```

The examples above will return the value `7` to the variable `myVar` and `4` to the variable `myVar2`.

Logical Operators with VBA

Logic as applied to a computer program is evaluating an expression as true or false. An expression is typically, but not always, a comparison of two variables such as `var1>var2` or `var1=var2` (see Table 3.1 for a list of available comparison operators). A programmer reads these expressions as follows:

- The value of var1 is greater than the value of var2.
- The value of var1 equals the value of var2.

The statements are evaluated as true or false.

Imagine a simple device that takes a single expression as input, evaluates that expression as true or false, spits out the answer, and then moves on to the next expression. The evaluation of the expression is a simple task since there are only two choices and computers are very good at assigning 1's (true) or 0's (false) to things. The difficulty arises from trying to make sense out of the expressions that have been evaluated as true or false. This is where Boolean (after the nineteenth century mathematician George Boole) algebra comes in to play. Boolean algebra refers to the use of the operators `AND`, `OR`, `NOT`, and a few others to evaluate one or more expressions as true or false. Then, based on the result of the logic, the program selects a direction in which to proceed.

TABLE 3.1 COMPARISON OPERATORS IN VBA

Operator	Function
=	Tests for equality
<>	Tests for inequality
<	Less than
>	Greater than
<=	Less than or equal to
>=	Greater than or equal to

AND, OR, and NOT Operators

VBA uses logical `AND` to make a decision based on the value of two conditions. The value of each condition can be one of two values, true or false. Consider the following two conditions.

Condition 1	Condition2
`myVar > 10`	`myVar < 20`

The expression `Condition1 AND Condition2` evaluates as true only if `Condition1` and `Condition2` are both true. If either or both conditions evaluate to false then the overall result is false. The evaluation of expressions using logical operators is easily displayed in truth tables. Table 3.2 shows the truth table for logical `AND`.

TABLE 3.2 TRUTH TABLE FOR THE AND OPERATOR

Condition1	Condition2	Condition1 AND Condition2
True	True	True
True	False	False
False	True	False
False	False	False

The logical operator `OR` returns true from an expression when at least one of the conditions within the expression is true.

The expression `Condition1 OR Condition2` evaluates as true when either `Condition1` or `Condition2` is true or if both conditions are true. Table 3.3 shows the truth table for logical `OR`.

TABLE 3.3 TRUTH TABLE FOR THE OR OPERATOR

Condition1	Condition2	Condition1 OR Condition2
True	True	True
True	False	True
False	True	True
False	False	False

The `NOT` operator simply returns the opposite logic of the condition; so if the condition is false, `NOT` will return true and vice versa. Table 3.4 shows the truth table.

There are a few other logical operators (`Xor`, `Eqv`, and `Imp`) but they are seldom used or needed, so let's turn our attention to the practical use of Boolean algebra within the code structures `If/Then/Else` and `Select Case`.

Table 3.4 Truth Table for the NOT Operator

Condition I	NOT Condition I
True	False
False	True

Conditionals and Branching

It may seem like I've covered a fair amount of VBA programming, but in reality, I've barely scratched the surface. Right now, you can't really do much with the VBA programs you've written, because you haven't learned any programming structures; however, that is about to change as I begin to examine a simple yet very useful VBA code structure. The `If/Then/Else` structure is known as both a conditional and branching structure because it uses conditional statements to change the flow or direction of program execution.

If/Then/Else

There are several ways to implement this code structure. The most basic uses the two required keywords `If` and `Then`.

```
If (condition) Then Code statement
```

In the example above, the code statement following `Then` will execute if `condition` evaluates as true; otherwise code execution proceeds with the next statement. The entire structure takes just one line of code. It's convenient when you have just one brief code statement that needs to be executed if the condition is true. Multiple statements can be entered on the same line if you separate them with colons (:), but then your code may be hard to read. If you need more than one code statement executed, then for the sake of readability, you should use the block form of `If/Then`.

```
If (condition) Then
    'Block of code statements
End If
```

Again, the condition must be true or the block of code statements will not execute. When using more than one line in the program editor for `If/Then`, you must end the structure with `End If`.

The following procedure is a simple number-guessing game where the computer comes up with a number between 0 and 10 and asks the user for a guess. Three `If/Then` structures are used to determine what message is output to the user depending on their guess.

```
Private Sub NumberGuess()
    Dim userGuess As Integer
    Dim answer As Integer
    answer = Rnd * 10
    userGuess = Val(InputBox("Guess a number between 0 and 10.", "Number Guess"))
    If (userGuess > answer) Then
        MsgBox ("Too high!")
        MsgBox ("The answer is " & answer)
    End If
    If (userGuess < answer) Then
        MsgBox ("Too low!")
        MsgBox ("The answer is " & answer)
    End If
    If (userGuess = answer) Then MsgBox ("You got it!")
End Sub
```

A random number generated by the `Rnd` function returns a random number of type single between 0 and 1. The random number is multiplied by 10 and assigned to the variable `answer` to make it fall between `0` and `10`. Using an integer data type for the variable `answer` ensures that the calculated value is rounded and stored as an integer.

The `If/Then` structures each use one condition that compares the values stored in the `userGuess` and `answer` variables. Only one of these conditions can be true, and the message box in the `If/Then` structure with the true condition executes.

Previously, you saw the = operator used as an assignment operator. For example, a value is assigned to a variable.

In the context of conditional expressions, the = operator is a comparison operator. Using the same character for more than one type of operation is known as overloading an operator.

If you know you want one block of code executed when a condition is true and another block of code executed when the same condition is false, then use the `Else` keyword.

```
If (condition)
    'This block of code executes if the condition is true
```

```
Else
     'This block of code executes if the condition is false.
End If
```

The `If/Then` structures in the number guess procedure can also be written as follows, where `<>` is the "not equal" operator (see Table 3.1):

```
If (userGuess <> answer) Then
    MsgBox ("Wrong! The answer is " & answer)
Else
    MsgBox ("You got it!")
End If
```

This time, instead of using additional `If/Then` statements, the keyword `Else` is used to direct the program to another block of code that is executed if the condition `(userGuess <> answer)` evaluates to false.

There is no limit on the number of conditions you can use with an `If/Then` code structure. The condition

```
If (userGuess <> answer) Then
```

can also be written as

```
If (userGuess < answer) Or (userGuess > answer) Then
```

Where the logical operator `Or` is used in the expression for the conditional. Thus, if only one conditional evaluates as true, then the expression returns true and the logic is maintained. You can use more than two conditionals if needed; however, your code will get harder to read as the number of conditionals in one line of code increases. You will see an excessive use of conditionals in the Poker Dice project at the end of this chapter.

There are numerous possibilities for achieving the same logic when using `If/Then/Else` and conditionals. You can also nest the `If/Then/Else` code structure if you want to. The procedure below outputs a short message to the user depending on the current time and day of the week. After some variable declarations, a few familiar date functions are used to determine the current time and day of the week.

```
Private Sub myTime()
    Dim time As Date
    Dim theHour As Integer
    Dim theDayOfTheWeek As Integer
    time = Now
    theHour = Hour(time)
```

```
    theDayOfTheWeek = Weekday(time)
    If (theHour > 8) And (theHour < 17) Then
        If (theDayOfTheWeek > 0) And (theDayOfTheWeek < 6) Then
            MsgBox ("You should be at work!")
        Else
            MsgBox ("I love weekends.")
        End If
    Else
        MsgBox ("You should not be at work!")
    End If
End Sub
```

The first `If/Then/Else` structure is checking if the time of the day is between 8:00 A.M. and 5:00 P.M., since the variable `theHour` holds an integer value between `0` and `23`. If the expression is true then another `If/Then/Else` structure will execute. This `If/Then/Else` structure is *nested* in the first one and is checking the value for the day of the week. If the day of the week is Monday through Friday, then a message box is used to display the string "`You should be at work!`". (Remember that it had to be between 8:00 A.M. and 5:00 P.M. to get to this point.) Otherwise, the nested `If/Then/Else` outputs the message `"I love weekends."` If the time of day is not between 8:00 A.M. and 5:00 P.M., then the string `"You should not be at work!"` is displayed in a message box.

There is no limit to the number of nested `If/Then` statements you can use; however, after three or four levels, keeping track of the logic can be difficult and your program may be difficult to read and debug.

It is a good idea to indent your code with each level of logic. You will find your programs much easier to read and debug if indented properly.

Another option regarding `If/Then/Else` structures is the `ElseIf` clause. The `ElseIf` clause is used like the `Else` clause with a conditional expression. You must also include `Then` when using `ElseIf`. The following example uses a series of `ElseIf` clauses to display the day of the week in a message box.

```
If (theDayOfTheWeek = 0) Then
    MsgBox ("It's Sunday!")
ElseIf (theDayOfTheWeek = 1) Then
    MsgBox ("It's Monday!")
ElseIf (theDayOfTheWeek = 2) Then
```

```
    MsgBox ("It's Tuesday!")
ElseIf (theDayOfTheWeek = 3) Then
    MsgBox ("It's Wednesday!")
ElseIf (theDayOfTheWeek = 4) Then
    MsgBox ("It's Thursday!")
ElseIf (theDayOfTheWeek = 5) Then
    MsgBox ("It's Friday!")
Else
    MsgBox ("It's Saturday!")
End If
```

There is no limit to the number of `ElseIf` clauses that can be used; however, `ElseIf` cannot be used after an `Else` clause. You can also nest more `If/Then/Else` structures inside an `ElseIf` clause.

Select/Case

There are innumerable ways to accomplish the same task with `If/Then/Else` and `ElseIf` code structures. But keep in mind that using a large number of `If/Then/Else` and `ElseIf` statements can make it difficult to follow the logic of your program. You should consider using the `Select/Case` code structure in situations where you find yourself using a large number of `ElseIf` statements. The `Select/Case` code structure is used when you need to test the value of a variable multiple times and, based on the outcome of those tests, execute a single block of code. The `Select/Case` syntax is fairly simple and easy to understand.

```
Select Case expression
     Case condition1
          'This block of code executes if condition1 is true.
     Case condition2
          'This block of code executes if condition2 is true.
          'There is no limit on the number of cases you can use
     Case Else
     'This block of code executes if none of the other conditions were true.
End Select
```

A `Select/Case` structure must begin with `Select Case` and end with `End Select`. The expression immediately following `Select Case` is typically a variable of numerical or string data type. Next, a list of one or more code blocks is entered just beneath the keyword `Case` and a condition. The condition is a comparison to the expression in the opening line of the structure. VBA proceeds down the list until it finds a condition that evaluates as true, then executes the block of code within that case element. Any additional case elements following one that evaluates as true are ignored, even if their conditions are also true. Thus, order of the case elements is important. The last case element should use `Case Else`. This ensures that at least one block of code executes if all other conditions are false.

The following example uses a `Select/Case` structure in a VBA function designed to work with an Excel spreadsheet. The input value should be numerical and expressed as a percentage. This percentage represents a student's score and is passed into the function and stored in the variable `studentScore`. The variable `studentScore` is used as the test expression for the `Select/Case` structure.

```
Public Function AssignGrade(studentScore As Single) As String
    Select Case studentScore
        Case 90 To 100
            AssignGrade = "A"
        Case Is >= 80
            AssignGrade = "B"
        Case 70 To 80
            AssignGrade = "C"
        Case Is >= 60
            AssignGrade = "D"
        Case Else
            AssignGrade = "F"
    End Select
End Function
```

There are two forms for writing the conditionals in the case elements; both are shown in this example. The first case element uses `Case 90 To 100`. This condition is specified as a range of values with the lower value inserted first followed by the `To` keyword and then the upper value of the range. This condition evaluates as true if the value stored in the variable `studentScore` is greater or equal to `90` and less than or equal to `100`.

If the value of `studentScore` is less than `90`, VBA proceeds to the next case element which is `Case Is >= 80`. This is the other form for a condition using the `Is` keyword to specify a range with a comparison operator >= (greater than or equal to). If the value of `studentScore` is greater than or equal to `80`, this condition is true and the block of code within this element executes (assuming the previous condition was false). Again, VBA proceeds down the list until it finds a true condition and then evaluates that case element's code block. If `Case Is >= 60` in the `AssignGrade()` function is placed at the top of the `Select/Case` structure, then all students with a percentage higher than `60` would be assigned a grade of `D` even if they have a score of `100`.

CONSTRUCTING THE POKER DICE PROGRAM

Poker Dice is a variation on five-card draw using dice instead of cards. Since each die offers six possible values instead of thirteen and no suits, you will get better hands with this game. This program illustrates the use of conditionals with `If/Then/Else` and `ElseIf` code structures, as well as sub and function procedures. *Poker Dice* will also introduce you to a couple of new ActiveX controls, the Image control and the Check Box control. Please find the project along with the images of the dice on the accompanying CD.

Requirements for Poker Dice

I want to create a program that simulates five card draw using dice instead of cards. The spreadsheet is preformatted in the Excel application for color, font, and borders. The requirements of the program are as follows:

1. The user interface shall consist of a single spreadsheet formatted to simulate a game board with five Image controls, five Check Box controls, two Command Button controls, and a merged area of cells for outputting messages to the user.
2. A new game shall be initiated by clicking a button and clearing the game board (spreadsheet) of images, check marks, and text.
3. The button that clears the game board shall be disabled after each use and another button that is used to roll the dice enabled.
4. Clicking the roll dice button (enabled in requirement three) shall simulate the roll of five dice.
5. When simulating a roll of the dice, the program shall display five dice images. Each image shall be randomly selected from one of six images.
6. After the initial roll of the dice, the program shall report the result of the hand as text in a spreadsheet cell.
7. The user shall have one chance to discard dice and roll again.
8. The Image and Check Box controls shall be disabled for the first roll of the dice and enabled for the second roll.
9. The user shall select dice to save by clicking on a check box or a dice's image.
10. After the second roll, the program shall display the new images of the dice and display the new result.
11. After the second roll, the button used to roll the dice shall be disabled and the button used to clear the game board enabled.

Designing Poker Dice

Figure 3.9 shows my design for the *Poker Dice* program's user interface. I formatted the cells for width, height, and background colors of black or green from the Excel application. I also merged cells C12:E13 into one cell and formatted its border as shown in Figure 3.9. The merged cells will serve to display the result of the hand for each roll to the user. I added ActiveX controls for displaying dice images (Image controls), selecting dice to hold (Check Box controls), and playing the game (Command Button controls).

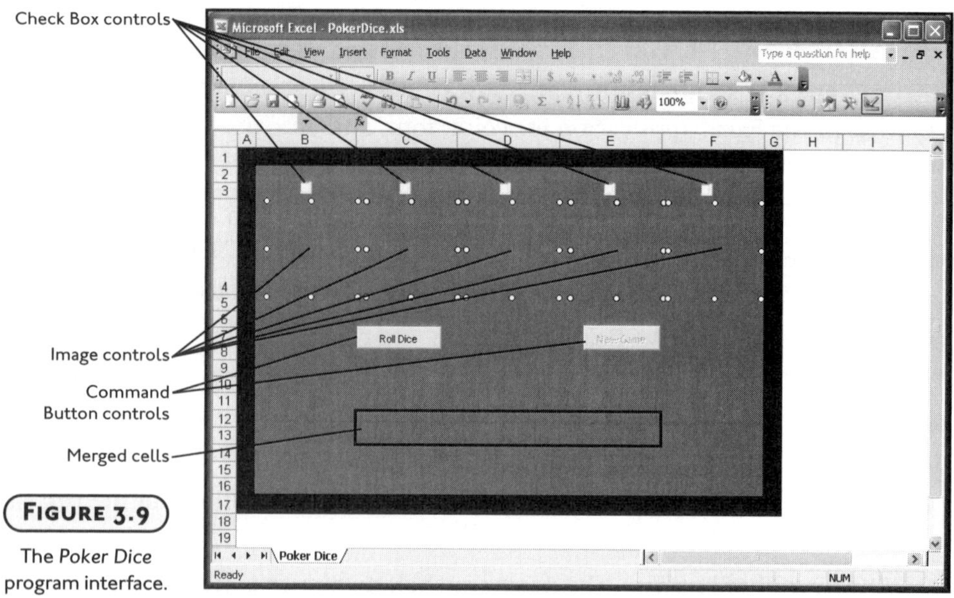

FIGURE 3.9

The *Poker Dice* program interface.

The Image Control

The Image control is used to display image files (most commonly bitmaps, jpegs, or gifs). The Image control can be added to a worksheet from the control toolbox like any other ActiveX control. Figure 3.10 shows the icon for the Image control.

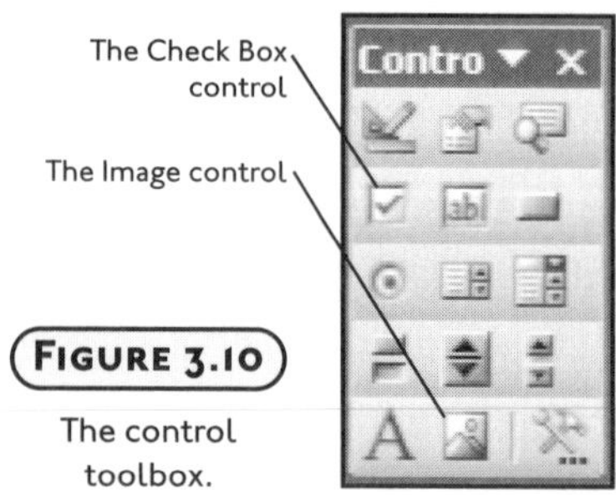

FIGURE 3.10

The control toolbox.

Image files can be loaded into the Image control at Design Time or run time via the `Picture` property. Some of the more important properties of the Image control are summarized in Table 3.5

TABLE 3.5 SELECTED PROPERTIES OF THE IMAGE CONTROL

Property	Function
`Name`	Used for referencing the control in your program
`AutoSize`	If true, the control will automatically resize itself to fit the image size.
`BackStyle`	Use the transparent setting if you don't want the user to know it's there until an image is loaded.
`Picture`	The path to the image file to be displayed
`PictureAlignment`	Aligns the image to the specified location
`PictureSizeMode`	`Clip`, `Stretch`, or `Zoom`. Not important if `AutoSize` is true. May distort the image.

Table 3.6 lists the properties of the Image controls I changed at Design Time for the Poker Dice program. With the `BackStyle` property set to transparent, the control cannot be seen unless an image is loaded or the control is selected while in design mode (see Figure 3.9). I matched the size of the Image controls (`Width` and `Height` properties) to that of the dice images.

TABLE 3.6 PROPERTY SETTINGS OF IMAGE CONTROLS IN THE POKER DICE PROGRAM

Property	Value
`Width, Height`	`75`
`Name`	`imgDice1, imgDice2`, etc.
`BackStyle`	transparent
`AutoSize`	`True`
`BorderStyle`	None
`SpecialEffect`	Flat

The Image control also has several event procedures; most notably the `Click()`, `BeforeDragOver()`, and `BeforeDropOrPaste()` event procedures. I will use the `Click()` event procedure of the Image controls to allow a user to select a dice; that is, when the user clicks on an image of a dice, its corresponding Check Box will toggle on or off.

The Check Box Control

The Check Box control is a familiar and relatively easy control to use. Figure 3.10 shows the icon for the Check Box control. Check Box controls are designed to give the user multiple selections from a group.

Use the Option Button control if you wish to limit the user to only one choice.

Table 3.7 lists the most important properties of the Check Box control.

TABLE 3.7 SELECTED PROPERTIES OF THE CHECK BOX CONTROL

Property	Function
`Name`	Used for referencing the control in your program
`Caption`	Displays text that describes a choice for the user.
`Value`	Boolean property. True if checked.

Most Check Box control properties relate to its appearance; you will have to use more than what is listed in Table 3.7; however, these are the properties most commonly manipulated at Design Time. The `Name` property is used to reference the Check Box control and the `Value` property tests whether or not the user has it selected. Table 3.8 lists the properties of the Check Box controls I changed at Design Time for the Poker Dice program.

The Check Box control has several event procedures associated with it, but you will seldom use anything other than its `Click()` event procedure.

Locating the Code for Poker Dice

Requirement 2 for the Poker Dice program specifies that a button will be used to initiate the program. Other requirements specify actions for mouse clicks on images as well as another button. Since all ActiveX controls are drawn on the same worksheet, the entire program can be written in the object module for the worksheet containing the game board. The `Click()`

Table 3.8 Property Settings of Check Box Controls in the Poker Dice Program

Property	Value
`Name`	`ckBox1`, `ckBox2`, etc.
`BackStyle`	Transparent
`Caption`	Empty
`SpecialEffect`	Sunken
`Value`	`False`

event procedures of the two Command Button controls and the Image controls must all contain code. Custom sub and function procedures will be added as needed to satisfy the remaining requirements and keep the event procedures from getting too long. You must keep in mind that the purpose of writing your own sub and function procedures is to compartmentalize your program into smaller and therefore more easily solved tasks.

Coding Poker Dice

The Poker Dice program code will be written in the object module of the worksheet containing the game board. The `Click()` event procedures of the Command Button controls will contain the code that initiates the game, whereas the `Click()` event procedures of the Image controls will simply toggle the Check Boxes.

Selecting the Dice

To begin, let's write code that allows a user to select a dice to hold when he or she clicks on its image. This means you have to change the `Value` property of the Check Box controls from the `Click()` event procedure of the Image controls. The user is allowed to toggle the Check Box on and off, so you should use the `Not` operator to change the Boolean value of the Check Box's `Value` property. The user can accomplish the same thing by clicking on the Check Box directly; however, you don't need to write any code for this as it's automatically handled by the Check Box.

```
Option Explicit
Private Sub imgDice1_Click()
    ckBox1.Value = Not ckBox1.Value
End Sub
```

```
Private Sub imgDice2_Click()
    ckBox2.Value = Not ckBox2.Value
End Sub
Private Sub imgDice3_Click()
    ckBox3.Value = Not ckBox3.Value
End Sub
Private Sub imgDice4_Click()
    ckBox4.Value = Not ckBox4.Value
End Sub
Private Sub imgDice5_Click()
    ckBox5.Value = Not ckBox5.Value
End Sub
```

Resetting the Game Board

Before a user can play a game of *Poker Dice*, he or she must reset the game board by clearing the dice, check marks, and text. I handle the resetting of the game board with the procedures `ToggleControls()` and the `Click()` event of the Command Button control named `cmdNewGame`. These procedures are fairly straightforward.

The `ToggleControls()` sub procedure is passed a Boolean parameter that is used to enable or disable all of the Check Box and Image controls on the game board. Set the `Enabled` property of an ActiveX control to true in order to activate the control for use. Set the `Enabled` property of an ActiveX control to false to make it unavailable to the user. Please note: the caption will be grayed out. These controls must be disabled prior to the first roll of the dice to prevent the user from accidentally selecting one of these controls. If a Check Box is selected prior to the first roll, the dice's image will not be loaded for its corresponding Image control (you will see why shortly). The `ToggleControls()` sub procedure must be called later in the program so that the Check Box and Image controls are enabled prior to the user making his or her second roll of the dice. Note that one Boolean value must be passed to the `ToggleControls()` sub procedure in order to specify enabling or disabling the controls. The procedure's scope is private since it only needs to be accessed from code in the object module.

The code in the `ToggleControls()` sub procedure could have been left in the `Click()` event procedure of the Command Button control; however, moving this code to a custom sub procedure serves to shorten the `Click()` event procedure, and prevents a code redundancy later in the program for re-enabling these controls.

```
Private Sub ToggleControls(toggle As Boolean)
'Toggle the Enabled property of the Check Box and Image controls.
    ckBox1.Enabled = toggle
    ckBox2.Enabled = toggle
    ckBox3.Enabled = toggle
    ckBox4.Enabled = toggle
    ckBox5.Enabled = toggle
    imgDice1.Enabled = toggle
    imgDice2.Enabled = toggle
    imgDice3.Enabled = toggle
    imgDice4.Enabled = toggle
    imgDice5.Enabled = toggle
End Sub
```

The `Click()` event of the Command Button control named `cmdNewGame` clears the Check Boxes, images, and text from the game board and calls the `ToggleControls()` sub procedure. You can remove any checks selected by the user by setting the `Value` property of all Check Box controls to false. To clear a cell's content you can set the `Value` property of the cell to an empty string as I have done with the merged cells on the game board. Note that when referring to cells that have been merged, use the row and column indices of the upper left cell in the merged group, in this case cell `C12`. To allow the user his or her first roll, you must enable and disable the Command Buttons `cmdRollDice and cmdNewGame`, respectively. Finally, you can remove the images from the Image controls by passing an empty string to VBA's `LoadPicture()` function.

```
Private Sub cmdNewGame_Click()
'Initialize ActiveX controls on the worksheet.
    '--------------
    'Clear check box controls.
    '--------------
    ckBox1.Value = False
    ckBox2.Value = False
    ckBox3.Value = False
    ckBox4.Value = False
    ckBox5.Value = False
    ToggleControls False    'Call sub to disable Image and Check Box controls
```

```
    '-------------------------------
    'Clear text from merged cells. Enable/disable buttons.
    'Clear images from Image controls.
    '-------------------------------
    Range("C12").Value = ""
    cmdRollDice.Enabled = True
    cmdNewGame.Enabled = False
    imgDice1.Picture = LoadPicture("")
    imgDice2.Picture = LoadPicture("")
    imgDice3.Picture = LoadPicture("")
    imgDice4.Picture = LoadPicture("")
    imgDice5.Picture = LoadPicture("")
End Sub
```

Figure 3.11 shows the *Poker Dice* game board while the user attempts to click on an Image control after it has been reset. The Image control is grayed while the user clicks it, but its associated Check Box is not and cannot be checked at this time.

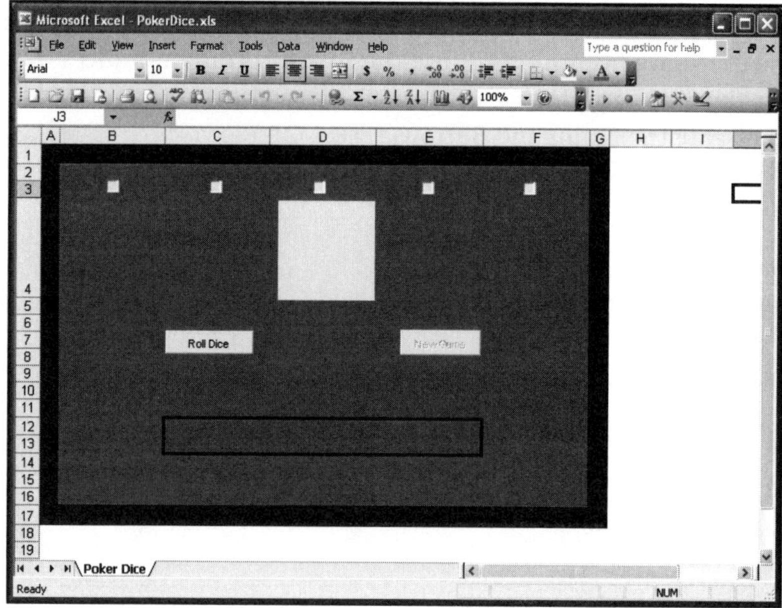

FIGURE 3.11

The Poker Dice game board after resetting.

Rolling the Dice

The Command Button control's (`cmdRollDice`) `Click()` event procedure loads images of dice into the Image controls. The image for each control is selected randomly from one of six choices.

The static integer variable `numRolls` keeps track of how many times the user has clicked on this button. The variable `numRolls` is incremented by one each time this procedure executes; however, the user is allowed only two clicks per game. For example, when `numRolls` reaches a value of two, it resets to zero near the end of the procedure.

The string variables `imageFile` and `imagePath` hold the name of the file and path to that file, respectively. The file path is stored in a variable; if it needs to be changed later, only one line of code needs editing. (The syntax used to get the file path string will make more sense after you have read Chapter 5.) When the workbook containing *Poker Dice* is loaded, Excel keeps track of the file path to the loaded workbook (PokerDice.xls). The line of code that stores the file path in the variable `imagePath` accesses this information using the `Path` property of the `Workbook` object. This will actually prevent a "file not found" error if the workbook is copied to a new location on the same, or another computer. An additional backslash is concatenated onto the string for later use.

The program must select an image of a dice randomly; therefore, I use the `Randomize()` function to initialize VBA's random number generator. Without any arguments passed to it, `Randomize()` will use the system clock to set a seed value for random number generation. Without the `Randomize()` function, the same seed value will be used for random number generation. As a result, the same random number sequence will be reproduced each time the program is run. Obviously, I do not want the same sequence of random numbers for each game; therefore, I have added the `Randomize()` function to the program.

To load an image, I have written several conditional blocks of code. An `If/Then/Else` code structure checks the `Value` property of the Check Box controls. If the value is false, then a randomly-chosen image is loaded into the Image control. If the value is true, then no image is loaded—this is why the Image and Check Box controls are cleared and disabled for the first roll. The random number is converted to an integer with the `Int()` function. As written, the value of the random number can only fall between 1 and 6. I store the random number in a spreadsheet cell because I will need to access this value in another procedure later in the program in order to check the result of the hand. Alternatively, I could use a set of module-level variables to hold the result from the random number generation. The entire path to the desired image file is stored in the string variable `imageFile`. I used filenames "1.bmp", "2.bmp", etc., for my image files in order to make the string concatenation easy. Finally, the image is loaded into the Image control by passing the file path to the `LoadPicture()` function. This `If/Then/Else` block is repeated for each of the five Image controls. (In Chapter 5, you will learn how to loop through a set of objects so that you will not have to write the redundant code I've written here.)

Another If/Then/Else structure is used to test the value of the variable numRolls. After the user has rolled twice, the Command Button controls named cmdRollDice and cmdNewGame are disabled and enabled, respectively. The Check Box and Image controls are enabled with a call to ToggleControls() sub procedure (if it's the user's first roll). If it's the user's second roll, the variable numRolls is reinitialized to zero for the next game.

The sub procedure DisplayResult() is called without passing parameters in order to determine the result of the user's hand. This procedure serves to simplify the program by compartmentalizing the larger problem into smaller and more manageable problems—in this case, scoring the hand.

```
Private Sub cmdRollDice_Click()
'Use random numbers to select an image of a die for each Image control
    Static numRolls As Integer
    Dim imageFile As String
    Dim imagePath As String

    '---------------
    'Set path to image files.
    '---------------
    imagePath = Workbooks("PokerDice.xls").Path & "\"
    numRolls = numRolls + 1
    Randomize    'Seed random number generator

    '-----------------------------------
    'For each image control, get a random number between 1 and 6.
    'Use the random number to load specific dice image.
    '-----------------------------------
    If ckBox1.Value = False Then
        Range("B2").Value = Int(Rnd * 6) + 1
        imageFile = imagePath & Trim(Str(Range("B2").Value)) & ".bmp"
        imgDice1.Picture = LoadPicture(imageFile)
    End If
    If ckBox2.Value = False Then
        Range("C2").Value = Int(Rnd * 6) + 1
        imageFile = imagePath & Trim(Str(Range("C2").Value)) & ".bmp"
        imgDice2.Picture = LoadPicture(imageFile)
    End If
    If ckBox3.Value = False Then
        Range("D2").Value = Int(Rnd * 6) + 1
```

```
        imageFile = imagePath & Trim(Str(Range("D2").Value)) & ".bmp"
        imgDice3.Picture = LoadPicture(imageFile)
    End If
    If ckBox4.Value = False Then
        Range("E2").Value = Int(Rnd * 6) + 1
        imageFile = imagePath & Trim(Str(Range("E2").Value)) & ".bmp"
        imgDice4.Picture = LoadPicture(imageFile)
    End If
    If ckBox5.Value = False Then
        Range("F2").Value = Int(Rnd * 6) + 1
        imageFile = imagePath & Trim(Str(Range("F2").Value)) & ".bmp"
        imgDice5.Picture = LoadPicture(imageFile)
    End If

    '-------------------
    'Use a static variable to ensure the
    'user only gets one draw per game.
    '-------------------
    If numRolls = 2 Then
        cmdRollDice.Enabled = False
        cmdNewGame.Enabled = True
        numRolls = 0
    Else
        ToggleControls True
    End If
    DisplayResult   'Call sub to display result of roll.
End Sub
```

Figure 3.12 shows an example of the *Poker Dice* game board after one roll of the dice.

Scoring the Hand

In order to score the user's hand, you first determine the number of dice with the same value (for example, three dice with a value of four and two dice with a value of six), then assign a result to the hand (for example, full house). Because I have not yet covered enough VBA programming structures, the process of evaluating the user's hand is somewhat cumbersome, a bit inefficient, and longer than is otherwise necessary; however, you will see several examples of decision structures and functions in the *Poker Dice* program. After you have read about VBA's looping structures in Chapters 4 and 5, you can come back to this program and improve it.

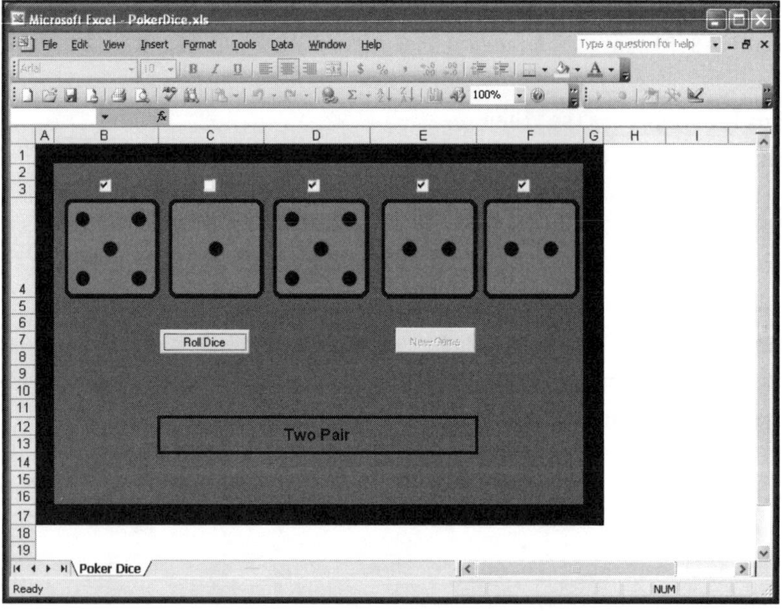

FIGURE 3.12

The *Poker Dice* game board after one roll.

The sub procedure `DisplayResult()` makes several function calls to determine the result of the user's hand. The first series of function calls (`GetNumOnes`, `GetNumTwos`, and so on) determine the number of dice with a particular value in the user's hand. These functions do not have any parameters, but they do return integers to a series of variables. These variables are passed to another series of functions (`IsNothingOrStraight`, `IsOnePair`, and so on) that score the hand and return a string. This is somewhat inefficient in that all seven function calls are made even if the hand has been properly scored by a previously called function. For example, if the first call to the `IsNothingOrStraight()` function procedure properly scores the hand, the code in the remaining functions still executes. This is why the variable `result` is passed to these functions—it must retain its string value if the function does not score the hand. The final result is then written to the merged cells on the game board (cell C12).

```
Private Sub DisplayResult()
'Evaluate the hand based on the value of the each die.
    Dim numOnes As Integer
    Dim numTwos As Integer
    Dim numThrees As Integer
    Dim numFours As Integer
    Dim numFives As Integer
    Dim numSixes As Integer
    Dim result As String
```

```
    '------------------------------------
    'Function calls to determine the number of die displaying each value.
    '------------------------------------
    numOnes = GetNumOnes
    numTwos = GetNumTwos
    numThrees = GetNumThrees
    numFours = GetNumFours
    numFives = GetNumFives
    numSixes = GetNumSixes

    '------------------------
    'Call functions for the result of the hand.
    '------------------------
    result = IsNothingOrStraight(numOnes, numTwos, numThrees, _
             numFours, numFives, numSixes, result)
    result = IsOnePair(numOnes, numTwos, numThrees, _
             numFours, numFives, numSixes, result)
    result = IsTwoPair(numOnes, numTwos, numThrees, _
             numFours, numFives, numSixes, result)
    result = IsThreeOfAKind(numOnes, numTwos, numThrees, _
             numFours, numFives, numSixes, result)
    result = IsFourOfAKind(numOnes, numTwos, numThrees, _
             numFours, numFives, numSixes, result)
    result = IsFiveOfAKind(numOnes, numTwos, numThrees, _
             numFours, numFives, numSixes, result)
    result = IsFullHouse(numOnes, numTwos, numThrees, _
             numFours, numFives, numSixes, result)

    Range("C12").Value = result
End Sub
```

The line continuation (_) character tells VBA that I really want just one line of code, but I need to type it on more than one line in the text editor. Make sure there is a single space between the last character and the underscore before proceeding to the next line.

The function procedures GetNumOnes(), GetNumTwos(), GetNumThrees(), GetNumFours(), GetNumFives(), and GetNumSixes() are called from the DisplayResult() sub procedure and they determine the number of dice with a particular value. These functions use numerous If/Then code structures to check the values of the dice stored in the second row of the spreadsheet (cells B2 through F2). The random number function `Rnd()` generated these values earlier in the program. A variable is then incremented if its associated value is found in a spreadsheet cell. These functions effectively determine how many dice show the value 1, 2, 3, 4, 5, or 6.

```
Private Function GetNumOnes() As Integer
'Determine the number of dice displayed with a value of 1
    Dim numOnes As Integer

    If Range("B2").Value = 1 Then numOnes = numOnes + 1
    If Range("C2").Value = 1 Then numOnes = numOnes + 1
    If Range("D2").Value = 1 Then numOnes = numOnes + 1
    If Range("E2").Value = 1 Then numOnes = numOnes + 1
    If Range("F2").Value = 1 Then numOnes = numOnes + 1
    GetNumOnes = numOnes
End Function

Private Function GetNumTwos() As Integer
'Determine the number of dice displayed with a value of 2
    Dim numTwos As Integer

    If Range("B2").Value = 2 Then numTwos = numTwos + 1
    If Range("C2").Value = 2 Then numTwos = numTwos + 1
    If Range("D2").Value = 2 Then numTwos = numTwos + 1
    If Range("E2").Value = 2 Then numTwos = numTwos + 1
    If Range("F2").Value = 2 Then numTwos = numTwos + 1
    GetNumTwos = numTwos
End Function

Private Function GetNumThrees() As Integer
'Determine the number of dice displayed with a value of 3
    Dim numThrees As Integer

    If Range("B2").Value = 3 Then numThrees = numThrees + 1
    If Range("C2").Value = 3 Then numThrees = numThrees + 1
    If Range("D2").Value = 3 Then numThrees = numThrees + 1
    If Range("E2").Value = 3 Then numThrees = numThrees + 1
    If Range("F2").Value = 3 Then numThrees = numThrees + 1
    GetNumThrees = numThrees
End Function
```

```
Private Function GetNumFours() As Integer
'Determine the number of dice displayed with a value of 4
    Dim numFours As Integer

    If Range("B2").Value = 4 Then numFours = numFours + 1
    If Range("C2").Value = 4 Then numFours = numFours + 1
    If Range("D2").Value = 4 Then numFours = numFours + 1
    If Range("E2").Value = 4 Then numFours = numFours + 1
    If Range("F2").Value = 4 Then numFours = numFours + 1
    GetNumFours = numFours
End Function

Private Function GetNumFives() As Integer
'Determine the number of dice displayed with a value of 5
    Dim numFives As Integer

    If Range("B2").Value = 5 Then numFives = numFives + 1
    If Range("C2").Value = 5 Then numFives = numFives + 1
    If Range("D2").Value = 5 Then numFives = numFives + 1
    If Range("E2").Value = 5 Then numFives = numFives + 1
    If Range("F2").Value = 5 Then numFives = numFives + 1
    GetNumFives = numFives
End Function
Private Function GetNumSixes() As Integer
'Determine the number of dice displayed with a value of 6
    Dim numSixes As Integer

    If Range("B2").Value = 6 Then numSixes = numSixes + 1
    If Range("C2").Value = 6 Then numSixes = numSixes + 1
    If Range("D2").Value = 6 Then numSixes = numSixes + 1
    If Range("E2").Value = 6 Then numSixes = numSixes + 1
    If Range("F2").Value = 6 Then numSixes = numSixes + 1
    GetNumSixes = numSixes
End Function
```

The function procedures `IsNothingOrStraight()`, `IsOnePair()`, `IsTwoPair()`, `IsThreeOfAKind()`, `IsFourOfAKind()`, `IsFiveOfAKind()`, `IsSixOfAKind()`, `IsFullHouse()` are called from the `DisplayResult()` sub procedure, and effectively score the hand and return a string result.

Each of these functions tests for a particular score (for example, one pair, two pair, and so on) indicated by the function name. These functions use `If/Then/Else` structures with numerous conditional statements. I said earlier in the chapter there would be an excessive use of conditionals—at this point, it can't be helped much, but I have used a line continuation character (`_`) in an effort to make the code easier to read.

Consider the `IsNothingOrStraight()` function procedure. The six conditionals in the first `If/Then/Else` structure are all linked with logical `And`. This means that all conditionals must be true if the block of code within the first `If/Then` statement is to be executed. If the number of occurrences of each die's value is equal to or less than one, a nested `If/Then/Else` code structure is then used to determine if the hand is a `"6 High Straight"`, a `"6 High"`, or a `"5 High Straight"`. If one of these conditional statements is true, then the function is assigned the value of one of the aforementioned strings which is returned to the calling procedure. If none of the conditionals are true, the original result is returned. Similar logic applies to the remaining functions and their determination of a score. You should study each function carefully noting the use of logical operators, parentheses, and `If/Then/Else` code structures.

Parentheses can be used to change the order of operator execution in VBA expressions. For example the conditional statement `(5 > 4 Or 6 > 3) And 7 < 3` evaluates to false whereas the expression `5 > 4 Or 6 > 3 And 7 < 3` evaluates to true.

```
Private Function IsNothingOrStraight(numOnes As Integer, numTwos As Integer, _
                  numThrees As Integer, numFours As Integer, numFives As Integer, _
                  numSixes As Integer, result As String) As String

    If (numOnes <= 1) And (numTwos <= 1) And (numThrees <= 1) And _
       (numFours <= 1) And (numFives <= 1) And (numSixes <= 1) Then
        If (numSixes = 1) And (numOnes = 0) Then
            IsNothingOrStraight = "6 High Straight"
        ElseIf (numSixes = 1) And (numOnes = 1) Then
            IsNothingOrStraight = "6 High"
        Else
            IsNothingOrStraight = "5 High Straight"
        End If
    Else
        IsNothingOrStraight = result
    End If
End Function
```

```
Private Function IsOnePair(numOnes As Integer, numTwos As Integer, _
                  numThrees As Integer, numFours As Integer, numFives As Integer, _
                  numSixes As Integer, result As String) As String

    If (numOnes = 2) And (numTwos <= 1) And (numThrees <= 1) And _
       (numFours <= 1) And (numFives <= 1) And (numSixes <= 1) Then
        IsOnePair = "Pair of Ones"
    ElseIf (numOnes <= 1) And (numTwos = 2) And (numThrees <= 1) And _
            (numFours <= 1) And (numFives <= 1) And (numSixes <= 1) Then
        IsOnePair = "Pair of Twos"
    ElseIf (numOnes <= 1) And (numTwos <= 1) And (numThrees = 2) And _
            (numFours <= 1) And (numFives <= 1) And (numSixes <= 1) Then
        IsOnePair = "Pair of Threes"
    ElseIf (numOnes <= 1) And (numTwos <= 1) And (numThrees <= 1) And _
            (numFours = 2) And (numFives <= 1) And (numSixes <= 1) Then
        IsOnePair = "Pair of Fours"
    ElseIf (numOnes <= 1) And (numTwos <= 1) And (numThrees <= 1) And _
            (numFours <= 1) And (numFives = 2) And (numSixes <= 1) Then
        IsOnePair = "Pair of Fives"
    ElseIf (numOnes <= 1) And (numTwos <= 1) And (numThrees <= 1) And _
            (numFours <= 1) And (numFives <= 1) And (numSixes = 2) Then
        IsOnePair = "Pair of Sixes"
    Else
        IsOnePair = result
    End If
End Function
Private Function IsTwoPair(numOnes As Integer, numTwos As Integer, _
                  numThrees As Integer, numFours As Integer, numFives As Integer, _
                  numSixes As Integer, result As String) As String

    If (numOnes = 2 And numTwos = 2) Or _
        (numOnes = 2 And numThrees = 2) Or _
        (numOnes = 2 And numFours = 2) Or _
        (numOnes = 2 And numFives = 2) Or _
        (numOnes = 2 And numSixes = 2) Or _
        (numTwos = 2 And numThrees = 2) Or _
        (numTwos = 2 And numFours = 2) Or _
        (numTwos = 2 And numFives = 2) Or _
```

```
        (numTwos = 2 And numSixes = 2) Or _
        (numThrees = 2 And numFours = 2) Or _
        (numThrees = 2 And numFives = 2) Or _
        (numThrees = 2 And numSixes = 2) Or _
        (numFours = 2 And numFives = 2) Or _
        (numFours = 2 And numSixes = 2) Or _
        (numFives = 2 And numSixes = 2) Then

        IsTwoPair = "Two Pair"
    Else
        IsTwoPair = result
    End If

End Function
Private Function IsThreeOfAKind(numOnes As Integer, numTwos As Integer, _
                 numThrees As Integer, numFours As Integer, numFives As Integer, _
                 numSixes As Integer, result As String) As String

    If (numOnes = 3 And numTwos < 2 And numThrees < 2 And numFours < 2 _
            And numFives < 2 And numSixes < 2) Then
        IsThreeOfAKind = "Three Ones"
    ElseIf (numOnes < 2 And numTwos = 3 And numThrees < 2 And _
            numFours < 2 And numFives < 2 And numSixes < 2) Then
        IsThreeOfAKind = "Three Twos"
    ElseIf (numOnes < 2 And numTwos < 2 And numThrees = 3 And _
            numFours < 2 And numFives < 2 And numSixes < 2) Then
        IsThreeOfAKind = "Three Threes"
    ElseIf (numOnes < 2 And numTwos < 2 And numThrees < 2 And _
            numFours = 3 And numFives < 2 And numSixes < 2) Then
        IsThreeOfAKind = "Three Fours"
    ElseIf (numOnes < 2 And numTwos < 2 And numThrees < 2 And _
            numFours < 2 And numFives = 3 And numSixes < 2) Then
        IsThreeOfAKind = "Three Fives"
    ElseIf (numOnes < 2 And numTwos < 2 And numThrees < 2 And _
            numFours < 2 And numFives < 2 And numSixes = 3) Then
        IsThreeOfAKind = "Three Sixes"
    Else
        IsThreeOfAKind = result
    End If
```

```
End Function
Private Function IsFourOfAKind(numOnes As Integer, numTwos As Integer, _
                 numThrees As Integer, numFours As Integer, numFives As Integer, _
                 numSixes As Integer, result As String) As String

    If numOnes = 4 Then
        IsFourOfAKind = "Four Ones"
    ElseIf numTwos = 4 Then
        IsFourOfAKind = "Four Twos"
    ElseIf numThrees = 4 Then
        IsFourOfAKind = "Four Threes"
    ElseIf numFours = 4 Then
        IsFourOfAKind = "Four Fours"
    ElseIf numFives = 4 Then
        IsFourOfAKind = "Four Fives"
    ElseIf numSixes = 4 Then
        IsFourOfAKind = "Four Sixes"
    Else
        IsFourOfAKind = result
    End If
End Function
Private Function IsFiveOfAKind(numOnes As Integer, numTwos As Integer, _
                 numThrees As Integer, numFours As Integer, numFives As Integer, _
                 numSixes As Integer, result As String) As String

    If numOnes = 5 Then
        IsFiveOfAKind = "Five Ones"
    ElseIf numTwos = 5 Then
        IsFiveOfAKind = "Five Twos"
    ElseIf numThrees = 5 Then
        IsFiveOfAKind = "Five Threes"
    ElseIf numFours = 5 Then
        IsFiveOfAKind = "Five Fours"
    ElseIf numFives = 5 Then
        IsFiveOfAKind = "Five Fives"
    ElseIf numSixes = 5 Then
        IsFiveOfAKind = "Five Sixes"
    Else
```

```
        IsFiveOfAKind = result
    End If
End Function
Private Function IsFullHouse(numOnes As Integer, numTwos As Integer, _
                  numThrees As Integer, numFours As Integer, numFives As Integer, _
                  numSixes As Integer, result As String) As String

    If (numOnes = 3 And numTwos = 2) Or (numOnes = 3 And numThrees = 2) Or _
        (numOnes = 3 And numFours = 2) Or (numOnes = 3 And numFives = 2) Or _
        (numOnes = 3 And numSixes = 2) Or (numTwos = 3 And numOnes = 2) Or _
        (numTwos = 3 And numThrees = 2) Or (numTwos = 3 And numFours = 2) Or _
        (numTwos = 3 And numFives = 2) Or (numTwos = 3 And numSixes = 2) Or _
        (numThrees = 3 And numOnes = 2) Or (numThrees = 3 And numTwos = 2) Or _
        (numThrees = 3 And numFours = 2) Or (numThrees = 3 And numFives = 2) Or _
        (numThrees = 3 And numSixes = 2) Or (numFours = 3 And numOnes = 2) Or _
        (numFours = 3 And numTwos = 2) Or (numFours = 3 And numThrees = 2) Or _
        (numFours = 3 And numFives = 2) Or (numFours = 3 And numSixes = 2) Or _
        (numFives = 3 And numOnes = 2) Or (numFives = 3 And numTwos = 2) Or _
        (numFives = 3 And numThrees = 2) Or (numFives = 3 And numFours = 2) Or _
        (numFives = 3 And numSixes = 2) Or (numSixes = 3 And numOnes = 2) Or _
        (numSixes = 3 And numTwos = 2) Or (numSixes = 3 And numThrees = 2) Or _
        (numSixes = 3 And numFours = 2) Or (numSixes = 3 And numFives = 2) Then

        IsFullHouse = "Full House"
    Else
        IsFullHouse = result
    End If
End Function
```

Figure 3.13 shows an example of the *Poker Dice* game board after two rolls of the dice.

That concludes *Poker Dice*. It really is a pretty simple program. The difficulty lies in following the logic of the large number of conditions contained in the expressions with the `If/Then/Else` code structures. Some of the procedures are longer than I normally write them because of the number of conditionals involved and I have not yet discussed loops. As you may have already guessed, these procedures can be simplified significantly with the use of different programming structures and techniques. You will look at a couple of these structures in the next chapter.

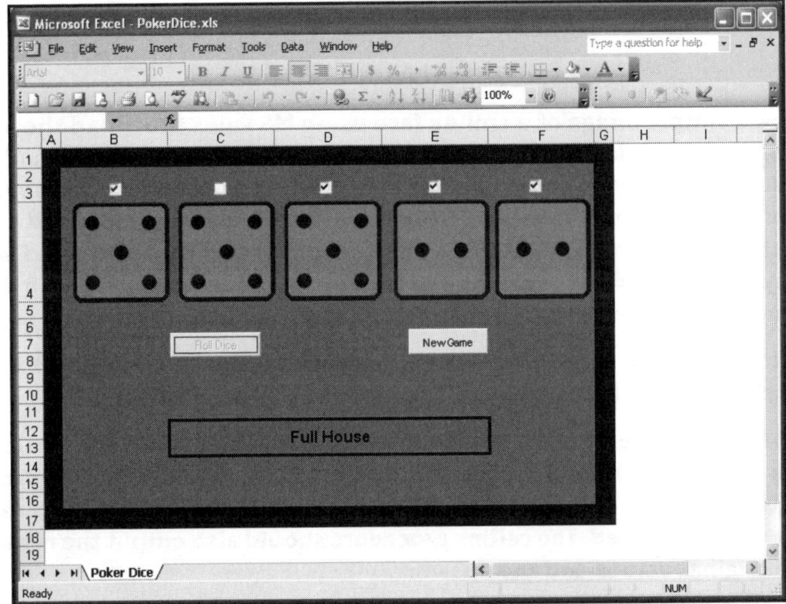

FIGURE 3.13

The *Poker Dice* game board after two rolls.

CHAPTER SUMMARY

In this chapter, you covered a considerable amount of material on some of the tools required to help you build a strong programming foundation. You started by taking an in-depth look at procedures in VBA; specifically, event, sub, and function procedures. You learned how to use and build these procedures while considering the procedure's scope, available parameters, and return values (function procedures). You even learned how to build new function procedures to use within formulas created in the Excel application. Finally, you saw two new code structures, `If/Then/Else` and `Select/Case` and you learned how to use Boolean logic within conditional expressions so a program could branch off in different directions in terms of code execution. In essence, you learned how to write a program that can make simple decisions.

Challenges

1. Draw a simple image of a smiley face using MS Paint then load the image into an Image control placed on a worksheet in Excel. Using the `MouseDown()` event procedure of the Image control, write a program that displays a message to the user every time the user clicks on the image. The message should tell the user if he or she clicked on the eyes, nose, mouth, or face of the image and which button they used. The message can be displayed with a message box, or in a Label control, or on the spreadsheet.
2. Write a function procedure in VBA that returns the square root of a number. The function should be made available to the Excel application.
3. Write a sub procedure in VBA that either adds, subtracts, multiplies, or divides two numbers. The procedure should be called by another sub procedure that collects the two numbers from the user and asks the user which mathematical operation is desired. The calling procedure should also output the result, displaying the original values and the answer.
4. Add a few Check Box controls or Option Button controls to a worksheet, then use a `Select/Case` code structure in a sub procedure that outputs a message to the user telling them which box or option has been selected.
5. Add some features to the *Poker Dice* program. For example, keep a record of a user's session (`n` games) by outputting the results of each game to a spreadsheet column off the game board. Use a static variable to track the row number of the cell you output the results to. You can also assign point values to each hand based on its value and track the user's point total for a session of *Poker Dice*. To make getting a good hand more difficult, you can create additional dice images using new colors (blue, green, and so on).

Loops and Arrays

In Chapter 3, "Procedures and Conditions," you started building your programming foundation with the branching structures `If/Then/Else` and `Select/Case`. In this chapter, you will significantly expand on that foundation by learning looping code structures and arrays. Loops and arrays are fundamental to all programming languages; they expand the capabilities of a program significantly and make them easier to write. You'll begin this chapter by looking at the different looping structures available in VBA before moving on to arrays.

Specifically, this chapter will cover:

- Do Loops
- For Loops
- Input Validation
- Arrays
- Multi-Dimensional Arrays
- Dynamic Arrays
- Recording Macros
- The Forms Toolbar Controls

PROJECT: MATH GAME

The *Math Game* program is a natural choice for programming with a spreadsheet application like Excel. The *Math Game* requires only basic math skills; it may be more fun for kids to play, but it's a lot of fun for adults to write. To play the *Math Game*, you answer as many questions as you can in the allotted time. After you finish, the questions are reviewed and scored. The *Math Game* spreadsheet is shown in Figure 4.1.

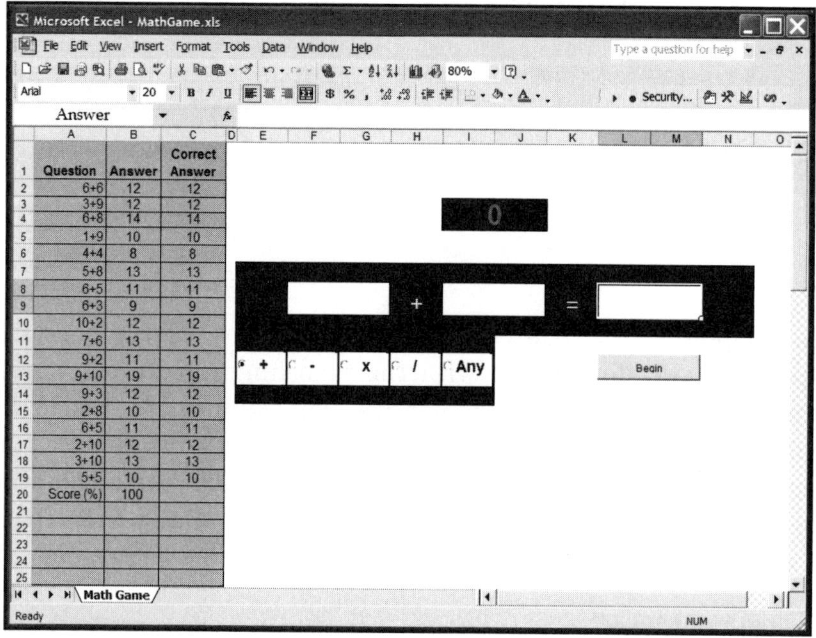

Question	Answer	Correct Answer
6+6	12	12
3+9	12	12
6+8	14	14
1+9	10	10
4+4	8	8
5+8	13	13
6+5	11	11
6+3	9	9
10+2	12	12
7+6	13	13
9+2	11	11
9+10	19	19
9+3	12	12
2+8	10	10
6+5	11	11
2+10	12	12
3+10	13	13
5+5	10	10
Score (%)	100	

FIGURE 4.1

The *Math Game* program worksheet.

LOOPING WITH VBA

Program looping is the repetition of a block of code a specified number of times. The number of times the block of code is repeated may be well defined or based on a conditional statement. All computer languages contain looping structures because these structures are excellent at solving problems that would otherwise require repetitive code. Imagine a program whose function it is to search for a specific name in a column of data with one hundred entries. A program with one hundred `If/Then` statements testing the value of each cell for the required name will solve the problem. The program would be technically easy to create, but cumbersome to type the repetitive code and it would look awful. Fortunately, we have looping code structures to help us.

Each execution of the block of code inside a looping structure represents one iteration of the loop.

Do Loops

Do loops will execute a given block of code repetitively based on the value of a conditional expression. All `Do-Loops` require the keywords `Do` and `Loop`, plus one additional keyword (`While` or `Until`) depending on the desired action. The keywords are used to build four basic representations of the `Do-Loop`. The first two representations use the keyword `Until` with a conditional statement that determines if, and how many times the code inside the loop executes. With the conditional statement at the end of the loop, the code inside the loop executes at least one time.

```
Do
     'Block of code executes at least once and continues to loop if condition is
'false.
Loop Until (condition)
```

When the conditional statement is at the beginning of the loop, the code inside the loop will not execute unless the logic of the conditional statement allows it. When using `Until`, the code inside the loop executes if the conditional statement is false.

```
Do Until (condition)
     'Block of code executes only if condition is false.
Loop
```

The next two representations of the `Do-Loop` use the keyword `While` with a conditional statement that determines if, and how many times the code inside the loop executes. When `While` is used, the code inside the loop executes when the conditional statement is true.

```
Do
     'Block of code executes at least once and continues to loop if condition is
'true.
Loop While (condition)
```

When deciding on which representation of the `Do-Loop` to use, ask yourself whether you need the code inside the loop to execute at least once. If you do, then put the conditional at the end. The choice of `While` or `Until` depends on the logic of the conditional expression.

```
Do While (condition)
     'Block of code executes only if condition is true.
Loop
```

Beware of creating loops that never stop repeating, otherwise known as *infinite loops*. When constructing your Do-Loop, create it with a conditional expression that will change its logical value (true to false and vice versa) at some point during the code's execution within the loop. It is easier to create an infinite loop than you might think. The following example is suppose to find the first occurrence of the string Flintstone in the first column of a worksheet, output a message to the screen, and then quit.

```
Dim I As Integer
I = 1
Do
        If (Cells(I, "A").Value = "Flintstone") Then
                MsgBox ("Yabba Dabba Do! I found a Flintstone in row " & Str(I))
        End If
        I = I + 1
Loop Until (Cells(I, "A").Value = "Flintstone")
```

You can use the Cells property to return all or just one cell on a worksheet. Using the Cells property without any parameters returns all cells on the worksheet.

```
ActiveSheet.Cells
```

To return a specific cell, you can specify a row and column index. For example, the following line of code returns cell D1.

```
ActiveSheet.Cells(1,4)
```

The Cells property is convenient for using inside of loops when the indices for the row and column are replaced with looping variables. Alternatively, you can specify the column parameter with a string.

```
ActiveSheet.Cells(1,"D")
```

The loop will always fail for two reasons. First, if the string Flintstone does not appear in the first column of the worksheet, then the loop is infinite because the conditional statement at the end of the loop (Cells(I, "A").Value = "Flintstone") will never be true. Second, even if the string Flintstone does appear in the first column of the worksheet, the output from the MsgBox() function will not appear because the conditional statement at the end of the loop will be true before the conditional statement associated with the If/Then structure.

If you find your program stuck in an infinite loop, use Ctrl-Alt-Break to suspend program execution.

In most cases you can construct a loop with logical expressions that will work with both `While` or `Until`, so using one or the other is simply a matter of personal preference. The following `Do-Loops` have the exact same function, but the first loop uses `While` and the second uses `Until`.

```
Dim I As Integer
I = 1
Do
        If (Cells(I, "A").Value = "Flintstone") Then
                MsgBox ("Yabba Dabba Do! I found a Flintstone in row " & Str(I))
        End If
        I = I + 1
Loop While (Cells(I, "A").Value <> "")
```

If I change the conditional operator to =, then I change the logic of the conditional statement, so I must use the keyword `Until` to get the same result from the loop.

```
Dim I As Integer
I = 1
Do
        If (Cells(I, "A").Value = "Flintstone") Then
                MsgBox ("Yabba Dabba Do! I found a Flintstone in row " & Str(I))
        End If
        I = I + 1
Loop Until (Cells(I, "A").Value = "")
```

Both of these loops search the first column for the string `Flintstone`. Once the desired string is found, a message box outputs a statement with the index of the worksheet row in which the string was found. In both examples, the `Do-Loop` continues until an empty cell is found. Both loops will execute at least once because the conditional expression is at the end of the loop. Neither loop will be infinite because Excel will always add empty rows to the end of a spreadsheet as more rows of data are added.

For Loops

When you know the number of iterations required from a loop, the `For/Next` loop is the best choice of structures. The syntax is very simple.

```
For variable = start To end Step value
      'Block of code
Next variable
```

The required keywords are For, To, and Next. To keep track of the number of iterations through the loop requires a counting variable as well as starting and ending values. The keyword Step is optional but if it's used, the value that follows it is used to denote the step size of the counting variable with each iteration through the loop. The step's value can be any positive or negative integer; the default value is +1 when Step is omitted. Table 4.1 lists a few examples of For/Next loops.

TABLE 4.1 EXAMPLES OF FOR/NEXT LOOPS IN VBA

Loop Example	Output from Message Box
For I = 0 To 10 MsgBox (I) Next I	11 iterations: 0, 1, 2, 3, 4, 5, 6, 7, 8, 9, and 10
For I = 0 To 10 Step 2 MsgBox (I) Next I	6 iterations: 0, 2, 4, 6, 8, and 10
For I = 0 To 10 Step 3 MsgBox (I) Next I	4 iterations: 0, 3, 6, and 9
For I = 10 To 0 Step –5 MsgBox (I) Next I	3 iterations: 10, 5, and 0

The variable I in Table 4.1 should be declared as an integer prior to use and the ending value for the loop is usually another variable rather than a constant. In most cases, you will use the default step size of +1, so the keyword Step is omitted.

Use the statement Exit Do or Exit For to force code execution to leave a looping structure and proceed with the first line of code after the loop. Normally, Exit Do or Exit For will be within a branching structure (If/Then or Select/Case) inside of the loop.

The following example of a VBA function mimics the FACT() function in the Excel application by calculating the factorial of an integer.

```
Public Function Factorial(myValue As Integer) As Long
    Dim I As Integer
    Dim factorialValue As Long

    factorialValue = 1
    For I = 2 To myValue
        factorialValue = factorialValue * I
    Next I
    Factorial = factorialValue
End Function
```

In the Real World

The factorial function can also be written as a recursive procedure. A *recursive* procedure is one that calls itself.

```
Public Function Factorial(N As Integer) As Integer
    If N <= 1 Then
        Factorial = 1
    Else
        Factorial = Factorial(N - 1) * N
    End If
End Function
```

Although the factorial example above is a nice illustration of recursion, it is not a practical example. Recursive procedures can be very demanding on system resources and they must contain logic that will eventually stop the procedure from calling itself.

Recursive procedures are most often and most effectively applied to tree-like data structures such as the file system on a computer.

The `For/Next` loop is a natural choice, because you need the looping variable to increment by one with each iteration until it reaches the value of the integer passed into the function. Each iteration through the `For/Next` loop multiplies the next factor by the previous result, effectively producing the factorial of the value stored in the variable `myValue`. For example, if `myValue` is 5 then the variable `factorialValue` will be calculated as 1*2*3*4*5.

Finally, consider the most obvious example of looping in spreadsheet applications, which is looping through a range of cells in a worksheet. For now, I will illustrate looping through a worksheet range using a `For/Next` loop.

```
For I = 1 To 10
    For J = 4 To 7
        Cells(I, Chr(64 + J)).Value = I * J
    Next J
Next I
```

The looping structures discussed so far are not the best choice for looping through a range of cells—even though doing so is a simple enough task. A better looping structure for handling this task is the `For/Each` loop discussed in Chapter 5, "Basic Excel Objects."

The example above uses one `For/Next` loop nested inside another `For/Next` loop to loop through the worksheet range D1:G10. The nested (inside) loop will execute 4 iterations with each iteration of the outer loop. In the example just given, the value of `J` iterates from 4 through 7 for each value of `I`. The code loops through the range by rows, as the variable used for the row index (`I`) is also the counting variable for the outer loop. The `Chr()` function is used to convert a numerical input representing an ASCII (American Standard Code for Information Interchange) value to its corresponding keyboard character; in this case the values 68 through 71 will be converted to the uppercase letters D through G. The `Chr()` function in VBA works with values 0-255. Table 4.2 lists a few of the more common characters in the set. Alternatively, you could replace the `Chr()` function with the looping variable `J`; which, in this case, would make for easier and cleaner code; however, I wanted to introduce the `Chr()` function since it can be quite useful when working with the `Cells` and `Range` properties.

TABLE 4.2 SELECTED ASCII CONVERSION CHARACTERS

ASCII Value	Keyboard Character
8	backspace
9	tab
10	line feed
13	carriage return
32	space
48-57	0-9
65-90	A-Z
97-122	a-z

Input Validation

Trusting that a user will input the type of data required by your program is a leap of faith. You can, and should, provide hints to the user indicating the type of data and format your program requires; however, you should also include code in your program to check what the user enters against a required format. The process of checking user input for accuracy is known as *validation*. Validation should be included whenever input is required from the user and the format of that input cannot be guaranteed. Examples discussed thus far in this book include: the `InputBox()` function, the Text Box control, and spreadsheet cells. This may seem like a daunting task at first, but asking where the validation code needs to be entered in a program and when it needs to run, simplifies the task considerably.

Validation with the InputBox() Function

In the Chapter 2 project, the program asked the user to input his or her name and birthday. The program assumed the user would enter the information in the proper format. For the user's name, the desired format was first name-space-last name and for the user's birthday, a date format of month, day, and year (e.g., 3/4/86 or 3-4-1986). The `DateValue()` function handled some of the input validation for us by allowing multiple date formats, but more validation is required.

Consideration of where the validation code should go and when it should run is easy with the `InputBox()` function. The validation should occur as soon as the user enters data. The best way to determine this is to put the `InputBox()` function inside a `Do-Loop`. In the Biorhythms and Time of Your Life project in Chapter 2, user validation could be added as follows:

```
Dim userName As String
Dim userBirthday As Date
Dim nameOk As Boolean
nameOk = True
Do
        userName = InputBox("What is your first and last name?", "Name")
        If (userName <> "") Then nameOk = ValidateName(userName)
Loop While (nameOk = False) Or (userName <> "")
```

The `InputBox()` function is inserted inside a `Do-Loop` where the return value is tested by the function procedure `ValidateName()`. The `ValidateName()` procedure returns true if the name satisfies the desired format, otherwise it returns false. The loop is repeated if the `ValidateName()` name procedure returns false, or the user hits the cancel button (`InputBox()` returns an empty string) on the input box.

The `ValidateName()` function procedure accepts the string entered by the user as input and tests for the number of spaces inside the string.

```
Private Function ValidateName(userName As String) As Boolean
    Dim strLength As Integer
    Dim I As Integer
    Dim numSpaces As Integer
    Dim tempString As String
    Dim msb As Integer
    userName = Trim(userName)
    strLength = Len(userName)
    For I = 1 To strLength
        If Left(userName, 1) = " " Then
            numSpaces = numSpaces + 1
        End If
        userName = Right(userName, Len(userName) - 1)
    Next I
    If  (numSpaces > 1) Then
        ValidateName = False
        msb = MsgBox("Please enter just two names separated by one space", _
vbCritical, "Error")
    Else
        ValidateName = True
    End If
End Function
```

Any leading or trailing spaces on the string entered by the user are removed using the `Trim()` function so extra spaces before or after the names are forgiven. The length of the resulting string is then stored in the `strLength` variable for use in the subsequent `For/Next` loop.

The `For/Next` loop tests the leftmost character for equality to a space before removing this character. If the character is a space then a variable keeping track of the number of spaces in the string is incremented by one. Essentially, the `For/Next` loop iterates through each character in the string and counts the number of spaces found within that string. If more than one space is found in the string entered by the user, then the function returns false, otherwise it returns true.

For example, if the user enters either of the strings `FredFlintstone` or `Fred J Flintstone` in the input box, then the `ValidateName()` function returns false to the calling procedure just after outputting the message `Please enter just two names separated by one space` in a message box.

Obviously, the `ValidateName()` function procedure does not test for all possible mistakes users might make entering in their names, but it does illustrate how to use input validation with the `InputBox()` function. To test for other potential errors by the user, simply add more code (specific to the type of error you are looking for) to the `ValidateName()` function procedure.

Validation with a Spreadsheet Cell

In older versions of Excel, validation of spreadsheet content meant writing a lot of code to ensure the data was of proper type and/or format. With the latest versions of Excel, this is no longer the case. Data validation is now included in the Excel application, so you don't necessarily have to write any code. Figure 4.2 to shows the data validation dialog box (select Data, Validation from the Excel application menu). Use this tool in your spreadsheets to force validation of data entered by the user. If your project creates new worksheets that require data validation, you can use the record macro tool discussed later in this chapter to learn how to add it to your program.

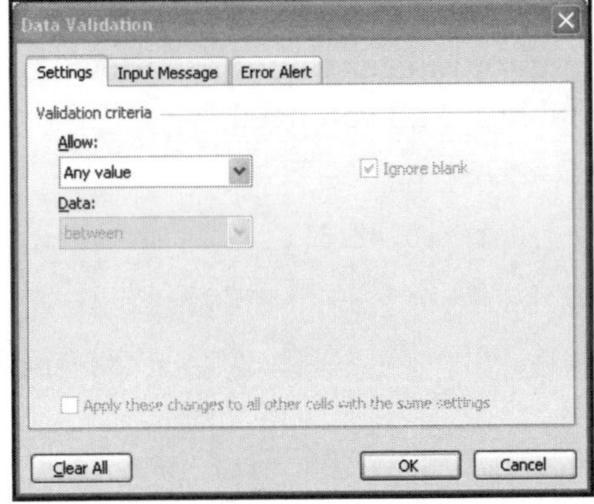

FIGURE 4.2

The Data Validation dialog.

ARRAYS

Normally, arrays are not discussed until the end of introductory programming books; however, as you are already familiar with spreadsheet applications, the concept of an array should come easily. An *array* is a variable that can hold multiple values. You should use arrays when a related set of values is to be stored in a variable. Doing so relieves you from having to declare a new variable with a unique name for each value in the set. Arrays are convenient as they simplify programming code tremendously.

A spreadsheet column that contains data is basically the same thing as an array—it's a group of related values. Each cell within a spreadsheet column containing the related set of values is referenced by a row and column index. Values in an array are also referenced using indices.

I assume that you organize your spreadsheets in the normal way—by placing data inside columns rather than rows—but the argument is the same whether you equate a spreadsheet column or row to an array.

Before starting with the simplest example of an array (the one-dimensional array), consider a sub procedure that uses a worksheet column much as a programmer would use an array in an application that does not work with a spreadsheet.

In previous chapters, and throughout this chapter I use the `Cells` property of the Excel `Application` object in code examples. The `Cells` property is straightforward, with a row and column index that corresponds to a single spreadsheet cell. Although discussed in detail in Chapter 5, be aware as you look at the examples in this chapter that the `Cells` property acts like a function that returns a `Range` object consisting of a single spreadsheet cell. I have used the `Value` property of the `Range` object extensively thus far, but the `Range` object has many other properties for the VBA programmer to use besides the `Value` property, and you will see many examples in this chapter and subsequent chapters.

The `BubbleSort()` procedure sorts a column of integer values from lowest to highest value. Two integer variables and a Boolean variable are all you need.

```
Public Sub BubbleSort()
'Sorts data in A2:A11 and writes sorted data to B2:B11
    Dim tempVar As Integer
    Dim anotherIteration As Boolean
    Dim I As Integer

    Range("A2:A11").Copy Range("B2:B11")     'Copy all data to column B
    Range("B1").Value = "Sorted Data"
    Do
        anotherIteration = False
        For I = 2 To 10
            'Compare and swap adjacent values
            If Cells(I, "B").Value > Cells(I + 1, "B").Value Then
                tempVar = Cells(I, "B").Value
                Cells(I, "B").Value = Cells(I + 1, "B").Value
                Cells(I + 1, "B").Value = tempVar
                anotherIteration = True
            End If
        Next I
    Loop While anotherIteration
End Sub
```

A `For/Next` loop nested inside a `Do-Loop` will iterate through a column of 10 values until the data is sorted from lowest to highest value. The nested `For/Next` loop effectively pushes the largest value from wherever it is located to the last position, much like a bubble rising from the depths to the surface. The `For/Next` loop starts at the beginning of the data list and compares two successive values. If the first value is larger than the second value, then the position of the two values are swapped with help from the variable `tempVar`. The next two values are then compared, where the first of these values was the second value in the previous comparison (or first if it had been swapped). Please note: the row index in the `Cells` property uses `I + 1`, so the looping variable in the `For/Next` loop works from 2 to 11 so that the procedure sorts ten values. If a swap of two values has to be made, then the Boolean variable `anotherIteration` is set to true to ensure the outer `Do-Loop` continues with at least one more iteration.

Each iteration through the `Do-Loop` moves the next largest value in the set down the column to its correct position. Thus, it will take up to *n* iterations to sort the data, where *n* is the number of values in the set. This does not make the `BubbleSort()` procedure terribly efficient, but it works well for small data sets. The worksheet shown in Figure 4.3 illustrates what happens to a set of numbers after iteration through the `Do-Loop` loop. The `BubbleSort()` procedure sorts values from column A and copies them to column B.

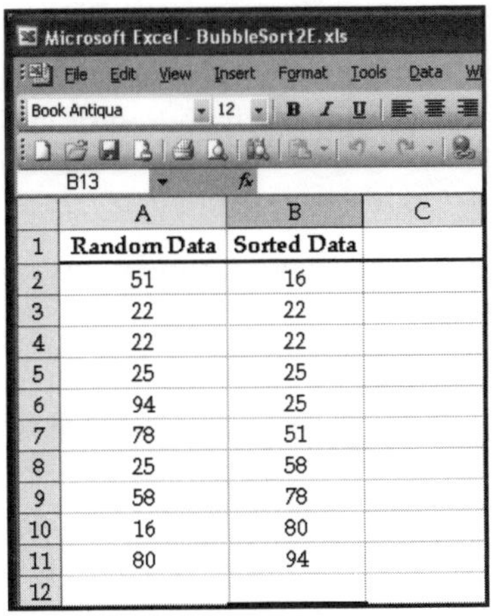

Microsoft Excel - BubbleSort2E.xls

	A	B	C
1	Random Data	Sorted Data	
2	51	16	
3	22	22	
4	22	22	
5	25	25	
6	94	25	
7	78	51	
8	25	58	
9	58	78	
10	16	80	
11	80	94	
12			

FIGURE 4.3

Worksheet illustration of the `BubbleSort()` sub procedure.

One-Dimensional Arrays

An array is a variable used to hold a group of related values; it must be declared just as a variable is declared. An array is declared with a single name and the number of elements (values) that can be stored in the array.

```
Dim myArray(number of elements) As Type
```

You may also declare arrays using the `Public` or `Private` keywords to define the scope as you would with a regular variable declaration. If you do not specify a data type, then, like a variable, the array will be a variant type. Arrays may be declared as any available data type in VBA. All elements in arrays with numerical data types are initialized with the value 0. Elements of string arrays are initialized with an empty string. When specifying the number of elements, you must consider the lower bound of the array. The default lower bound is zero.

```
Dim myArray(10) As Integer
```

When you need multiple array declarations of the same size, use a constant to specify the size of the arrays in the declarations.

```
Const ARRAYSIZE=10
Dim myArray1(ARRAYSIZE) As Integer
Dim myArray2(ARRAYSIZE) As Integer
Dim myArray3(ARRAYSIZE) As Integer
Etc.
```

This way, if you have to edit the size of your arrays, you only need to change the value of the constant.

Thus, the integer array `myArray` declared above has 11 elements accessed with the indices 0 through 10. To override the default, set the lower bound of the array in the declaration.

```
Dim myArray(1 To 10) As Integer
```

The array `myArray` now has just 10 elements because the lower bound has been explicitly set to one.

Use the statement `Option Base 1` in the general declarations section of a module to change the default lower bound of all arrays declared in the module to 1.

You can initialize a single element in the array as you would a variable, but you must include the index of the element you wish to change.

```
myArray(5) = 7
```

However, arrays are typically initialized inside a loop. To insert the spreadsheet's values of the first 10 cells of column A into an array, do the following:

```
Dim I As Integer
Dim myArray(10) As Integer
```

```
For I = 0 To 9
     myArray(I) = Cells(I + 1, "A").Value
Next I
```

Then use another loop to output the values of the array. The following loop squares the values stored in the array `myArray` before copying them to column B of the spreadsheet.

```
For I = 0 To 9
     Cells(I + 1, "B").Value = myArray(I)^2
Next I
```

Now let's revisit the `BubbleSort()` procedure, this time using an array. The sub procedure `BubbleSort2()` works exactly like the `BubbleSort()` procedure, except that the tests and swaps are performed on the values in the set after they have been loaded into an array rather than just using the worksheet column.

```
Public Sub BubbleSort2()
     Dim tempVar As Integer
     Dim anotherIteration As Boolean
     Dim I As Integer
     Dim myArray(10) As Integer
     For I = 2 To 11
          myArray(I - 2) = Cells(I, "A").Value
     Next I
     Do
          anotherIteration = False
          'Compare and swap adjacent values
          For I = 0 To 9
               If myArray(I) > myArray(I + 1) Then
                    tempVar = myArray(I)
                    myArray(I) = myArray(I + 1)
                    myArray(I + 1) = tempVar
                    anotherIteration = True
               End If
          Next I
     Loop While anotherIteration = True
     Range("B1").Value = "Sorted Data"
     For I = 2 To 11
          Cells(I, "B").Value = myArray(I - 1)
     Next I
End Sub
```

After variable declarations, the values in column A of the worksheet are loaded into the array with a simple `For/Next` loop. The `For/Next` loop nested in the `Do-Loop` is just as it was in the `BubbleSort()` procedure, except now the `Cells` property has been replaced with the array named `myArray`. The looping variable in the `For/Next` loop now runs from 0 to 9 because the lower bound for the array is 0 not 1. When the first value is greater than the second, the values are swapped. Finally, the sorted values are written to column B in the worksheet.

Multi-Dimensional Arrays

If one-dimensional arrays are analogous to a single column in a spreadsheet, then two-dimensional arrays are analogous to multiple columns in a spreadsheet. Three-dimensional arrays are analogous to using multiple worksheets and higher dimensions than three are a bit difficult to imagine, but nevertheless are available. You can declare multi-dimensional arrays in VBA with up to 60 dimensions. Unless you're comfortable imagining multi-dimensional spaces greater than dimension three, I suggest keeping the number of dimensions in an array to three or less.

```
Dim myArray(10, 2) As Integer
```

The above declaration creates a two-dimensional integer array with 11 rows and 3 columns (remember the lower-bound is 0). Access the individual elements of the array using the row and column indices.

```
myArray(5, 1) = Cells(6, "B").Value
```

This example assigns the value of the spreadsheet cell B6 to the sixth row and second column in the array `myArray`.

As with one-dimensional arrays, multi-dimensional arrays are typically accessed within loops; however, you need to use nested loops in order to access both indices in a multi-dimensional array.

The sub procedure below transposes the values of a group of cells in a worksheet. This sub procedure takes input from the first ten rows and three columns in a worksheet and transposes the values to the first three rows and ten columns in the same worksheet. See Figure 4.4 and Figure 4.5 for depictions of the initial spreadsheet and the spreadsheet resulting from running the `Transpose()` sub procedure.

After variable declarations, the values in the spreadsheet are loaded into the two-dimensional array named `transArray`.

Microsoft Excel - Transpose2E.xls

	A	B	C	D
1	61	21	43	
2	75	76	92	
3	98	33	50	
4	63	75	26	
5	94	77	39	
6	93	26	50	
7	65	61	59	
8	54	24	5	
9	61	81	17	
10	98	32	57	
11				

FIGURE 4.4

An Excel spreadsheet prior to running the `Transpose()` sub procedure.

Microsoft Excel - Transpose2E.xls

	A	B	C	D	E	F	G	H	I	J
1	61	75	98	63	94	93	65	54	61	98
2	21	76	33	75	77	26	61	24	81	32
3	43	92	50	26	39	50	59	5	17	57

FIGURE 4.5

An Excel spreadsheet after running the `Transpose()` sub procedure.

A three-dimensional array is declared with three values within the parentheses of its declaration (for example, `Dim myArray(9, 2, 2)`). You could use a three-dimensional array to keep track of rows and columns from multiple worksheets, whereas a two-dimensional array would keep track of rows and columns from a single worksheet.

The looping variables in the nested `For/Next` loops are used to access the row and column indices of the array `transArray`. The looping variables `I` and `J` are used as the column and row indices, respectively, in both the array and worksheet. Next, the contents of the worksheet are cleared using the `ClearContents` method of the `Range` object. (The `Range` object will be covered in detail in Chapter 5.)

To transpose the values, the looping variables `I` and `J` are now used to access the opposite index (i.e., `I` is used for the row index; `J` is used for the column index) in the `Cells` property; however, the array `transArray` uses the indices as in the previous `For/Next` loop. These nested `For/Next` loops effectively transpose the values, as shown in Figure 4.5.

```
Public Sub Transpose()
'Transposes first 10 rows and first 3 columns of worksheet
'to first 3 rows and first 10 columns.
    Dim I As Integer
    Dim J As Integer
    Dim transArray(9, 2) As Integer
    For I = 1 To 3
        For J = 1 To 10
            transArray(J - 1, I - 1) = Cells(J, I).Value
        Next J
    Next I
    Range("A1:C10").ClearContents
    For I = 1 To 3
        For J = 1 To 10
            Cells(I, J).Value = transArray(J - 1, I - 1)
        Next J
    Next I
End Sub
```

Dynamic Arrays

The `BubbleSort2()` and `Transpose()` sub procedures use arrays with fixed lengths. The number of values in fixed length arrays cannot be changed while the program is running. This is fine as long as the required length of the array is known before running the program; however, the use of dynamic arrays allows programmers to create a more robust program. Wouldn't the `BubbleSort2()` procedure be more useful if it sorted data with any number of values rather than just ten values? A similar question can be asked of the `Transpose()` procedure —wouldn't it be more useful if it worked with any size data set rather than just a set with 10 rows and 3 columns? If you do not want to limit the `BubbleSort2()` and `Transpose()` sub procedures to constant-sized data sets, then you must use dynamic arrays.

The size of a dynamic array can be changed (increased or decreased) as necessary while the program runs. To declare a dynamic array, use empty parentheses instead of a value for the bound(s).

```
Dim myArray() As Integer
```

After the required length of the array has been determined then the array is re-dimensioned using the `ReDim` keyword.

ReDim can also be used as a declarative statement with arrays, but potential conflicts may arise if there are variables of the same name within your project—even if they are of different scope. Therefore, avoid using ReDim as a declarative statement, but use it to re-size previously declared arrays.

```
ReDim myArray(size)
```

The ReDim statement will re-initialize (erase) all elements of the array. If you need to preserve the existing values then use the Preserve keyword.

```
ReDim Preserve myArray(size)
```

If the new size of the array is smaller than the original size, then the values of the elements at the end of the array are lost. Normally, an array is re-dimensioned with the Preserve keyword only when the new size is larger than the previous size of the array. When re-sizing an array with the Preserve keyword, you can only change the size of the last dimension; you cannot change the number of dimensions, and you can only change the value of the upper bound. You will see an example of using ReDim Preserve in the *Math Game* project at the end of the chapter.

The BubbleSort2() and Transpose() sub procedures are now rewritten using dynamic arrays.

```
Public Sub DynamicBubble()
    Dim tempVar As Integer
    Dim anotherIteration As Boolean
    Dim I As Integer
    Dim arraySize As Integer
    Dim myArray() As Integer

    '-------------
    'Get the array size.
    '-------------
    Do
        arraySize = I
        I = I + 1
    Loop Until Cells(I, "A").Value = ""
    ReDim myArray(arraySize - 1)

    '-----------------------
    'Get the values. Convert text to numbers.
    '-----------------------
```

```
    For I = 1 To arraySize
        myArray(I - 1) = Val(Cells(I, "A").Value)
    Next I
    Do
        anotherIteration = False
        For I = 0 To arraySize - 2
            If myArray(I) > myArray(I + 1) Then
                tempVar = myArray(I)
                myArray(I) = myArray(I + 1)
                myArray(I + 1) = tempVar
                anotherIteration = True
            End If
        Next I
    Loop While anotherIteration = True

    '--------------
    'Write data to column B.
    '--------------
    For I = 1 To arraySize
        Cells(I, "B").Value = myArray(I - 1)
    Next I
End Sub
```

After declaring the dynamic array, you must determine the required size of the array. A `Do-Loop` is used to iterate through the cells in the worksheet's column A until an empty cell is found. By keeping track of the number of iterations with the variable `I`, the number of values in the column—and hence the required size of the array—is discovered. Then the array is re-dimensioned with the appropriate variable and `ReDim` statement.

This is not the best method for learning how many values the user has entered into column A of the worksheet, as the potential for error is high. For example, any text entered into a cell will be converted to a numerical value with the `Val()` function—ususally zero. The procedure also limits the sort to data entered into column A of the worksheet. In the next chapter, I'll discuss additional methods for allowing the user more flexibility in terms of where the data can be input, and gathering user input such that ambiguities in the data are minimized.

The rest of the `DynamicBubble()` procedure is the same as the `BubbleSort2()` procedure except the upper limit of all looping variables are set to the same value as the size of the array.

The `DynamicTranspose()` sub procedure is re-written using a dynamic array that is re-dimensioned with two dimensions. One dimension is for the number of rows in the grid of values to be transposed and the other dimension is for the number of columns.

Once again, `Do-Loops` are used to determine the number of rows and columns holding values in the worksheet. The array `transArray` is then re-dimensioned to the same number of rows and columns. Don't forget the lower bound on each dimension is 0. The rest of the procedure is the same, with the exception of the upper limit on the looping variables used in the `For/Next` loops.

```
Public Sub DynamicTranspose()
    Dim I As Integer
    Dim J As Integer
    Dim transArray() As Integer
    Dim numRows As Integer
    Dim numColumns As Integer

    '----------------
    'Get rows for dynamic array.
    '----------------
    Do
        numRows = I
        I = I + 1
    Loop Until Cells(I, "A").Value = ""

    '------------------
    'Get columns for dynamic array.
    '------------------
    I = 0
    Do
        numColumns = I
        I = I + 1
    Loop Until Cells(1, Chr(I + 64)).Value = ""
    ReDim transArray(numRows - 1, numColumns - 1)

    '-------------------
    'Copy data from worksheet to array.
    '-------------------
```

```
    For I = 1 To numColumns
        For J = 1 To numRows
            transArray(J - 1, I - 1) = Val(Cells(J, Chr(I + 64)).Value)
        Next J
    Next I
    Range("A1:C10").ClearContents

    '-----------------------
    'Copy data from array to worksheet transposed.
    '-----------------------
    For I = 1 To numColumns
        For J = 1 To numRows
            Cells(I, Chr(J + 64)).Value = transArray(J - 1, I - 1)
        Next J
    Next I
End Sub
```

Programming Formulas into Worksheet Cells

If you are going to be an Excel VBA programmer, then it is inevitable that you will have to create programs that enter formulas into worksheet cells. Thankfully, it is a pretty simple thing to do; however, you must decide on the reference style you wish to use–A1 type, or R1C1 type.

A1 Style References

The A1 style uses the column and row headings (letters and numbers, respectively) as indices to reference a particular worksheet cell (for example, A1, B5, $C$2, etc.). Dollar signs in front of an index denote an absolute reference; the lack of a dollar sign on an index denotes a relative reference. The A1 style reference is the preferred style of most Excel users.

Creating a formula using VBA is easy. Instead of using the `Value` property of the range returned by the `Cells` property, you use the `Formula` property and assign a string value. The string should be in the form of an Excel formula.

In reality, you can also assign formula strings to the `Value` property of a range; however, it makes your code easier to read if you use the `Formula` property when assigning formulas to a range.

The following example inserts a formula in cell A11 of a worksheet that calculates the sum of the values in the range A2:A10 using the Excel application's SUM() function.

```
Dim formulaString As String
formulaString = "=SUM($A$2:$A$10)"
Cells(11, "A").Formula = formulaString
```

If you want to create a set of related formulas in a column, you can use a looping structure to iterate through the cells that receive the formula. The following example uses formulas inserted into the cells of column B in a worksheet to calculate a running sum of column A.

```
Dim formulaString As String
Dim I As Integer
Cells(1, "B").Value = Cells(1, "A").Value
For I = 2 To 10
      formulaString = "=A" & Trim(Str(I)) & "+B" & Trim(Str(I - 1))
      Cells(I, "B").Formula = formulaString
Next I
```

Looping through the cells is not the most efficient method available in VBA for inserting formulas. Using loops to insert formulas can slow your program down considerably, especially if it is running on an older machine with a relatively slow processor. You would not enter individual formulas in the Excel application when it is possible to copy and paste, so why do it with your VBA code? Instead, you can use Copy() and Paste() or AutoFill() methods that run much faster.

```
Dim formulaString As String
Dim I As Integer
Cells(1, "B").Value = Cells(1, "A").Value
formulaString = "=A2+B1"
Cells(2, "B").Formula = formulaString
```

To use the Copy() and Paste() methods, first insert the formula in the original cell as before, execute the Copy() method on the range returned by the Cells property, select the desired range, and paste the formula.

```
Cells(2, "B").Copy
Range("B2:B10").Select
ActiveSheet.Paste
```

A method is yet another type of procedure that performs a specific action on a program component or *object*. The Paste() method performs its action on an Excel worksheet by pasting the contents of the clipboard onto the worksheet.

Another option is to use the `AutoFill()` method by specifying the destination range. The term `Destination` is a named argument predefined for the `AutoFill()` method in VBA. *Named arguments* allow the programmer to pass values to a function without having to worry about the order of the arguments, or how many commas must be included for optional arguments that are not used. Use the named argument operator (:=) to assign the value to the name.

```
Cells(2, "B").AutoFill Destination:=Range("B2:B10")
```

Or, if you prefer, you can still pass the arguments in a list.

```
Cells(2, "B").AutoFill Range("B2:B10")
```

The second line of code using the `AutoFill()` method works because `Destination` is the first argument/parameter that must be passed to the method. (As it turns out, the `Destination` argument is the only required parameter of the `AutoFill()` method.) Using the named argument with the named argument operator makes the code more readable; therefore, the first example with the `AutoFill()` method is probably better. You can use named arguments with any procedure in VBA.

Specifically, the `Copy()` and `AutoFill()` methods are associated with the `Range` object and the `Paste()` method with the `Worksheet` object. I'll discuss these objects in detail in the next chapter.

R1C1-Style References

The R1C1 style uses the letters R for row and C for column followed by numbers to reference spreadsheet cells. For example, R[-1]C[2] is a relative reference to the cell one row lower and two columns higher than the cell that contains this reference in a formula. To denote an absolute reference, leave off the brackets (for example, R-1C2). The R1C1 reference style can be turned on in the Excel application by clicking Tools, Options, General, and then clicking R1C1 reference style as shown in Figure 4.6.

You can use the R1C1 reference style in your VBA code any time. It can be a preferable style to use when dealing with references to columns, as the indices use a numerical value. The value of the string variable `formulaString` in the previous example can be assigned as shown here:

```
formulaString = "=R[0]C[-1]+ R[-1]C[0]"
Cells(2, "B").FormulaR1C1 = formulaString
```

Although the `Formula` property of the `Range` object returned by the `Cells` property would work just as well, I have used the `FormulaR1C1` property for consistency.

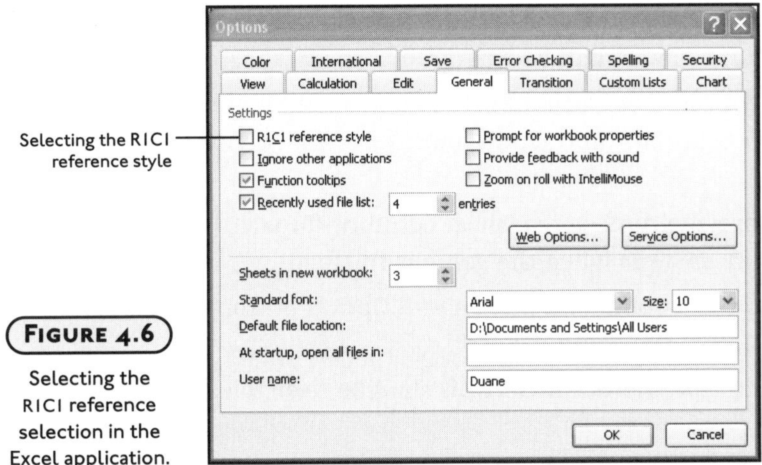

FIGURE 4.6

Selecting the R1C1 reference selection in the Excel application.

Whether you use the A1 style or R1C1 reference style in your VBA code is of no consequence to the user. The user will see whichever style they have set their Excel application to use.

CONSTRUCTING THE MATH GAME

The *Math Game* is designed as an exercise in basic math skills suitable for an elementary school child. The game gives the player one minute to correctly answer as many questions as possible with the selected operation (addition, subtraction, multiplication, or division). After the one-minute interval, the user's answers are scored and the result displayed on the worksheet. The game uses several programming structures and techniques discussed in this chapter, including loops and arrays.

Requirements for the Math Game

If you have young children or teach in elementary school, then you can use the *Math Game* as a testing tool of basic math skills (probably first and second graders). Your kids may not enjoy the test, but you can have a lot of fun writing it—and after you are comfortable with VBA, add more features to the program to suit your needs. The requirements of the Math Game as I have defined them follow:

1. The user interface shall consist of a single spreadsheet formatted to accentuate the numerical question. The operands, operator, and answer shall all have a large spreadsheet cell formatted with a large, easy to read font.
2. The user interface shall contain a Command Button control for initiating the program.

3. The user interface shall contain a timer that counts down to zero from 60 seconds (displaying each second). The timer shall be written to a spreadsheet cell.
4. The user interface shall contain five Option Button controls that allow the user to select a specific operator (addition, subtraction, multiplication, division, or random) for the game.
5. The user interface shall provide three spreadsheet columns for writing the questions, user's answers, and correct answers when the game is finished.
6. When the program begins, the Command Button and Option Button controls shall be disabled for the duration of the game.
7. The Command Button and Option Button controls shall be re-enabled when the game ends.
8. When the game begins, the program shall automatically select the worksheet cell in which the user enters his or her answers to the questions.
9. Operands for each question shall be randomly selected integers between zero and ten.
10. The mathematical operator for each question shall be chosen from the user's selection of the Option Button controls. If the user selects the Option Button labeled "Any," then the operator shall be selected randomly for each question and written to the proper spreadsheet cell.
11. The user shall proceed to the next question by pressing the Enter key.
12. The user must enter an answer to the question before proceeding to the next question.
13. When the user enters an answer, the question shall be cleared and the worksheet cell containing the answer is re-selected; that is, the cursor shall remain in the same worksheet cell for the duration of the game.
14. The game is over when the timer reaches zero.
15. When the game ends, the questions, user's answers, and correct answers shall be written to the spreadsheet.
16. When the game ends, the user's score shall be calculated and written to the spreadsheet.
17. Incorrect answers shall be highlighted in the worksheet with a different font color.

Designing the Math Game

The program interface is built from a single Excel worksheet. The worksheet is formatted with colors and a large font to make it easy for the user to see the questions. The macro recording tool is activated while formatting the worksheet in order to save most of the interface design as VBA code. ActiveX controls (Option Buttons and a Command Button control) are drawn on the worksheet in a convenient location to provide the user with a selection of mathematical operators, and an easy way to start the program. The *Math Game* worksheet is shown in Figure 4.7.

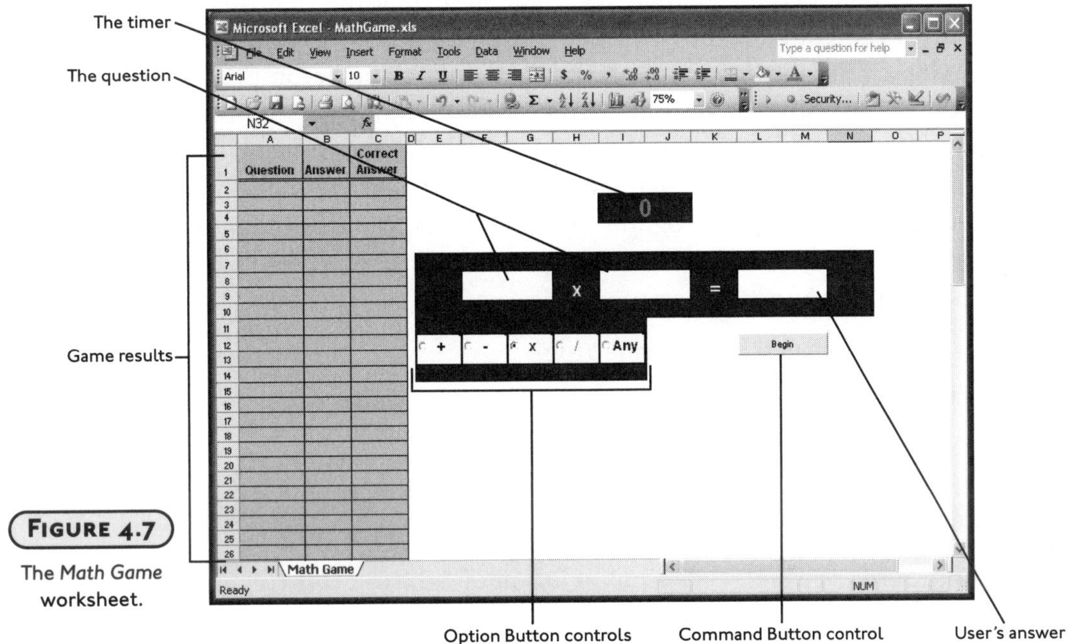

FIGURE 4.7

The *Math Game* worksheet.

The only input required by the *Math Game* program is the user's answers to the questions as they are entered from the keyboard. The program must make it convenient for the user to quickly enter his or her answers in the required worksheet cell, so the program must keep the answer cell selected through the duration of the game. This can be accomplished programmatically by selecting the cell when the user starts the game and setting the direction in which the selection moves after Enter is pressed on the keyboard (see Tools, Options, Edit, and the Move selection after Enter Check Box from the Excel application).

Program outputs include a timer written to a worksheet cell that counts down from 60 seconds, and the questions and score of the user's game. VBA contains an `OnTime()` method of the `Application` object that can handle the program's timer. The questions and answers can simply be written to the worksheet. Arrays are convenient tools for storing the questions and answers as the game is played.

As with previous programming projects, the program code can be entirely contained within the object module for the game's worksheet. The program must be initiated from the `Click()` event of the Command Button control. Other programming tasks will be assigned to various event, sub, and function procedures in order to properly compartmentalize the program.

The *Math Game* program is considerably more complex than the first three projects in this book; therefore, as you might expect, it's going to be longer. With slightly longer programs, I typically write a brief outline of the tasks that need to be accomplished based on the requirement list. Generally, the outline defines the sub and function procedures I need to write for the program. The `Click()` event of the Command Button control will serve as the main procedure for the program, looking very much like a program outline with procedure calls that follow the flow of the program. Other event procedures that are needed include the `Click()` events of the Option Button controls that are used to set the operator for each question. The project outline follows:

1. Format the worksheet (record formatting)
2. Add ActiveX controls and set their Design Time properties
3. Disable the ActiveX controls (sub procedure)
4. Clear the results from a previous game (`Click()` event of Command Button control)
5. Initialize variables (`Click()` event of Command Button control)
6. Select the answer cell (`Click()` event of Command Button control)
7. Get operands for the question (sub procedure)
8. Get an operator for the question (sub procedure)
9. Start the program timer (sub procedure)
10. Collect the user's answers and repeat steps 7 and 8 (`Change()` event of the worksheet)
11. Disable the timer (use the same sub procedure that starts the timer)
12. Enable ActiveX controls (use the same sub procedure that disables the controls)
13. Clear the game board (sub procedure)
14. Score the user's answers and write the results to the worksheet (`Click()` event of Command Button control)

Recording Macros

Up to this point, all chapter projects have been preformatted with no specific instructions on how it was done. I assume you are an experienced Excel user and are comfortable with formatting worksheets; however, there will be occasions when you need to create new formatted worksheets programmatically. You could write VBA code that formats the worksheet as you want, but this is often a tedious exercise and is not really necessary. You will know how you want the worksheet formatted; you just don't want it done until the user has reached a certain stage in your program. This is one example of when recording a macro is very handy. The basic steps for recording a macro are as follows:

1. Turn on Excel's macro recorder.
2. Format the worksheet as desired.
3. Stop the recorder.
4. Proceed to the VBA IDE and find the VBA code you just recorded.
5. Clean the recorded code for readability and add it to your program.

Another situation in which recording macros is useful is when you need to learn how to use a particular VBA function. If you can't find what you need in the online help or get your code to run correctly, simply record a macro that uses the desired function of the Excel application. Of course, you must know how to perform the same task within the Excel application that you are trying to add to your VBA code. Once the task is recorded, return to the VBA IDE and examine the recorded VBA code.

To begin recording a macro, in the Excel application select Tools, Macros, and Record New Macro, as shown in Figure 4.8. You can also select the Record Macro button on the Visual Basic toolbar.

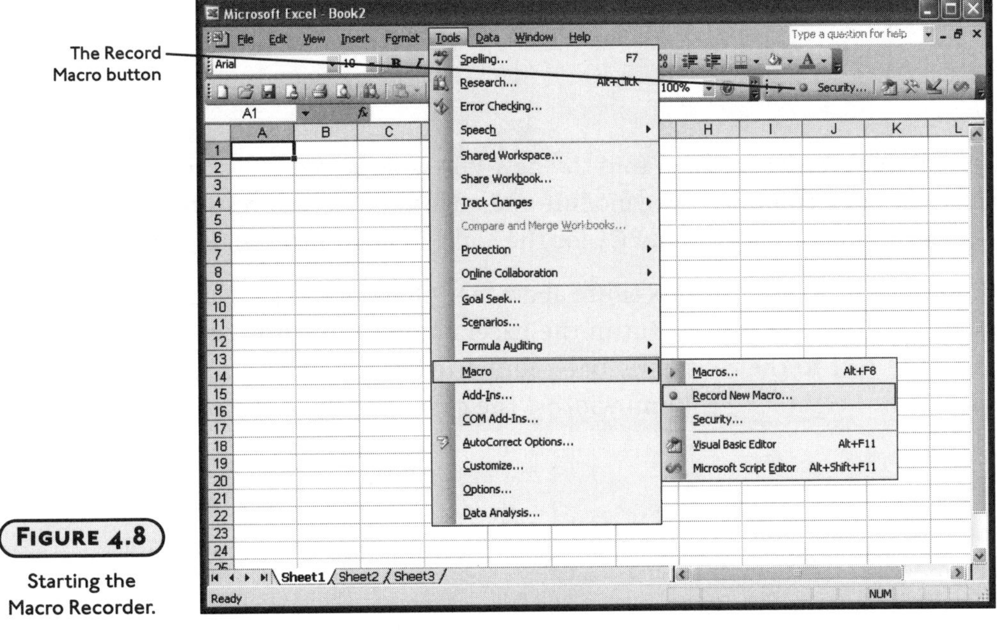

FIGURE 4.8

Starting the Macro Recorder.

A dialog box will appear, as shown in Figure 4.9, asking you to input a name for your macro, where you want to store the code (a new workbook, the current workbook, or a personal macro workbook), and for a description of the macro. You can enter in new values or use the default. I recommend at least changing the name of the macro to something meaningful. Store the macro in whatever workbook you want, but keep in mind the macro will be saved with the workbook you choose, and will only be available when this workbook is open.

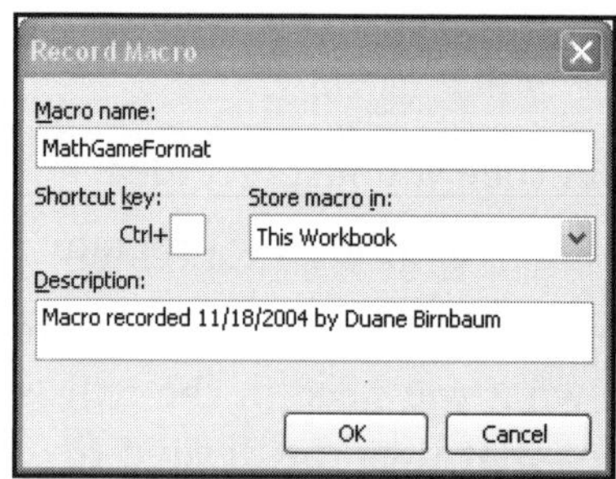

FIGURE 4.9

Naming and storing the macro.

After selecting the name and location of the macro, a small toolbar with a small square button will appear, as shown in Figure 4.10. After you are finished recording the macro, click this button to stop the recorder. Until you click the stop button, every action you perform in the Excel application is recorded as VBA code.

FIGURE 4.10

The Stop Recording button.

After stopping the recorder, you can find the new VBA code stored in a standard module in the previously designated project. The module and code window that results from recording a macro that formats cells A1, B1, and C1 for the *Math Game* is shown in Figure 4.11.

To record this macro, I follow the procedure above, and then format the cells before stopping the recorder. Specific tasks carried out in the Excel application while the recorder was on were: adding the text to the cells, specifying font size, bold, centered text, word wrapped text, a border, row height, and column widths. The code, exactly as recorded, is as follows:

```
Sub MathGameFormat()
'
' MathGameFormat Macro
' Macro recorded 11/16/2004 by Duane Birnbaum
'
```

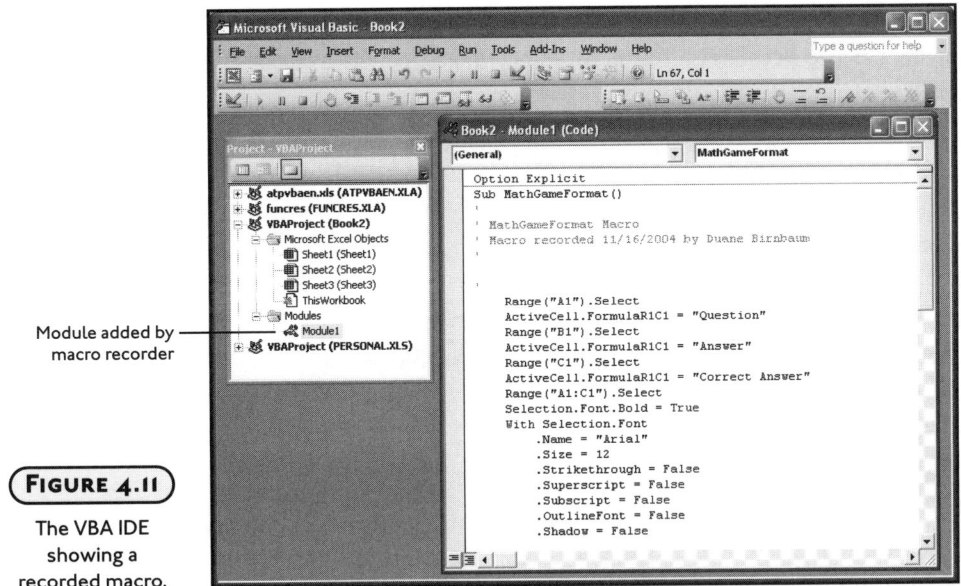

FIGURE 4.11

The VBA IDE showing a recorded macro.

```
'
    Range("A1").Select
    ActiveCell.FormulaR1C1 = "Question"
    Range("B1").Select
    ActiveCell.FormulaR1C1 = "Answer"
    Range("C1").Select
    ActiveCell.FormulaR1C1 = "Correct Answer"
    Range("A1:C1").Select
    Selection.Font.Bold = True
    With Selection.Font
        .Name = "Arial"
        .Size = 12
        .Strikethrough = False
        .Superscript = False
        .Subscript = False
        .OutlineFont = False
        .Shadow = False
        .Underline = xlUnderlineStyleNone
        .ColorIndex = xlAutomatic
    End With
    Selection.Borders(xlDiagonalDown).LineStyle = xlNone
```

```
    Selection.Borders(xlDiagonalUp).LineStyle = xlNone
    Selection.Borders(xlEdgeLeft).LineStyle = xlNone
    Selection.Borders(xlEdgeTop).LineStyle = xlNone
    With Selection.Borders(xlEdgeBottom)
        .LineStyle = xlDouble
        .Weight = xlThick
        .ColorIndex = xlAutomatic
    End With
    Selection.Borders(xlEdgeRight).LineStyle = xlNone
    Selection.Borders(xlInsideVertical).LineStyle = xlNone
    Rows("1:1").RowHeight = 32.25
    Columns("A:A").ColumnWidth = 10.71
    Columns("B:B").ColumnWidth = 9
    Columns("C:C").ColumnWidth = 10.86
    With Selection
        .HorizontalAlignment = xlCenter
        .VerticalAlignment = xlBottom
        .WrapText = False
        .Orientation = 0
        .AddIndent = False
        .IndentLevel = 0
        .ShrinkToFit = False
        .ReadingOrder = xlContext
        .MergeCells = False
    End With
    Range("C1").Select
    With Selection
        .HorizontalAlignment = xlCenter
        .VerticalAlignment = xlBottom
        .WrapText = True
        .Orientation = 0
        .AddIndent = False
        .IndentLevel = 0
        .ShrinkToFit = False
        .ReadingOrder = xlContext
        .MergeCells = False
    End With
End Sub
```

As you can see, recording just a few tasks will generate a considerable amount of code. (I even took care to minimize my worksheet cell selections knowing it would reduce the amount of recorded code.) Because of the volume of code generated by the macro recorder, I do not recommend recording many tasks at any one time. You want to be able to record small pieces, then clean up the recorded code and proceed to the next task.

Much of the recorded code can be eliminated by deleting the setting of default values and compressing multiple statements into one line of code. You will get better at this as you gain experience with VBA programming. The macro I just showed you can be quickly reduced to the following:

```
Sub MathGameFormat()
' Revised macro

    Range("A1").Select
    ActiveCell.FormulaR1C1 = "Question"
    Range("B1").Select
    ActiveCell.FormulaR1C1 = "Answer"
    Range("C1").Select
    ActiveCell.FormulaR1C1 = "Correct Answer"
    Range("A1:C1").Select
    Selection.HorizontalAlignment = xlCenter
    With Selection.Font
        .Bold = True
        .Name = "Arial"
        .Size = 12
    End With
    With Selection.Borders(xlEdgeBottom)
        .LineStyle = xlDouble
        .Weight = xlThick
    End With
    Rows("1:1").RowHeight = 32.25
    Columns("A:A").ColumnWidth = 10.71
    Columns("B:B").ColumnWidth = 9
    Columns("C:C").ColumnWidth = 10.86
    Range("C1").Select
    Selection.WrapText = True
End Sub
```

The macro is public by default and is contained inside a standard module.

The `With/End With` code structure is used to execute a series of statements on the same Excel object. This removes the requirement of constantly qualifying the object before setting one of its properties. The `With/End With` programming structure will be covered in Chapter 5.

To run a recorded macro in the Excel application, select Tools, Macro, Macros or press Alt+F8. A dialog box displaying a list of available macros will appear, as shown in Figure 4.12.

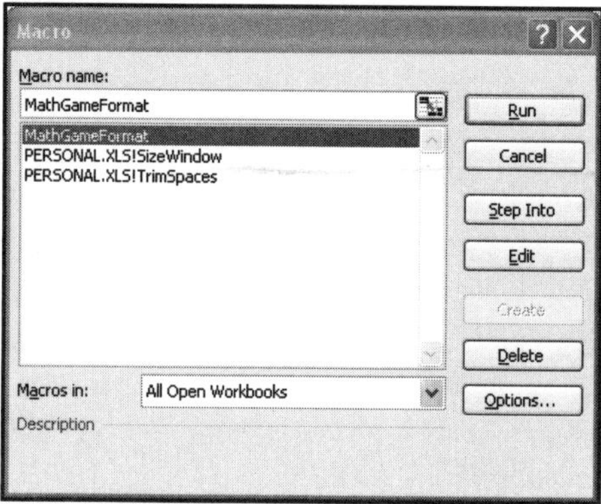

FIGURE 4.12

Selecting an available macro.

Select the macro you want and press the Run button to execute the code in the macro.

Any public procedure (recorded or not) stored in a standard or object module will appear in the list of available macros.

After recording the formatting of the worksheet cells A1 through C1, I record another manageable amount of formatting, clean up the code and paste it within the previously recorded procedure. After all recording is completed and the code is reduced, it can be copied to any sub procedure necessary to fulfill the algorithm for the program. For example, the recorded code may be needed inside the `Click()` event procedure of a Command Button control. Although the formatting macro is not a required part of the Math Game program, I have included the recorded macro (after editing) on the book's accompanying CD.

The macro-recording tool in Excel was really designed for non-programming users as a method to extend the capabilities of their spreadsheets and eliminate the tedium of repetitive tasks. As it turns out, the macro-recording tool can also serve the VBA programmer as a method of eliminating tedious programming tasks and learning how to carry out specific tasks in Excel with VBA code.

The Forms Toolbar

Along with the macro recorder, Excel comes with a few other controls similar to ActiveX controls that are designed for use with recorded macros. The controls are available from the Forms toolbar and can be accessed through the View menu in the Excel Application (see Figure 4.13).

FIGURE 4.13

The Forms toolbar.

Most of these controls are the same as the controls on the Control toolbox and their functions are basically the same. The difference: how the controls on the Forms toolbar are used. These controls are designed for non-programmers to use with recorded macros; therefore, they do not have code windows other than the module containing the recorded macro. To attach a macro to a control from the Forms toolbar, first draw the control on a worksheet and right click on the control to view its menu, then select Assign Macro. The Assign Macro dialog box, shown in Figure 4.14, will appear with a list of all available procedures (any procedure declared with the `Public` keyword) currently open in Excel.

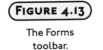

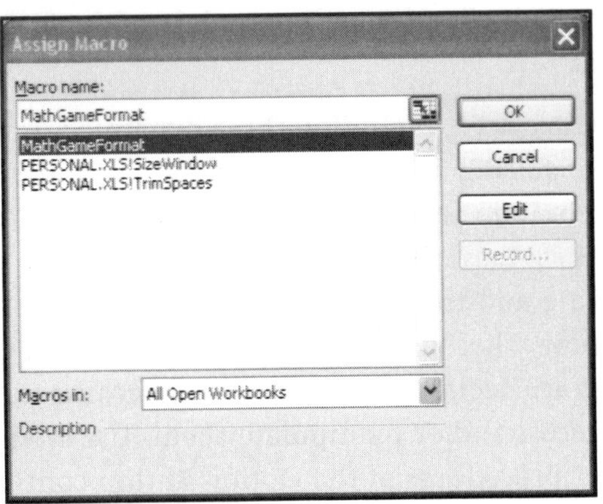

FIGURE 4.14

The Assign Macro Dialog Box.

Select the procedure you want to execute and click the OK button. The macro will be assigned to the major event of the control (typically a `Click()` event).

You can use these controls to initiate VBA procedures just as you would with controls from the Control toolbox; however, you sacrifice considerable flexibility with respect to properties and events associated with the control. Nevertheless, if all you need is code initiation, the Forms toolbar controls offer a simple set of tools.

Coding the Math Game Program

The *Math Game* was written following the design algorithm I have already discussed; all code was written in the object module of the worksheet. The program starts when the user clicks on the Command Button control and ends when the timer reaches zero. Option Button controls are used to select the operator. You should begin writing your programs by setting the properties of the ActiveX controls (if any are used).

Adding the ActiveX Controls

The program design calls for one Command Button and five Option Button controls. You should be quite familiar with the Command Button control. The Option Button control is similar to a Check Box except that a user can only select one button from a group. A group of Option Button controls is defined by their container—in this case, a worksheet. It does not matter how many Option Button controls I add to a worksheet, the user will only be able to select one. Table 4.3 shows selected properties of the ActiveX controls for the *Math Game* program that I changed at design time. (Size and display properties are not shown in the table, but, as is usually the case were edited from their default values.)

Addition is set as the default operator for the game by setting the `Value` property of `optAdd` to true. The controls are initially enabled so that the user may choose an operator and start the game. The entire program is contained in the object module of the formatted worksheet that contains the ActiveX controls.

Several module level variables are declared, including three dynamic arrays (`mathQuestions`, `mathOperators`, and `userAnswers`) for storing the questions, operators, and the user's answers. The variable `opType` will tell the program what mathematical operation is currently being used in the question. The variables `numQuestions`, `curDate`, and `gameRunning` store the number of questions asked, the current date and time (used later to set the timer), and a Boolean value used by the program to know whether or not the `Change()` event of the worksheet should be ignored. These variables are declared at module level because more than one procedure in the program needs to access and/or manipulate them. The module level variable declarations and the `Click()` event procedures of the Option Button controls follow:

Keep the number of module level variables in your program to an absolute minimum. A common trap novice programmers make is to create most of the variables module level (and later global when you include more modules in your program). Although module level variables may seem convenient, they can make your program prone to logic errors that are difficult to debug.

Table 4.3 Selected Properties of the ActiveX Controls Used in the Math Game

ActiveX Control	Property	Value
Command Button	Name	cmdBegin
	Caption	Begin
Option Button	Name	optAdd
	Value	True
	Caption	+
Option Button	Name	optSubtract
	Value	False
	Caption	-
Option Button	Name	optMultiply
	Value	False
	Caption	x
Option Button	Name	optDivide
	Value	False
	Caption	/
Option Button	Name	optAny
	Value	False
	Caption	Any

```
Option Explicit
Private mathQuestions() As Integer
Private mathOperators() As String
Private userAnswers() As Integer
Private opType As Integer
Private numQuestions As Integer
Private curDate As Date
Private gameRunning As Boolean
```

```
Private Sub optAdd_Click()
    Range("Operator").Value = "+"
    opType = 1
End Sub
Private Sub optSubtract_Click()
    Range("Operator").Value = "-"
    opType = 2
End Sub
Private Sub optMultiply_Click()
    Range("Operator").Value = "x"
    opType = 3
End Sub
Private Sub optDivide_Click()
    Range("Operator").Value = "/"
    opType = 4
End Sub
Private Sub optAny_Click()
    Range("Operator").Value = ""
End Sub
```

The purpose of these `Click()` event procedures is to write the operator (+, -, ×, and /) to the appropriate worksheet cell (merged cells H8:H9). Please note: I defined a named range for cells H8:H9 in the Excel application calling it `Operator`. I can now use this name in my program to refer to the range. This makes the code easier to read (otherwise known as self-documenting). The module level variable `opType` is assigned a designated integer (1 = addition, 2 = subtraction, 3 = multiplication, and 4 = division) with each click of an Option Button control. The program will need to read the value of `opType` when storing each question.

Starting and Initializing the Math Game Program

The `Click()` event procedure of the `cmdBegin` Command Button control serves as the main procedure in the *Math Game* program. This procedure initializes a few variables, clears the worksheet, and makes several calls to sub procedures that get the game started.

```
Private Sub cmdBegin_Click()
    '-------------------
    'Initialize variables and controls.
    '-------------------
    EnableControls False
    numQuestions = 0
```

```
    gameRunning = True
    Range("A2:C" & UsedRange.Rows.Count).ClearContents
    Range("Answer").Select
    Application.MoveAfterReturn = False

    '-------------------------------
    'Get the operator type and operands for the question.
    '-------------------------------
    GetOperatorType
    GetOperands

    '----------------------
    'Mark the start time and start the clock.
    '----------------------
    curDate = Now
    MathGame
End Sub
```

Examination of the `Click()` event procedure of the Command Button control `cmdBegin` shows an immediate call to the sub procedure `EnableControls()`. This procedure is used to enable or disable the ActiveX controls on the worksheet via a Boolean value (passed in to the parameter `ctrlsEnabled`, see next sub procedure). At this stage of the program, I want to disable all ActiveX controls so the user doesn't accidentally select one while the game runs; therefore, I pass in the value false.

After the ActiveX controls are disabled, a couple more module-level variables are initialized (`numQuestions` and `gameRunning`) before the first three columns of the spreadsheet are cleared. The `UsedRange` property of the `Application` object returns exactly what its name implies—the range on the worksheet containing the data. I use this range along with the `Rows` and `Count` properties of the `Range` object to tell me how many rows are used on the spreadsheet so they can be cleared (see Chapter 5 for a discussion of the `Application` object, `Range` object, and their properties). This effectively clears the results of a previous game from the worksheet.

After clearing the worksheet of the previous game's results, the range of cells in which the user must enter his/her answer is selected. This is the range L8:M9 which I merged and defined a name for (`Answer`) in the Excel application. The `MoveAfterReturn` property of the `Application` object is set to false to prevent the cursor from moving (usually down one cell) after the user presses enter on the keyboard. This feature can be found in the Excel application under Tools, Options, and the Edit tab (see Figure 4.15).

I only had a vague memory of setting the cursor direction after Enter feature in Excel, so I searched Options dialog (because it seemed like the most reasonable place) in the Excel application until I found it. Then, with the macro recorder turned on, I deselected the *Move selection after Enter* check box (see Figure 4.15) and examined the resulting VBA code to learn how to program this feature.

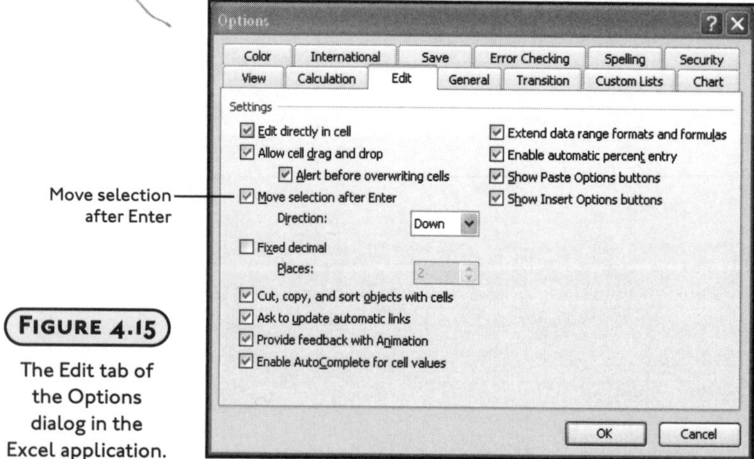

FIGURE 4.15

The Edit tab of the Options dialog in the Excel application.

```
Private Sub EnableControls(ctrlsEnabled As Boolean)
'Enables/Disables ActiveX controls on the worksheet.
    cmdBegin.Enabled = ctrlsEnabled
    optAdd.Enabled = ctrlsEnabled
    optSubtract.Enabled = ctrlsEnabled
    optDivide.Enabled = ctrlsEnabled
    optMultiply.Enabled = ctrlsEnabled
    optAny.Enabled = ctrlsEnabled
End Sub
```

After the game's variables and controls are initialized, the first question is randomly generated before starting the timer.

Generating Random Questions and Operators

You have already seen how to generate random numbers in VBA. The *Math Game* program requires the operands for each question to be randomly generated and the operator is randomly generated if the user selects the proper Option Button control (the button labeled "Any," see Figure 4.7).

The GetOperatorType() procedure tests the Value property of the Option Button controls to see which operator has been selected by the user. If the user selects the option "Any," then the GetRandomOperator() procedure is called to generate a random number between 1 and 4. This procedure writes the operator to the merged cells I defined with the name Operator, and is only used when the operator is randomly chosen by the program. You should recall that when a user selects a specific operator, the Click() event procedure of the Option Button control writes that operator to the Operator range.

```
Private Sub GetOperatorType()
'Gets the operator selected by the user.
    If optAdd.Value = True Then opType = 1
    If optSubtract.Value = True Then opType = 2
    If optMultiply.Value = True Then opType = 3
    If optDivide.Value = True Then opType = 4
    If optAny.Value = True Then GetRandomOperator
End Sub
Private Sub GetRandomOperator()
'Randomly selects the type of operator for the question.
    Randomize
    opType = Int(4 * Rnd) + 1
    Select Case opType
        Case Is = 1
            Range("Operator").Value = "+"
        Case Is = 2
            Range("Operator").Value = "-"
        Case Is = 3
            Range("Operator").Value = "x"
        Case Is = 4
            Range("Operator").Value = "/"
        Case Else
            Range("Operator").Value = "+"
    End Select
End Sub
```

A question's operands are written to the appropriate cell locations (F8:G9, defined name LeftOperand and I8:I9, defined name RightOperand) with the GetOperands() sub procedure that calls the GetRandomNumber() function procedure in order to generate and return the operands randomly. If the mathematical operation is division, the GetRandomNumber() function uses a loop that will continue to iterate until a second operand is found that results in a non-fractional answer. The VBA operator Mod is used to test the two random numbers for a remainder of zero.

The GetOperands() sub procedure is called from the Click() event of the Command Button control cmdBegin and the Change() event of the worksheet (listed later).

```
Private Sub GetOperands()
'Adds randomly choosen operands to the worksheet.
    Dim rightOperand As Integer

    rightOperand = GetRandomNumber(1)
    Range("RightOperand").Value = rightOperand
    Range("LeftOperand").Value = GetRandomNumber(rightOperand)
End Sub

Private Function GetRandomNumber(divisibleBy As Integer) As Integer
'Generates the random numbers for the operands.
    Dim ranNum As Integer
    Const upperLimit = 10

    Randomize
    '--------------------------------
    'Generate the random integer. If operation is division,
    'then make sure the two operands are evenly divisible.
    '--------------------------------
    Do
        ranNum = Int(upperLimit * Rnd) + 1
    Loop Until ((opType <> 4) Or (ranNum Mod divisibleBy = 0))

    GetRandomNumber = ranNum
End Function
```

The game is now ready for the user to enter his or her answer, so the timer must start counting down.

Starting the Timer

The essence of the *Math Game* program is contained within the sub procedure appropriately named MathGame(). This procedure controls the game's clock and calls the sub procedures that score the user's answers when the clock reaches zero. The clock is controlled with a very special method of the Application object—the OnTime() method. You can use the OnTime() method to set up repetitive calls to the same procedure based on a given time increment; in this case, one second.

To begin, the MathGame() procedure uses the integer variable numSeconds to hold the amount of time left in the game. The length of the game is held in the constant TIMEALLOWED. The number of seconds left in the game is calculated by the VBA function DateDiff() using the current time and the time the program was initiated with the click of the Command Button control cmdBegin (stored in the module level variable curDate). This value is written to cell I3 on the worksheet with a defined name of Clock.

In order to count down in one second intervals, a date one second later than the current time is calculated by adding the two dates returned from VBA's Now() and TimeValue() functions. This date is then assigned to the variable nextTime. The Now() function returns the current date and time and the TimeValue() function returns a date converted from a string (formatted using hours:minutes:seconds). I passed the TimeValue() function a string specifying one second ("00:00:01"). As you are about to see, the nextTime variable is used to specify the next time the MathGame() procedure executes.

The most interesting statement in the MathGame() procedure comes next. The OnTime() method that belongs to the Application object is set up to repeatedly call the MathGame() sub procedure. The OnTime() method takes up to four parameters for input, two of which are required. Because I only need to pass the OnTime() method three parameters, I am using named arguments. The EarliestTime parameter represents the next time the system will call the procedure specified by the Procedure parameter, in this case the MathGame() procedure. The EarliestTime and Procedure parameters are required. The other two parameters, both of which are optional are LatestTime and Schedule. The LatestTime parameter represents the latest time the procedure specified by the Procedure parameter can be called; however it is not required here. The Schedule parameter is used to schedule a new call to the procedure specified by the Procedure parameter. In this case, Schedule must be used and set to true in order to ensure the next call to the MathGame() procedure occurs. It is important to point out that between calls to the MathGame() procedure, the system is allowed to process other events; thus, the system is not locked up processing code as it would be if we used a looping structure to handle the timer. This allows the user to enter answers into the appropriate worksheet cell. The MathGame() procedure is now set up to execute every second. Figure 4.16 shows the *Math Game* program worksheet during a game. The timer started at 60 seconds.

Following the initial use of the OnTime() method, an If/Then decision structure is used to check the value of the timer. If the timer is less than or equal to zero, then the OnTime() method is used to disable the timer by setting the Schedule parameter to false; thus, the MathGame() procedure will no longer be called. Without this statement, the MathGame() procedure will be called every second and drastic action (ctrl+alt+break) will have to be taken to stop the program.

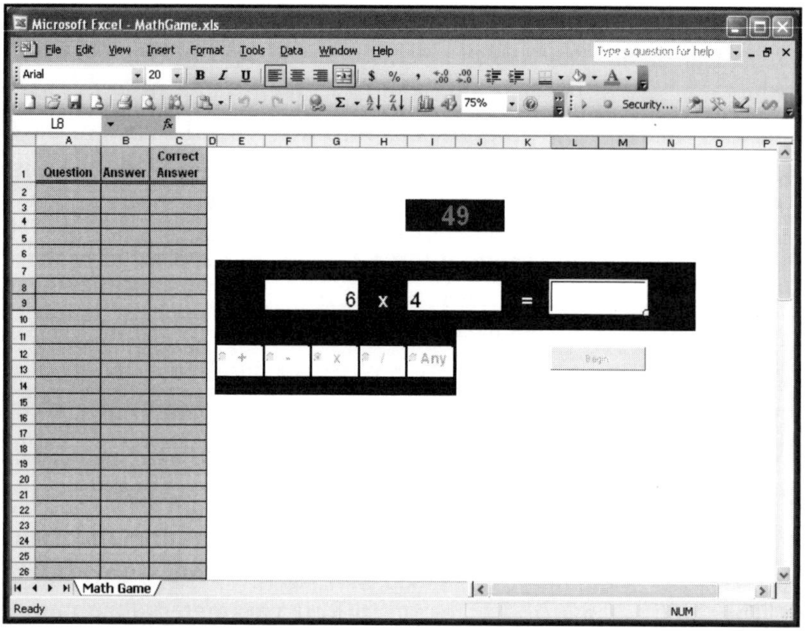

FIGURE 4.16

The *Math Game* worksheet as the program is running.

After the timer reaches zero, calls to the procedures `EnableControls()`, `ClearBoard()`, and `ScoreAnswers()` are made to enable the ActiveX controls, clear the values in the spreadsheet cells containing the question and answer, and score the results of the game.

```
Private Sub MathGame()
'Manages the clock while testing. Calls scoring procedures when test is over.
    Dim numSeconds  As Integer
    Dim nextTime As Date
    Const TIMEALLOWED = 60

    numSeconds = DateDiff("s", curDate, Now)
    '-----------
    'Start the clock.
    '-----------
    Range("Clock").Value = TIMEALLOWED - numSeconds
    nextTime = Now + TimeValue("00:00:01")
    Application.OnTime EarliestTime:=nextTime, Procedure:="MathGameSheet.MathGame", _
Schedule:=True
```

```
    '---------------------------------------
    'Disable timer when it reaches zero, score results, and clean up
    'worksheet controls/cells.
    '---------------------------------------
    If (TIMEALLOWED - numSeconds <= 0) Then
        gameRunning = False
        Application.OnTime EarliestTime:=nextTime, Procedure:="MathGameSheet.MathGame", _
Schedule:=False
        EnableControls True
        ClearBoard
        ScoreAnswers
        Application.MoveAfterReturn = True
    End If
End Sub
```

The `MathGame()` procedure handles the timer and scoring when the game is over, but it does not collect the questions or user's answers. Instead, these values are captured in the `Change()` event of the worksheet.

Collecting Answers

The `Change()` event of a worksheet triggers when the content of cells on the worksheet are changed by the user. In the *Math Game* program, this event will trigger every time the user enters an answer. Excel passes the altered cell's range to the `Change()` event via the `Target` parameter. The user's answers are entered into the merged range L8:M9 defined with the name `Answer`; therefore, the value of the `Target` parameter will be $L$8.

If the user has entered the answer in the correct cell, a series of statements are executed. A modicum of input validation is included in the conditional for the `If/Then` decision structure. If the user presses Enter without typing in an answer, then no code inside the `If/Then` decision structure is executed. This forces the user to enter an answer for each question. Furthermore, the `gameRunning` variable must be true or the code in the decision structure will not execute. (This prevents the program from displaying a question when the game is over.)

If the user does answer a question, then the `numQuestions` variable is incremented by one, the `StoreQuestions()` sub procedure is called, and a new question is obtained from calls to the `GetRandomOperator()` (if required) and `GetOperands()` procedures and displayed.

```
Private Sub Worksheet_Change(ByVal Target As Range)
'Stores answer entered by the user and gets next question.
```

```
    If (Target.Address = "$L$8") And (Range("Answer").Value <> "") And gameRunning Then
        numQuestions = numQuestions + 1
        StoreQuestions
        If optAny.Value = True Then
            GetRandomOperator
        End If
        GetOperands
        Range("Answer").Select
        Selection.Value = ""
    End If
End Sub
```

The `StoreQuestions()` sub procedure is called from the `Change()` event of the worksheet, so the code within is executed every time the user enters an answer to a question. The dynamic variable arrays declared at module level are re-dimensioned to increase their size by one with each call to this procedure. The `Preserve` keyword is used to ensure that previously stored values are not lost.

The two-dimensional array `mathQuestions` maintains the same number of dimensions, and only the upper bound of the last dimension changes, as required when using the `Preserve` keyword. Thus, the `mathQuestions` array can be thought of as containing two rows (indexed by 0 and 1) and *n* columns where *n* is equal to the number of questions asked during the game.

The operands (cells F8 and I8 defined as `LeftOperand` and `RightOperand`, respectively) for each question are stored in rows 0 and 1 of the `mathQuestions` array. The mathematical operator used and the user's answers are stored in the arrays `mathOperators` and `userAnswers`, respectively. The index value in the arrays used to store the mathematical operators and the user's answers is identical to the index value in the array used to store the corresponding question. This is critical for outputting these values to the correct worksheet cells later in the program.

The user's answer is passed to the `Val()` function before storing in the array. This serves as more input validation. If the user enters a non-numerical string, then the answer will usually be set to zero depending on the string, as discussed earlier in this chapter.

```
Private Sub StoreQuestions()
'Stores the questions and answers in dynamic arrays.
    ReDim Preserve mathQuestions(1, numQuestions) As Integer
    ReDim Preserve mathOperators(numQuestions) As String
    ReDim Preserve userAnswers(numQuestions) As Integer
```

```
    mathQuestions(0, numQuestions - 1) = Range("LeftOperand").Value
    mathQuestions(1, numQuestions - 1) = Range("RightOperand").Value
    mathOperators(numQuestions - 1) = Range("Operator").Value
    userAnswers(numQuestions - 1) = Val(Range("Answer").Value)
End Sub
```

After the timer has reached zero, the game is over and the last question is cleared with the `ClearBoard()` sub procedure before the user's results are scored and tabulated.

```
Private Sub ClearBoard()
'Clears the operands and the answer from the worksheet cells.
    Range("LeftOperand").Value = ""
    Range("RightOperand").Value = ""
    Range("Answer").Value = ""
End Sub
```

Scoring the Answers

The `ScoreAnswers()` sub procedure called at the end of the game from the `MathGame()` procedure reads the questions asked during the game from variable arrays and displays them on the worksheet. This procedure also checks the user's answers and outputs the score as a percentage of questions answered correctly.

I use a `For/Next` loop to iterate through the arrays holding the questions and answers, because I know the number of questions that were asked during the game is stored in the module level variable `numQuestions`. The lower bound on the arrays are zero, so the looping variable ranges from zero to the number of questions less one.

String concatenation is used to output the questions asked during the game to column A on the worksheet. The user's answers are output to column B on the worksheet. Using the looping variable as the indices for the arrays guarantees that the questions match their corresponding answer.

To display the correct answer in column C of the worksheet, a formula string is created and copied to the appropriate cell using the `Formula` property of the cell range. Because a x was used to display multiplication in column A, an `If/Then` decision structure replaces it with Excel's required multiplication operator (*) in the formula for column C. If the user entered a wrong answer, the answer is displayed in red and the integer variable `numWrong` is incremented by one. Finally, the user's score is calculated and output to the end of column B on the worksheet as a formula.

```
Private Sub ScoreAnswers()
'After the test is over, the user's answers are scored and the
'results written to the worksheet.
    Dim I As Integer
    Dim numWrong As Integer

    '-----------------------------------------
    'Loop through the arrays and score answers. Mark wrong answers in red.
    'Write the questions, user answers, and correct answers to the worksheet.
    '-----------------------------------------
    For I = 0 To numQuestions - 1
        Cells(I + 2, "A").Value = mathQuestions(0, I) & mathOperators(I) & _
mathQuestions(1, I)
        Cells(I + 2, "B").Value = userAnswers(I)
        If mathOperators(I) = "x" Then  'Excel requires asterisk (*) for multiplication.
            Cells(I + 2, "C").Formula = "=" & mathQuestions(0, I) & "*" & _
mathQuestions(1, I)
            Cells(I + 2, "B").Font.Color = RGB(0, 0, 0)
        Else
            Cells(I + 2, "C").Formula = "=" & mathQuestions(0, I) & _
mathOperators(I) & mathQuestions(1, I)
            Cells(I + 2, "B").Font.Color = RGB(0, 0, 0)
        End If

        If Cells(I + 2, "B").Value <> Cells(I + 2, "C").Value Then
            Cells(I + 2, "B").Font.Color = RGB(255, 0, 0)
            numWrong = numWrong + 1
        End If
    Next I
    '----------------------------
    'Compute % correct and write to the worksheet.
    '----------------------------
    Cells(I + 2, "A").Value = "Score (%)"
    Cells(I + 2, "B").Font.Color = RGB(0, 0, 0)
    Cells(I + 2, "B").Formula = "=" & (numQuestions - numWrong) / numQuestions & "*100"
End Sub
```

Figure 4.17 shows the *Math Game* program worksheet immediately after a game is played.

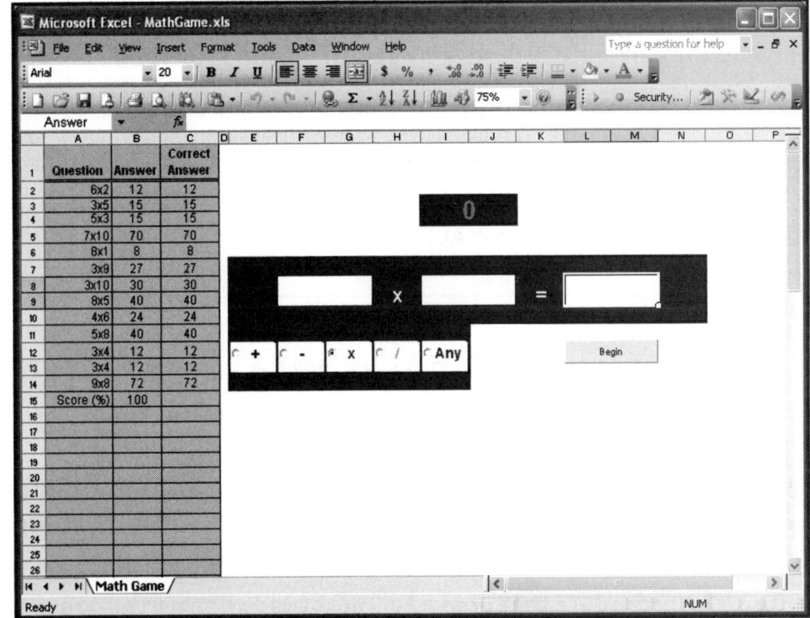

FIGURE 4.17

The *Math Game* program.

This concludes the *Math Game* program. I wrote the program following the algorithm described earlier. I added small details usually related to formatting the spreadsheet to the appropriate procedures after the program was working to satisfaction.

I wrote the *Math Game* program using a single code module. To add a small amount of complexity to the program, you could separate the procedures listed earlier into two or more code modules. For example, some programmers prefer to leave only event procedures in object modules and locate all of their custom procedures in standard modules. Splitting the code for the *Math Game* program into an object and standard module is left and an exercise for the reader. As a hint, be aware of variable scope for those variables required in both modules.

CHAPTER SUMMARY

You covered a significant number of topics concerning VBA programs in this chapter. The looping code structures (`Do-Loop` and `For/Next`) and variable arrays provide enormous power by allowing us to write more efficiently and significantly shorten the code.

You also examined a number of methods used for interaction with an Excel worksheet including input validation, entering formulas in spreadsheet cells, and using the `Change()` event procedure of a worksheet.

The *Math Game* used all of these tools plus a special method (`OnTime()`) of the application object to repeatedly call a procedure at a specified time interval.

You also examined the macro recorder and Forms toolbar controls.

The next chapter introduces the Excel object model concentrating on the objects at the top of the hierarchy. You have seen many examples of Excel objects in the first four chapters of this book. Now it is time to take an in depth look at these objects, their properties, and their methods.

CHALLENGES

1. **Write a procedure that outputs a random number to the first 100 cells in column A of an Excel worksheet.**
2. **Add a statement to the procedure from the previous question that inserts a formula into cell A101 and that calculates the sum of the first 100 cells. If you can't get it on your own, record a macro and examine the code.**
3. **Write a VBA procedure that uses a `For/Next` loop to store the contents of the first 10 cells in row 1 of an Excel worksheet to a variable array.**
4. **Write a VBA procedure that uses nested `For/Next` loops to store the contents of the range A1:E5 in an Excel worksheet to a two-dimensional array.**
5. **Write a VBA procedure that uses nested `For/Next` loops to store the contents of the range A1:E5 in each of three Excel worksheets to a three-dimensional array.**
6. **Change the procedures above using an input box to ask the user for the number of rows and/or columns and/or worksheets in which to retrieve values for storage in the same arrays. Use `Do-loops` and dynamic arrays. Add validation to the input box.**
7. **Record a macro that formats a worksheet to look like the worksheet in the *Math Game*, less the ActiveX controls.**
8. **Modify the *Math Game* program so that its timer starts at the specified number of seconds entered by the user in cell I3.**
9. **Modify the *Math Game* program so that the questions and answers are written to the spreadsheet as the user enters each answer.**
10. **Change the *Math Game* program such that it uses two code modules. The same object module for the worksheet and a standard module. Leave only the event procedures in the object module for the worksheet. Hint: You will have to increase the scope of those variables and procedures referenced in both modules to public.**

Basic Excel Objects

The preceding chapters concentrated on fundamental programming constructs common to all languages. Now it is time to introduce some VBA- and Excel-specific programming concepts and capabilities. You will be using programming tools referred to as *objects*, specifically some of the objects available in VBA and Excel.

In this chapter you will learn about:

- Objects
- VBA Collection Objects
- The Object Browser
- The Application Object
- Workbook and Window Objects
- The Worksheet Object
- The Range Object
- With/End With and For/Each
- Adding sound to your VBA program

Project: Battlecell

The *Battlecell* program will familiarize you with many of Excel's top level and most common objects, as well as reinforce code and data structures previously discussed. You will also become familiar with the Object Browser, in order to access all of the objects in the available libraries, not just in the Excel library. The *Battlecell* program relies heavily on Excel's `Application`, `Workbook`, `Worksheet`, and `Range` objects. The program is a computer simulation of the classic Battleship game you may have played as a kid, and a natural choice for a spreadsheet application. Figure 5.1 shows the Battlecell game board designed from an Excel worksheet with a game in progress.

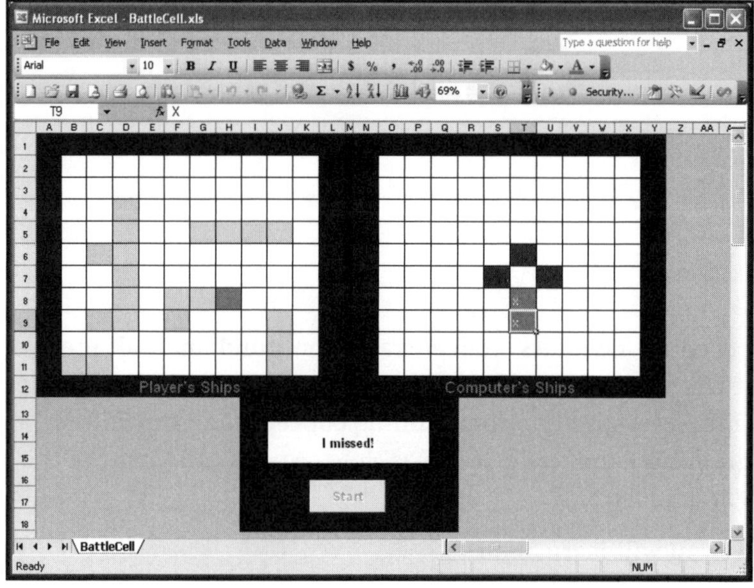

FIGURE 5.1

The Battleship game sheet.

VBA and Object-Oriented Programming

If VBA is your first programming language, then chances are you have not heard of object-oriented programming. Don't worry if you haven't heard of it; VBA does not qualify as an object-oriented language. There are some technicalities that disqualify VBA from calling itself "object-oriented," but VBA still shares many of the same concepts as genuine object-oriented languages. Mainly, object-oriented languages and VBA commonly share the existence of objects and some of the tools used to manipulate these objects. These tools include properties, events, and methods. (Other languages may call these tools something different, but they are really the same thing.) You have already seen several VBA objects in action. For example, in Chapter 1, the project code contained many references to Excel objects and some of their properties. Objects must be discussed in VBA at a relatively early stage. Objects show up early, often, and everywhere in your VBA code. This is a good thing, because your programs can't really do much without them.

In the Real World

Although C++ has been around for a few years, most object-oriented languages are relatively new. Java is an object-oriented language that gained a strong following with the rise in popularity of the World Wide Web. Other languages such as VBA, and some web-based languages (e.g., JavaScript, Perl) do not satisfy all the definitions required for the object-oriented label; however, all of these languages use objects extensively and thus serve as a good introduction to object-based programming, if they aren't totally object-oriented.

Program objects, such as ActiveX controls in VBA, allow greater flexibility and power in software development because they can be developed by one group of programmers and used by other groups in virtually any application. It is this ability to re-use program objects and the time savings it creates that make objects so popular among programmers.

The requirements for a language to be designated as object-oriented are really quite strict. One requirement is that object-oriented languages must allow programmers to build new classes (object definitions). Furthermore, the objects created from a new class must support inheritance. Inheritance refers to the ability of one class to inherit from another. This simply means that the new class (also known as the derived class) will have all the members of the inherited class (also known as the parent class). Although VBA allows programmers to define new classes, it does not support inheritance and for this reason (and others not beyond the scope of this text), VBA is not considered object-oriented.

The latest version of Visual Basic (VB .net) and the relatively new development language C# satisfy object-oriented requirements. The popularity of object-oriented languages is likely to continue and the migration of object-based languages to true object-oriented status is also probable (if they survive). However, it appears that for the time being, VBA will remain object-based, and not object-oriented.

Objects Defined

There is no need to get too abstract here with the definition of an object. It really is a pretty simple thing to understand. You can think of objects as separate computer programs with specific (and often common) functions that are available for repeated use in your programs. Objects are dynamic in that they can be easily manipulated in code with the various parameters used to define them.

In one common analogy, objects are equated as nouns in the English language. A programming object can be described with adjectives (properties), be capable of performing different actions with verbs (methods), and be built out of other objects. As an example, consider a bicycle. A bicycle can be described by its size, color, and type (among other things). For example, it might be a 26" blue ten-speed. The color, size, and type are all adjectives that describe the bicycle. Thus, they are all *properties* of the bicycle. A bicycle can also perform various actions; it can move straight or turn when ridden. Moving and turning are action verbs that tell you what tasks the bicycle can perform. Moving and turning are *methods* of the bicycle. Finally, the bicycle is built out of other objects such as a frame, wheels, handlebars, and pedals. These objects, in turn, have their own properties and methods. For example, a bicycle wheel is of a certain diameter, is built out of aluminum or titanium alloys, and it turns or rolls. The diameter and type of material are properties of the wheel object, and to turn or roll would be two of its methods. So you see, there is sort of a hierarchy to the objects in your bicycle and the bicycle object itself sits at the top of the hierarchy.

I could take it further. For example, a wheel is built from a tire, rim, and spoke objects. The tires are built from organic polymers, and so on, and so on. The description continues until eventually you will get to the objects at the very bottom of the hierarchy. These objects may have properties and methods, but they are not built out of any other objects. It may take you awhile to get to this level if you really think about your bicycle. Eventually you could break the bicycle down to its subatomic components. Of course, then you would have to stop because you would reach the limit of human knowledge. Fortunately, in any program, the object hierarchy does not extend that far and is well defined by the programmer. In this case, you get help from Excel and VBA in defining the objects, but it is still up to you to choose which objects you want or need to use in your program.

Now there is one more attribute of an object that has not yet been mentioned (at least not here; but it was discussed in Chapter 3). Consider what happens when a tire on your bicycle goes flat; or when the rider pedals the bicycle; or when the rider turns the handlebars on the bicycle. These are all *events* that occur when some action is carried out. Don't be confused with the method of the bicycle turning and the event of the rider turning the handlebars. They are not the same—one depends on the other. In this particular case, the bicycle turns when the rider turns the handlebars. Events are actions triggered by an external stimulus of the object. You write code to use the `turn_bicycle()` method when the rider triggers the `handlebar_turn()` event. The code that is executed (invoking the `turn_bicycle()` method) is a coded response to the user's stimulus (`handlebar_turn()` event).

Object events are very powerful programming tools, as they allow for a much more interactive experience between the program and the user. Think about what a program would be like without events. Once you started the program running, you would not do anything else except maybe type in some information when prompted by the program. That is, the programmer would completely dictate the flow of the program. If you remember computers prior to GUI's then you may remember this kind of programming. You have already seen some of the events associated with a couple of Excel's objects in previous chapters. Now, you should have a little better understanding as to why events exist.

Now let's consider some of the objects in Excel. If you are a regular user of Excel or any spreadsheet program, then you are already familiar with many of its objects. For example, there are `Workbook` objects, `Worksheet` objects, `Range` objects, `Chart` objects, and many more. The rest of this chapter is devoted to showing you how to use a few of Excel's objects, and in particular, some of its top-level objects.

VBA Collection Objects

Collection objects in VBA are fairly straightforward—they are exactly what the name implies: a group or collection of the same object types. Referring to the bicycle example again, consider a collection of bicycles. The bicycle objects in your bicycle collection can be different sizes, colors, and types, but they are all bicycles.

Collection objects allow you to work with objects as a group rather than just working with a single object. In VBA, collection objects are typically denoted with the plural form of the object types that can belong to a collection (not all can). For example, any `Workbook` object belongs to a `Workbooks` collection object. The `Workbooks` collection object contains all open `Workbook` objects. The Excel window shown in Figure 5.2 contains three open `Workbook` objects (`Book1`, `Book2`, and `Book3`).

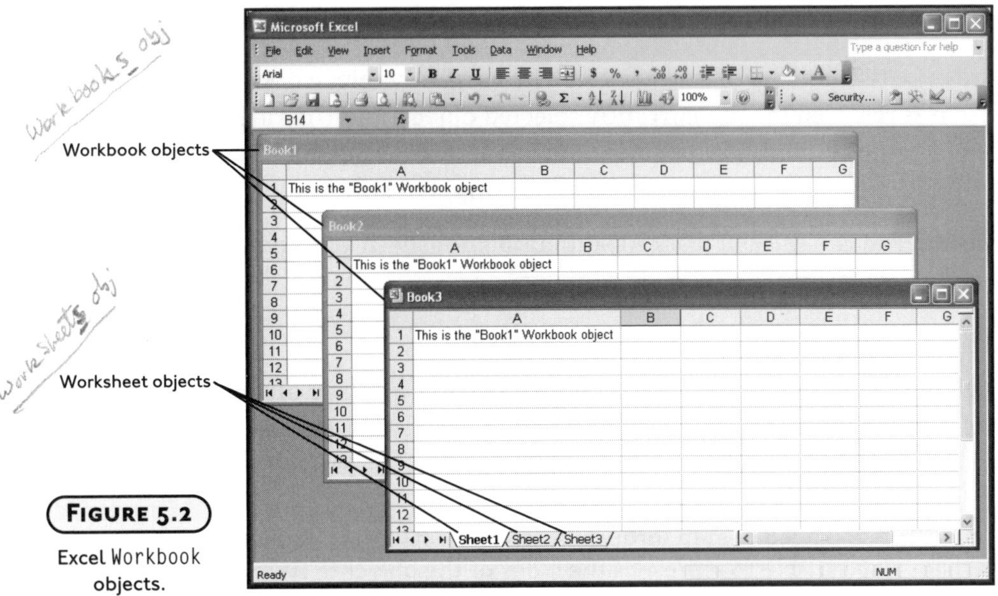

Figure 5.2

Excel `Workbook` objects.

To select a `Workbook` object from the `Workbooks` collection object, the code would look like this:

```
Workbooks(2).Activate
```

This line of code uses the Workbooks property of the Application object (more on this later) to return a single Workbook object from the Workbooks collection object and then uses the Activate() method of the Workbook object to select the desired object.

The required syntax when addressing objects in VBA is object.property or object.method. You may also specify multiple properties in order to reach the desired property or method. For example, Application.ActiveSheet .Range("A1").Font.Bold = True is of the form object.property.property.property .property because ActiveSheet, Range("A1"), and Font all represent properties that return objects. Bold is a Boolean property of the Font object and its value is set to true. As you may have guessed, this line of code turns on bold formatting in cell A1 of the current worksheet.

So, from the collection of Workbook objects shown in Figure 5.2, which Workbook object does the previously mentioned line of code return? If you answered Book2, you'd be wrong, although that is the intuitive answer. The number in parentheses refers to a relative index number for each Workbook object as it was created. (In this case, Book1 was created first, Book2 second, and Book3 third.) The confusing part is that an index value of 1 is reserved for the currently selected Workbook object, regardless of when that Workbook object was created. So to select Book2 you would actually have to use an index value of 3 in the above line of code. An index value of 2 would return Book1 and an index value of 1 or 4 would return Book3.

There will always be two choices of an index for the currently selected Workbook object, the value 1 because it is reserved for the currently selected object, and the value corresponding to its sequence in being created. The behavior of the Workbooks collection object can be confusing, but with practice, patience, and above all, testing, I'm sure you can figure it out.

To avoid confusion, you can select a workbook unambiguously—if you know the name of the desired Workbook object—using the following line of code.

```
Workbooks("Book2").Activate
```

Here you simply include the name of the object as a string in place of the index number. Obviously, this is much less confusing and makes your code easier to read, so I recommend doing it this way whenever possible.

When you need to step through several objects in a collection, use a loop and a looping variable to represent the index of the object to be returned.

```
For I=1 To 3
    If Workbooks(I).Saved Then Workbooks(I).Close
Next I
```

Other examples of collection objects include `Worksheets`, `Windows`, and `Charts`. For example, each of the `Workbook` objects in Figure 5.2 contains three `Worksheet` objects that belong to separate `Worksheets` collection objects. There are three `Worksheets` collection objects in this example because they are lower in the object hierarchy than the `Workbook` object.

The Object Browser

The VBA IDE includes a convenient and very useful tool for browsing through all available objects for a project and viewing their properties, methods, and events. It is called the Object Browser, and you'll use it to view Excel's object model and learn about what objects are available for you to use in your programs. You can also view all procedures and constants from your current project.

To open the Object Browser, select View, Object Browser, as shown in Figure 5.3, or simply hit F2. Figure 5.4 shows the Object Browser.

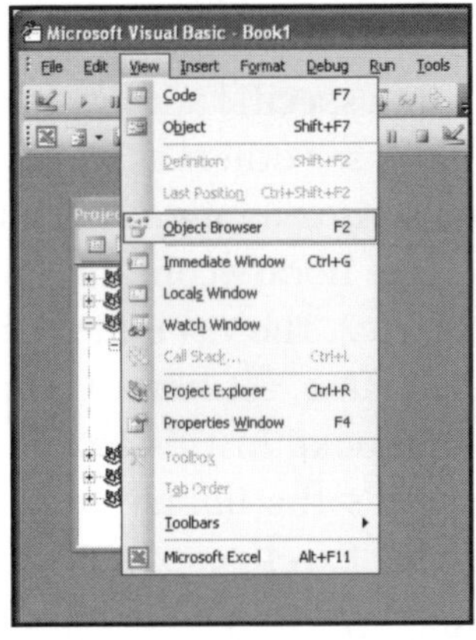

Figure 5.3

Selecting the Object Browser from the VBA IDE.

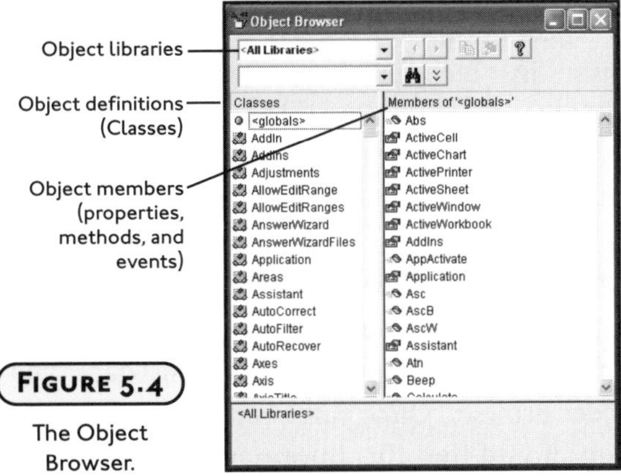

Figure 5.4

The Object Browser.

To use the object browser, first select the library from which you need to view the desired object, or select All Libraries (see Figure 5.5).

FIGURE 5.5

Selecting an object library.

An object library is a collection of objects provided by a specific application. You may notice libraries for `Excel`, `Office`, `VBA`, and `VBAProject`. You may see others as well, but it is these specific libraries that are of the most interest to you now. As you might have guessed, the `Excel` library contains objects specific to Excel and the `Office` library contains objects common to all MS Office applications (Word, PowerPoint, Excel, etc.). The `VBA` library adds a few objects specific to the VBA programming language, and the `VBAProject` library represents objects in the project currently open in Excel (that is, a workbook). In this chapter, it is the `Excel` library that is of the most interest to you because it's the library that contains specific objects that will allow you to interact with and extend Excel's capabilities.

After selecting the `Excel` library you'll see a list of all available objects within Excel in the bottom left window of the Object Browser (see Figure 5.4 or 5.5). The window is labeled Classes but don't let that confuse you. A class is just an object definition. A class definition is used to create an instance of the object it defines. This is all just technical jargon that you don't need to worry about right now—just remember that when you see the word *class*, you should immediately think "object." Also, remember that the class/object list represents all objects available for you to use in your program. After selecting an object from the list, the available properties, methods, and events of the selected object will be displayed in the window on the bottom right side of the Object Browser (refer to Figure 5.4). This window is labeled Members, because these items belong to, or are members of the selected object. When you select an item in the members list, information about that member—the member type, required syntax, and data type—will be displayed at the very bottom of the Object Browser. Once you become more familiar with the Object Browser, and VBA in general, you should find this information more helpful.

To learn more about a specific object or one of its members, simply select an item in the Object Browser and press F1. The Help window will appear, displaying the result for the selected item in much more detail than what you see in the Object Browser.

If you prefer a more graphical representation of the Excel object model, look for the Object Model chart in the Help window under Microsoft Excel Objects. The chart, shown in Figure 5.6, displays the object hierarchy and provides links to documentation on the entire Excel Object Model.

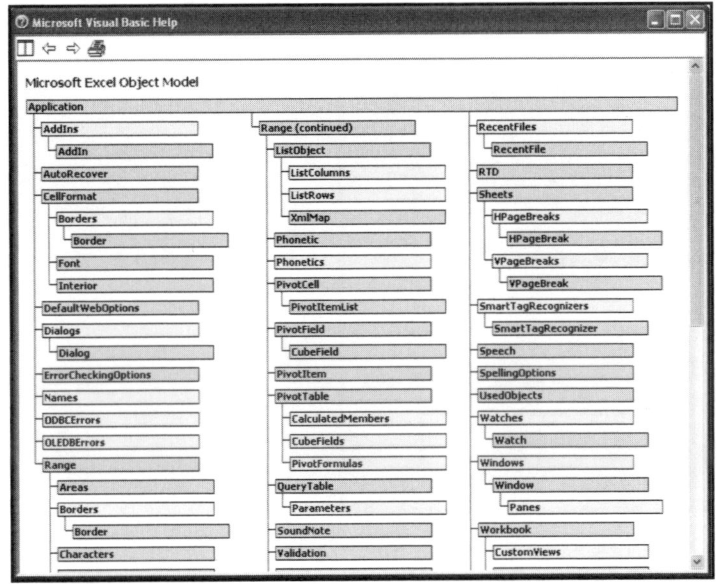

FIGURE 5.6

The Excel Object Model.

Whatever tool you prefer to use (the Object Browser or Object Model chart), keep in mind that there is a hierarchy of objects that must be followed. You should think of the object hierarchy as a path to the object of interest much like a file path in a computer's operating system. It is a good idea to use these tools to set a specific object property or invoke an object's method when you're having difficulty navigating through the object hierarchy.

Consider a simple example. How do we insert the string `"VBA is fun!"` into cell `A4` of `Sheet2` in `Book2` from the project shown in Figure 5.2? From examples in previous chapters, you know that you can use the `Range` property of the `Application` object.

```
Range("A4").Value = "VBA is fun!"
```

However, the line of code above will insert the string into the current or active worksheet, and this may not be your target worksheet. To ensure the string finds the correct target, first select the desired workbook.

```
Workbooks("Book2").Activate
```

To find the next object in the desired path to cell `A4` of `Sheet2` of `Book2`, look at the Object Browser. Since the above line of code gets you to the `Workbook` object, start by selecting the Excel object library and `Workbook` from the list of objects. Immediately, the members of the `Workbook` object are displayed on the right. If you scroll through this list you will eventually come to a property called `Worksheets`, as shown in Figure 5.7.

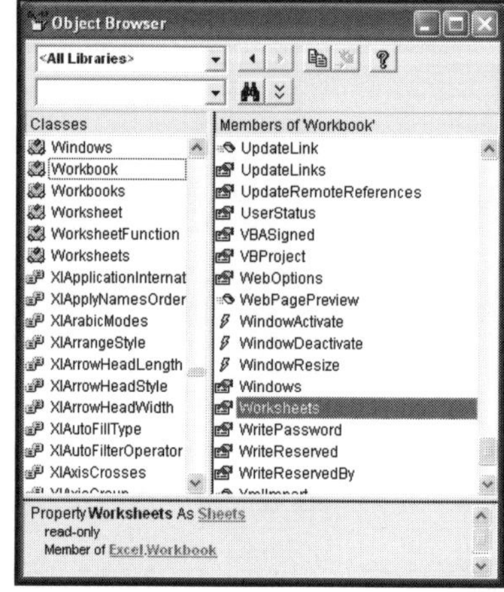

FIGURE 5.7

Viewing the `Worksheets` property of the `Workbook` object.

To select `Sheet2`, use the following code.

```
Workbooks("Book2").Worksheets("Sheet2").Activate
```

The second part of this statement (`Worksheets("Sheet2")`) is really the same code as written for selecting the `Workbook` object from the `Workbooks` collection object. The `Worksheet` object `Sheet2` is selected from the `Worksheets` collection object. This code uses the `Worksheets` property of the `Workbook` object to return a `Worksheet` object from the `Worksheets` collection object. Since the `Worksheet` object is lower in the object hierarchy than the `Workbook` object, it follows it in the line of code above. Finally, the `Activate()` method of the `Worksheet` object selects `Sheet2` within the workbook `Book2`. That was a mouthful, but if you work through the hierarchy slowly, and view each of these components through the Object Browser, it will make sense.

To add the string `"VBA is fun!"` to cell `A4`, use the following code:

```
Workbooks("Book2").Sheets("Sheet2").Range("A4").Value = "VBA is fun!"
```

The Range property is found in the list of members for the Worksheet object, as shown in Figure 5.8. Note that the Cells property could have also been used.

```
Workbooks("Book2").Sheets("Sheet2").Cells(4, "A").Value = "VBA is fun!"
```

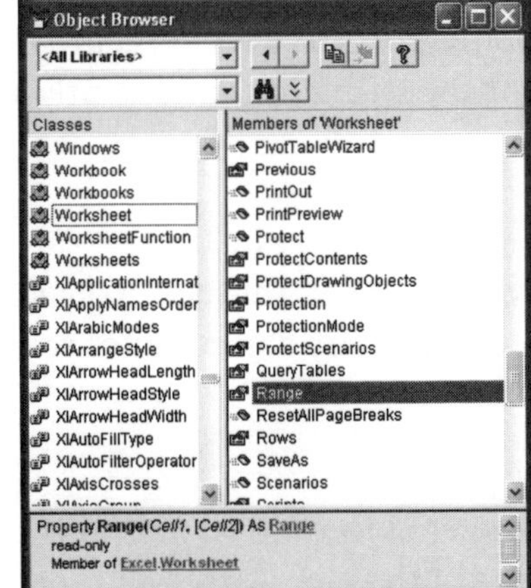

FIGURE 5.8

Viewing the Range property of the Worksheet object.

The Range property returns a Range object that represents one or more cells in a continuous block on a worksheet. In this case, the Range property returns the Range object that represents cell A4. Next, the Value property of the Range object is used to set the contents of cell A4 to the desired string "VBA is fun!", as shown in Figure 5.9.

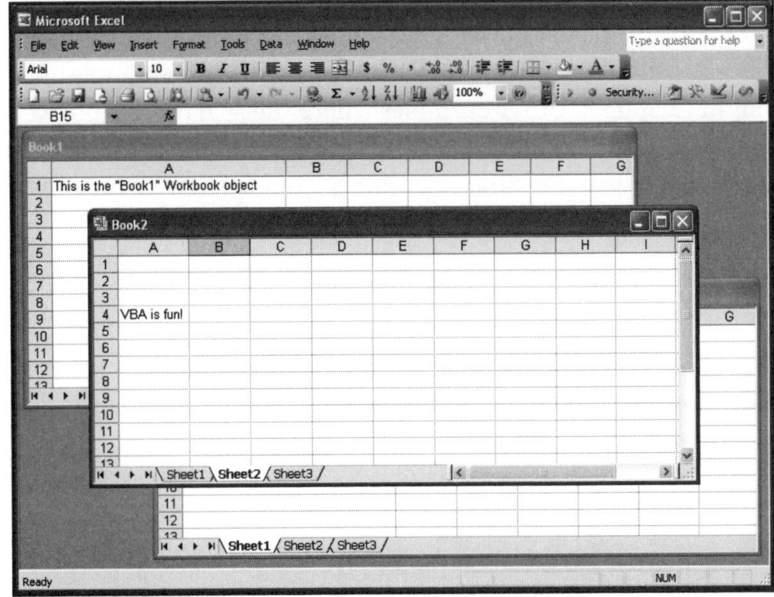

FIGURE 5.9

Inserting a string in a worksheet cell.

You may be wondering if you really need to work your way through the entire object hierarchy to set one property? The answer is yes, but only if each object referenced in the code needs to be identified out of a collection of objects. For example, if there is only one Workbook object open, then

```
Sheets("Sheet2").Range("A4").Value = "VBA is fun!"
```

works just as well as the previous code. Actually, this code will execute regardless of how many Workbook objects are open, but it will put the string in the currently selected or active workbook. Likewise,

```
Range("A4").Value = "VBA is fun!"
```

executes, but it will put the string in the active worksheet; thus, each object qualifier is necessary only as long as it is needed to identify one specific object out of several possibilities.

Top-Level Excel Objects

I will start at the top of the hierarchy in the Excel object model and work my way through the first few objects. There are too many objects in the model to cover them all, but the goal of this chapter is to get you comfortable navigating through the object model and learning how to use new objects on your own.

The Application Object

The Application object is the top-level object in Excel's object model. It represents the entirety of the Excel application (see Figure 5.6). As the top-level object it is unique and thus, seldom needs to be addressed in code; however, there are a few occasions when you must use the Application object's qualifier in code. One example is the OnTime() method used in the Math Game program in Chapter 4. Other examples where the Application object must be explicitly referenced in code include the Width and Height properties used to set the size of the application window, and the DisplayFormulaBar property used to show or hide the formula bar.

```
Application.Width = 600
Application.Height = 450
Application.DisplayFormulaBar = True
```

For the most part, you need to use the Application object qualifier to set properties pertaining to the appearance of the Excel window, such as shown above, or the overall behavior of Excel as shown below.

```
Application.Calculation = xlManual
Application.EditDirectlyInCell = False
Application.DefaultFilePath = "C:\My Documents"
```

The Application object qualifier must also be used with the very helpful ScreenUpdating and WorksheetFunction properties.

```
Application.ScreenUpdating = False
Range("A11") = Application.WorksheetFunction.Sum(Range("A1:A10"))
```

However if you just need to set properties of lower-level objects, then the Application object qualifier is not needed.

```
ActiveCell.Formula = "=SUM(A1:A10)"
```

The line of code above uses the ActiveCell property of the Application object to return a Range object. The Range object returned by this line of code is the currently selected spreadsheet cell. The Formula property of the Range object is then set with the given string. The formula is then entered into the cell and the result calculated as normal by Excel. To view all the Application object's properties, methods, and events, select it from the Classes list in the Object Browser, as shown in Figure 5.10.

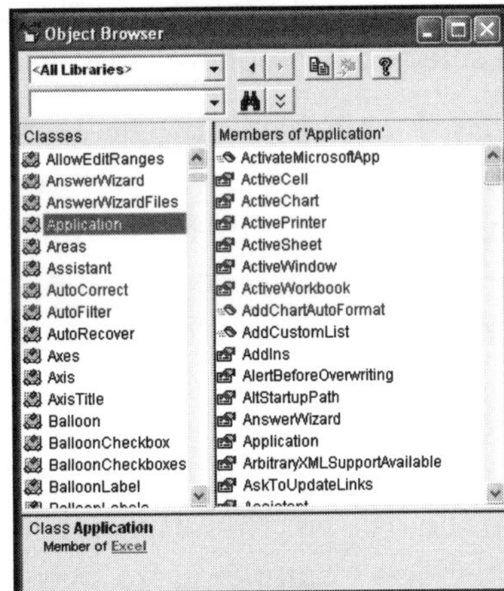

FIGURE 5.10

The Application object as viewed through the Object Browser.

The events associated with the Application object are not enabled by default so they will not work like other Excel object event procedures. Enabling events for the Application object involves the use of a class module and other advanced methods that are beyond the scope of this book and will not be discussed.

The Workbook and Window Objects

You have already seen in action, in some of the examples in this chapter, the Workbooks, and Worksheets collection objects, as well as the Workbook and Worksheet objects. The difference between collection objects and regular objects was discussed earlier. When working with these objects, keep in mind that the Workbook object is higher in the hierarchy than the Worksheet object. If you are familiar with Excel, this makes sense to you because a single workbook can hold multiple worksheets.

However, the Window object may be unfamiliar and/or a bit confusing. Window objects refer to instances of windows within either the same workbook, or the application. Within the Excel application, the Windows collection object contains all Window objects currently opened; this includes all Workbook objects and copies of any Workbook objects. The Window objects are indexed according to their layering. For example, in Figure 5.2, you could retrieve Book2 with the following code:

```
Application.Windows(2).Activate
```

because Book2 is the center window in a total of three Window objects. After Book2 is retrieved and thus brought to the top layer its index would change to 1 when using the Windows collection object. This is different from accessing Book2 using the Workbooks collection object. As stated previously, Workbook objects are indexed according to the order of their creation after the value of 1, which is reserved for the selected, or top-level Workbook object.

You may be thinking that the Windows collection object within the Application object is essentially the same as the Workbooks collection object. This may or may not be true depending whether or not the user creates a new window by selecting New Window from the Window menu in the Excel application. This effectively makes a copy of the currently selected workbook. You may also use the NewWindow() method of either the Window or Workbook object in your code to accomplish the same task.

```
Application.Windows(1).NewWindow
```

When a new window is created, the caption in the title bar from the original window is concatenated with a colon and an index number. For example, Book1 becomes Book1:1 and Book1:2 when a new window is created (see Figure 5.11). These captions can be changed in code by manipulating the Caption property of the Window object.

Do not confuse the creation of a new window from the Window menu with that of a new workbook. New workbooks are created when the user selects New from the File menu, or by using the Add() method of the Workbooks collection object. Of course, creating a new workbook also creates a new window, but the reverse is not true. If a new Window object is created through the use of the Window menu in Excel (or NewWindow() method in VBA), then this window does not belong to the Workbooks collection object and thus, cannot be accessed in code by using the following:

```
Application.Workbooks("Book1:2").Activate
```

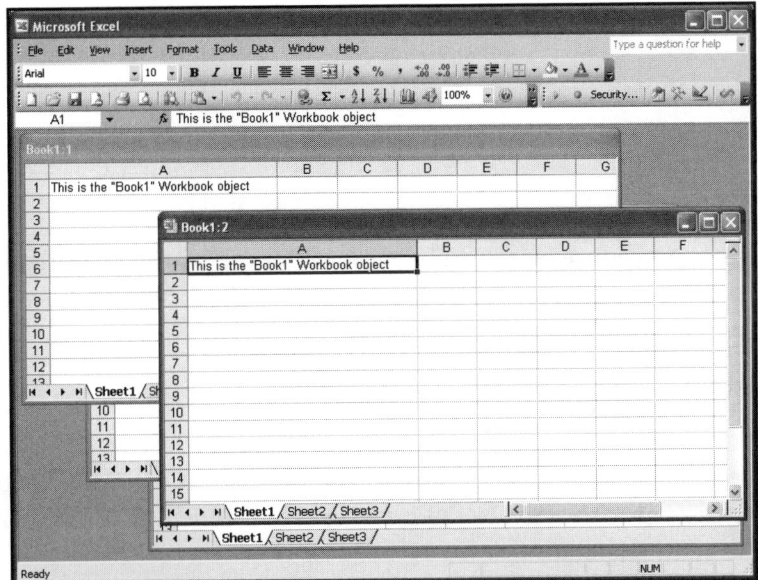

FIGURE 5.11

Creating a new window in Excel.

This code fails because `Book1:2` does not belong to the `Workbooks` collection object but to the `Windows` collection object of either the `Application` object or the `Workbook` object named `Book1`. It could be accessed with either of the following lines of code:

```
Workbooks("Book1").Windows("Book1:2").Activate
```

Or,

```
Application.Windows("Book1:2").Activate
```

These examples and the above descriptions demonstrate that there may be more than one path to retrieving an object of interest in your code, and that differences between some objects may be quite subtle. I recommend that you play with these examples and create instances of new windows and new workbooks in your code. Then access these objects through as many paths as you can think of. You will find that it doesn't take long to get comfortable working with the `Workbooks` collection, `Windows` collection, `Workbook`, and `Window` objects.

All properties, methods, and events for these objects can be viewed in the Object Browser. Let's take a closer look at a few of them via an example, starting with the `Workbooks` collection object, shown in Figure 5.4.

There are only a few properties and methods of the `Workbooks` collection object and their functions are straightforward. Add the following procedure to a standard module in a workbook.

```
Public Sub AddWorkbooks()
    Dim I As Integer
    For I = 1 To 3
        Workbooks.Add
    Next I
End Sub
```

If you execute this procedure by selecting `AddWorkbooks` from the Macro menu in Excel, you will immediately see three new workbooks opened in Excel. To select a specific workbook, insert the following line of code after the `For/Next` loop in the `AddWorkbooks()` sub procedure.

```
Workbooks(Workbooks.Count).Activate
```

This is another example of nesting, and it will activate the last workbook to be opened in Excel. The statement `Workbooks.Count` returns the number of open workbooks in Excel and is then used as the index to activate the last workbook added. If you prefer, edit the above code to make it more readable:

```
Dim numWorkbooks as Integer
NumWorkbooks = Workbooks.Count
Workbooks(NumWorkbooks).Activate
```

Through the Object Browser, you will notice that the `Workbooks` collection object only has a few members. They are relatively straightforward to use, and you have already seen a couple of them (the `Add()` method and `Count` property). You may find the `Open()` and `Close()` methods and `Item` property useful as well. Some of these members will be addressed later, albeit with different objects. You will find that many of the collection objects share the same properties and methods. This is not unusual, but be aware that depending on the object you use, the parameters that are either available or required for these members may vary. Figures 5.12 and 5.13 show that the `Workbooks` collection object and the `Workbook` object both have `Close()` methods.

If you look at the bottom of the Object Browser windows displayed in Figure 5.12 and Figure 5.13, you will see that the `Close()` method of the `Workbooks` collection object does not accept any arguments, but the `Close()` method of the `Workbook` object can accept up to three arguments, all of which are optional (denoted by the brackets).

Consider the following VBA procedure illustrating the use of the `Close()` method of the `Workbook` object. The code can be placed in a standard or object module.

```
Public Sub CloseFirstLast()
    Workbooks(Workbooks.Count).Close SaveChanges:=False
    Workbooks(1).Close SaveChanges:=False
End Sub
```

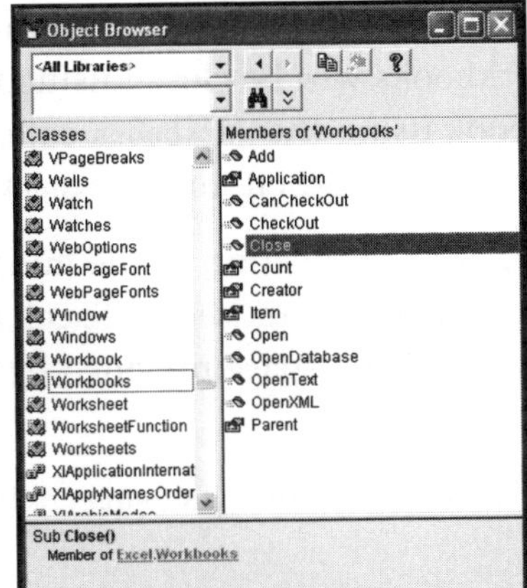

FIGURE 5.12

The `Close()` method of the `Workbooks` collection object.

FIGURE 5.13

The `Close()` method of the `Workbook` object.

This procedure will close the first and last workbooks opened in Excel without prompting the user to save changes. However, if this procedure is contained somewhere in a code module for the last workbook to be opened, then only the last workbook will be closed. This is because the module containing this code will close before the last line (`Workbooks(1).Close SaveChanges:=False`) is executed. In the example above, the `Close()` method of the `Workbook` object is used, not the `Close()` method of the `Workbooks` collection object. This must be the case because an index value was specified, and therefore only the `Workbook` object designated by an index of `1` is available. Because the `Workbook` object is used, optional arguments can be used with the method. In this case, the prompt to the user for saving changes to the workbook is set to false (the default is true), so the workbook closes immediately. If you want to close all workbooks simultaneously, then use the `Close()` method of the `Workbooks` collection object.

```
Workbooks.Close
```

In this case, there are no optional arguments allowed, so the user will be prompted to save the currently selected workbook. All open workbooks will be closed using the line of code above. There is no way to close a single workbook using the `Workbooks` collection object. To close just one workbook, you need to use the `Close()` method for a `Workbook` object.

Now consider an example that sizes and centers the application in the middle of the user's screen such that one-eighth of the screen on every side is unused by Excel. In addition, the workbook is sized so that it just fits inside the available space provided by the application window.

The following code was added to an open workbook and saved as `Center.xls` on this book's CD-ROM.

```
Option Explicit

Private Sub Workbook_Open()
    Application.WindowState = xlMaximized
    CenterApp Application.Width, Application.Height
    CenterBook
End Sub

Private Sub CenterApp(ByVal maxWidth As Integer, maxHeight As Integer)
'This procedure is used to center the application window
    Application.WindowState = xlNormal
    Application.Left = maxWidth / 8
    Application.Top = maxHeight / 8
    Application.Width = 3 * maxWidth / 4
    Application.Height = 3 * maxHeight / 4
End Sub

Private Sub CenterBook()
'This procedure will center the workbook within the application with no extra space
'below or above the workbook window
    ActiveWindow.WindowState = xlNormal
    Workbooks("Center.xls").Windows(1).Width = Application.UsableWidth
    Workbooks("Center.xls").Windows(1).Height = Application.UsableHeight
    Workbooks("Center.xls").Windows(1).Left = 0
    Workbooks("Center.xls").Windows(1).Top = 0
End Sub
```

```
Private Sub Workbook_WindowResize(ByVal Wn As Window)
'Display 20-21 rows of the workbook.
    If (Wn.VisibleRange.Rows.Count < 21) Then
        Do
            Wn.Zoom = Wn.Zoom - 1
        Loop Until (Wn.VisibleRange.Rows.Count >= 21)
    Else
        Do Until (Wn.VisibleRange.Rows.Count <= 21)
            Wn.Zoom = Wn.Zoom + 1
        Loop
    End If
End Sub
```

Explicit variable declaration is turned on as usual in the general declarations section of the code window. The main procedure is the `Open()` event of the `Workbook` object to ensure that the program is executed immediately after the workbook is opened. You can access the object module for the workbook through the `ThisWorkbook` selection in the project explorer, as shown in Figure 5.14.

HINT The name of the module `ThisWorkbook` can be changed via the `Name` property in the properties window for the `Workbook` object.

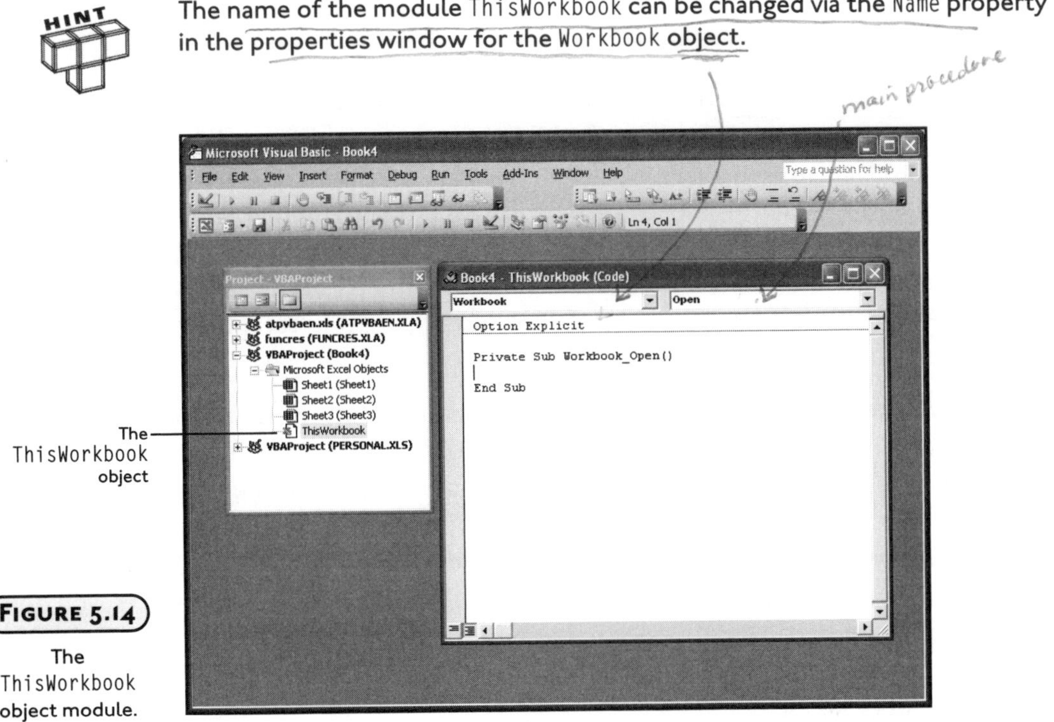

FIGURE 5.14

The ThisWorkbook object module.

The `WindowState` property (`xlMaximized` is a constant defined by VBA) of the `Application` object is used to maximize the Excel window (fill the user's screen). The application window is set to fill the user's screen so that its maximum size can be determined. The `Width` and `Height` properties of the `Application` object are then passed to the `CenterApp()` sub procedure while the application is maximized.

Different users will have different monitor resolution settings. To ensure consistency from one machine to another, you must first learn the dimensions of the user's screen. Most languages provide a `Screen` object from which to determine these properties. VBA has no `Screen` object; therefore, you have to be a bit less elegant about getting the desired width and height.

The `CenterApp()` sub procedure receives two arguments, `maxWidth` and `maxHeight`. The function of the `CenterApp()` procedure is to center the application window within the user's screen, leaving one-eighth of the screen (on all sides) unoccupied by Excel. The `CenterApp()` sub procedure begins by setting the `WindowState` property to `xlNormal`. This is the equivalent of the user clicking the middle window icon at the top-right corner of the workbook window. The application window must be returned to a normal state because you cannot move a maximized window; thus, trying to set the `Left` property of the `Application` object will cause an error and the program will crash. After returning the window state to normal, the application window is resized by setting the `Left`, `Top`, `Width`, and `Height` properties accordingly.

Next, the `Open()` event procedure calls the `CenterBook()` sub procedure without passing arguments. The `CenterBook()` procedure is called for the purpose of filling the workbook within the Excel application window. The workbook window is set to a normal state just like the application window so that it may be resized. The `UsableWidth` and `UsableHeight` properties of the `Application` object are used to set the values for the `Width` and `Height` properties of the `Window` object representing the workbook. The `Windows` property of the `Workbook` object is used to return the top-level window (`Windows(1)`). Finally, the position (`Left`, `Top`) properties of the window are set to the upper-left corner of the application window (0,0).

It is not necessary to use `Workbooks("Center.xls")` qualifier in the `CenterBook()` procedure. I did this only to illustrate the path to the desired object. If the reference to the `Workbook` object `Center.xls` were to be omitted, then VBA would simply use the default object path. The default object path is to the active window of the current workbook. Since this code runs immediately after opening `Center.xls`, it is the current workbook. An index of `1` is used to select the active or top-level window. As there is only one window in `Center.xls`, you don't have to worry about getting to the desired window; however, if you created multiple windows in the `Center.xls` workbook, then you might want to use the `Window` object's `Caption` property instead of an index number.

The last procedure in the Center.xls project is the WindowResize() event of the Workbook object. This event procedure accepts one argument representing the Window object associated with the workbook being centered. The WindowResize() event triggers whenever the workbook window is resized; thus, the previous code in the CenterBook() procedure will trigger this event. The code in the WindowResize() event serves to increase or decrease the Zoom property of the Window object such that approximately 21 rows of the worksheet are displayed in the window. The VisibleRange property of the Window object returns a Range object (discussed later) representing those cells that are visible to the user in the Excel application. The Rows property of the Range object then returns another Range object representing the visible rows. Finally, the Count property (a property common to collection objects) of the Range object returns the number of cells in the Range object returned by the Rows property. The entire object/property path effectively returns the number of rows in the range of cells visible to the user.

The Worksheet Object

The Worksheet object falls just under the Workbook object in Excel's object hierarchy. To investigate some of the events of the Worksheet object, the following code has been added to the SelectionChange() event procedure of Sheet1 in the Center.xls workbook.

```
Private Sub Worksheet_SelectionChange(ByVal Target As Range)
    Dim msgOutput As String
    msgOutput = "The name of this worksheet is " & Worksheets(1).Name
    MsgBox (msgOutput)
    Worksheets(2).Select
End Sub
```

The SelectionChange() event procedure was first introduced in Chapter 2, and is found in the object module of a worksheet. The SelectionChange() event procedure is triggered whenever the user changes the current selection in the worksheet. The Target argument passed to the SelectionChange() event procedure is a range that represents the cells selected by the user. I will discuss the Range object shortly; for right now, ignore it because the current example does not use the passed argument.

The code in the SelectionChange() event procedure is straightforward. First, a string variable is created and assigned a value ("The name of this worksheet is") that is then concatenated with the name of the worksheet obtained from the Name property of the Worksheet object. The full object path is not used to return the name of the worksheet, as this code will only be executed when the user changes the selection in the first worksheet of the Worksheets collection object (Sheet1). Therefore, the object path travels through the current Workbook object.

This is why index numbers can be used with the Worksheets property of the Workbook object without having to worry about returning the wrong sheet. After displaying the concatenated string in a message box, the Select() method of the Worksheet object is used to select the second worksheet in the Worksheets collection object. (This will generate an error if only one worksheet exists in the collection.)

Next, code is added to the Worksheet_Activate() event procedure of Sheet2. The Worksheet_Activate() event procedure is triggered when a worksheet is first selected by the user or, in this case, by selecting the worksheet using program code (Worksheets(2).Select). The code is essentially the same as the previous example.

```
Private Sub Worksheet_Activate()
    Dim msgOutput As String
    msgOutput = "This worksheet is " &  Worksheets(2).Name
    MsgBox (msgOutput)
End Sub
```

The Worksheet_Activate() event procedure is not triggered when a workbook is first opened, so it is not a good place for initialization routines intended to run as soon as a workbook is opened. These procedures should be placed in the Workbook_Open() event procedure.

You may have noticed in the object browser an object called Sheets. The Sheets collection object is nearly identical to the Worksheets collection object and the two objects can often be used interchangeably (as is the case in the previous two examples). The difference between these two objects is that the Sheets collection object will also contain any chart sheets open in the active workbook. So, if you expect chart sheets to be open in the workbook of interest, you should access worksheets using the Sheets collection object; otherwise, either collection object will suffice.

The Range Object

The Range object represents a group of one or more contiguous cells in an Excel worksheet. The Range object is one level beneath the Worksheet object in Excel's object hierarchy, and it is extremely useful, as it allows us to manipulate the properties of an individual cell or collection of cells in a worksheet. You will probably find yourself using the Range object in every program you write using VBA for the Excel application.

Consider the following code examples that use properties of the Range object.

```
Range("A1").Value="Column A"
Range("A1:G1").Columns.AutoFit
Range("A1:C1", "E1:F1").Font.Bold = True
```

The Range object is one example of a VBA collection object that does not use the plural form of an existing object for its name. The Range object is a collection object in the sense that it represents a collection of cells in a worksheet, even if the collection represents only one cell.

First, note that a long object path is omitted from the examples above; thus, these lines of code will operate on the currently selected worksheet. The first line inserts the text Column A into cell A1 by setting its Value property. The Range property was used to return a Range object representing a single cell (A1) in this example. You have already seen several examples of the Value property in this book. Although the Value property exists for several objects, it is the Range object for which it is most commonly used. The second line of code above uses the AutoFit() method of the Range object to adjust the width of columns A through G such that the contents of row 1 will just fit into their corresponding cells without overlapping into adjacent columns. This is equivalent to the user selecting Format, Column, AutoFit Selection from the Excel application menu.

Entries in other rows that are longer than the entries in row 1 will still run into the next column. To automatically adjust the width of these columns such that the contents of every cell in the columns fit within cell boundaries, use the range A:G instead of A1:G1. The third and last example demonstrates setting the Bold property of the Font object to true for two distinct ranges in the active worksheet. The two ranges are A1:C1 and E1:F1. You are allowed to return a maximum of two ranges, so adding a third range to the arguments in the parentheses would generate a run-time error.

The examples above demonstrate just a couple of formatting methods and properties belonging to the Range object (AutoFit(), Columns, and Font). If you are a regular user of Excel, then you have probably surmised that there are numerous other properties and methods related to formatting spreadsheet cells. You can either search the Object Browser or the online help for more examples on how to use formatting options of interest; however, when you know what formatting options you want to include in your VBA program, record a macro. It is a quick and easy way to generate the code you need without having to search the documentation for descriptions of the desired objects, properties and methods. After you have recorded the macro in a separate module, you can clean up the recorded code and then cut and paste into your program as needed.

You may have noticed that the range arguments used in the examples above (A1, A1:G1, etc.) are of the same form used with cell references in the Excel application. The identical syntax is highly convenient because of its familiarity.

Finally it is time to take a closer look at the Cells property, specifically the Cells property of the Application, Range, and Worksheet objects.

Using the Cells Property

The Cells property returns a Range object containing all (no indices used) or one (row and column indices are specified) of the cells in the active worksheet. When returning all of the cells in a worksheet, you should only use the Cells property with the Application and Worksheet objects, as it would be redundant, and thus confusing, to use it with the Range object. For example,

```
Range("A1:A10").Cells
```

returns cells A1 through A10, thus making the use of the Cells property unnecessary.

The Cells property will fail when using it with the Application object unless the active document is a worksheet.

To return a single cell from a Worksheet object you must specify an index. The index can be a single value beginning with the left uppermost cell in the worksheet (for example, Cells(5) returns cell E1) or the index can contain a reference to the row and column index (recommended) as shown below.

```
Cells(1, 4).Value=5
Cells(1, "D").Value =5
```

This is the familiar notation used throughout this book. Both lines of code will enter the value 5 into cell D1 of the active worksheet. You can either use numerical or string values for the column reference. You should note that the column reference comes second in both examples and is separated from the row reference by a comma. I recommend using the second example above, as there is no ambiguity in the cell reference—though on occasion it's convenient to use a numerical reference for the column index.

Now consider some examples using the Cells property of the Range object.

```
Range("C5:E7").Cells(2, 2).Value = 50
Range("C5:E7").Cells(2, "A").Value = 50
```

This code may confuse you because they appear to be trying to return two different ranges within the same line of code; however, that is not the case, but you can use these examples to more carefully illustrate how the `Cells` property works.

Before reading on, guess in what worksheet cell each of these lines places the value `50`. If you guessed cells `B2` and `A2`, respectively, you're wrong. Instead, the value `50` is entered in cells `D6` and `A6`, respectively, when using the previous lines of code. Why? It's because the `Cells` property uses references relative to the selected range. Without the reference to the `Range` object in each statement (`Range("C5:E7")`), the current range is the entire worksheet, thus `Cells(2,2)` returns the range `B2`; however, when the selected range is `C5:E7`, `Cells(2,2)` will return the second row from this range (row 6) and the second column (column D). Using a string in the `Cells` property to index the column forces the selection of that column regardless of the range selected. The row index is still relative; therefore, the second example above returns the range `A6`.

Working with Objects

You have now seen numerous examples of objects and how to set their properties and invoke their methods and events, but there are a couple more tools that can be of tremendous use when working with objects: the `With/End With` code structure that, although never required, works well to simplify code; and the object data type, which allows you to reference existing objects or even create new objects. The object data type is not as easy to use as the numerical and string data types you're now familiar with, but it is an essential tool for the creation of useful and powerful VBA programs.

The With/End With Structure

VBA includes a programming structure designed to reduce the number of object qualifiers required in your code. Although the `With/End With` structure discussed in this section is not required under any circumstances, its use is often recommended because it makes your programs more readable. Also you will often see the `With/End With` structure in recorded macros. Consider the following code:

```
Range("A1:D1").Select
With Selection.Font
    .Bold = True
    .Name = "Arial"
    .Size = 18
End With
```

```
With Selection
    .HorizontalAlignment = xlCenter
    .VerticalAlignment = xlCenter
End With
```

When executed, this code selects the range `A1:D1` of the active worksheet using the `Select()` method of the `Range` object. The `Select()` method applies to several objects including the `Worksheet` and `Chart` objects. You will notice that using the `Select()` method with the `Range` object will cause the selected range to be highlighted in the worksheet, just as if the user used the mouse to make the selection.

Immediately after invoking the `Select()` method, the `With/End With` structure appears. The `With` statement requires an object qualifier to immediately follow. In this case, the `Selection` property of the `Window` object is used to return a `Range` object from which the `Font` property returns a `Font` object associated with the selected range. The statement could have just as easily been written without the `Select()` method and `Selection` property and entered using the `Range` property to return the desired `Range` object (for example, `With Range("A1:D1").Font`).

Once inside the structure, any property of the object can be set without having to qualify the object in each line of code. Subordinate objects and their properties can also be accessed. Each line within the structure must begin with the dot operator followed by the property or object name, then the method or assignment.

After all desired properties and/or methods have been invoked for the given object, the structure closes with `End With`.

You will note that a second `With/End With` structure is used to set the horizontal and vertical alignment of the selected range. This is because I recorded this code and cleaned it up by deleting lines of code created by the macro recorder for default assignments. The example can be compressed further as shown below:

```
With Range("A1:D1")
    .HorizontalAlignment = xlCenter
    .VerticalAlignment = xlCenter
    .Font.Bold = True
    .Font.Name = "Arial"
    .Font.Size = 18
End With
```

The `With/End With` structure is straightforward and particularly useful when a large number of properties or methods of one object are to be addressed sequentially in a program.

The Object Data Type

A chapter on Excel objects would not be complete without a discussion of the object data type. If you find multiple instances of the same object in your program, then you can use an object variable to handle the reference rather than constantly retyping the qualifiers. Also, variables can be assigned meaningful names, making the program easier to interpret. Object variable are similar to other VBA data types in that they must be declared in code. For example,

```
Dim myObject as Object
```

declares an object variable named `myObject`; however, assigning a value to an object variable differs from assignments to more common data types. The `Set` keyword must be used to assign an object reference to a variable.

```
Set myObject = Range("A1:A15")
```

This will assign the `Range` object representing cells A1 through A15 to the variable `myObject`. Properties of the object can then be initialized in the usual way.

```
myObject.Font.Bold = True
```

This sets the values in cells `A1` through `A15` to be displayed in bold-face type. Declaring variables as above using the general object data type is not recommended because the object will not be bound to the variable until run-time. If VBA has trouble resolving references to various properties and methods when checking them at run-time, it can significantly slow down execution of a program. I recommend that you use object-specific data types whenever possible. Any object type can be used—just consult the Object Browser for a list of available types. Using the `Range` object, the above example can be rewritten thusly:

```
Dim myRange as Excel.Range
Set myRange=Range("A1:A15")
myRange.Font.Bold = True
```

You may also include the library (`Excel`) in your declaration to avoid any ambiguity; however, it is the object type (`Range`) that is important. Now the object will be referenced at compile time and VBA will have no trouble working out references to the properties and methods of the object, as the type of object and the library to which it belongs have been explicitly declared. You will see more examples of object variable types in the next section, in subsequent chapters, and in the Battlecell program.

For/Each and Looping through a Range

As stated at the beginning of this chapter, objects are often built from other objects. For example a `Workbook` object usually contains several `Worksheet` objects, which in turn contains multiple Range objects. It may be necessary, on occasion, to select individual objects contained within other objects. For example, you may want to access each individual Worksheet object in a Worksheets collection object in order to set certain properties. If you are thinking *loops* then you are right on track, but you're not going to use any of the looping structures previously discussed. Instead, you'll use a looping structure specifically designed to iterate through collections. The loop is the For/Each loop, and its use is illustrated in the example that follows:

```
Dim myRange As Excel.Range
Dim myCell As Excel.Range

Randomize
Set myRange = Range("A1:B15")
For Each myCell In myRange
        myCell.Interior.ColorIndex = Int(Rnd * 56) + 1
Next
```

In this example, the background of a group of cells is changed to all different colors. To accomplish this, each cell is accessed individually as a Range object before setting the ColorIndex property of the Interior object. The For/Each loop is used for this purpose.

Two object references are required with the For/Each loop; one for the individual objects, and the other for the collection of objects. In this example, the object variable myRange represents a collection of cells while the object variable myCell represents each individual cell within myRange.

The reference to the object variable myRange must be set (cells A1 through B15 in this example) before it can be used in a For Each loop.

The loop begins with the keywords For Each, followed by the variable that is to represent the individual elements in the collection—myCell in this example. The keyword In is followed by the name of the collection—myRange in this example. Note, that it is not necessary to set the object reference to the variable myCell, as VBA handles this automatically in the For Each loop.

Inside the loop, properties and methods of the individual elements can be addressed. In this case, the ColorIndex property of the Interior object is changed using a randomly generated number between 1 and 56 (there are 56 colors in Excel's color palette). Once each statement within the loop is executed, the Next keyword is used to continue the loop.

VBA iterates through the cells in the collection first by row and then by column. Therefore, in this example, the order follows A1, B1, A2, B2, A3, B3, and so on.

When all elements of the collection have been accessed and each statement executed, program execution resumes at the end of the loop as normal. The above code was added to a standard module in a sub procedure named `CellColors()` and executed. Figure 5.15 shows the result.

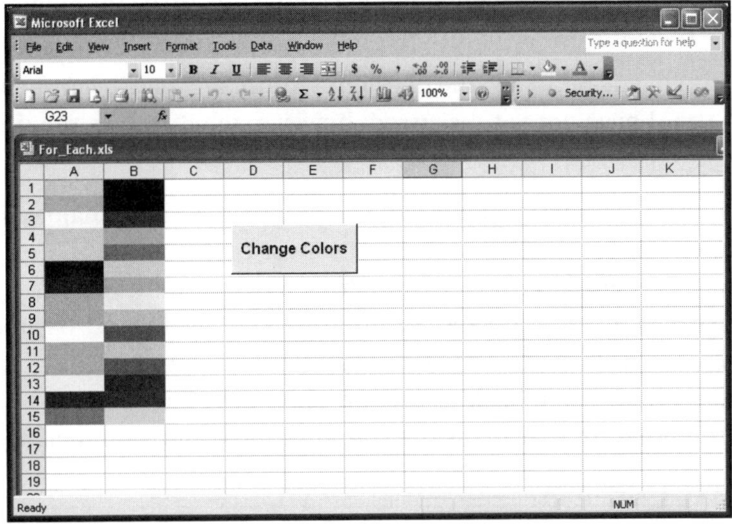

FIGURE 5.15

The result of executing the `CellColors()` sub procedure.

This a common technique for iterating through a collection of spreadsheet cells. You will see more examples of this technique in the *Battlecell* program.

CONSTRUCTING BATTLECELL

The *Battlecell* game is a simplified computer simulation of the classic board game Battleship. It is a natural choice for a game program using Excel because the grid-like layout used in the original game can easily be duplicated on a worksheet.

Requirements for Battlecell

Even if you never played Battleship as a kid, you are probably familiar with the game. Either your siblings played it, or your friends, or perhaps your own children play it now. You can also find several versions of the game on the Internet and in many department stores.

If you are familiar with the game, you might think that defining a list of requirements for the game to be a pretty easy task, but this is not necessarily the case as this program will be considerably more complex than anything you've written so far. The biggest problem is that Battlecell is the first project in this book that actually requires a bit of intelligence on the part of the computer (that is, your program) in order to properly mimic the original. Some intelligence is required by the program when selecting a target on the user's grid. Knowing, if a ship has been previously hit, what direction a ship has been placed, and how many hits are required to sink a ship all require some thought. You and I might take these things for granted when playing the game, but a computer must have instructions from the program as to the most likely location of an opponent's ship. As it turns out, adding even rudimentary intelligence to a program isn't an easy task.

Programming intelligence into a game does not require any new or immensely complicated VBA structures that I have not yet discussed; however, what it does require is a clever algorithm (plan).

Because it would likely double the length of the program, and the major goal of the *Battlecell* program is to give you experience with Excel's most common VBA objects, I've decided to skip adding the intelligence to this program. Instead, I will walk you through the use of the `Workbook`, `Worksheet`, and `Range` objects to program the layout and basic operation of the game. I will even add a little multimedia in the form of sound to make it more exciting. I highly encourage you to come back to this program at some point and add an intelligent component to the program that helps the computer play more competitively.

In the Real World

The term *artificial intelligence* (AI) was first coined at the Massachusetts Institute of Technology in the mid 1950s and refers to the branch of computer science that tries to make computers think like humans. In reality, there is no such thing (at least not yet). Instead, AI is mimicked in a computer by very clever algorithms designed by computer scientists and then written into a program. At this point in time, human understanding of our own brain function is much too inadequate in order to properly write a program that can generate thoughts in a computer that are as complex as thoughts in our own minds. However, in 1997 computer scientists at IBM were able to write a program for a super-computer that defeated world chess champion Gary Kasparov.

The requirements for Battlecell as I have defined them follow:

1. The program shall use a single worksheet for the game board.
2. When the program file is opened or the workbook window is resized, the program shall maximize the application window and size the worksheet such that the game board fits within the application window.
3. The user's and computer's grid shall be 10 by 10 cells in size and defined in separate ranges on the worksheet.

4. A range of merged cells shall be used to output messages to the user.
5. The game shall begin from the click of a Command Button control.
6. The Command Button control shall be disabled while the game is played.
7. When the user places his or her ships, the program shall output a message to the user indicating what ship (name and number of cells) is to be placed on the game board.
8. The user shall place 5 ships on their game board by selecting the appropriate number of cells (5 = carrier, 4 = destroyer, 3 = battleship, 2 = submarine, 1 = patrol boat).
9. The program shall validate the user's ship selections for location (the entire ship must be within the user's grid and cannot overlap another ship) and size (the ship must be of the correct length and be contained entirely within one worksheet row or one worksheet column) and display a message box citing a reason for an invalid selection.
10. The program shall output error messages to the user for: wrong length, outside range, spans multiple rows and columns, overlap with another ship.
11. The program shall color the worksheet cell light blue when the user selects a valid location for a ship.
12. After the player has finished placing his or her ships, then the program shall randomly choose locations for its ships following the same validation rules as the player (within its own grid).
13. The computer shall mark the location of its ships with an X entered into the cells. The font format shall match the color of the background so the user cannot see the location of the computer's ships.
14. The user shall fire at the computer's ships by selecting an individual cell on the computer's grid.
15. The user's selection of a target shall be validated for range length (only one cell allowed) and location (must be within the computer's grid). An appropriate error message shall be output if the user's target selection is invalid.
16. When the user selects a target, the program shall play a sound file simulating cannon fire.
17. When the user selects a target, the program shall play a sound file simulating an explosion if it's a hit.
18. If the user scores a miss, the target cell shall be colored blue.
19. If the user scores a hit, the target cell shall be colored red.
20. The computer shall fire a random shot at the user's grid after each shot taken by the user.

21. If the computer scores a miss, then the target cell shall be colored green.
22. If the computer scores a hit, then the target cell shall be colored red.
23. When the game is over (either the user or computer has scored 17 hits), the program shall output a message to the game board.
24. When the game is over, the program shall play one of two different sound files depending on the winner.
25. When the workbook file is closed, the program shall clear the game board, enable the Command Button control, and resave the workbook file.

Designing Battlecell

As stated in previous chapters, when designing a program, you need to consider the user interface and all inputs and outputs required by the program. The *Battlecell* program interface shown in Figure 5.16 is fairly simple, consisting of two 10 by 10 grids in which the user and computer must place their ships. The user will input ship and target selections via mouse clicks on worksheet cells. Clicking the Command Button control will initiate the game and an area of merged cells will serve as a message board to help the user know what to do. Other program inputs and outputs include help messages output to the worksheet and sound files that are played during the course of the game.

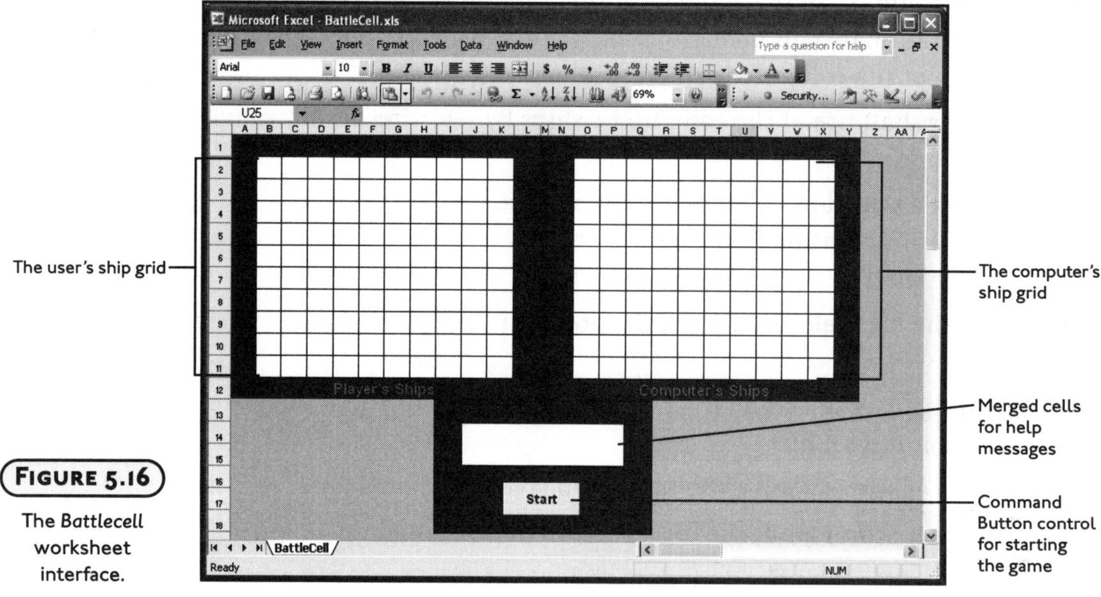

FIGURE 5.16

The Battlecell worksheet interface.

The program will require at least two modules, including the object modules for the `Workbook` and `Worksheet` objects containing the game. The object module for the `Workbook` object is required for its `Open()`, `BeforeClose()`, and `WindowResize()` events that will be used to satisfy the requirements for clearing, resizing, and resaving the workbook. The object module for the `Worksheet` object is needed for its `SelectionChange()` event that will satisfy the requirements for the user's selection of ship locations and targets. Standard modules may be used as well in order to better organize the code.

The *Battlecell* program's design is summarized in the following:

1. Format the worksheet with two 10 by 10 grids, merged cells for help messages, and a Command Button control. Use colors, borders, and large fonts to make the grids, merged cells and Command Button control stand out. Define names for the two grids and the merged cells in order to make the code that references these ranges easier to read.
2. Resize the workbook window via the `Zoom` property of the `Window` object (sub procedure). The workbook should automatically resize when the user opens the workbook file or resizes the workbook window (`Open()` and `WindowResize()` events of the `Workbook` object).
3. Clear the user's and computer's grids (sub procedure) of color and values, and save the workbook when the user closes the workbook file (`BeforeClose()` event of the `Workbook` object).
4. Initialize the game (sub procedure) when the user clicks the Command Button control (`Click()` event of the Command Button control).
5. Capture the user's selections for ship placement (`SelectionChange()` event of the `Worksheet` object) and color the selection light blue if valid (several custom sub procedures that validate the selection for the following: location within the user's grid, length, one row or one column, overlap with another ship). The validation procedures should return an error message if the user's selection is invalid.
6. Randomly generate locations for the computer's ships and mark them with an X after validation. This will require several sub procedures that generate the row and column indices for the computer's ships. The same sub procedures that validate the user's ship selections should also validate the randomly generated selections used for the computer's ships.
7. Capture the user's selections for targeting the computer's ships (`SelectionChange()` event of the `Worksheet` object) and color the validated target blue for a miss and red for a hit. The target must be validated for the following: location within the computer's grid, only one cell selected, and the target has not been previously selected. Use custom sub procedures that return an error message if the target is not validated.

8. Play a sound file if the user's target is valid.
9. Play another sound file (explosion) if the user scores a hit, and test for the end of the game. Play another sound file (specific for the user winning the game) if the game is over.
10. Immediately following the user's target selection, simulate the computer's return fire. Randomly generate a target (sub procedure) and color the validated target green for a miss and red for a hit. Validate the target using the same validation procedures used to validate the user's target.
11. If the computer scores a hit, then test for the end of the game and play another sound file (specific for the computer winning the game) if the game is over.
12. Re-enable the Command Button control and terminate the program when a winner is declared (sub procedure).

Coding Battlecell

As requirement lists get longer and designs more complex, so do programs. *Battlecell* will have to be written in multiple code modules. The `Workbook` object's code module contains the event procedures necessary for handling open, close, and window resizing events. The `Worksheet` object's code module will also be required for its `SelectionChange()` event as well as the `Click()` event of the Command Button control. Since a worksheet serves the program interface, much of the program will be contained within its code module. Standard code modules are optional, but with longer programs, are usually good ideas for organizing the various procedures that make up the program.

Opening and Closing the Battlecell Workbook

Several of the requirements for the *Battlecell* program can best be satisfied using the `Open()`, `BeforeClose()`, and `WindowResize()` events of the `Workbook` object. The `Open()` event is triggered when a workbook file (.xls extension) is first opened, thus making it an ideal location for sizing both the application and workbook windows. The `WindowResize()` event procedure is triggered whenever the user resizes the workbook window, so it must also include code that ensures the *Battlecell* game board is in the user's viewable range. Since two event procedures must resize the game board, I will write a custom sub procedure that handles this task and call it from the event procedures. To resize the workbook window such that the game board is completely visible, I can increase or decrease the zoom (found on the Standard toolbar) programmatically.

You may be wondering how I knew the `Open()`, `BeforeClose()`, and `WindowResize()` events of the `Workbook` object existed. Part of it is experience, but requirement number 2 clearly tells me to look for an event procedure associated with the `Workbook` object; thus, I opened a code module for the `Workbook` object and searched the names of the event procedures in the drop-down list box. After searching the online help describing these event procedures, I settled on these three events for satisfying the program requirements.

As you gain experience with VBA, you will not only remember more tools available to use in your programs, but you will also learn how to find what is available and find it quickly.

The code I have written for the `Workbook` object's code module follows:

```
Option Explicit

Private Sub Workbook_Open()
    '-----------------------------------
    'Maximize the application and workbook windows, then use the
    'worksheet zoom to change the viewable area of the worksheet
    '-----------------------------------
    Application.ScreenUpdating = False
    Range("A1").Select
    Application.WindowState = xlMaximized
    ActiveWindow.WindowState = xlMaximized
    ZoomGameBoard
End Sub
```

The `Open()` event of the `Workbook` object is triggered when the Excel file is opened by the user. It's an excellent location for code that initializes the appearance of the workbook and/or specific worksheets. I have used it here to maximize the Excel application window and the workbook window by setting the `WindowState` property of the `Application` and `Window` objects to the VBA-defined constant `xlMaximized`. The `ZoomGameBoard()` sub procedure (listed later) is called in order to zoom in or out on the workbook window such that the game board fits within the user's visible range.

```
Private Sub Workbook_BeforeClose(Cancel As Boolean)
    '----------------------
    'Reset the board and save the workbook.
    '----------------------
    Dim cmdObj As OLEObject
    Battlesheet.ClearBoard
```

```
    Set cmdObj = ActiveSheet.OLEObjects("cmdStart")
    cmdObj.Enabled = True

    If Not Me.Saved Then Me.Save
End Sub
```

The BeforeClose() event of the Workbook object is triggered when the user closes the workbook. This procedure actually executes before the workbook is closed. I have used this event to clear the Battlecell game board and re-save the workbook file that contains the game. The board is cleared by calling the ClearBoard() sub procedure listed in the object module for the Worksheet object named Battlesheet. The ClearBoard() sub procedure must have public scope because it is accessed from more than one code module. The object module containing the ClearBoard() procedure must be qualified in the path (Battlesheet.ClearBoard) because the procedure is contained in an object module.

Take a close look at the BeforeClose() event procedure as it contains an element that is probably unfamiliar. You will notice that I have declared an object variable of type OLEObject. ActiveX controls placed on worksheets are part of the OLEObjects collection object. Thus, in order to enable the Command Button control named cmdStart, I must access the control by setting an object reference to a variable (cmdObj in this case) via the OLEobjects collection object. Once the variable reference is set, I can change its Enabled property to true.

The last task before closing the workbook is to save it using the Save() method of the Workbook object. If the Saved property of the Workbook object returns false, then the Save() method is used to resave the Battlecell.xls workbook.

You can use the Me keyword to refer to the current instance of an object currently in scope. All procedures associated with the current object have access to the object referred to by Me. For example, when the Me keyword is used in the BeforeClose() event procedure of the Workbook object, it references the Workbook object. You could also reference the Workbook object in the Battlecell game using Workbooks("BattleCell.xls").Saved or ThisWorkbook.Saved.

```
Private Sub Workbook_WindowResize(ByVal Wn As Window)
    '-------------------------------------
    'Use the worksheet zoom to change the viewable area of the sheet.
    '-------------------------------------
    Application.ScreenUpdating = False
    Range("A1").Select
    ZoomGameBoard
End Sub
```

The WindowResize() event is triggered whenever the user resizes the workbook window via its window icons in the upper-right corner, or by dragging an edge or corner of the window. I have used the WindowResize() event procedure to call the ZoomGameBoard() sub procedure. Note that the SreenUpdating property of the Application object is set to false so that the changes made to the appearance of the workbook will not be seen by the user until the procedure as ended (End Sub).

```
Private Sub ZoomGameBoard()
    '---------------------------------
    'Set worksheet zoom such that about 600 cells are visible.
    '---------------------------------
    Const NUMCELLS = 550
    Select Case ActiveWindow.VisibleRange.Cells.Count
        Case Is <= NUMCELLS
            Do Until (ActiveWindow.VisibleRange.Cells.Count >= NUMCELLS)
                ActiveWindow.Zoom = ActiveWindow.Zoom - 2
            Loop
        Case Else
            Do Until (ActiveWindow.VisibleRange.Cells.Count <= NUMCELLS)
                ActiveWindow.Zoom = ActiveWindow.Zoom + 2
            Loop
    End Select
End Sub
```

The ZoomGameBoard() sub procedure increases or decreases the workbook zoom (found on the Standard toolbar) in order to keep the Battlecell game board within the user's viewable range. The game board uses rows 1 through 18 and columns A through Y, which represents 450 total cells. So I use the Count property of the Range object to return the number of cells in the range returned by the VisibleRange property of the Window object. If the visible range is too small (not enough cells are visible), then the zoom is decreased and vice versa. I increase the number to 550 to ensure a little cushion around the range of cells used by the game.

Initializing Battlecell and Starting the Game

The worksheet module named Battlesheet contains most of the game's code because this worksheet serves as the user interface and contains the Command Button control that starts play. The code begins with a few module-level variables that are used in multiple procedures in this module.

```
Option Explicit

Private allowSelection As Boolean
Private gameStarted As Boolean
Private ships As Variant
Private Const NUMSHIPS = 5
```

The module level variables `allowSelection` and `gameStarted` are used by the program to distinguish between the two different types of cell selections made by the user and whether or not the game is active. The first type of selection occurs when the user places his or her ships and the second type of selection occurs when the user selects a target on the computer's grid. These variables should be initialized at the start of the game and altered after the user has placed his/her ships.

You may recall in Chapter 2 that I recommended you not use variant variables because variants can slow program execution speed and make your program more difficult to read. Well, sometimes variant variables are just a little too convenient, and here is one example. The variable `ships` is declared as a variant because I intend to use this variable to hold an array of strings representing the types of ships (carrier, battleship, and so on). Unlike most programming languages, VBA does not allow arrays to be initialized in a declaration, so I have to use a variant variable and VBA's `Array()` function to initialize the array (see `InitializeGame()` sub procedure). Alternatively, I could declare a string array with five elements (`Private ships(4) As String`), but then I have to initialize each element separately (`ships(0) = "Carrier"`, `ships(1) = "Battleship"`, and so on) and I find that annoying (decide your own preference).

```
Private Sub cmdStart_Click()
    cmdStart.Enabled = False
    InitializeGame
    ClearBoard
    Range("Output").Value = "Place your " & ships(numShipsPlaced) & _
            ": Select " & shipSize(numShipsPlaced) & " contiguous cells"
End Sub
```

The code entered in the `Click()` event of the Command Button control is short and simple. First the Command Button control is disabled before two sub procedures are called to initialize program variables and clear the game board. The `ClearBoard()` sub procedure is the same procedure called from the `BeforeClose()` event of the `Workbook` object. The last statement outputs a message to the user indicating what ship must be placed. The variables `shipSize` and `numShipsPlaced` are global variables declared in a standard module (listed later) and represent the total number of cells that make up each ship and the number of ships already placed by the user, respectively. The variable `shipSize` is another array variable of type variant.

```
Private Sub InitializeGame()
    '-------------------------
    'Initialize variables for starting the game.
    '-------------------------
    ships = Array("Carrier", "Battleship", "Destroyer", "Submarine", "Patrol Boat")
    shipSize = Array(5, 4, 3, 3, 2)
    Set pRange = Range("Player")
    Set cRange = Range("Computer")
    numShipsPlaced = 0
    allowSelection = True
    gameStarted = False
End Sub
```

The InitalizeGame() sub procedure initializes the module level and global variables used by the program. The only two variables I have not already discussed are pRange and cRange which are both global variables (type range) used to represent the 10 by 10 grids for the player and computer, respectively. Note that the range B2:K11 was defined in the Excel application with the name "Player" and the range O2:X11 was defined with the name "Computer". Figure 5.17 shows the *Battlecell* worksheet with the "Player" range selected.

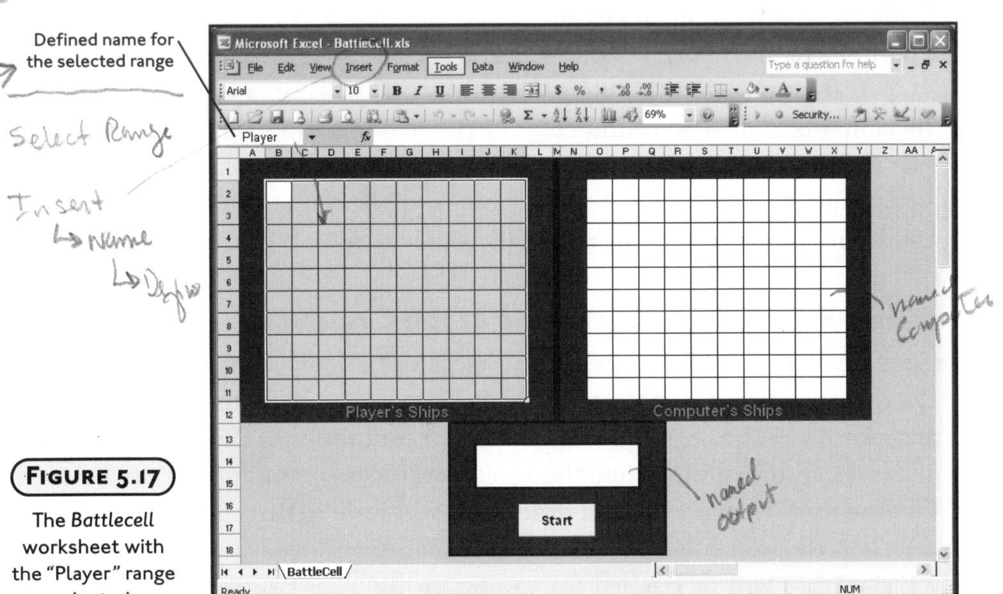

FIGURE 5.17

The *Battlecell* worksheet with the "Player" range selected.

```
Public Sub ClearBoard()
    '----------------------
    'Clear the game grids and output cell.
    '----------------------
    Dim bothGrids As Range

    Set bothGrids = Application.Union(Range("Player"), Range("Computer"))
    With bothGrids
        .ClearContents
        .Interior.ColorIndex = xlNone
    End With
    Range("Output").Value = ""
End Sub
```

The code in the sub procedure `ClearBoard()` effectively clears the player's and computer's grids of colors and values, and also clears the merged cells (`J14:P15` defined with the name `"Output"` in the Excel application) of any help message that might be displayed. This procedure must have public scope so that it may be called from the `BeforeClose()` event of the `Workbook` object.

The range variable `bothGrids` is set to reference the combination of two ranges (the two ranges defined with the names `"Player"` and `"Computer"` in the application) using the `Union()` method of the `Application` object. This object variable is then used in a `With/End With` structure to clear the contents and background color of the player's and computer's grids. Note that I cannot use the `pRange` and `cRange` variables here because it is possible that this code may be triggered from the `BeforeClose()` event of the `Workbook` object before a game is started when these variables have not been initialized.

Player Selections: Placing Ships and Firing at the Computer

The program requirements state that the user must select his or her choices for ship and target locations by selecting specific cells on the worksheet. The user's selections for ship locations and targets are captured by the `SelectionChange()` event procedure of the `Worksheet` object. Specifically, the `Target` argument passed to the `SelectionChange()` event procedure holds the range selected by the user. The code in this procedure will have to distinguish between the two types of selections the user might make (i.e., ship placement or targeting of computer's ships). Custom procedures will be needed for validating the user's selection, marking the location of the user's ships, and marking the location of the user's targets.

```
Private Sub Worksheet_SelectionChange(ByVal Target As Range)
```

```
    '---------------------------
    'Test if player is firing at the computer.
    'This is first because LocatePlayerShip will turn gameStarted variable to true.
    '---------------------------
    If gameStarted Then PlayerFire Target

    '---------------------------------------------
    'Test if player is setting his/her ships before game starts.
    '---------------------------------------------
    If allowSelection Then LocatePlayerShip Target
End Sub
```

The `SelectionChange()` event procedure consists of two procedure calls based on the values of the `allowSelection` and `gameStarted` variables. If `allowSelection` is true, then the user is selecting worksheet cells for locating his or her ships. If `gameStarted` is true, then the user has placed his/her ships and is firing at targets on the computer's grid. It is critical that at no time during the execution of the program that the values of both variables are true.

```
Private Sub LocatePlayerShip(Target As Range)
    '---------------------------------------------
    'Capture user's selections for ship locations. If selection is
    'valid then color it blue and display message for next ship.
    '---------------------------------------------
    Dim errMsg As String

    If RangeValid(Target, "Player", errMsg) Then
        Target.Interior.Color = RGB(0, 255, 255)
        numShipsPlaced = numShipsPlaced + 1
        If (numShipsPlaced < NUMSHIPS) Then
            Range("Output").Value = "Place your " & ships(numShipsPlaced) & _
            ": Select " & shipSize(numShipsPlaced) & " contiguous cells"
        Else
            allowSelection = False
            PlaceComputerShips
            gameStarted = True
            Range("Output").Value = "You may begin"
        End If
    Else
        MsgBox errMsg
    End If
End Sub
```

The `LocatePlayerShip()` sub procedure is called from the `SelectionChange()` event procedure and passed the user's cell selection in the form of the range variable `Target`. The primary goal of the `LocatePlayerShip()` sub procedure is to validate and mark the user's selection for a ship. To accomplish this goal, the Boolean value returned by the `RangeValid()` function procedure (listed later) is used as the conditional statement in an `If/Then/Else` code block. If the user's selection is valid then the interior color of the selection is colored light blue, and the `numShipsPlaced` variable is incremented by one. If the user's selection is invalid then the `RangeValid()` procedure sets the value of the string variable `errMsg` that was passed (by reference) as an argument. This error message is then output to the user in a message box. The nested `If/Then/Else` code block tests if the user has placed all five ships. If not, then a message is output to place the next ship. If the user has placed all five ships, then the `PlaceComputerShips()` sub procedure is called in order to generate the location of the computer's ships, the `gameStarted` variable is set to true, and the user is informed that he/she can begin firing. Figure 5.18 shows the *Battlecell* worksheet after the user has placed four ships.

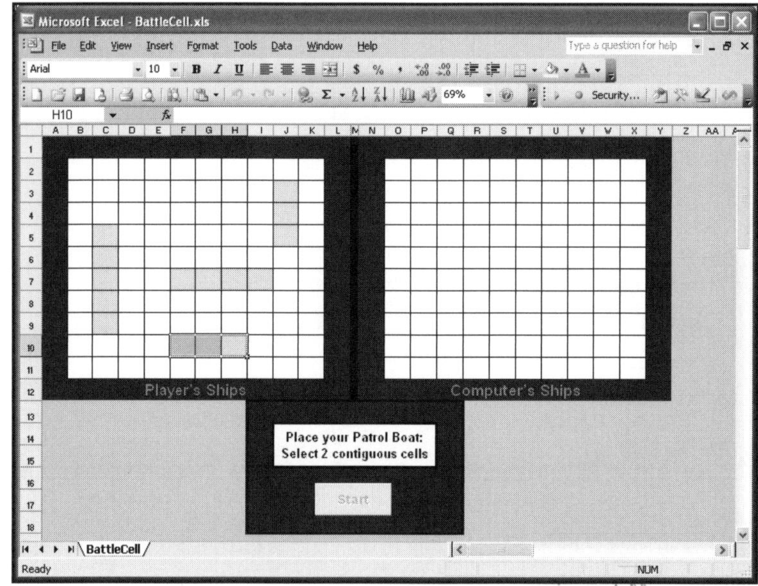

FIGURE 5.18

The *Battlecell* worksheet after the user has placed four of five ships.

```
Private Sub PlayerFire(Target As Range)
    '-------------------------------
    'If player is firing at computer, then record the shot as
    'a hit or miss and track the number of hits.
    '-------------------------------
    Dim errMsg As String
```

```
    If TargetValid(Target, "Computer", errMsg) Then
        PlayWav ActiveWorkbook.Path & "\Sounds\cannon.wav"
        HitOrMiss Target
        ComputerFire
    Else
        MsgBox errMsg
    End If
End Sub
```

The PlayerFire() sub procedure is used to validate and mark the user's target selection when firing at the computer. This procedure is also called from the SelectionChange() event procedure and passed the user's cell selection as the range variable Target. It is also very similar in form to LocatePlayerShip() sub procedure with an If/Then/Else code block that first validates the user's selection. If the selection is valid, a sound file is played (more later) and the procedure marks the user's targets on the computer's grid by coloring them green or red via a call to the HitOrMiss() sub procedure. This is immediately followed by a call to the ComputerFire() sub procedure which simulates the computer's turn at firing back at the user. If the user's selection is invalid, then a message box outputs an error message.

```
Private Sub HitOrMiss(Target As Range)
'Tests if player scores a hit. If so, then game ends
    Static numTargetHits As Integer

    '--------------------
    'Test if players attack scored a hit.
    '--------------------
    If Target.Value = "X" Then
        Target.Interior.Color = RGB(255, 0, 0)
        PlayWav ActiveWorkbook.Path & "\Sounds\explode.wav"
        numTargetHits = numTargetHits + 1
        If (numTargetHits = 17) Then  'Test for end of game.
            Range("Output").Value = "You've sunk all of my ships."
            PlayWav ActiveWorkbook.Path & "\Sounds\playerwins.wav"
            GameOver
        End If
    Else
        Target.Interior.Color = RGB(0, 0, 255)
    End If
End Sub
```

The `HitOrMiss()` sub procedure is called from `PlayerFire()` and serves to test whether or not the user has scored a hit against the computer. Hits are scored by coloring the cell red when the target cell holds an X; otherwise the cell is colored blue. The procedure also tracks the number of hits scored by the user with the static integer variable `numTargetHits`. When the number of hits reaches 17, then the user wins and the game is over. Figure 5.19 shows the *Battlecell* worksheet after the user and computer have each scored several misses and one hit.

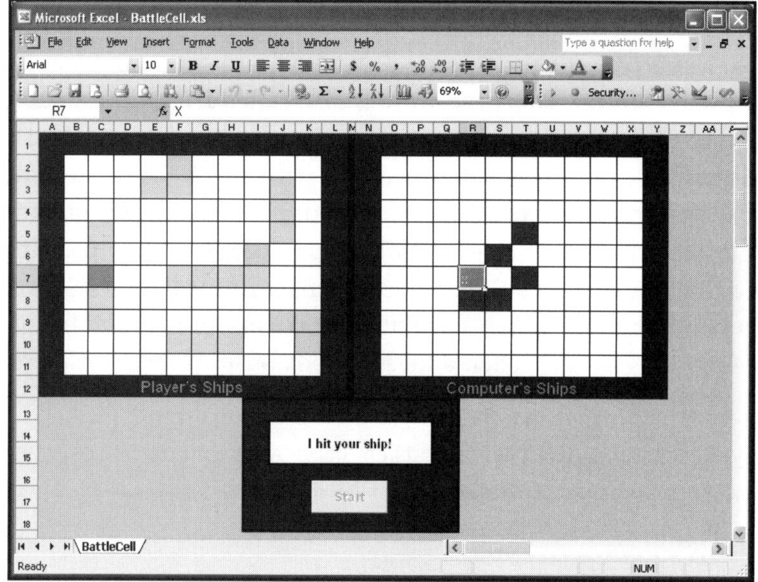

FIGURE 5.19

The *Battlecell* worksheet for a game in progress.

Computer Selections: Placing Ships and Firing at the Player

Selecting locations for the computer's ships is a more challenging problem in that the randomly selected locations must be validated using the same rules as for the user's ships. To randomly generate a ship's location, I need two numbers that represent a single cell's row and column index. These two numbers will have to be bound such that the cell falls within the computer's grid. One additional random number (0 or 1) is required to determine the direction (0 = horizontal, 1 = vertical) the ship is placed. The location of a ship is only valid if all of its cells fall within the computer's grid. That is, it is possible for the random numbers to represent a valid cell, but one or more of the remaining cells may fall outside the range or overlap with another ship that was already placed. The program must not proceed to placing the next ship until the current ship is in a valid location; therefore, the process of placing a ship for the computer will require a loop that executes until the location is validated.

```
Private Sub PlaceComputerShips()
    Dim rowIndex As Integer, colIndex As Integer
    Dim isRow As Boolean
    Dim rangeStr As String, compSelection As Range

    numShipsPlaced = 0
    '------------------------------------
    'Loop through the placement of each ship. This loop
    'iterates an unknown number of times depending on random numbers.
    '------------------------------------
    Do
        SetFirstCell rowIndex, colIndex, isRow

        If isRow Then
            rangeStr = Chr(colIndex + 64) & rowIndex & ":" & _
                       Chr(colIndex + 64) & _
                       (rowIndex + shipSize(numShipsPlaced) - 1)
        Else
            If (colIndex + shipSize(numShipsPlaced) - 1) < 25 Then
                rangeStr = Chr(colIndex + 64) & rowIndex & ":" & _
                           Chr(colIndex + 64 + shipSize(numShipsPlaced) - 1) & _
                           rowIndex
            Else
                'Columns after column Z cause problems.
                rangeStr = Chr(colIndex + 64) & rowIndex & ":" & "Z" & rowIndex
            End If
        End If
        Set compSelection = Range(rangeStr)
        If (AssignShipToLocation(compSelection)) Then _
            numShipsPlaced = numShipsPlaced + 1
    Loop While (numShipsPlaced < NUMSHIPS)
End Sub
```

The `PlaceComputerShips()` sub procedure mostly consists of a `Do-Loop` that iterates until all five of the computer's ships are placed. The loop begins with a call to the `SetFirstCell()` sub procedure (listed next) which generates the random numbers for the cell's row and column index (`rowIndex`, `colIndex`) and the direction of the ship (`isRow`). Next, the large `If/Then/Else` code block builds a string in the form of an Excel range (for example, `R6:U6`). The number of cells represented in this string matches the length of the ship being placed.

The nested `If/Then/Else` structure is required to handle situations where the range extends past column `Z` on the worksheet. Excel labels the next column after `Z` with `AA`; therefore, the character returned by the `Chr()` function will not represent a valid column label and the `rangeStr` variable will not represent a syntactically correct Excel range. This will generate a run-time error when the range variable `compSelection` is set immediately following the `If/Then/Else` code block. To avoid this error, the second column reference in the `rangeStr` variable is set to `Z` in order to generate a syntactically correct range, albeit an invalid range for the game (the computer's grid ends at column `X`).

The location of the computer's ships must be kept hidden from the user. To do this, the program can simply enter a value into the cells representing the location of a ship. The value is not important since the worksheet cells are formatted for the same font color as the background. I will use an X just to make testing the program easier. Later it should be replaced by a space so that the user can't cheat and highlight all cells in the computer's grid in order to see where the X's are. Figure 5.20 shows the *Battlecell* worksheet (with the computer's grid highlighted) immediately following the random placement of the computer's ships.

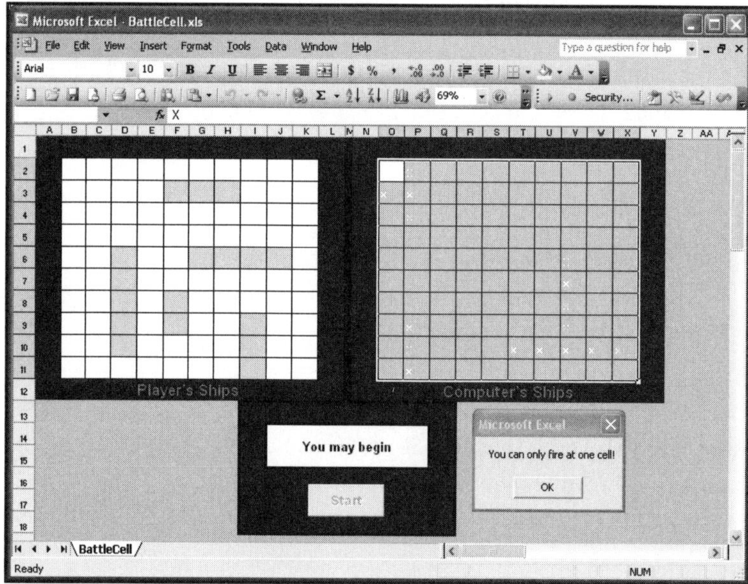

FIGURE 5.20

The *Battlecell* worksheet showing the location of the computer's ships.

Misses and hits scored by the user against the computer are color coded for visual confirmation and to make it easy to validate new targets.

Finally, just before the `Do-Loop` ends, a call to the `AssignShipToLocation()` function procedure tests the selection and marks it with X's if it is valid before the variable `numShipsPlaced` is incremented by one.

```
Private Sub SetFirstCell(rIndex As Integer, cIndex As Integer, isRow As Boolean)
'Randomly select a row and column index within the computer's grid
'to place the first cell for a ship.

    Dim lowerRow As Integer, upperRow As Integer
    Dim lowerCol As Integer, upperCol As Integer

    Randomize
    '------------------------------
    'Initialize values for range of random numbers.
    '------------------------------
    lowerRow = cRange.Row
    upperRow = cRange.Row + cRange.Rows.Count - 1
    lowerCol = cRange.Column
    upperCol = cRange.Column + cRange.Columns.Count - 1

    '------------------------------------------
    'Generate random numbers for cell location and direction of ship placement.
    '------------------------------------------
    rIndex = Int((upperRow - lowerRow + 1) * Rnd + lowerRow)
    cIndex = Int((upperCol - lowerCol + 1) * Rnd + lowerCol)
    If (Int(2 * Rnd) = 0) Then isRow = True Else: isRow = False
End Sub
```

The `SetFirstCell()` sub procedure is quite simple and is used to generate the random numbers for the initial cell and direction of the computer's ship. The bounds for the random numbers are set using the `Row`, `Rows`, `Column`, and `Columns` properties of the `Range` object. The values are effectively returned to the calling procedure (`PlaceComputerShips()`) by passing the variables `rowIndex`, `colIndex`, `isRow` by reference. Note that the value for `isRow` is converted to a Boolean from a random number generated between 0 and 1.

```
Private Function AssignShipToLocation(compSelection As Range) As Boolean
    '----------------------
    'Mark ship location if selection is valid.
    '----------------------
    Dim c As Range

    If RangeValid(compSelection, "Computer") Then
        For Each c In compSelection
            c.Value = "X"
```

```
        Next
        AssignShipToLocation = True
    End If
End Function
```

The AssignShipToLocation() function procedure first validates the randomly generated range representing the computer's ship (passed as the range variable compSelection) and marks the cells with an X if the selection is valid. The procedure returns a Boolean value to the PlaceComputerShips() procedure indicating the validity of the range. Note that the same validation procedure is used here (RangeValid()) as was used to validate the user's ship locations.

The computer's target selection is also done randomly. This makes it easy for the user to win the game, but you can add an intelligent targeting algorithm later. Random numbers representing the cell row and column are generated for a target. If the target's background color is white then the computer scores a miss. If it's cyan, the computer scores a hit.

```
Private Sub ComputerFire()
    Dim targetCell As String, targetRange As Range
    Static numTargetHits As Integer
    Dim tryAgain As Boolean

    '------------------------------------
    'Generate a random target, validate it, then test for hit or miss
    'Also test for end of game.
    '------------------------------------
    Do
        targetCell = SetTargetCell
        Set targetRange = Range(targetCell)

        If TargetValid(targetRange, "Player") Then
            tryAgain = False
            If targetRange.Interior.Color = RGB(0, 255, 255) Then
                Range("Output").Value = "I hit your ship!"
                targetRange.Interior.Color = RGB(255, 0, 0)
                numTargetHits = numTargetHits + 1
                If (numTargetHits = 17) Then
                    Range("Output").Value = "I've sunk all of your ships!"
                    PlayWav ActiveWorkbook.Path & "\Sounds\computerwins.wav"
                    GameOver
                End If
```

```
            Else
                Range("Output").Value = "I missed!"
                targetRange.Interior.Color = RGB(0, 255, 0)
            End If
        Else
            tryAgain = True
        End If
    Loop While (tryAgain)
End Sub
```

The ComputerFire() sub procedure is called from PlayerFire() and simulates the computer's return fire at the user's grid. The logic is essentially the same as the PlayerFire() and HitOrMiss() sub procedures listed earlier except that the target is now randomly generated using the SetTargetCell() function procedure. The target is validated using the same sub procedure that validated the user's target selection (TargetValid()).

```
Private Function SetTargetCell() As String
    Dim cIndex As Integer, rIndex As Integer
    Dim lowerRow As Integer, upperRow As Integer
    Dim lowerCol As Integer, upperCol As Integer

    '--------------------------------
    'Use random numbers for selecting a row and columns,
    'then convert it to a string in A1 notation.
    '--------------------------------
    lowerRow = pRange.Row
    upperRow = pRange.Row + pRange.Rows.Count - 1
    lowerCol = pRange.Column
    upperCol = pRange.Column + pRange.Columns.Count - 1
    Randomize

    rIndex = Int((upperRow - lowerRow + 1) * Rnd + lowerRow)
    cIndex = Int((upperCol - lowerCol + 1) * Rnd + lowerCol)

    SetTargetCell = Chr(cIndex + 64) & rIndex
End Function
Public Sub GameOver()
    cmdStart.Enabled = True
    End
End Sub
```

The game ends when either the user or computer scores 17 hits. The Command Button control is enabled and the `End` keyword is used to terminate the program and clear all variables.

Validating Selections

Custom validation procedures should test the user's and computer's ship and target selections for proper location and size. Because there are several validation procedures, I have placed them in their own standard code module. This is not really necessary as all of the remaining code could have been included with the object module for the `Worksheet` object; however, the code in the object module was getting a bit long and more difficult to navigate, so a new module was added and named `Validation` in order to better organize the program's procedures.

The standard code module contains several global variable declarations previously discussed. These variables are given public scope because they must be accessed in multiple code modules.

It is worth repeating that it is best to avoid the use of global variables as they make your code harder to read and leave your data unprotected; however, at this level of programming, it is difficult to avoid the use of global variables and they are acceptable as long as their number is kept to a minimum.

```
Option Explicit
Public pRange As Range, cRange As Range
Public numShipsPlaced As Integer
Public shipSize As Variant
```

The two main validation procedures in the `Validation` code module are `RangeValid()` and `TargetValid()` which are used to validate the user's and computer's ship locations and target selections, respectively. Each of these functions calls several subordinate function procedures that validate a specific requirement of the range.

These two procedures were designed to handle validation for both the user's and computer's ships and targets; therefore, the argument `msg` is declared in the argument list for each function using the VBA keyword `Optional`. Using `Optional` indicates that the argument is not required in the calling statement. (Error messages are only required for the user's selections.) If `Optional` is used, then all subsequent arguments in the parameter list must also be optional and declared using the `Optional` keyword.

```
Public Function RangeValid(shipLocation As Range, grid As String, _
                           Optional msg As String) As Boolean
```

```
'Validates players selections when placing ships.
    Dim tempRange As Range

    RangeValid = True

    '-------------
    'Define range for tests.
    '-------------
    If (grid = "Player") Then
        Set tempRange = pRange
    Else
        Set tempRange = cRange
    End If

    '------------------------------
    'Call several functions testing for specific errors.
    'Exit function immediately with any failed test.
    '------------------------------
    RangeValid = TestLength(shipLocation, msg)
    If (Not RangeValid) Then Exit Function

    RangeValid = TestIfInRange(shipLocation, tempRange, msg)
    If (Not RangeValid) Then Exit Function

    RangeValid = TestForMultipleRowsOrCols(shipLocation, msg)
    If (Not RangeValid) Then Exit Function

    RangeValid = TestForOverlap(shipLocation, msg)
    If (Not RangeValid) Then Exit Function
End Function
```

The functions listed here rely heavily on the `Range` object and a few of its properties; but by now, you should be getting more comfortable with the `Range` object. The `RangeValid()` function procedure tests the user's and computer's ships for valid length, location within the correct grid, spanning multiple rows or columns, and overlap with a previously placed ship—using a separate function for testing each criteria (`TestLength()`, `TestIfInRange()`, `TestForMultipleRowsOrCols()`, and `TestForOverlap()`). If each criteria passes, then the function returns true to the calling procedure, otherwise it returns false.

```
Private Function TestLength(shipLocation As Range, msg As String) As Boolean
    '--------------------
    'Check if length of selection is correct
    '--------------------
    TestLength = True
    If shipLocation.Count <> shipSize(numShipsPlaced) Then
        msg = "Please select " & shipSize(numShipsPlaced) & " cells"
        TestLength = False
    End If
End Function

Private Function TestIfInRange(shipLocation As Range, tempRange As Range, msg As _
String) As Boolean
    '--------------------------------
    'Check if selection is in player's/computer's range and that
    'either column index or row index is identical across the range.
    '--------------------------------
    Dim col1 As Integer, col2 As Integer
    Dim row1 As Integer, row2 As Integer

    TestIfInRange = True
    col1 = shipLocation.Column
    col2 = shipLocation.Column + shipLocation.Columns.Count
    row1 = shipLocation.Row
    row2 = shipLocation.Row + shipLocation.Rows.Count
    If (row1 < tempRange.Row) Or (row2 > tempRange.Row + tempRange.Rows.Count) _
            Or (col1 < tempRange.Column) _
            Or (col2 > tempRange.Column + tempRange.Columns.Count) Then
        msg = "Selection out of range"
        TestIfInRange = False
    End If
End Function

Private Function TestForMultipleRowsOrCols(shipLocation As Range, msg As String) As _
Boolean
    '--------------------------
    'Check if selection spans multiple rows or columns.
    '--------------------------
```

```
    TestForMultipleRowsOrCols = True
    If (shipLocation.Columns.Count > 1) And (shipLocation.Rows.Count > 1) Then
        msg = "Selection must be within the same row or column"
        TestForMultipleRowsOrCols = False
    End If
End Function

Private Function TestForOverlap(shipLocation As Range, msg As String) As Boolean
    '-------------------------------
    'Check to see if selection overlaps a previous selection.
    '-------------------------------
    Dim c As Range

    TestForOverlap = True
    For Each c In shipLocation
        If c.Interior.Color = RGB(0, 255, 255) Or c.Value = "X" Then
            msg = "Selection cannot overlap another ship!"
            TestForOverlap = False
        End If
    Next
End Function
```

The `TargetValid()` function procedure tests the user's and computer's targets for proper length (one cell) and location (within each other's grids, and not previously selected). The subordinate functions `TestForOneCell()` and `TestLocation()` handle the specific tests for validating the target.

```
Public Function TargetValid(shotSelection As Range, grid As String, _
                                Optional msg As String) As Boolean
'Tests user's/computer's selection of target.
    Dim tempRange As Range

    '-------------
    'Define range for tests.
    '-------------
    If (grid = "Player") Then
        Set tempRange = pRange
    Else
        Set tempRange = cRange
    End If
```

```
    msg = "Select one cell within the computer's grid."
    '--------------------
    'Test if only one cell is selected.
    '--------------------
    TargetValid = TestForOneCell(shotSelection, msg)

    '----------------------------------
    'Test if player's/computer's selection is in computer's grid or
    'if player/computer already selected the target cell.
    '----------------------------------
    TargetValid = TestLocation(shotSelection, tempRange, msg)
End Function

Private Function TestForOneCell(shotSelection As Range, msg As String) As Boolean
    TestForOneCell = True
    If shotSelection.Count > 1 Then
        msg = "You can only fire at one cell!"
        TestForOneCell = False
    End If
End Function

Private Function TestLocation(shotSelection As Range, tempRange As Range, msg As
String) As Boolean
    Dim c As Range

    'TestLocation = True
    For Each c In tempRange
        If c.Address = shotSelection.Address Then
            TestLocation = True
            If c.Interior.Color = RGB(0, 0, 255) Or _
                    c.Interior.Color = RGB(255, 0, 0) Or _
                    c.Interior.Color = RGB(0, 255, 0) Then
                msg = "You have already selected that cell!"
                TestLocation = False
                Exit Function
            End If
        End If
    Next
End Function
```

Adding Sound to Your VBA Program

Microsoft removed support for playing sound files in Excel several versions ago. This leaves two choices for playing sounds in Excel applications with VBA: ActiveX controls and the Windows API (application programming interface).

As there are no ActiveX controls for playing sound that currently ship with VBA, the Windows API will be used for adding sound to your VBA programs in this book.

There is a multimedia control that comes with Windows and it can be used to play sound files in your VBA programs; however, it cannot be accessed from the Control toolbox, so its use is beyond the scope of this book. That's really just as well, because using it to play sound files is actually more difficult than using the Windows API.

The Windows API

The Windows Application Programming Interface (API) is the interface used to programmatically control the Windows operating system. The Windows API is comprised of numerous procedures that provide programmatic access to the features of the Windows operating system (for example, windows functions, file functions, and so on). The API procedures are stored in the system directory of Windows as .dll (dynamic link library) files. There can be dozens of procedures stored within a single .dll file. The API procedures are conceptually the same as procedures used in any programming language, including VBA; however, because the API procedures are written in C/C++, accessing them via the VBA programming environment can be difficult–in some cases, impossible.

Normally, the Windows API is left as an advanced programming topic for some very good reasons. Using the Windows API can be dangerous as it bypasses all of the safety features built into VBA to prevent the misuse of system resources and the subsequent system crashes they usually cause (but nothing that can't be fixed by rebooting your computer); however, the API can greatly extend the ability and therefore, the power of a program.

Fortunately, tapping into the Windows API to play a .wav file (Wave Form Audio) is about as easy as it gets. This section of the book will only show you how to play .wav files using the Windows API and will not discuss the Windows API in any detail. Instead, the Windows API is left as an advanced topic for you to consider after becoming comfortable with VBA. The Windows API is the best (and probably easiest) tool available to all VBA programmers for adding sound to a program, but it should not be used extensively by beginning programmers; therefore, I will only show you how to use it to add sound to a VBA program.

To use a function from the Windows API in VBA, open a code module and use a `Declare` statement in the general declarations section to create a reference to the external procedure (Windows API function). Note that line continuation character has been used in the declaration below due to its length.

```
Public Declare Function sndPlaySoundA Lib "winmm.dll" _
(ByVal lpszSoundName As String, ByVal uFlags As Long) As Long
```

In reality, this is a relatively short API declaration. This declaration creates a reference to the `sndPlaySoundA()` function found in the file `winmm.dll`. It looks a lot like a function call in VBA, but it is only a declaration; the call to the function will come later. Capitalization is important and will not be corrected automatically if typed incorrectly.

The function accepts two arguments as listed in the declaration. The argument `lpszSoundName` represents the string specifying the filename and path to the .wav file to be played, and the argument `uFlags` represents the integer used to denote whether or not program execution should proceed immediately (`1`) or wait until after the file is done playing (`0`). The `sndPlaySoundA()` function returns a value of type `Long` that may be discarded. Hence, calls to the `sndPlaySoundA()` function from a VBA procedure can appear as follows.

```
sndPlaySoundA "Path to .wav file", 1
returnVal = sndPlaySoundA("Path to .wav file", 0)
```

Playing Wav Files Via the Windows API

I entered the code for playing these files in a new standard module named `General`. (I used a new module to make it easy to export this code to other VBA projects.) The code is very simple, consisting of the declarative statement for the API function and a short sub procedure with one argument representing a file path. The `PlayWav()` sub procedure consists of one line of code that calls the `sndPlaySoundA()` API function passing the file path to the .wav file and the value for the `uFlags` argument (`0` indicates that program execution will pause while the sound file is playing). The `PlayWav()` sub procedure is called when the user selects a target to fire at and when the game ends (see the `PlayerFire()`, `HitOrMiss()`, and `ComputerFire()` procedures).

```
Option Explicit

Public Declare Function sndPlaySoundA Lib "winmm.dll" _
(ByVal lpszSoundName As String, ByVal uFlags As Long) As Long

Public Sub PlayWav(filePath As String)
    sndPlaySoundA filePath, 0
End Sub
```

The .wav files used in the Battlecell program are courtesy of http://www.a1freesoundeffects.com.

You can see how easy it is to play sound files using the Windows API. Although programming via the Windows API is an advanced technique, there really is nothing simpler for the VBA programmer to use for playing sound files.

This concludes the *Battlecell* program. The program is not terribly long or complex, but is starting to approach a level of programming that makes the game fun even for adults. The intention of the program is to help you get comfortable using VBA objects and navigating through Excel's object hierarchy. The `Range` object is used extensively in the *Battlecell* program and that will be typical of the VBA programs you write. The use of `Workbook` and `Worksheet` object event procedures is also prevalent in the *Battlecell* program. To take full advantage of the power of VBA, you should get comfortable identifying and using these procedures.

Chapter Summary

This chapter represents a critical phase in your development as a VBA programmer. Understanding objects and their role in creating dynamic and powerful applications is critical in any programming language including VBA.

In this chapter, we learned how to use several of Excel's top-level objects and how to navigate through its object model. Specifically, you looked at the `Application`, `Workbook`, `Window`, `Worksheet`, and `Range` objects in detail. Some of the event procedures, methods, and properties of these objects were also introduced.

Next, you learned about some of the tools available in VBA for working with objects. This included the Object Browser for navigating through the object hierarchy and getting fast help to an object of interest. The `With/End With` code structure, object data type, and `For/Each` loop were also introduced.

Finally, the *Battlecell* program illustrated a practical and fun programming example that relied heavily on Excel's top-level objects. As there is a tendency for such things to occur, a few subordinate objects also appeared in the program.

Challenges

1. Write a VBA procedure that outputs a range after being selected by the user (one statement will do it).
2. Write a VBA procedure that first asks the user to input some text and then changes the caption of the current window to the text value input by the user.
3. Write a VBA procedure that adds three additional workbooks to the application and 10 additional worksheets to each workbook added. Hint: Use object variables and nested `For/Each` loops.
4. Write a VBA procedure that deletes all but one worksheet in all workbooks currently open in the Excel application. Again use nested `For/Each` loops. To turn off prompts to the user, use the `DisplayAlerts` property of the `Application` object.
5. Open a workbook with more than one worksheet. Write a procedure that inserts a string in each cell in the range A1:E5 in every worksheet. Make the string a concatenation of the worksheet name and cell address (for example, Sheet1:$A$3).
6. Use the `Worksheet_Change()` event procedure to alter the properties of the `Font` object (`Bold`, `Size`, `Color`, and so on) after the user enters text into a cell. Use a `With/End With` code structure.
7. Create a spreadsheet that contains several names in multiple rows and columns. Write a VBA procedure that finds a specific name within a highlighted range on the spreadsheet. Use the `Find()` method of the `Range` object and the `Worksheet_SelectionChange()` event procedure of the `Worksheet` object. Refer to the Object Browser or on-line help for syntactic requirements. Then record a macro with a similar function and compare the recorded procedure to your own.
8. Design an algorithm for adding intelligence to the *Battlecell* program, then implement your algorithm by writing the code that will make the computer a more competitive player. Add your code to a new standard module inserted into the Battlecell project. The initial procedure for simulating intelligence should be called from the `ComputerFire()` procedure in the *Battlecell* program. You can remove the `SetTargetCell()` procedure from the *Battlecell* program that is used to randomly generate a target for the computer. This is a tough one, so be sure to take plenty of time designing your algorithm before writing any code!

VBA UserForms and Additional Controls

UserForms are programmable containers for ActiveX controls. They enable you to build customized windows to serve as a user interface in any VBA application. UserForms are similar to other VBA objects in that they have properties, methods, and events that you use to control the appearance and behavior of your interface window; but the main function of a UserForm is to serve as a container for other ActiveX controls. UserForms are part of the VBA object library, and therefore, are available to use in all MS Office applications (Excel, Word, PowerPoint, and so on). In this chapter you will learn how to design UserForms using ActiveX controls for inclusion in your VBA programs.

In this chapter I will examine:

- UserForms
- The Option Button Control
- The Scroll Bar Control
- The Frame Control
- The RefEdit Control
- The MultiPage Control
- The List Box and Combo Box Controls
- Custom Data Types and Enumerations

Project: Blackjack

Blackjack is a standard on most computers. You can find numerous versions of this game in Windows, Java, and JavaScript. This chapter reproduces the game using VBA UserForms with Excel, which is something you probably have not seen before. Figure 6.1 shows the *Blackjack* game in the Excel application.

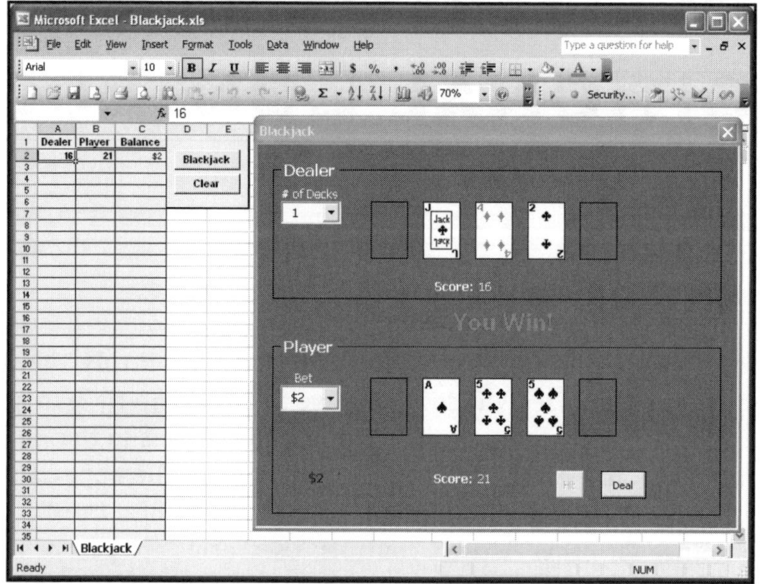

Figure 6.1

The *Blackjack* game.

Designing Forms with VBA

If you have previous programming experience in Visual Basic (even as a novice), then UserForms (hereafter referred to as a VBA form or just form when used in the general sense) will be very familiar, because they will remind you of Visual Basic forms. If you have never used Visual Basic, then VBA forms will probably look just like another Window; however, VBA forms are not quite VB forms or regular windows because they don't have as many features. For example, there are no minimize and maximize buttons in the upper-right corner. Also, there are fewer properties and methods available for altering the appearance and behavior of the `UserForm` object. Nonetheless, VBA forms are invaluable for adding custom user interfaces to your applications.

Forms are included in VBA to allow programmers to build custom user interfaces with their office applications. Up to this point, input from the user via dialog boxes has been limited to `InputBox()` and `MsgBox()` functions. Because forms can be customized using a number of ActiveX controls, they greatly extend the ability of VBA programmers to collect user input.

In the Real World

The graphical user interface (GUI) that made operating systems, such as Macintosh and Windows, so popular was first made available in the early 1980s by Apple Computer; however, the technology was actually developed by researchers at Xerox.

Macintosh computers remained extremely popular until Microsoft's release of Windows 95, the first version of Windows that matched Macintosh for ease of use.

Adding a Form to a Project

To add a form to a project, select Insert/UserForm from the menu bar in the VBA IDE as shown in Figure 6.2.

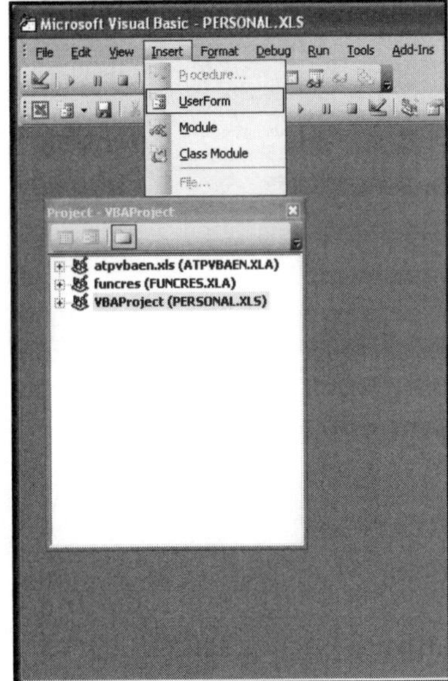

Figure 6.2

Inserting a VBA form into a project from the VBA IDE.

A new folder labeled Forms will appear in the Project Explorer window. An example of a form just added to a project is shown in Figure 6.3.

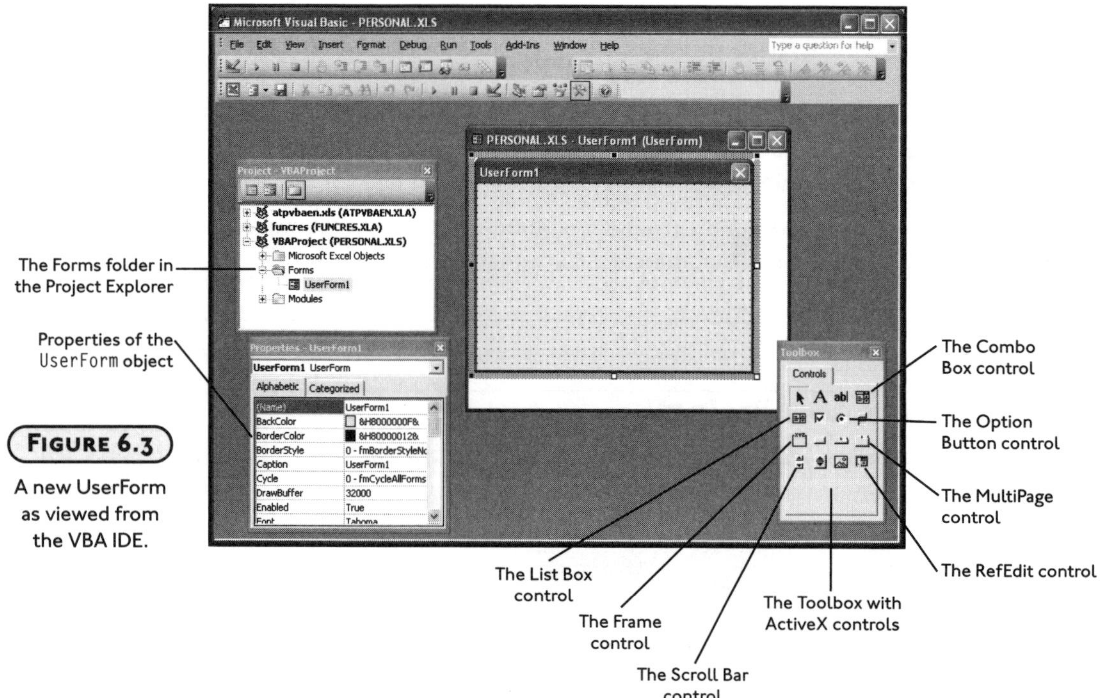

FIGURE 6.3

A new UserForm as viewed from the VBA IDE.

Components of the UserForm Object

In the same manner as ActiveX controls, when you select a form, its properties appear in the Properties window in the VBA IDE (see Figure 6.3). Table 6.1 lists some of the properties of the `UserForm` object that you will commonly set at Design Time.

TABLE 6.1 SELECTED PROPERTIES OF THE USERFORM OBJECT

Property	Description
Name	Sets the name of the `UserForm` object for use as a code reference to the object.
BackColor	Sets the background color of the form.
Caption	Sets the text displayed in the title bar.
Height	Sets the height of the form.
StartUpPosition	Sets the position of the form on the screen when displayed.
Width	Sets the width of the form.

The `UserForm` object has several additional appearance properties besides those listed in Table 6.1. These properties include `BorderColor`, `BorderStyle`, and `SpecialEffect` which are used for aesthetic appeal.

Forms represent separate entities in a VBA project and have their own code window. To view the code window (module) associated with the `UserForm` object, select the View Code icon from the Project Explorer; or select View, Code from the menu bar; or hit F7 (all with the form selected). You can also double click on the form to open its code window. The structure of a form code window (sometimes referred to as a form module) is the same as any other module window. The upper-left corner contains a dropdown list with all objects contained within the form, including the `UserForm` object. The upper-right corner contains a dropdown list of all event procedures associated with the various objects that may be contained in the form. There is also a general declarations section for making module level declarations in the form module. An example code window for a form is shown in Figure 6.4.

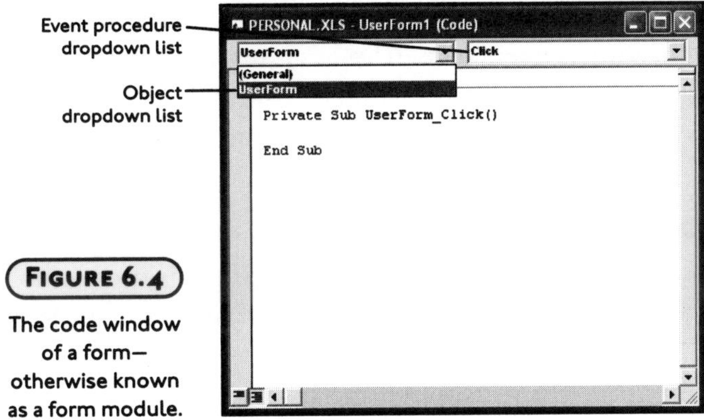

FIGURE 6.4

The code window of a form—otherwise known as a form module.

The behavior of variables and procedures declared with the `Dim`, `Private`, and `Public` keywords in a form module are identical to that of an object module as discussed in Chapter 3. Thus, the scope of variables and procedures declared as `Public` in the general declarations section of a form module are global, but must be accessed from other modules using the variable's module identifier (for example, `moduleName.variableName` or `moduleName.procedureName`).

The `UserForm` object has several event procedures, including `Click()`, `Activate()`, and `QueryClose()` among others. To view the full list of event procedures of the `UserForm` object, select the `UserForm` object in the object dropdown list and then select the event procedure dropdown list from the form module (see Figure 6.4). Some of these event procedures should be familiar, as they are common to several ActiveX controls. Table 6.2 lists a few of the more commonly used event procedures of the `UserForm` object.

TABLE 6.2 SELECTED EVENT PROCEDURES OF THE USERFORM OBJECT

Event	Description
Activate()	Triggered when the UserForm is activated (i.e., shown).
Initialize()	Triggered when the UserForm is loaded.
QueryClose()	Triggered when the UserForm is closed or unloaded.
Terminate()	Triggered when the UserForm is closed or unloaded.

The `Initialize()` event of the `UserForm` object is triggered when the form is first loaded, and therefore, is an excellent location for code that initializes program variables and controls. The `Activate()` event is also used for initialization; however, it is not triggered when the `UserForm` object is loaded, but only when the form is made active. The `QueryClose()` and `Terminate()` events are triggered when the `UserForm` is unloaded from memory, making these event procedures good locations for code that clears memory and/or ends the program.

Adding ActiveX Controls to a Form

Like the `Worksheet` object, the `UserForm` object is a container object, meaning it is used to hold other objects. When a form is added to a project, the Control Toolbox should automatically appear (see Figure 6.3). If the Control Toolbox does not appear, select View/Toolbox from the menu bar. There will be a few additional controls displayed in the control toolbox when viewed with a form (relative to a worksheet), including the MultiPage and Frame controls (discussed later).

ActiveX controls are added to a form in the same manner that they are added to worksheets. When added to a form, you access the properties of an ActiveX control via the Properties window and you access event procedures associated with ActiveX controls via the form module that contains them. To practice using ActiveX controls on forms, open Excel and from the VBA IDE, insert a form into a new VBA project. Adjust the size properties (`Width` and `Height`) of the `UserForm` object and change its `Caption` property to `"Hello"`. Add Label and Command Button controls to the form and change their `Name` properties to something meaningful (for example, `lblOutput`, and `cmdHello`). Also, adjust the size and appearance properties of the Label and Command Button controls to suit your taste. Next, double-click on the Command Button control to access its `Click()` event procedure in the code module of the `UserForm` object and add one line of code such that the entire procedure appears as follows:

```
Private Sub cmdHello_Click()
    lblOutput.Caption = "Hello!"
End Sub
```

The form, as viewed at Design Time, from the VBA IDE is shown in Figure 6.5.

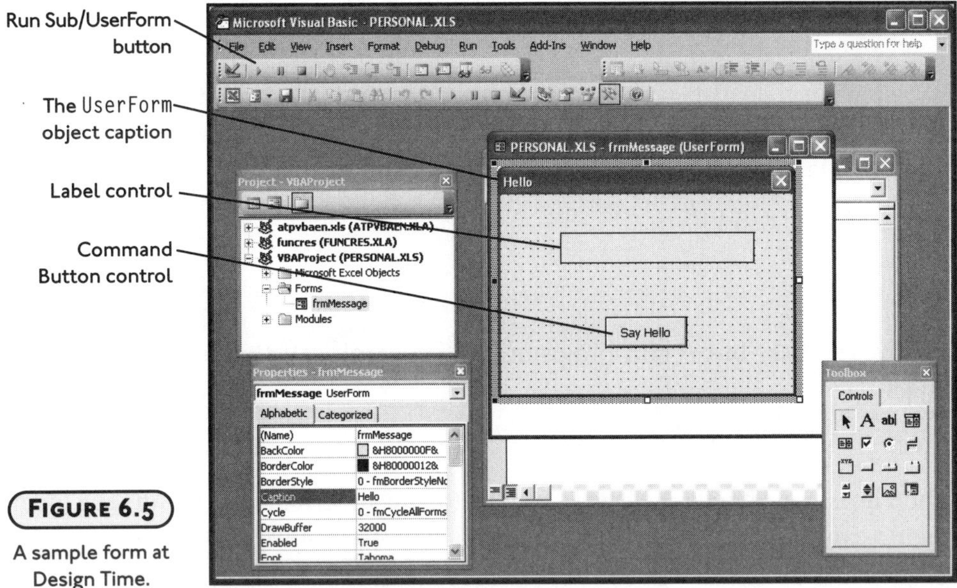

FIGURE 6.5

A sample form at Design Time.

When the user clicks the Command Button control name `cmdHello`, the preceding procedure is triggered, and the `Caption` property of the Label control named `lblOutput` is changed.

To test the application, select the form and click on Run/Sub UserForm from the IDE standard toolbar (see Figure 6.5) or menu bar, or press F5 on the keyboard. The form appears as a window above the Excel application. Click the Command Button control to output the simple message to the Label control. To close the form, click on the X in the upper-right corner of the window.

Showing and Hiding Forms

To display a form from the Excel application, call the `Show()` method of the `UserForm` object in a procedure that can be triggered from Excel (a public procedure in a standard module or an event procedure from an object module). The basic syntax follows:

```
UserFormName.Show [Modal]
```

To load a form into system memory without displaying it, call VBA's `Load()` method.

```
Load UserFormName
```

The `UserForm` object and all of its components can be accessed programmatically after loading it into memory. Note that the `Show()` method will also load a form if it has not been previously loaded into memory.

For example, the following code displays a `UserForm` object named `frmMessage` when the `Click()` event procedure of a Command Button control named `cmdShowForm` is triggered. The Command Button control can be placed on a worksheet or another form.

```
Private Sub cmdShowForm_Click()
    frmMessage.Show
End Sub
```

To hide a form from the user but retain programmatic control, call the `Hide()` method of the `UserForm` object.

```
UserFormName.Hide
```

The `Hide()` method does not remove the `UserForm` object from system memory, thus the form and its components can still be accessed programmatically. To remove a form from system memory, call VBA's `UnLoad()` method.

```
UnLoad UserFormName
```

Modal Forms

The `Show()` method of the `UserForm` object takes an optional Boolean parameter that specifies whether or not the form is modal. The default value of the modal parameter is true, which creates a modal form. A modal form is one that must be addressed by the user, and subsequently closed (by the user or the program) before any other part of the Excel application can be accessed. If the form is modeless, then the user may select between any open windows in the Excel application.

Modeless forms are only supported in MS Office 2000, and later versions. Trying to create a modeless form in an earlier version of MS Office will generate a runtime error.

Use the VBA-defined constants `vbModal` and `vbModeless` with the `Show()` method to show modal and modeless forms, respectively.

A modal form is safest, unless user interaction with the Excel application is required while the form is displayed. The form can be displayed via the `Show()` method from anywhere in a VBA program; however, be aware that program execution may proceed differently depending on where in a procedure the form is shown and whether the form is modal. For example, the two procedures below will yield different results.

In the first example, the `Show()` method is called for a `UserForm` object in order to display a modeless form. Next, a `MsgBox()` function displays some text. In this example, code execution proceeds through the entire procedure—first displaying the form, then the message box—so both dialogs are displayed to the user at the same time.

```
Private Sub MyProcedure()
    frmMyUserForm.Show vbModeless
    MsgBox("The message box is displayed immediately after the UserForm")
End Sub
```

In the second example, the form is displayed modally, enabling code execution within the procedure to pause while the form is displayed. After the user closes the form, program execution proceeds to the next line of code; thus, when using a modal form, program behavior is identical to the `MsgBox()` and `InputBox()` functions.

```
Private Sub MyProcedure()
    frmMyUserForm.Show vbModal
    MsgBox("The message box is displayed after the UserForm is closed.")
End Sub
```

To determine which version of Excel is running on a user's computer, test the `Version` property of the `Application` object. The `Version` property returns a read-only string containing a number that represents the version of Excel currently running on your computer (for example, 11.0 for Excel 2003).

Now that you know how to display a form in a program, it's time to look at a few specific ActiveX controls that are used with forms and see how they interact with the Excel application.

Designing Custom Dialog Boxes Using Forms

As mentioned earlier, forms are generally used as dialog boxes to collect user input relevant to the current application. You use ActiveX controls to expand the capabilities of forms well beyond that of the `InputBox()` and `MsgBox()` functions.

Some of the ActiveX controls available for forms are identical to those used with an Excel worksheet, but there are also a few new controls as well as others I have not yet discussed; therefore, with the aid of a couple of examples, I will illustrate the use of several ActiveX controls that have not yet been introduced.

The Option Button Control

The Option Button control is similar to that of the Check Box control in that it offers the user a selection from a group of possibilities. The difference between the two: the Option Button control gives the user one selection; therefore, when the user selects an Option Button from a group of Option Buttons, a previously selected Option Button is automatically deselected.

Option Button controls are grouped by the container on which they have been added. So no matter how many Option Button controls are added to the form shown in Figure 6.6, only one can be selected at any given time.

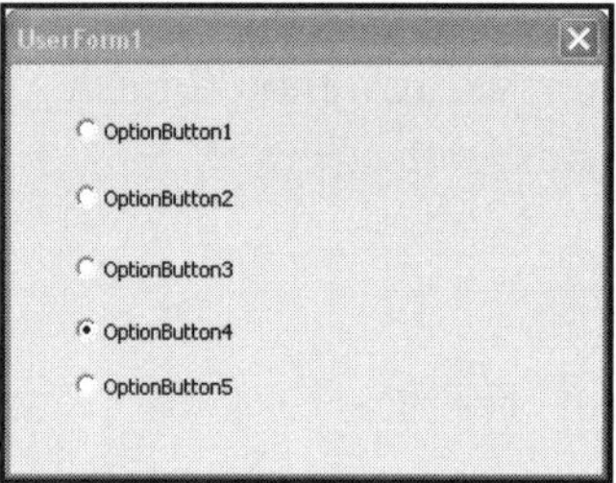

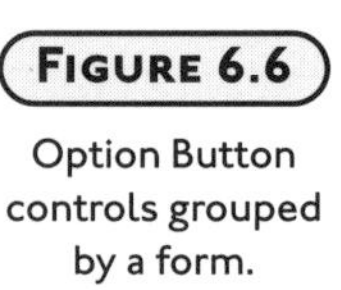
FIGURE 6.6

Option Button controls grouped by a form.

The most common Option Button control properties that you will set (excluding size and appearance properties) include the `Name`, `Caption`, and `Value` properties. The Boolean `Value` property represents the selection state of the control (selected=true) and is the property most commonly addressed in your VBA code. The `Name` and `Caption` properties are typically set at Design Time.

The `Click()` event is the most commonly used event procedure of the Option Button control. The `Click()` event is triggered whenever the user changes the state of an Option Button; thus, it is a good location for code that processes the user's change made to the `Value` property of the control.

The Scroll Bar Control

You have undoubtedly seen and used scroll bars in numerous applications for scrolling through lengthy documents or large figures. Scroll bars sometimes automatically appear on the sides and/or the bottom of VBA controls so the user can view the entire content displayed in a control. Situations such as these require nothing extra from you, or your program—the scroll bars are simply there to provide the user with a method of seeing the complete content of the control; however, VBA also provides a Scroll Bar control that you may add to forms in your project to enhance an interface, such that the user may do more than just scroll through content.

There are several properties of the Scroll Bar control that are of interest to you as a VBA programmer (other than the usual appearance and size properties). Table 6.3 summarizes the major properties of the Scroll Bar control.

Table 6.3 Selected Properties of the Scroll Bar Control

Property	Description
`Name`	The name used for programmatic access to the control.
`Min`	The minimum allowed value of the Scroll Bar. The minimum occurs when the scroll box is located at its minimum location.
`Max`	The maximum allowed value of the scroll bar. The maximum occurs when the scroll box is located at its maximum location.
`SmallChange`	Defines the amount the value of the Scroll Bar is incremented or decremented when the user clicks on either scroll arrow.
`LargeChange`	Defines the amount the value of the Scroll Bar is incremented or decremented when the user clicks on the Scroll Bar on either side of the scroll box.
`Value`	The value of the Scroll Bar as defined by range set by the `Min` and `Max` properties

You may use the Scroll Bar control to read or set the value for the property of another control or program object. Typically, the Scroll Bar control sets a value from a large range of choices. For example, you may use a Scroll Bar control on a form to provide the user with a method of activating a worksheet from all possible worksheets in a workbook.

The `Change()` and `Scroll()` events are the two most common event procedures associated with the Scroll Bar control. The `Change()` event procedure is triggered when the value of the Scroll Bar control is changed by the user. The `Scroll()` event procedure is triggered when the user drags the scroll box on the Scroll Bar control. The following code uses the `Initialize()` event of a `UserForm` object, and the `Change()` and `Scroll()` events of a Scroll Bar control (named `scrWorksheet`) to select distinct worksheets in the active workbook.

```
Private Sub scrWorksheet_Change()
    Worksheets(scrWorksheet.Value).Select
End Sub
Private Sub scrWorksheet_Scroll()
    Worksheets(scrWorksheet.Value).Select
End Sub
Private Sub UserForm_Initialize()
    scrWorksheet.Max = Worksheets.Count
    scrWorksheet.LargeChange = Worksheets.Count / 5
End Sub
```

In this example, the `Max` and `LargeChange` properties of the Scroll Bar control cannot be set at Design Time because the number of worksheets in the active workbook is an unknown; therefore, these properties are set in the `Initialize()` event of the `UserForm` object. The program uses both the `Change()` and `Scroll()` events of the Scroll Bar control to select a `Worksheet` object from the `Worksheets` collection object of the active `Workbook` object (not qualified in code). If the `Scroll()` event is not used, then the user will not see which worksheet is selected if he or she moves the scroll box by dragging. Instead, the user will not see the selected worksheet until the scroll box is released.

To test this code, open Excel and create a new workbook with multiple worksheets. Next, from the VBA IDE add a form and draw a Scroll Bar control onto it. Note that you can make a vertical or horizontal scroll bar by dragging the sizing handles of the Scroll Bar control horizontally or vertically on the form. Set the `Name` property of the Scroll Bar control and add the code to the form module's code window. Then, with the form selected, press F5 to run the program.

The Frame Control

The Frame control groups ActiveX controls on a form. The ActiveX controls grouped within a Frame control may be related by content, or in the case of Option Button controls, be made mutually exclusive. The properties of the Frame control are seldom referenced in code. The `Name` and `Caption` properties along with a couple of appearance properties (`BorderStyle`, `Font`, etc.) are typically set at Design Time.

You will seldom (if ever) programmatically access the Frame control. The Frame control organizes or groups controls on a form for aesthetic appearance; in the case of Option Button controls, behavior. A sample form using two Frame controls, each grouping a set of Option Button controls, is shown in Figure 6.7. A Scroll Bar and two Label controls have also been added to the UserForm.

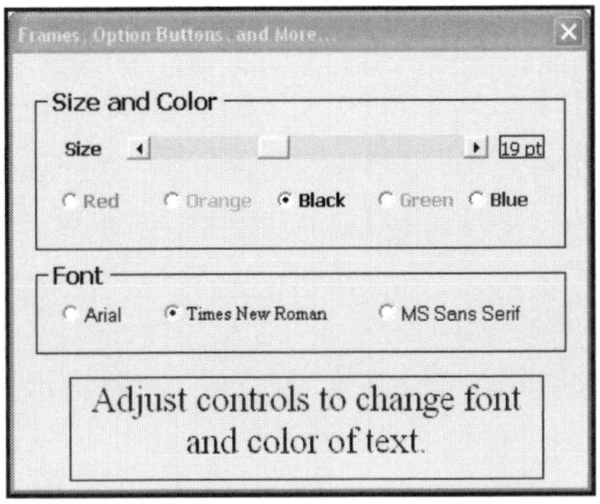

FIGURE 6.7

Using the Frame control on a form.

The purpose of the form shown in Figure 6.7 is to give the user a selection between different font types, sizes, and colors. The result of the user's selections is displayed in the Label control at the bottom of the form. The font size of the text in this Label control is adjusted by the Scroll Bar control (the value of which is displayed in the adjacent Label control). The Frame controls group the Option Button controls by content and make each set mutually exclusive. Without at least one Frame control, the user would only be allowed to select one of the eight Option Buttons.

I set the usual properties of these controls at Design Time. This includes the `Name`, `Caption`, size, and appearance properties (fonts, colors, borders, and so on) of each control. The `Min` and `Max` properties of the Scroll Bar control were set to `6` and `40`, respectively.

The code for this demonstration program is contained entirely in event procedures of the `UserForm` object and ActiveX controls. The `Initialize()` event of the `UserForm` object sets the initial `Caption` property of the Label control that displays the font size (in pts), and the `Click()` event procedure of each Option Button control sets the `ForeColor` and `Font` properties of the Label control at the bottom of the form. Finally, the `Change()` event of the Scroll Bar control adjusts the font size of the Label control at the bottom of the form and writes this size to the adjacent Label control. The entire program entered into the form module follows:

```
Option Explicit
Private Sub UserForm_Initialize()
    lblFontSize.Caption = scrFontsize.Value & " pt"
End Sub
Private Sub optBlack_Click()
    lblResult.ForeColor = vbBlack
End Sub
Private Sub optBlue_Click()
    lblResult.ForeColor = vbBlue
```

```
End Sub
Private Sub optGreen_Click()
    lblResult.ForeColor = vbGreen
End Sub
Private Sub optOrange_Click()
    lblResult.ForeColor = RGB(255, 125, 0)
End Sub
Private Sub optRed_Click()
    lblResult.ForeColor = vbRed
End Sub
Private Sub optArial_Click()
    lblResult.Font = "Arial"
End Sub
Private Sub optSans_Click()
    lblResult.Font = "MS Sans Serif"
End Sub
Private Sub optTimes_Click()
    lblResult.Font = "Times New Roman"
End Sub
Private Sub scrFontsize_Change()
    lblResult.Font.Size = scrFontsize.Value
    lblFontSize.Caption = scrFontsize.Value & " pt"
End Sub
```

Note that, when possible, I use VBA color constants to set the `ForeColor` property of the Label control; however, orange is not a defined constant, so I call VBA's `RGB()` function to set the red, green, and blue components (integers between 0 and 255) to return the long integer representing orange.

The RefEdit Control

A common requirement for custom dialog boxes is providing an interface in which the user can select a range of cells from a worksheet. Your program then uses the selected range for some specific task. The RefEdit control makes it easy to acquire a worksheet range from a form.

Several of Excel's dialogs and wizards contain RefEdit controls, including the chart wizard shown in Figure 6.8.

The RefEdit control allows the user to select a range from an existing Excel worksheet, and have the textual reference for the selected range automatically entered into the edit region of the control. You can also enter the range manually by typing in the text area of the control.

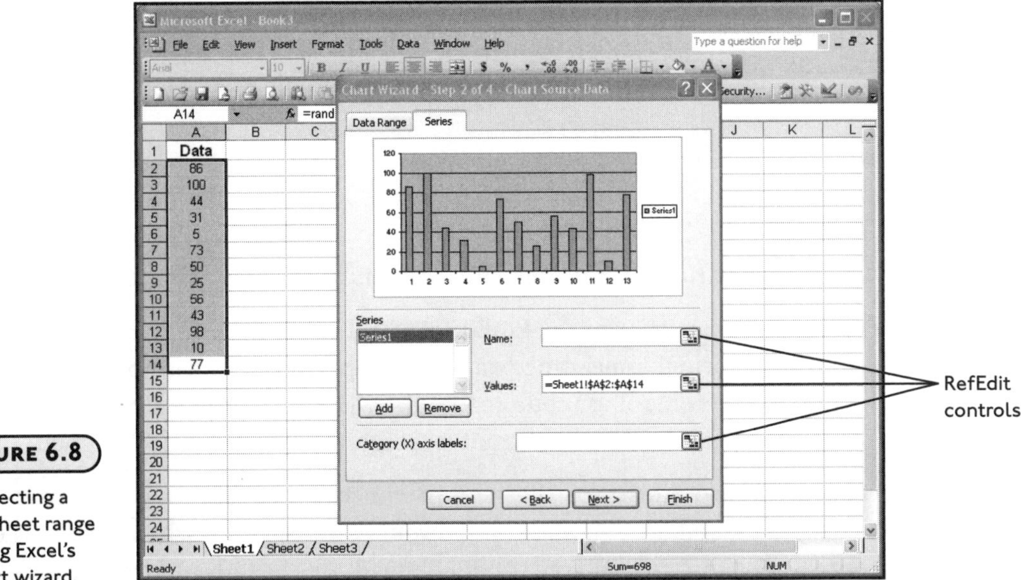

FIGURE 6.8

Selecting a worksheet range using Excel's chart wizard.

To test how a RefEdit control works, you don't even need any code. Just add a form to any VBA project. Draw a RefEdit control on the form and press F5 on your keyboard. Next, select a range from any worksheet and the reference will be added to the RefEdit control as shown in Figure 6.9.

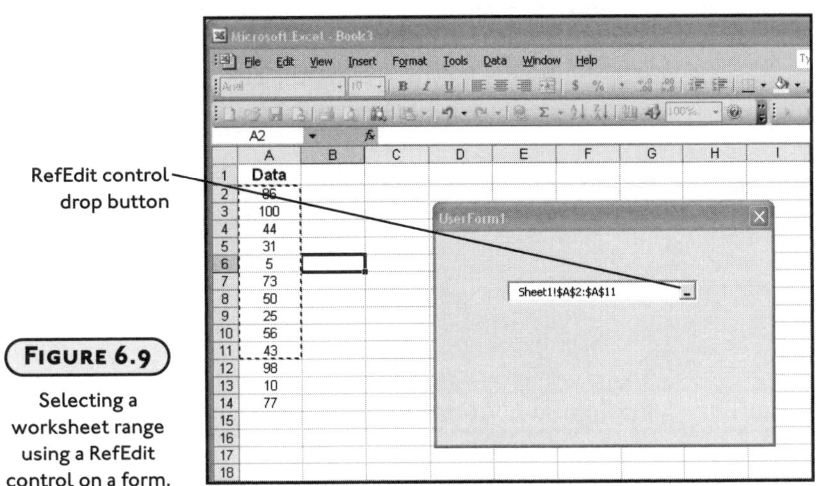

FIGURE 6.9

Selecting a worksheet range using a RefEdit control on a form.

You can also collapse the form by clicking on the drop button at the right of the RefEdit control prior to selecting the range.

You read the selected range from the RefEdit control with the `Text` or `Value` properties. Both properties are strings, so it doesn't matter which one you read. For example, the following line of code reads the value of the `Text` property of a RefEdit control named `RefEdit1` to create a `Range` object:

```
Dim selRange As Range
Set selRange = Range(RefEdit1.Text)
```

After the `selRange` object variable is set, you can access its properties and methods as needed.

You will seldom use any properties of the RefEdit control other than the `Name`, `Text`, or `Value` properties (excluding the usual appearance and size properties). The `Name` property provides a meaningful name to the control for code readability. The `Text` or `Value` property provides you with the selected range, which is the task for which this control was designed.

There are several event procedures of the RefEdit control that you may find useful. The `Enter()`, `Exit()`, `Change()`, and `DropButtonClick()` events are triggered when the focus enters or exits the control, the text in the control is changed, or the drop button is pressed (as implied by their names); but be wary of referencing the RefEdit control in any of its own event procedures, as this may cause your program to lock up. The RefEdit control has a history of bugs (see the MSDN developer Web site at http://msdn.microsoft.com and search for RefEdit control) that have not yet been resolved. Instead, you have to find workarounds.

I recommend using the RefEdit control when you need a range selection from the user entered in a form; however, I further suggest that you do not try to read the range text entered in the RefEdit control from any of its own event procedures. Instead, you should read the text from the event procedure of another ActiveX control. The `Click()` event of a Command Button control works quite well as you will see later in this chapter.

You cannot use the RefEdit control on a modeless form. Doing so will cause Excel and VBA to lock up after showing the form and selecting a worksheet range.

The MultiPage Control

The MultiPage control is another example of a container control that groups or organizes the user interface on a form into multiple categories. An example of the MultiPage control in the Excel application is the Options dialog box shown in Figure 6.10. The Options dialog can be selected in the Excel application from the Tools menu. You can see from this example that the MultiPage control allows you to cram a lot of options onto a single form.

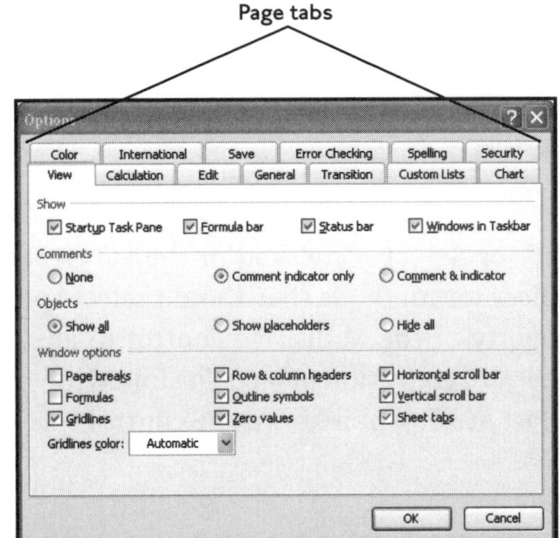

FIGURE 6.10

The Options dialog in Excel.

The MultiPage control allows you to design an interface with multiple pages that group a related set of controls. The different pages are selected using the page tabs.

The MultiPage control is a container for a `Pages` collection object; each page on a MultiPage control is a `Page` object contained in the `Pages` collection. As with most container controls, you generally set their appearance at Design Time and you only write a minimum amount of code for them (if any), unless a specific path to a `Page` object is required.

By default, when you add a MultiPage control to a form, two pages are included. To add more pages, right click on a page tab while in Design Mode and select New Page from the shortcut menu. Figure 6.11 shows a form in Design Mode containing a MultiPage control.

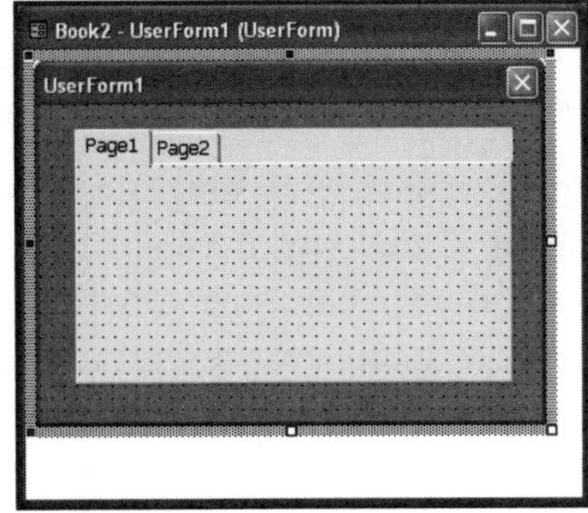

FIGURE 6.11

VBA's MultiPage control.

Properties of the MultiPage control that you will want to investigate include the `Style`, `TabOrientation`, and `MultiRow` properties which set the appearance and location of the tabs.

The `SelectedItem` property returns the currently selected `Page` object. It is useful for identifying what page on the MultiPage control is active. For example:

```
If MultiPage1.SelectedItem.Caption = "Page 1" Then
    MsgBox "You are viewing page 1."
End If
```

Interestingly, there is no `Activate()` or `Select()` method of the `MultiPage` or `Page` objects. These seem like the consistent choices for methods that should select specific `Page` objects. Instead, you can set the `Value` property of the MultiPage control to an index value representing a specific `Page` object in the `Pages` collection object. The following line of code selects the second page (index numbers start at zero) of a MultiPage control.

```
MultiPage1.Value = 1
```

If you select a page on the MultiPage control while in Design Mode, you will have access to the Design Mode properties of a `Page` object. There aren't many properties, but the `Name` and `Caption` properties of each `Page` object should be changed from their default values.

The `Page` object has no events, and the event procedures unique to the MultiPage control are seldom used except in more advanced applications; thus, they will not be discussed. However, the MultiPage control does have a few common event procedures such as `Click()` and `Change()` with which you should already have some familiarity.

The List Box and Combo Box Controls

The List Box control displays data in the form of a list from which the user may select one or more items. The Combo Box control combines the features of a List Box control with a Text Box control, allowing the user to enter a new value if desired. Properties of the List Box and Combo Box controls commonly set at Design Time and Run Time are listed in Table 6.4.

The List Box control may be drawn on the form with varying height and width such that it displays one or more items in the list. If there are more items in the list that can be displayed in the area provided, scroll bars will automatically appear. Normally the List Box control is drawn with its `Height` property set to a value large enough for several values to be displayed, because it is difficult to see the scroll bar when the control is at a minimum height. If space on the form is at a premium, use a Combo Box control and set the `Style` property to dropdown list.

Data is added to the List Box and Combo Box controls at run time using their `AddItem()` method.

```
ControlName.Additem (item)
```

Table 6.4 Selected Properties of the List Box and Combo Box Controls

Property	Description
`Name`	Sets the name of the control to use as a code reference to the object.
`MultiSelect`	List Box control only. Indicates whether of not the user will be able to select multiple items in the list.
`ColumnCount`	Sets the number of data columns to be displayed in the list.
`ListStyle`	Indicates whether option buttons (single selection) or check boxes (multi selection) should appear with items in the list.
`Value`	Holds the current selection in the list. If a multi-select List Box control is used, the `BoundColumn` property must be used to identify the column from which the `Value` property is set.
`BoundColumn`	Identifies the column that sets the source of the `Value` property in a multi-select List Box.
`List`	Run-time only. Used to access the items in the control.
`ListCount`	Run-time only. Returns the number of items listed in the control.
`ListIndex`	Run-time only. Identifies the currently selected item in the control.
`Style`	Combo Box control only. Specifies the behavior of the control as a combo box or a dropdown list box.

The `AddItem()` method must be called for every row of data added to the list. A looping code structure will often work well to complete this task. Other methods belonging to both the List Box and Combo Box controls include, `Clear()` and `RemoveItem()` which remove all or one item from the control's list, respectively. The Combo Box control also includes a `DropDown()` method that, when invoked, displays the control's list.

The most useful event procedure of the List Box and Combo Box controls is the `Change()` event. Although you may find the `DropButtonClick()` event procedure of the Combo Box control quite useful as well. The `Change()` event is triggered when the `Value` property of the control changes. (The `Value` property of the List Box and Combo Box control is the selected item from the list.) The `DropButtonClick()` event of the Combo Box control is triggered when the controls dropdown button is clicked signaling that the user is viewing the list of items in the control.

Be sure to check the Object Browser for a complete list of properties, methods, and events associated with the ActiveX controls discussed in this chapter.

A Custom Dialog for Quick Stats

The following example of a custom dialog is built from a `UserForm` object and several ActiveX controls. The form window allows a user to quickly select a worksheet range and calculate some basic statistics. Furthermore, the form allows the user to summarize their work by writing the statistics for each selected range to a List Box control for later review. Figures 6.12 and 6.13 show the two pages of the MultiPage control used in the form's design.

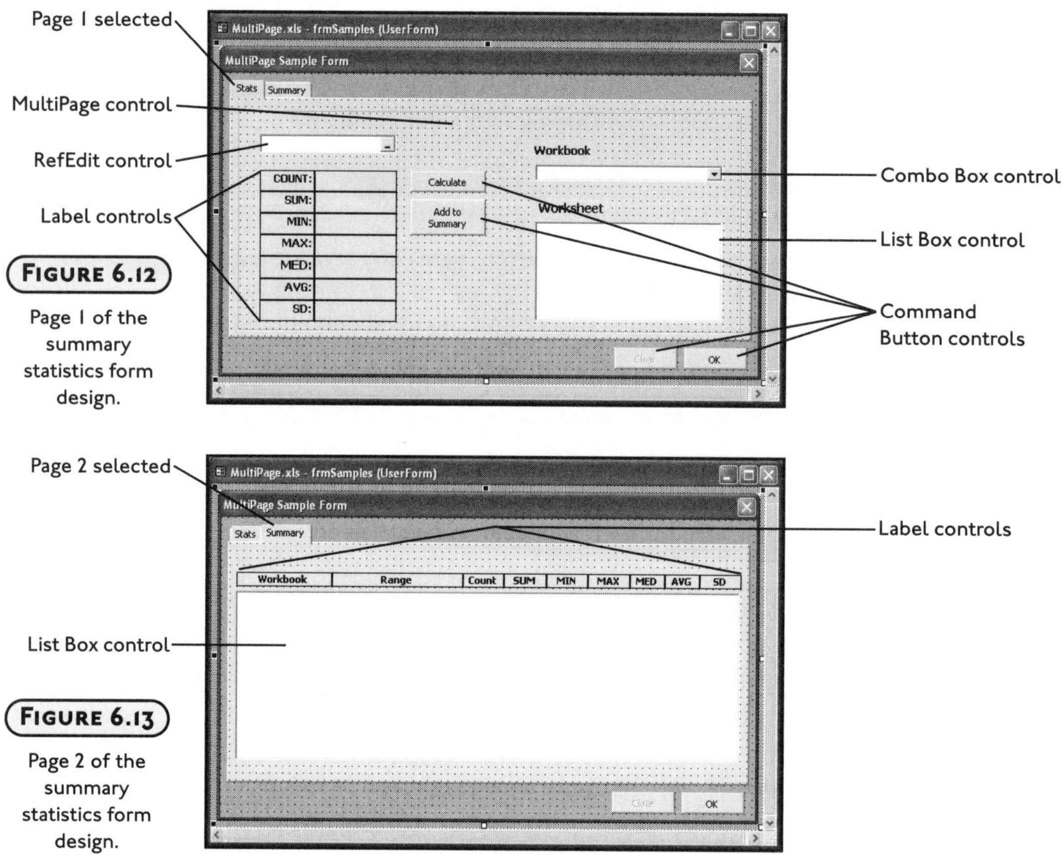

FIGURE 6.12

Page 1 of the summary statistics form design.

FIGURE 6.13

Page 2 of the summary statistics form design.

The form contains a Combo Box, a List Box, and a RefEdit control that allow a user to select a workbook, worksheet, and cell range from the Excel application. Basic statistics are calculated from the selected range when the Command Button control with `Caption` property `"Calculate"` is clicked. The Command Button control with `Caption` property `"Add to Summary"` adds the stats to the List Box control on the second page of the MultiPage control. Two additional Command Button controls at the bottom of the form (`Caption` properties `"Clear"` and `"OK"`) close the custom dialog and clear the List Box control on page 2 of the MultiPage control.

Table 6.5 summarizes the properties of the ActiveX controls that were changed from their default values at Design Time. Label controls that only serve to provide a textual label for other controls, and are not referenced in the program, are not listed in Table 6.5. Table 6.5 does not list any of the appearance properties that were changed in these controls. You should be able to recognize different fonts, colors, borders, and you will probably want to change them anyway to suit your personal preference.

Table 6.5 Property Settings of ActiveX Controls for the Summary Stats Custom Dialog

Control	Property	Setting
Label	Name	lblCount, lblSum, lblMin, lblMax and so on
Label	TextAlign	fmTextAlignCenter
Label	BorderStyle	fmBorderStyleSingle
Command Button	Name	cmdCalcStats, cmdSummary, cmdClear, cmdOk
Command Button	Caption	"Calculate", "Add to Summary", "Clear", "Ok"
Command Button	Enabled	False for cmdClear, True for other three Command Buttons
RefEdit	Name	refStats
Combo Box	Name	cmbWorkbooks
Combo Box	Style	fmStyleDropDownList
Stats Page List Box	Name	lstWorksheets
Summary Page List Box	Name	lstSummary
Summary Page List Box	ColumnCount	9
Summary Page List Box	ColumnWidths	84 pt; 115 pt; 36 pt; 36 pt; 36 pt; 36 pt; 30 pt; 30 pt; 36 pt
MultiPage	Name	mpgSummary
MultiPage	TabOrientation	fmTabOrientationTop
MultiPage	Style	fmTabStyleTabs
Page 1 on MultiPage control	Name	pgStats
Page 1 on MultiPage control	Caption	"Stats"
Page 2 on MultiPage control	Name	pgSummary
Page 2 on MultiPage control	Caption	"Summary"

The `Style` property of the Combo Box control can take one of two constant values; `fmStyleDropDownCombo`, and `fmStyleDropDownList`. If the `Style` property is `fmStyleDropDownCombo`, the user can enter a value in the Combo Box control as well as choose from the list. If the `Style` property is `fmStyleDropDownList`, the control is essentially a List Box and the user must choose only from the list provided.

You can also change the number of data columns in the Combo Box and List Box controls from their default value of one. The `ColumnCount` and `ColumnWidths` properties set the number of data columns, and their widths (in points), respectively. Be sure to separate the different widths in the `ColumnWidths` property with a semicolon (;).

Microsoft uses the *point* for the size properties of the ActiveX controls in VBA. A point is 1/72 of an inch. You are probably more familiar with the point as a size unit for fonts. It's the same unit that describes the `Width`, `Height`, and `ColumnWidths` properties (and many others) of ActiveX controls.

The code for the Summary Stats dialog is contained entirely within its form module. All program code is entered into several event procedures of the ActiveX controls on the form. These procedures follow:

```
Option Explicit

Private Sub UserForm_Initialize()
    Dim wb As Workbook

    For Each wb In Workbooks
        cmbWorkbooks.AddItem wb.Name
        If ActiveWorkbook.Name = wb.Name Then
            cmbWorkbooks.Value = wb.Name
        End If
    Next

    mpgSummary.Value = 0
End Sub
```

The `Initialize()` event of the `UserForm` object serves to add the names of all open workbooks to the Combo Box control named `cmbWorkbooks`. A `For/Each` loop iterates through all the `Workbook` objects in the `Workbooks` collection and the `AddItem()` of the Combo Box control adds the name of each workbook to the list. When the active workbook is found, an `If/Then` decision structure ensures that the name of the active workbook is displayed in the edit area of the Combo Box control by setting the `Value` property of the control.

The last statement in the Initialize() event procedure uses the Value property of the MultiPage control to ensure that the first page (index 0) of the MultiPage control is selected when the form is shown. If this statement is omitted, then the form is shown with the page that is selected while in design view of the VBA IDE.

```
Private Sub mpgSummary_Change()
    If mpgSummary.SelectedItem.Caption = "Summary" Then
        cmdClear.Enabled = True
    Else
        cmdClear.Enabled = False
    End If
End Sub
```

The Change() event of the MultiPage control is triggered whenever the user selects a different page on the control. I use this event to enable or disable the Command Button control named cmdClear. This is the Command Button that clears the List Box on the second page of the MultiPage control. Since this Command Button only applies to the second page of the MultiPage control, it is disabled when the first page of the MultiPage control is selected. The Caption property of the Page object that is returned by the SelectedItem property of the MultiPage control tells the program what page is currently selected.

```
Private Sub cmbWorkbooks_Change()
    Dim ws As Worksheet

    Workbooks(cmbWorkbooks.Value).Activate
    lstWorksheets.Clear
    For Each ws In Worksheets
        lstWorksheets.AddItem ws.Name
        If ActiveSheet.Name = ws.Name Then
            lstWorksheets.Value = ws.Name
        End If
    Next
End Sub
```

The Change() event of the Combo Box control is triggered when the value of the control is changed. This trigger occurs when the user selects a new workbook from the list, and when the Initialize() event of the UserForm object sets the Value property of the control; therefore, the code that adds the names of the worksheets in the active workbook to the List Box control is best placed in this event procedure.

First, a For/Each loop iterates through all Worksheet objects in the Worksheets collection and the AddItem() method of the List Box control adds the name of each worksheet to the list. Because I did not specify a Workbook object in the opening statement of the For/Each loop only the names of the worksheets from the active workbook are added to the List Box. An If/Then decision structure nested in the For/Each loop tests for equality between the name of the active worksheet and the Name property of the Worksheet object currently identified in the loop. When the condition is true, the Value property of the List Box control sets this name to be the selected item in the list.

```
Private Sub lstWorksheets_AfterUpdate()
    Worksheets(lstWorksheets.Value).Select
End Sub
```

The AfterUpdate() event is triggered after data in a control is changed through the user interface; therefore, when the user selects a new worksheet in the List Box control, the Value property of the List Box control is changed and the AfterUpdate() event is triggered. The single line of code in the AfterUpdate() event simply passes the new value of the List Box control to the Worksheets property of the Application object in order to select the new worksheet.

```
Private Sub refStats_DropButtonClick()
    refStats.Text = ""
End Sub

Private Sub refStats_Enter()
    refStats.Text = ""
End Sub
```

Earlier, I suggested that you avoid using the event procedures of the RefEdit control. For the most part, that recommendation remains; however, I have used the DropButtonClick() and Enter() event procedures in this program to clear text from the RefEdit control. These two event procedures trigger when the user selects the RefEdit control (either the drop button or edit area of the control). It's important that the text is removed from the RefEdit control before the user selects another worksheet range; otherwise, the new selection may be inserted into, rather than replace, the previous selection. After testing the program, these two events behaved—at least with these very simple program statements.

```
Private Sub cmdCalcStats_Click()
    Const NUMFORMAT = "#.00"

    On Error Resume Next
    lblCount.Caption = Application.WorksheetFunction.Count _
                        (Range(refStats.Text))
```

```
    lblSum.Caption = Application.WorksheetFunction.Sum _
                         (Range(refStats.Text))
    lblMin.Caption = Application.WorksheetFunction.Min _
                         (Range(refStats.Text))
    lblMax.Caption = Application.WorksheetFunction.Max _
                         (Range(refStats.Text))
    lblMedian.Caption = Application.WorksheetFunction.Median _
                         (Range(refStats.Text))
    lblAvg.Caption = Format(Application.WorksheetFunction.Average _
                         (Range(refStats.Text)), NUMFORMAT)
    lblStanDev.Caption = Format(Application.WorksheetFunction.StDevP _
                         (Range(refStats.Text)), NUMFORMAT)
End Sub
```

In the `Click()` event procedure of the Command Button control named `cmdCalculate`, Excel worksheet functions calculate the statistics that are written to the Label controls. The worksheet functions are passed `Range` objects created from the text entered in the RefEdit control. Note the use of line continuation characters with the excessively long statements and the `Format()` function to format the numerical output for the average and standard deviation such that only two decimal places are shown.

You probably noticed the statement `On Error Resume Next` in the `Click()` event of the Command Button control `cmdCalcStats`. Adding this statement to a procedure prevents the program from crashing when it generates a Run Time error by sending program execution to the next line of code. I will discuss debugging and error handling in the next chapter.

```
Private Sub cmdSummary_Click()
    Dim curRow As Integer

    curRow = lstSummary.ListCount

    lstSummary.AddItem cmbWorkbooks.Value
    lstSummary.List(curRow, 1) = refStats.Text
    lstSummary.List(curRow, 2) = lblCount.Caption
    lstSummary.List(curRow, 3) = lblSum.Caption
    lstSummary.List(curRow, 4) = lblMin.Caption
    lstSummary.List(curRow, 5) = lblMax.Caption
    lstSummary.List(curRow, 6) = lblMedian.Caption
```

```
    lstSummary.List(curRow, 7) = lblAvg.Caption
    lstSummary.List(curRow, 8) = lblStanDev.Caption
End Sub
```

The `AddItem()` method of the List Box and Combo Box controls only adds values to the first column of the control. When the `ColumnCount` property is greater than one, the `List` property must be used to add data to the other columns in the control. You can think of the `List` property as a two-dimensional array with the first index represented by the control's rows and the second index represented by the control's columns; thus, the code in the `Click()` event procedure of the Command Button control named `cmdSummary` makes perfect sense as it uses a row and column index with the `List` property to write the workbook name, selected range, and statistical values to the List Box. The `ListCount` property of the List Box control returns the number of items listed in the control and serves as the row index for setting the value of the `List` property. Index values for the `List` property start at zero, so the final column index representing the ninth column in the control is 8.

```
Private Sub cmdClear_Click()
    lstSummary.Clear
End Sub

Private Sub cmdOk_Click()
    Unload frmSamples
    End
End Sub

Private Sub UserForm_QueryClose(Cancel As Integer, CloseMode As Integer)
    Unload frmSamples
    End
End Sub
```

The last three procedures listed for the program are short and simple. The `Click()` event procedure of the Command Button control named `cmdClear` invokes the `Clear()` method of the List Box control to remove all of its listed items. The `Click()` event of the Command Button control named `cmdOk` and the `QueryClose()` event of the `UserForm` object are both used to close the form. They unload the form from system memory and end the program.

Figures 6.14 and 6.15 show both pages of the Summary Stats dialog form after running the program with some test data.

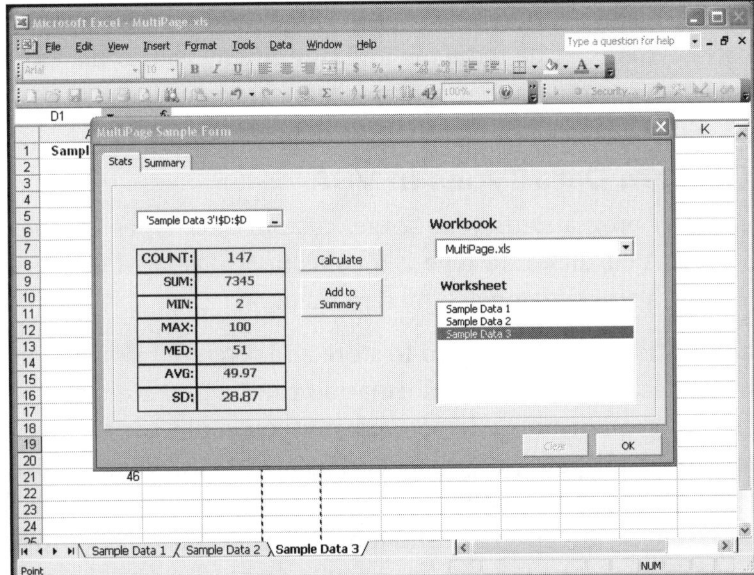

FIGURE 6.14

The Stats page on the Summary Statistics dialog.

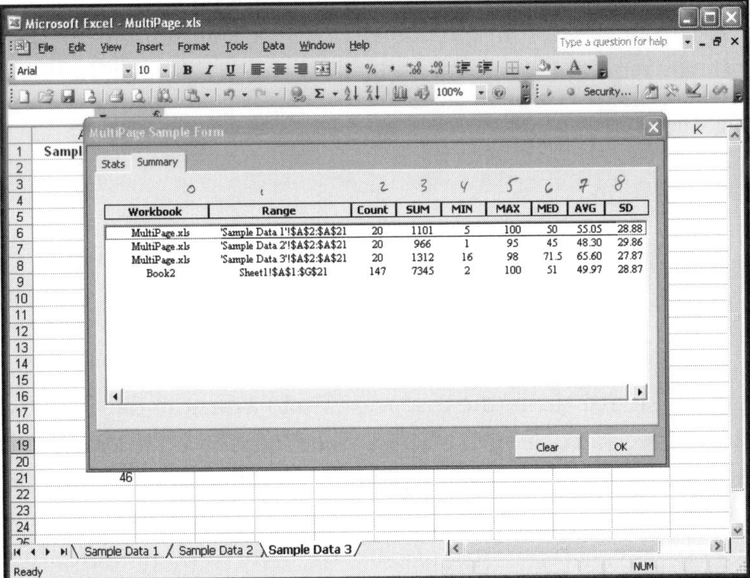

FIGURE 6.15

The Summary page on the Summary Statistics dialog.

DERIVED DATA TYPES IN VBA

You have come far enough along in your VBA programming experience that I can now introduce you to derived data types. The two derived types I will discuss are custom data types and enumerations. Custom data types are powerful data structures that allow you to handle more complicated systems while reducing and simplifying your code. Enumerated types are relatively simple data structures that produce more readable code.

Defining Custom Data Types in VBA

As is the case in any programming language, custom data types in VBA are derived from existing data types. A custom data type is a collection of related elements, possibly of different types, having a single name assigned to them.

Consider an application that is required to store and retrieve information about customers in a database. The database contains information that includes a customer's identification number, name, age, gender, and address. Certainly you could declare five separate variables for each of these items and your program could read/write information from/to the database using the five separate variables; however, this is a cumbersome approach that will end with a program that is longer, less efficient, and more difficult to read—not to mention, more difficult to write.

Of course, the answer to this problem is a custom data type derived from the data types of the original five variables. Custom data types in VBA are defined using the `Type` and `End Type` statements with the required elements declared between as shown in the following example:

```
Public Type CustomerInfo
    ID As Integer
    Name As String * 30
    Age As Integer
    Gender As String * 1
    Address As String * 50
End Type
```

In this example, I assigned the name `CustomerInfo` to a custom data type with five elements: two integer and three fixed length strings (see Chapter 2). A custom data type must be defined in the general declarations section of a module. The `Private` and `Public` keywords define the scope of the definition; private types are available only within the module where the declaration is made, and public types are available in all modules in the project.

It is important to distinguish between a variable declaration and a custom data type definition. The latter only defines the data type and does not create any variables. That is, defining a custom data type does not expose any data; therefore, assigning public scope to the definition of a custom data type is a perfectly reasonable thing to do. Just as you want to be able to declare integer variables throughout your program, you may also want to create variables of a custom type throughout your program.

To declare a variable of type `CustomerInfo` is like any other variable declaration. The following declaration creates a `CustomerInfo` variable named `customer`.

```
Dim customer As CustomerInfo
```

Individual elements for a variable of a custom data type are accessed using the dot (`.`) operator as shown in the following:

```
customer.ID = 1234
customer.Name = "Fred Flintstone"
customer.Gender = "M"
customer.Age = 40
```

Some other things you can do with custom data types include: declaring variable arrays, defining elements as arrays, and passing variables, or elements of variables, to procedures. In the *Blackjack* project, you will see a variable array declared from a custom data type with elements that are also declared as arrays.

Defining Enumerated Types in VBA

Like custom data types, enumerated types contain multiple elements; however, enumerated types are derived only from the integer data type. In an enumerated type, each integer is assigned an identifier called an enumerated constant. This allows you to use symbolic names rather than numbers, making your program more readable.

You must define an enumerated type in the general declarations section of a module. Once an enumeration is defined, you can declare variables, parameters, or a procedure's return value with its type.

Enumerated types are defined with their elements listed between the `Enum` and `End Enum` statements. The following definition reproduces VBA's `VbDayOfWeek` enumerated type.

```
Public Enum Weekdays
    Sunday = 1
    Monday
    Tuesday
    Wednesday
    Thursday
    Friday
    Saturday
End Enum
```

The elements of an enumerated type are initialized to constant values within the Enum statement. You can assign the elements of an enumerated type both positive and negative integers. If no specific assignment is made, then VBA assigns the first element 0, the second element 1, and so on. Alternatively, you can assign a value to the first element and VBA will make subsequent assignments to all other elements by incrementing each value by one. In the Weekdays enumerated type, I assigned 1 to Sunday and made no assignments for the remaining elements; however, VBA automatically assigns the value 2 to Monday, 3 to Tuesday, and so on.

The assigned values in an enumerated type are constants and therefore can't be modified at run time.

Variables of an enumerated type are declared in the usual way using the name of enumerated type. They can be assigned any integer value, but it defeats the purpose of using an enumerated type if you assign the variable anything other than one of the enumerated constants.

```
Dim wkDay As Weekdays
wkDay = Tuesday
```

In effect, you should treat the variable wkDay as a highly constrained integer that can only be assigned values between 1 and 7, even though it can store any value of type integer.

Next, consider the following function called GetDayOfWeek() that is declared public in a standard module. The return type of the GetDayOfWeek() function is that of the previously defined enumerated type Weekdays. When called in a worksheet formula, this function returns an integer value between 1 and 7 depending on the value of the string passed to the function. Certainly, an identical function can be written without using an enumerated type; however, the purpose of an enumerated type is to make your program more readable and the Weekdays enumerated type achieves that goal.

```
Public Function GetDayOfWeek(wkDay As String) As Weekdays
    wkDay = LCase(wkDay)
    Select Case wkDay
        Case Is = "sunday"
            GetDayOfWeek = Sunday
        Case Is = "monday"
            GetDayOfWeek = Monday
        Case Is = "tuesday"
            GetDayOfWeek = Tuesday
```

```
        Case Is = "wednesday"
            GetDayOfWeek = Wednesday
        Case Is = "thursday"
            GetDayOfWeek = Thursday
        Case Is = "friday"
            GetDayOfWeek = Friday
        Case Is = "saturday"
            GetDayOfWeek = Saturday
    End Select
End Function
```

Chapter Project: Blackjack

The *Blackjack* game is a favorite for beginning programmers because it is relatively straightforward programming and can be a lot of fun to customize. The game is saved as Blackjack.xls on the CD-ROM accompanying this book. I added some sound to the game, but it could easily be dressed up with features such as animation or odd rule twists. This particular version uses an Excel UserForm and various ActiveX controls to simulate the card game. There are two players, the user and the computer, and the game follows most of the standard rules of Blackjack. The computer serves as the dealer. The idea is to draw as many as five cards with a total value that comes as close to 21 as possible without going over. Face cards are worth 10 and aces are 1 or 11. All other cards are face value. The game begins with two cards dealt to each player. One of the dealer's cards is dealt face down so it is unknown to the player (i.e., user). The player draws cards until the hand's value exceeds 21 or the player decides to stop. After the player is finished, the dealer takes its turn.

Requirements for Blackjack

Because of my familiarity with the game, the requirement list for the *Blackjack* game was relatively easy to compile. Due to project length, I did not add many of the rules normally found in Blackjack such as doubling down, splitting, insurance for dealer blackjack, and so on. If you are unfamiliar with these features, you can find descriptions in the challenges at the end of the chapter. It would be great practice for you to add some of these features to the game.

The requirements for the *Blackjack* game, as I've defined them, follow:

1. The program interface shall be split between a worksheet and a VBA form with the form simulating the game board and the worksheet storing the results of each hand.
2. The form shall be displayed when the player clicks a Command Button located on the worksheet that stores the results of each hand.

3. The game shall begin with the shuffling of the deck when the player clicks a Command Button located on the form.
4. When the cards are shuffled, a second form shall be momentarily displayed indicating that the cards are being shuffled. The code that simulates the shuffling shall be executed at this time.
5. When the cards are shuffled, the program shall play a sound file suggestive of a deck being shuffled.
6. The game shall simulate shuffling between one and three decks as selected by the player.
7. The program shall run the shuffling simulation whenever the player changes the number of decks used in the game. The default number of decks shall be one.
8. The player shall be able to place a bet on each hand only before the cards are dealt. The player can choose an amount for the bet from a list of choices or enter their own. The default amount for a bet shall be two dollars.
9. Dealing a new hand shall be triggered from the click of a Command Button control.
10. Whenever cards are dealt, the program shall play a sound file suggestive of a card being flipped from the deck.
11. When a new hand is dealt, the program shall simulate dealing two cards each to the dealer and player. The first card dealt to the dealer shall be face down.
12. Cards shall be displayed to the player as images using a set of 53 bitmaps (52 for the deck and one for the deck's back).
13. The player's hand shall be automatically scored by the program and the result displayed after the first two cards are dealt.
14. The player can choose to stand at any time after being dealt the first two cards from the click of a Command Button control.
15. Additional cards shall be drawn by the player (one at a time) from the click of a Command Button control. The player's score shall be updated after each draw.
16. Face cards shall count as 10 and Aces as one or eleven. All other cards shall count as face value.
17. The dealer's and the player's hand shall not exceed five cards.
18. After the player chooses to stand, the program shall display the dealer's hidden card, calculate and display the dealer's score, and simulate the dealer's play based on the following rule: the dealer must draw another card while its score is fifteen or less; otherwise, the dealer must stand.

19. The program shall evaluate the dealer's and player's scores and display a message indicating the winner, or push if it's a tie.
20. The program shall calculate and display the player's balance from the amount of the bet and the result of each hand.
21. The program shall output the result of each hand to the worksheet. The result consists of the dealer's and player's final score, and the player's new balance.
22. The program shall allow the player to quickly clear the results from the worksheet from a click of a Command Button control located on the worksheet.

Designing Blackjack

This project uses many of the tools discussed in previous chapters of this book, including various code structures and common ActiveX controls. In particular, the project includes additional tools discussed in this chapter. These tools include UserForms and their code modules, along with Frame, and Combo Box controls.

The *Blackjack* game runs from a VBA form that contains several ActiveX controls. The form is separated into a Dealer area and a Player area using Frame controls. The dealer frame contains these ActiveX controls:

- Five Image controls for displaying images of cards representing the dealer's hand.
- A Combo Box control (used as a dropdown list) so the player can choose the number of decks (52 cards per deck) used in the game.
- A Label control for displaying the score of the dealer's hand.

The player frame contains these ActiveX controls:

- Five Image controls for displaying images of cards representing the player's hand.
- A Combo Box control for the player to enter or select an amount to bet.
- A Label control for displaying the player's score.
- A Label control for displaying the player's current balance.
- A Command Button control for beginning and selecting a new game.
- A Command Button control for selecting another draw from the deck.

A single Label control displays the result of each hand. Figure 6.16 shows the *Blackjack* form (named `frmTable`) interface with the previously listed ActiveX controls. Table 6.6 lists the settings of a few select properties of the ActiveX controls added to the *Blackjack* form. In most instances, font, color, and size properties were also changed from their default values, but are not listed in the table.

Table 6.6 Select Properties of the Blackjack Form

Object	Property	Value
UserForm	Name	frmTable
...	BackColor	Green
...	Caption	"Blackjack"
...	StartUpPosition	CenterScreen
...	BorderStyle	fmBorderStyleNone
Frames	Name	frmDealer and frmPlayer
...	Caption	"Dealer" and "Player"
...	BorderStyle	fmBorderStyleSingle
Image	Name	imgDlr1 through imgDlr5 and imgPlayer1 through imgPlayer5
...	AutoSize	False
...	BorderStyle	fmBorderStyleSingle
Combo Box	Name	cmbNumDecks
...	Style	fmStyleDropDownList
...	Value/Text	"1"
Combo Box	Name	cmbBet
...	Style	fmStyleDropDownCombo
...	Value/Text	"$2"
Command Button	Name	cmdHit
...	Caption	"Hit"
...	Enabled	False
Command Button	Name	cmdDeal
...	Caption	"Begin"
...	Enabled	True
Labels	Name	lblPlayerScore and lblDealerScore
...	Caption	Empty String
...	BorderStyle	fmBorderStyleNone
...	ForeColor	White
...	TextAlign	fmTextAlignCenter

Table 6.6 Select Properties of the Blackjack Form (continued)

Object	Property	Value
Label	`Name`	`lblResult`
...	`ForeColor`	**Red**
...	`BorderStyle`	`fmBorderStyleNone`
...	`TextAlign`	`fmTextAlignCenter`
Label	`Name`	`lblEarnings`
...	`Caption`	`"$0"`
...	`ForeColor`	**Blue**
...	`BorderStyle`	`fmBorderStyleNone`
...	`TextAlign`	`fmTextAlignCenter`

To set the size of the Image controls, I first set the `AutoSize` property of one Image control to true. Then, I loaded an image of a card into the control at Design Time via its `Picture` property. The Image control automatically adjusts its `Width` and `Height` properties to fit the image exactly. Finally, I removed the image from the Image control by deleting the path from its `Picture` property and set the `Width` and `Height` properties of all other Image controls to match.

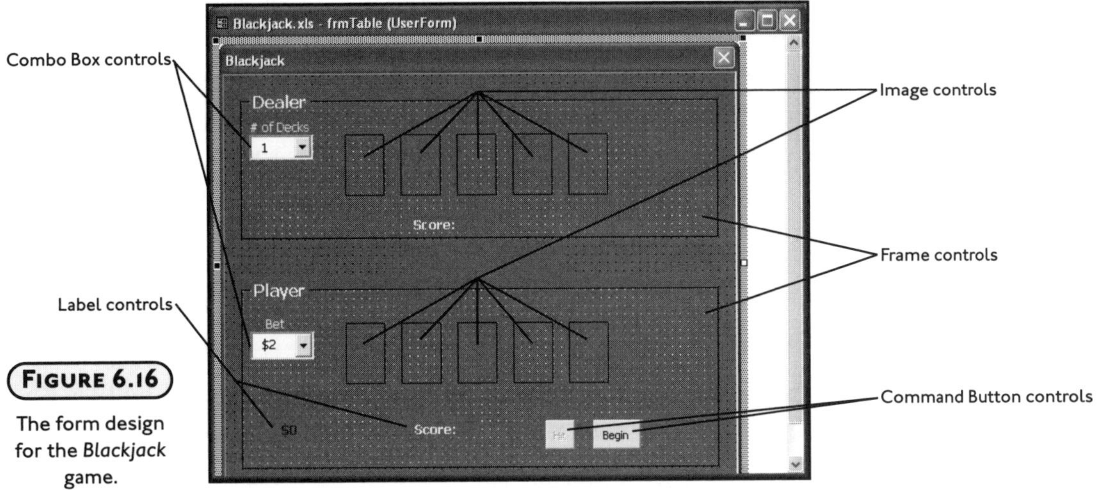

Figure 6.16

The form design for the *Blackjack* game.

In addition to the *Blackjack* form, a second form is added to the project to serve as a splash screen to distract the player as the code that simulates the shuffling of the deck executes. The code doesn't really take that long to run, but the delay in the game is a nice distraction that doesn't require the player to do anything, and it serves to inform the player that the end of the deck was reached and must be reshuffled. Figure 6.17 shows the deck shuffling form with two Label controls.

FIGURE 6.17

The Shuffling form.

The code module for the Shuffling form contains the code for initializing and shuffling the deck.

The last part of the interface for the *Blackjack* game is the worksheet that shows the form and stores the results of each hand. Figure 6.18 shows the worksheet for the *Blackjack* game. It contains two Command Button controls: one for showing the *Blackjack* form, and the second for clearing the content of the first three columns that store the result of each hand.

Program inputs include bitmap image files, Wave Form Audio (.wav) files, the number of decks in the game, an amount to bet on each hand and numerous mouse clicks. The image files represent a deck of cards, and are displayed in the Image controls on the *Blackjack* form. A total of fifty-three images are needed to represent the deck (52 for the faces and 1 for the card back). You can create simple images such as these shown using just about any drawing program (I used MS Paint). These images are loaded into the Image controls when a new hand is dealt and when the player or dealer draws additional cards. The .wav files are played whenever the deck is shuffled or cards are dealt. Combo Box controls on the *Blackjack* form allows the player to choose the number of decks and select an amount to bet on each hand.

Program outputs include the results of each hand and the playing of the .wav sound files. The results of each hand include the player's score, the dealer's score, and the player's new balance to columns A, B, and C of the worksheet, respectively. The sound files are played such that program execution is continuous (i.e., the program does not pause while the sound file plays).

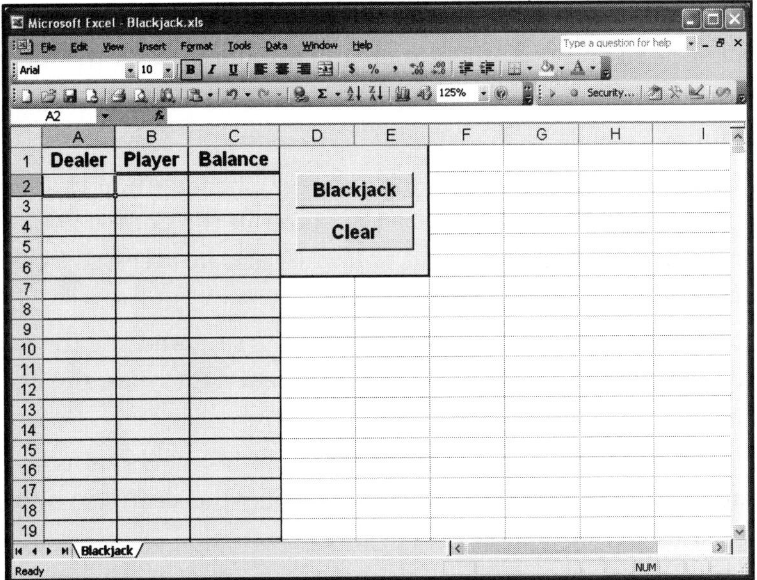

FIGURE 6.18

The *Blackjack* worksheet.

The outline of program execution follows:

- The game starts from the Command Button control on the worksheet labeled Blackjack. This displays the *Blackjack* form. A public procedure in a standard code module is connected to the Command Button (this button is from the Forms toolbar) and its code shows the form.

  The `Initialize()` event procedure of the *Blackjack* form should contain code that initializes its ActiveX controls.

- A single Command Button control on the form begins the game, deals each hand, and offers the player the choice to stand or hit on the current hand.
- The `Caption` property of this Command Button control starts with `"Begin"` and changes between `"Deal"` and `"Stand"` as the game proceeds.

  The `Click()` event of the Command Button control contains code that initializes the game (shuffles the cards and sets the `Caption` property to `"Deal"`) when the `Caption` property is `"Begin"`. If the `Caption` property is `"Deal"`, then the code should clear the *Blackjack* form of card images, and simulate the dealing of two cards each to the dealer and player. If the `Caption` property is `"Stand"`, then the code should display the dealer's hidden card and start the dealer's turn at drawing cards before ending the hand. At a minimum, custom sub procedures should be used to handle shuffling, clearing the form of images, dealing the hand, and drawing the dealer's cards. More custom procedures may be added to handle these tasks when the program is written.

- When the player changes the number of decks, the `Change()` event of the Combo Box control is triggered and the program forces an immediate shuffling of the deck.
- The code that simulates shuffling the deck is entered in the code module for the Shuffling form.

  The deck of cards is simulated using an array. The length of the array depends on the number of decks selected by the player in the Combo Box control. The deck array variable must be global as it must also be accessed by the code in the *Blackjack* form module.

  The array must store the value of each card, its suit, and the file path to the image representing the card. To handle these different data types, the deck should be constructed from a custom data type.

  The `Activate()` event procedure of the `UserForm` object contains the code for initializing and shuffling the deck. It should also play the shuffling .wav file and hide the form after a short delay.

  The deck is shuffled randomly by generating integer random numbers between 0 and the number of elements in the array. Next, two elements in the array (chosen randomly) representing two cards in the deck are swapped. The process of choosing two random numbers and swapping two elements in the deck array is contained within a loop such that it may be repeated. Figure 6.19 illustrates the process of swapping two cards in an array. When this process is repeated many times, the deck is effectively shuffled.

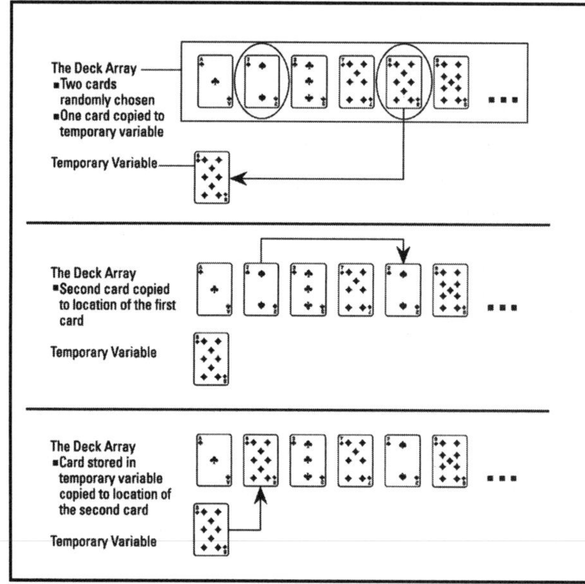

FIGURE 6.19

Swapping two cards in the deck.

- Four cards are dealt (two to the dealer and two to the player) with each new hand. The procedure that handles this task must loop through the image controls to find the correct control for displaying the card image, load the image of the card, store the value of each card for scoring, increment to the next card, play the draw card .wav file, and test if the deck needs shuffling. The first card drawn to the dealer must be displayed face down. Card information is stored in an array, so an array index must increment by one after each draw. The index representing the dealer's face-down card will have to be stored in a variable so its image and value can be called upon when the hand is over.
- A second Command Button control on the *Blackjack* form allows the player to draw more cards. This control must be initially disabled and then enabled when the player is allowed to draw more cards.

  The `Click()` event of this Command Button control should simulate drawing a single card to the player's hand. The code will have to display the card image in the appropriate Image control, play a .wav file, score the player's hand after each draw, and test for a bust.

  The code cannot allow the player to draw more than three cards while the player's score is less than twenty-one.

  If the player busts, then the dealer's cards are shown and score calculated before the hand is ended.

  The program must test if the deck needs reshuffling after each draw.
- After the player stands on a score of twenty-one or less, then the dealer draws cards until its score is sixteen or higher. The procedure that handles this task will have to load the card images, play a .wav file, score the dealer's hand, increment the deck array variable, and test if the deck must be shuffled after each draw. The dealer cannot draw more than three cards.
- A hand ends when either the player busts or the dealer finishes drawing cards. When the hand ends the program must test to see who won or if the hand is a push, then output the result to a Label control. The player's new balance is written to a Label control (win or lose) and the results of the hand are written to the worksheet.
- Results are cleared when the public procedure attached to the Command Button control labeled `"Clear"` (located on the worksheet) is executed.
- The game ends when the player closes the *Blackjack* form. This triggers the `QueryClose()` event of the `UserForm` object where the program removes the forms from system memory and ends the program.
- A majority of the code is entered in the code module for the *Blackjack* form. The remaining code is contained in the code module for the Shuffling form and two standard code modules.

Writing the Code for Blackjack

Since the *Blackjack* form is the major component of the user interface, its code module contains most of the program code. Much of this code is contained in event procedures of the `UserForm` object and the ActiveX controls it contains. Several procedures private to the *Blackjack* form's code module are added to support the tasks required for the game.

Program code for shuffling the cards is contained in the code module for the Shuffling form and public variable declarations and procedures are located in standard modules. I have included two standard modules for *Blackjack*: one for variables and procedures specifically created for the *Blackjack* game, and one for general purpose procedures that can be exported to other projects.

General Purpose Public Procedures

The procedures listed below could be used in just about any VBA project. You have already seen the `PlayWav()` procedure in the *Battlecell* program from Chapter 5. I have added one more procedure called `Delay()`. The entire content of the code module follows:

```
Option Explicit
Private Const DELAY_CODE = 0
Private Const CONTINUE_CODE = 1

Public Declare Function sndPlaySoundA Lib "winmm.dll" _
(ByVal lpszSoundName As String, ByVal uFlags As Long) As Long

Public Sub PlayWav(filePath As String)
    sndPlaySoundA filePath, CONTINUE_CODE
End Sub

Public Sub Delay(curTime As Single, pauseTime As Single)
    Do While Timer < pauseTime + curTime
        DoEvents
    Loop
End Sub
```

This module contains two short and simple public procedures, two module level constant declarations, and one API declaration for playing .wav sound files. The `PlayWav()` sub procedure is simply one line of code that calls the `sndPlaySoundA()` function in the winmm.dll system file. The constants (`DELAY_CODE` and `CONTINUE_CODE`) clarify the action of the API function call. In this case, program execution continues while the sound file is played. The `PlayWav()` procedure is called to play sound files when the program shuffles or deals cards.

The Delay() sub procedure is called to delay the execution of the *Blackjack* program. The delay is needed when a new hand is dealt and when the dealer draws more cards to give the game an appearance of dealing one card at a time. It is also called for an aesthetic affect when the Shuffling form is displayed because it only takes the program a fraction of a second (processor dependent) to effectively shuffle the cards. The delay is caused by a Do-Loop that executes until a specified number of seconds (indicated by the variable pauseTime) has passed. The VBA function DoEvents() yields the computer's processor so that the operating system can process other events. This allows the player to make other selections while the loop executes.

Public Procedures and Variables for the Blackjack Program

The second standard module included with the *Blackjack* program includes the variables and procedures specifically related to the *Blackjack* game and are not transferable to other applications.

The module uses two public enumerations named CardDeck and CardSuits to define related sets of constants that describe a deck of cards. The CardDeck enumeration defines the number of cards in a single deck, the number of cards in a suit, and the number of suits in a deck. The CardSuits enumeration defines integer constants that will be used later to initialize a deck of cards by suit. The suits are used in the filenames of the images so a card's suit must be known in order to load the correct image. The constants defined in these enumerations have public scope so they are available in all code modules. Since they are constants, and therefore cannot be changed elsewhere in the program, I don't have to worry about data contamination.

Next, a custom data type for the deck of cards is defined with two elements: value and filename. The integer element value represents the face value of a card. The string element filename stores the name of the image file associated with a card. All three elements of the custom data type are arrays with fifty-two elements (the number of cards in a single deck). The custom data type is named Deck and a public dynamic array variable of type Deck is declared and named theDeck. The array theDeck must be dynamic because its length will vary with the number of decks selected by the player.

```
Option Explicit

Public Enum CardSuits
    bjSpades = 1
    bjDiamonds = 2
    bjClubs = 3
    bjHearts = 4
End Enum
```

```
Public Enum CardDeck
    bjcardsindeck = 52
    bjCardsInSuit = 13
    bjNumSuits = 4
End Enum

Type Deck
    value(bjcardsindeck - 1) As Integer
    filename(bjcardsindeck - 1) As String
End Type

Public theDeck() As Deck

Public Sub Blackjack()
    frmTable.Show vbModal
End Sub

Public Sub ClearResults()
    Dim lastRow As Integer

    lastRow = ActiveSheet.UsedRange.Rows.Count
    Range("A2:C" & lastRow).ClearContents
End Sub
```

The two public procedures `Blackjack()` and `ClearResults()` are short and simple. Each procedure is attached to a Command Button control on the worksheet. The Command Button controls provide the player with an easy interface to show the *Blackjack* form and clear the results from the worksheet. The form is shown modally for no particular reason. If you prefer, you can certainly change it to a modeless form. The worksheet is cleared by calling the `ClearContents()` method of the `Range` object after determining the last used row in the worksheet via the `UsedRange` property of the `Worksheet` object. The `UsedRange` property returns a `Range` object representing the used range on the worksheet. The `Rows` property returns another `Range` object representing the rows in the range returned from the `UsedRange` property. Finally, the `Count` property returns an integer representing the number of rows in the range.

Shuffling the Deck for the Blackjack Program

The code module for the Shuffling form (named `frmShuffle`) contains the part of the *Blackjack* program that simulates the shuffling of the deck. The `Activate()` event procedure of the `UserForm` object is triggered when the form's `Show()` method is executed from elsewhere in the program. The custom sub procedures `InitDeck()` and `ShuffleDeck()` are called from the `Activate()` event procedure in order to initialize and shuffle the deck. A sound file simulating a deck being shuffled is played while program execution is delayed for one and a half seconds. The program is delayed so that the player can actually see the form before it is hidden again with the form's `Hide()` method.

```
Option Explicit

Private Sub UserForm_Activate()
     Const DELAY_TIME = 1.5
    '-----------------------
    'Initialize and shuffle the deck(s) values.
    '-----------------------
    InitDeck
    ShuffleDeck

    '--------------------------
    'Play shuffle sound while program delays long
    'enough to display the form.
    '--------------------------
    PlayWav (ActiveWorkbook.Path & "\Sounds\shuffle.wav")
    Delay Timer, DELAY_TIME
    frmShuffle.Hide
End Sub
```

The `InitDeck()` sub procedure first re-dimensions the size of the global `Deck` array variable `theDeck` to the number of decks selected in the Combo Box control (named `cmbNumDecks`) on the *Blackjack* form. Next, the custom array is filled with values, and filenames representing each card in a deck using nested `For/Next` loops. Note the use of array indices for the custom data type variable `theDeck` and each of its elements: `value` and `filename` because each deck has fifty-two cards.

For each deck, the card values are sequentially filled from one to ten, where aces are one, face cards are ten, and all other cards are face-value. Each deck is also filled with the strings for the filenames of the card images which are built using the enumerations, the `GetSuitLabel()` function procedure, and the card number (ranges from one to thirteen). Please note the use of line continuation characters in some of the longer program statements.

```
Private Sub InitDeck()
    Dim curCard As Integer, curSuit As Integer, curDeck   As Integer
    Dim numDecks As Integer, cNum As Integer
```

```
    '-----------------------------------
    'Initialize N decks with values 1-10. Fours suits per deck.
    'Ace=1, Jack=King=Queen=10
    '-----------------------------------
    numDecks = frmTable.cmbNumDecks.value - 1
    ReDim theDeck(numDecks)
    For curDeck = 0 To numDecks
        For curSuit = 1 To bjNumSuits
            For curCard = 0 To bjCardsInSuit - 1
                cNum = curCard + 1
                If (curCard + 1) < 10 Then
                    theDeck(curDeck).value(curCard + bjCardsInSuit * _
                         (curSuit - 1)) = curCard + 1
                Else
                    theDeck(curDeck).value(curCard + bjCardsInSuit * _
                         (curSuit - 1)) = 10
                End If

                theDeck(curDeck).filename(curCard + bjCardsInSuit * _
                         (curSuit - 1)) = cNum & GetSuitLabel(curSuit)
            Next curCard
        Next curSuit
    Next curDeck
End Sub

Private Function GetSuitLabel(suit As Integer) As String
    Select Case suit
        Case Is =bjSpades
            GetSuitLabel = "Spades"
        Case Is =bjDiamonds
            GetSuitLabel = "Diamonds"
        Case Is =bjClubs
            GetSuitLabel = "Clubs"
        Case Is =bjHearts
            GetSuitLabel = "Hearts"
    End Select
End Function
```

The `ShuffleDeck()` sub procedure performs five-hundred swaps per deck of two randomly selected cards in the deck array variable `theDeck` in order to effectively shuffle the deck. You can change the number of swaps at Design Time by simply changing the value of the `NUMSWAPS` constant. A series of variables serve as temporary storage locations for all the elements that describe a card (the index value for the deck, the value of the card, and the filename of the image representing the card) so two cards can be swapped as illustrated in Figure 6.19.

```
Private Sub ShuffleDeck()
    Dim ranCard1 As Integer, ranCard2 As Integer
    Dim ranDeck As Integer
    Dim tempCard As Integer, tempSuit As Integer
    Dim tempName As String
    Dim curSwap As Integer, numDecks As Integer
    Const NUMSWAPS = 500

    Randomize
    numDecks = frmTable.cmbNumDecks.value
    '-------------------------------
    'Shuffle the deck by swapping two cards in the array.
    '-------------------------------
    For curSwap = 0 To NUMSWAPS * numDecks
        ranCard1 = Int(Rnd * bjcardsindeck)
        ranCard2 = Int(Rnd * bjcardsindeck)
        ranDeck = Int(Rnd * numDecks)
        tempCard = theDeck(ranDeck).value(ranCard1)
        tempName = theDeck(ranDeck).filename(ranCard1)
        theDeck(ranDeck).value(ranCard1) = _
                        theDeck(ranDeck).value(ranCard2)

        theDeck(ranDeck).filename(ranCard1) = _
                        theDeck(ranDeck).filename(ranCard2)

        theDeck(ranDeck).value(ranCard2) = tempCard
        theDeck(ranDeck).filename(ranCard2) = tempName
    Next curSwap
End Sub
```

The Shuffling form only appears for a second or two, but it serves a very important purpose. First, it informs the player that the marker for the end of the deck was reached and the deck is being reshuffled. Second, the code contained within its code module effectively shuffles the array representing the deck(s).

Playing a Hand of Blackjack

Now it is time to get to the meat of the program which is contained in the *Blackjack* form code module. Module level variable declarations define a host of integers required by the program. Most of the names are self-explanatory. These variables are used in multiple procedures in the form module and store the following values: the number of cards drawn by the player and dealer (`numPlayerHits` and `numDlrHits`), the current deck and the current location in the deck (`curDeck` and `curCard`) from which the dealer draws the next card, the location and image for the dealer's face-down card (`hiddenCard`, `hiddenDeck`, `hiddenPic`), the value of the cards in the player's and dealer's hands (`scores`), and the dealing order for the first four cards dealt for a new hand (`dealOrder`).

```
Option Explicit

Private numPlayerHits As Integer
Private numDlrHits As Integer
Private curCard As Integer        'Track the location in the deck.
Private curDeck As Integer        'Track the location in the deck if there is more
                                  than one deck.
Private hiddenCard As Integer     'Temporary storage of the face-down card.
Private hiddenDeck As Integer
Private hiddenPic As Image
Private scores(4, 1) As Integer  'Track values of cards dealt to dealer and player.
Private dealOrder As Variant      'Set the order of Image controls for initial dealing
                                  of four cards.

Private Const PLAYER = 1          'Use to reference array index for scores.
Private Const DEALER = 0
Private Const DEALERSTAND = 16   'Dealer stands on this value or higher.
```

The `Activate()` event of the `UserForm` object initializes the variant array `dealOrder`. This array is a list of strings that match the `Name` property of four Image controls. The order of the strings is set to the order in which the initial four cards are dealt to the dealer and player for a new hand. I created this array so that I could simulate the dealing of the four cards using a loop (see `DealCards()` sub procedure); otherwise, a lot of repetitive code would be needed.

The `InitForm()` sub procedure is called to initialize some of the ActiveX controls on the form—namely, the Label and Combo Box controls.

```
Private Sub UserForm_Activate()
    dealOrder = Array("imgDlr1", "imgPlayer1", "imgDlr2", "imgPlayer2")
    InitForm
End Sub

Private Sub InitForm()
    Dim I As Integer

    '------------
    'Clear label controls.
    '------------
    lblResult.Caption = ""
    lblDlrScore.Caption = "0"
    lblPlyrScore.Caption = "0"

    '--------------------------------
    'Set values to be displayed in dropdown lists for the
    'number of decks, and the value of a bet.
    '--------------------------------
    cmbNumDecks.Clear
    cmbNumDecks.AddItem ("1")
    cmbNumDecks.AddItem ("2")
    cmbNumDecks.AddItem ("3")
    cmbBet.Clear
    cmbBet.AddItem ("$2")
    cmbBet.AddItem ("$5")
    cmbBet.AddItem ("$10")
    cmbBet.AddItem ("$25")
    cmbBet.AddItem ("$50")
    cmbBet.AddItem ("$100")
End Sub
```

The `Change()` event procedure of the `cmbNumDecks` Combo Box is triggered when the user changes its displayed value. This forces an immediate reshuffling of the deck with a call to the `NeedShuffle()` procedure that will show the Shuffling form and trigger its previously listed code. The `Caption` property of the Command Button control is set to `"Deal"` in case the player changes the number of decks immediately after the form is loaded and shown (i.e., when the Caption property reads "Begin").

The NeedShuffle() procedure accepts one optional Boolean argument that, when used, forces a reshuffling of the deck. If it is not forced, then the deck will still be shuffled if the current card location in the deck has reached the marker specified by the constant LASTCARD. If neither condition is met, then program execution exits the procedure without shuffling the deck. Remember, this procedure will have to be called after each card is dealt; so in most instances, the NeedShuffle() procedure will not cause the deck to be shuffled.

```
Private Sub cmbNumDecks_Change()
    NeedShuffle True
    cmdDeal.Caption = "Deal"
End Sub
Private Sub NeedShuffle(Optional forceShuffle As Boolean)
    Public Const LASTCARD = 10
    '--------------------------------
    'Test for the number of cards already played to
    'see if the deck needs reshuffling. Must increment the deck
    'and reset card number when using multiple decks.
    '--------------------------------
    If (curCard + (curDeck * 51) >= _
            Val(cmbNumDecks.value) * (bjcardsindeck - 1) - LASTCARD) _
            Or forceShuffle Then
        frmShuffle.Show
        curCard = 0     'Reset deck location after reshuffling.
        curDeck = 0
    ElseIf curCard > 51 Then
        curCard = 0
        curDeck = curDeck + 1
    End If
End Sub
```

The Click() event of the Command Button control cmdDeal is triggered from the *Blackjack* form, but the action taken depends on the value of its Caption property. If the Caption property is set to "Begin", then the deck is shuffled and the Caption property is reset to "Deal". The Caption property will only read "Deal" when the program is set to begin a new hand; therefore, when the Caption property is set to "Deal", the game table must be cleared with a call to the ClearBoard() sub procedure before a new hand is dealt by calling the DealCards() sub procedure.

The last possible value of the Caption property is "Stand". In this case, the player has decided to stand on the current score of his or her hand and it is the dealer's turn to draw. First, the dealer's hidden card is displayed and score calculated with a call to the CalcScore() procedure. The simulation of the dealer's turn to draw is handled by the DealerDraw() procedure. After the dealer's turn is over and program execution returns to the Click() event, the game is ended with a call to GameOver().

```
Private Sub cmdDeal_Click()
    If cmdDeal.Caption = "Begin" Then
        frmShuffle.Show
        cmdDeal.Caption = "Deal"
    ElseIf cmdDeal.Caption = "Deal" Then
        ClearBoard
        DealCards
    Else                                        'Player decides to stand.
        cmdHit.Enabled = False
        imgDlr1.Picture = hiddenPic.Picture
        CalcScore DEALER
        DealerDraw
        GameOver
    End If
End Sub
```

The ClearBoard() sub procedure serves to reset variables and ActiveX controls on the form. The images of the cards from the Image controls are removed by setting their Picture property with the LoadPicture() method while passing it an empty string. The For/Each loop iterates through all ActiveX controls on the form, identifying those controls whose name begins with "img" in order to find the Image controls. Since all ActiveX controls on the form are part of a Controls collection object, I use a For/Each loop to iterate through the controls on the *Blackjack* form (named frmTable); however, I need the decision structure to identify the first three letters in the name of each control because there is no collection object for control types, only for all controls on the form.

The dealer's and player's hands are stored in the two-dimensional variable array called scores. The array's size is five rows by two columns, where the first column is reserved for the dealer's hand, and the second column for the player's hand. The value of each card dealt to both players is stored in this array.

```
Private Sub ClearBoard()
    Dim I As Integer
    Dim imgCtrl As Control
```

```
    '-----------------------
    'Clear images of card from image controls.
    '-----------------------
    For Each imgCtrl In frmTable.Controls
        If Left(imgCtrl.Name, 3) = "img" Then
            imgCtrl.Picture = LoadPicture("")
        End If
    Next

    '-----------------
    'Reset variables and controls.
    '-----------------
    numPlayerHits = 0
    numDlrHits = 0
    lblDlrScore.Caption = "0"
    lblResult.Caption = ""
    For I = 0 To 4
        scores(I, DEALER) = 0
        scores(I, PLAYER) = 0
    Next I
    cmbBet.Enabled = False
End Sub
```

The `DealCards()` sub procedure handles the initial dealing of the four cards required to start a new hand. Since most of the required actions for each card dealt are the same, I wanted to handle this task with a loop; however, it is a bit more difficult to loop through four specific Image controls from a group of ten. This is why I declared the variant variable array named `dealOrder`—to identify these four Image controls. I also was careful to add the Image controls to the form in the same order specified in the `dealOrder` array (see `Activate()` event procedure). This way, I ensure that the `For/Each` loop iterates through the four Image controls in the desired order. (That is, once the first Image control listed in the `dealOrder` array is found.)

Once a proper Image control is identified, the program loads the card image into the Image control, the value of the card is stored in the variable array `scores`, the .wav file is played, and the program tests if the deck must be shuffled with a call to the `NeedShuffle()` procedure.

The first card is dealt face down to the dealer (represented by the image file Back.bmp); however, the program must remember the location of this card in the deck using the module level variables `hiddenCard` and `hiddenDeck` because it will be needed when the hand ends—at which time the program must display the card and calculate the dealer's score. The card image is also stored for later use by loading it into the `Picture` property of the image object variable `hiddenPic` with the `LoadPicture()` method. This does not display the image anywhere on the form because `hiddenPic` is an object variable, not an ActiveX control. This effectively stores the image in the computer's memory until it is needed. Alternatively, you could add another Image control to the form, set its `Visible` property to false, and load the image for the face-down card into its `Picture` property until it is needed. Figure 6.20 shows an example of the *Blackjack* form after the initial four cards of a hand are dealt.

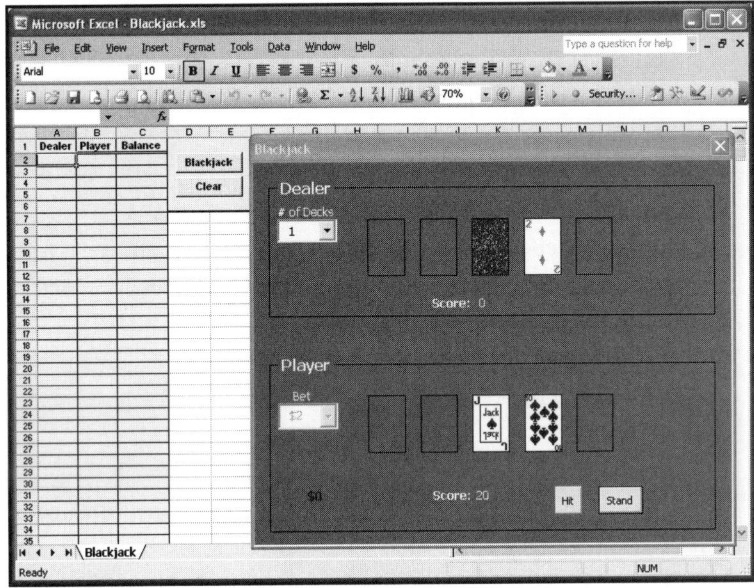

FIGURE 6.20

Starting a new hand of *Blackjack*.

```
Private Sub DealCards()
'--------------------------------
'Deals four cards; two each to the player and dealer.
'--------------------------------
    Dim fileCards As String
    Dim fileSounds As String
    Dim imgCtrl As Control
    Dim I As Integer

    fileCards = ActiveWorkbook.Path & "\Cards\"
    fileSounds = ActiveWorkbook.Path & "\Sounds\"
```

```
    '--------------------------------------------------------
    'Loop through the controls to find next image control. Load
    'the image of the card, store the value of the card for scoring,
    'increment to the next card, play the draw sound, and test if
    'the deck needs reshuffling.
    '--------------------------------------------------------
For Each imgCtrl In frmTable.Controls
        If I >= 4 Then Exit For    'Already found the 4 Image controls.
        If imgCtrl.Name = dealOrder(I) Then
            If (I = 0) Then
                imgCtrl.Picture = LoadPicture(fileCards & "Back.bmp")
                hiddenCard = curCard
                hiddenDeck = curDeck
                Set hiddenPic = New Image
                hiddenPic.Picture = LoadPicture(fileCards & _
                        theDeck(hiddenDeck).filename(hiddenCard) & ".bmp")
                scores(0, DEALER) = theDeck(curDeck).value(curCard)
            Else
                imgCtrl.Picture = LoadPicture(fileCards & _
                        theDeck(curDeck).filename(curCard) & ".bmp")
            End If
            If (I = 1) Then
                scores(0, PLAYER) = theDeck(curDeck).value(curCard)
            ElseIf (I = 2) Then
                scores(1, DEALER) = theDeck(curDeck).value(curCard)
            Else
                scores(1, PLAYER) = theDeck(curDeck).value(curCard)
            End If
            curCard = curCard + 1
            PlayWav (fileSounds & "\draw.wav")
            Delay Timer, 0.5
            NeedShuffle
            I = I + 1
        End If
    Next

    '--------------------
    'Score the player's hand.
    '--------------------
```

```
    CalcScore PLAYER
    cmdDeal.Caption = "Stand"
    cmdHit.Enabled = True
End Sub
```

The *Blackjack* program calculates the dealer's and player's score with the variable array scores and the `CalcScore()` sub procedure. A `For/Next` loop iterates through the scores array, identifying which player's score to sum using the `iPlayer` argument, and totals the values of each card in a hand. The number of Aces in a hand are counted and scored as eleven; unless the total score exceeds twenty-one, in which case the Aces are scored as one.

```
Private Sub CalcScore(iPlayer As Integer)
'-----------------------------
'Calculates the player's and dealer's score. Pass 0
'for the dealer and 1 for the player.
'-----------------------------
    Dim I As Integer
    Dim numAces As Integer
    Dim score As Integer
    Const MAXHANDSIZE = 5

    '-----------------------------
    'Calculates the score. Aces count one or eleven.
    '-----------------------------
    For I = 0 To MAXHANDSIZE - 1
        score = score + scores(I, iPlayer)
        If scores(I, iPlayer) = 1 Then numAces = numAces + 1
    Next I
    If (numAces > 0) Then
        score = score + 10 * numAces
        For I = 1 To numAces
            If (score > 21) Then score = score - 10
        Next I
    End If
    If (iPlayer = 0) Then
        lblDlrScore.Caption = score
    Else
        lblPlyrScore.Caption = score
    End If
End Sub
```

The Command Button control `cmdHit` is enabled after the first four cards of a new hand are dealt (see Figure 6.20). Its `Click()` event is triggered each time the player decides (and is allowed) to draw another card. This procedure loads a card image into the proper Image control and records the value of the card before playing the .wav file that sounds like a card being flipped. Next, the score of the player's hand is calculated using `CalcScore()`.

The module variable `numPlayerHits` was incremented by one early in the procedure. If the value of this variable reaches three, then the Command Button control `cmdHit` is disabled and this `Click()` event procedure cannot be triggered. The same is true if the player busts (score exceeds twenty-one). The screen shot in Figure 6.21 shows a hand where the player busted after drawing two cards (the two of hearts and king of clubs). Since the player busted, the dealer did not have to draw any more cards despite having a score less than sixteen.

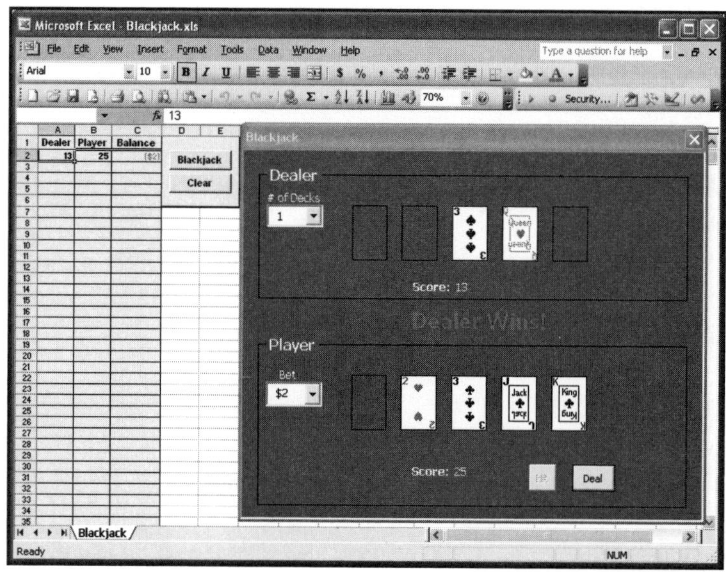

FIGURE 6.21

A player bust in a hand of *Blackjack*.

The player's turn at drawing cards is over when they bust, draw three cards (giving them a total of five cards), or choose to stand on their current hand. The action taken when the player stands is handled in the `Click()` event procedure of the Command Button control named `cmdDeal`. If the player busts, the hand is immediately ended by displaying the dealer's hidden card, calculating its score, and calling the `GameOver()` sub procedure. If the player manages to draw three cards without busting, then the player is forced to stand on his or her hand because it is the only enabled Command Button on the form.

As always, when a card is dealt, the `NeedShuffle()` procedure is called to test if the deck needs to be shuffled.

```
Private Sub cmdHit_Click()
'------------------------
'Player chooses to draw another card.
'------------------------
    Dim fileCards As String

    fileCards = ActiveWorkbook.Path & "\Cards\"

    '------------------------
    'Load the card image and record the score.
    '------------------------
    numPlayerHits = numPlayerHits + 1
    If (numPlayerHits = 1) Then imgPlayer3.Picture = _
        LoadPicture(fileCards & theDeck(curDeck).filename(curCard) & ".bmp")
    If (numPlayerHits = 2) Then imgPlayer4.Picture = _
        LoadPicture(fileCards & theDeck(curDeck).filename(curCard) & ".bmp")
    If (numPlayerHits = 3) Then imgPlayer5.Picture = _
        LoadPicture(fileCards & theDeck(curDeck).filename(curCard) & ".bmp")
    scores(numPlayerHits + 1, PLAYER) = theDeck(curDeck).value(curCard)
    PlayWav (ActiveWorkbook.Path & "\Sounds\draw.wav")

    '------------------------------------
    'Calculate player's score, increment deck to next card, and
    'test if the player has reached maximum number of allowed hits.
    '------------------------------------
    CalcScore PLAYER
    curCard = curCard + 1
    If numPlayerHits > 2 Then
        cmdHit.Enabled = False
        CalcScore DEALER
    End If
    NeedShuffle

    '------------------------------
    'If player busts, show dealer's hand and end the game.
    '------------------------------
    If lblPlyrScore.Caption > 21 Then
        imgDlr1.Picture = hiddenPic.Picture
```

```
        CalcScore DEALER
        GameOver
    End If
End Sub
```

After the player has selected to stand on his or her current hand, the `DealerDraw()` procedure is called in order to simulate the dealer's turn at drawing additional cards. This procedure uses a loop to draw up to three cards for the dealer as long as the dealer's score is less than sixteen. When a card is drawn, the card's image is loaded into the appropriate Image control, the card's value is stored, the dealer's score calculated, and the deck is tested to see if it needs shuffling.

```
Private Sub DealerDraw()
'------------------------------
'Call if dealer needs hits. Dealer must stand on
'16 or higher and hit with <16.
'------------------------------
    Dim fileCards As String

    fileCards = ActiveWorkbook.Path & "\Cards\"

    '-----------------------------------
    'Dealer takes hits while score is <16 to a max of five cards.
    '-----------------------------------
    Do While (lblDlrScore.Caption < DEALERSTAND)
        If (numDlrHits = 3) Then Exit Sub
        numDlrHits = numDlrHits + 1
        If (numDlrHits = 1) Then imgDlr3.Picture = LoadPicture( _
                fileCards & theDeck(curDeck).filename(curCard) & ".bmp")
        If (numDlrHits = 2) Then imgDlr4.Picture = LoadPicture( _
                fileCards & theDeck(curDeck).filename(curCard) & ".bmp")
        If (numDlrHits = 3) Then imgDlr5.Picture = LoadPicture( _
                fileCards & theDeck(curDeck).filename(curCard) & ".bmp")

        PlayWav (ActiveWorkbook.Path & "\Sounds\draw.wav")
        Delay Timer, 0.5

        scores(numDlrHits + 1, DEALER) = theDeck(curDeck).value(curCard)
        CalcScore DEALER
```

```
        curCard = curCard + 1
        NeedShuffle
    Loop
End Sub
```

A hand is over when the player busts or the dealer finishes drawing cards. In both cases, the `GameOver()` sub procedure is called to determine the winner, update the player's balance based on how much the player bet, and output the results to the form and the worksheet (calls `WorksheetOutput()` procedure) before resetting the ActiveX controls.

Figure 6.22 shows the *Blackjack* form after a hand won by the player when the dealer busted drawing the nine of diamonds.

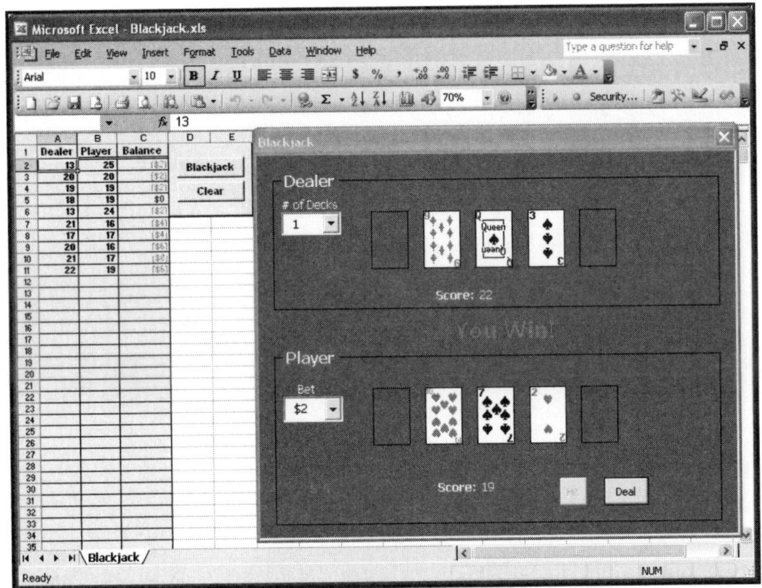

FIGURE 6.22

A dealer bust in a hand of *Blackjack*.

```
Private Sub GameOver()
'---------------------------
'Display results when the hand is finished.
'---------------------------
    Dim earningsLength As Integer
    Dim betLength As Integer
    Dim pScore As Integer, dScore As Integer
```

```
earningsLength = Len(lblEarnings.Caption)
betLength = Len(cmbBet.value)
pScore = lblPlyrScore.Caption
dScore = lblDlrScore.Caption

'-------------
'Dealer and player push.
'-------------
If (dScore = pScore) Then
    lblResult.Caption = "Push"
End If

'----------------------------
'Player wins if their score is higher than dealer's
'without busting or if dealer busts.
'----------------------------
If ((Val(dScore) < Val(pScore)) And (Val(pScore) < 22)) _
            Or ((Val(pScore) < 22) And (Val(dScore) > 21)) Then
    lblResult.Caption = "You Win!"
    lblEarnings.Caption = "$" & Val(Right(lblEarnings.Caption, _
        earningsLength - 1)) + Val(Right(cmbBet.value, betLength - 1))
End If

'----------------------------
'Dealer wins if their score is higher than player's
'without busting or if player busts.
'----------------------------
If ((Val(dScore) > Val(pScore)) And (Val(dScore) < 22) _
            Or (Val(dScore) < 22) And (Val(pScore) > 21)) Then
    lblResult.Caption = "Dealer Wins!"
    lblEarnings.Caption = "$" & Val(Right(lblEarnings.Caption, _
        earningsLength - 1)) - Val(Right(cmbBet.value, betLength - 1))
End If

'---------------
'Calculate player's balance.
'---------------
earningsLength = Len(lblEarnings.Caption)
```

```
    If Val(Right(lblEarnings.Caption, earningsLength - 1)) < 0 Then
        lblEarnings.ForeColor = RGB(255, 0, 0)
    Else
        lblEarnings.ForeColor = RGB(0, 0, 150)
    End If

    WorksheetOutput

    cmdHit.Enabled = False
    cmdDeal.Caption = "Deal"
    cmbBet.Enabled = True
End Sub
```

The last requirement of the program is to output the results of the hand to the worksheet. Most of this code should be quite familiar to you as it simply copies the `Caption` property of the Label controls to cells on the worksheet and formats the winning score in bold. The new technique here is using the `Find()` method of the `Range` object to locate the next empty cell in column A of the worksheet. The `Find()` method takes several arguments but the `What` argument is the only one required. The `What` argument identifies the string you are looking for in the specified range (in this case, `A:A`). The `After` argument is optional, but I use it here to tell the `Find()` method to start looking after cell A1.

The `Find()` method returns a `Range` object. I used the `Row` property of the `Range` object returned by the `Find()` method in order to return the index of the first empty row in column A to the variable `nextRow`. Next, I use the value stored in the `nextRow` variable to identify where to write the results of the hand.

```
Private Sub WorksheetOutput()
'----------------------------
'Output results of the hand to the worksheet.
'----------------------------
    Dim nextRow As Integer

    '---------------------------------------
    'Find first empty row in column A and write results to that row.
    '---------------------------------------
    nextRow = Range("A:A").Find(What:="", After:=Range("A1")).Row
    Range("A" & nextRow).value = lblDlrScore.Caption
    Range("B" & nextRow).value = lblPlyrScore.Caption
    Range("C" & nextRow).value = lblEarnings.Caption
```

```
    '-------------------------
    'Put the winner in bold font. Color the player's
    'balance to match the form.
    '-------------------------
    If lblResult.Caption = "Dealer Wins!" Then
        Range("A" & nextRow).Font.Bold = True
    ElseIf lblResult.Caption = "You Win!" Then
        Range("B" & nextRow).Font.Bold = True
    End If
    Range("C" & nextRow).Font.Color = lblEarnings.ForeColor
End Sub
```

Finally, the `QueryClose()` event of the `UserForm` object unloads the forms from the computer's memory before ending the program. The `QueryClose()` event is triggered when the player closes the form.

```
Private Sub UserForm_QueryClose(Cancel As Integer, CloseMode As Integer)
    Unload frmTable
    Unload frmShuffle
    End
End Sub
```

That's it for the *Blackjack* program. Take the code, play with it, change it, add to it, learn from it, and enjoy. If you have trouble, then focus on just a small piece of the program until you figure it out before moving on to the next problem.

Chapter Summary

This chapter introduced VBA UserForms and a few new ActiveX controls. Specifically, you learned how to add UserForms to a VBA project and show them in a program. This chapter discussed adding ActiveX controls to a form, including the Frame, Scroll Bar, Option Button, RefEdit, MultiPage, Combo Box, and List Box controls and how to use the code window of a form. You also learned how to create custom data types that are derived from existing VBA data types. Finally, you learned how to use modal and modeless UserForms.

Challenges

1. Add a modeless form (set the `ShowModal` property of the `UserForm` object) to a VBA project then add two Command Button controls to a worksheet. Using their `Click()` event procedures, use one Command Button control to show the form, and the other Command Button control to hide the form.
2. Add a RefEdit control and a Command Button control to the form created in the previous challenge. The RefEdit control is for the user to display a selected range. Then add code to the Command Button control such that it changes the format of the selected range by increasing its font size to 24 and its color to green (`vbGreen` or `RGB(0,255,0)`). You must show the form as modal or your program may lock up.
3. Create a form that contains a List Box control. Use the `AddItem()` method of the List Box control to display the contents of column A of the active worksheet. Hint: Use a `For/Each` to iterate through the cells in column A in the `Activate()` event procedure of the `UserForm` object.
4. Add a Command Button control to the form from the previous challenge and change the `MultiSelect` property of the List Box control to allow multiple selections. Add code to the `Click()` event procedure of the Command Button control that will copy the selected values of the List Box control to column B of the worksheet. Hint: Use the `Selected` property of the List Box control to return an array of Boolean values that can be used to determine which items are displayed in the control and have been selected by the user. Use the `ListCount` and `List` properties of the List Box control along with a `For/Next` loop to return the selected values of the List Box control if its `Selected` property is true.
5. Alter the *Blackjack* game to pay double the bet if the player is dealt a blackjack (one Ace and one card of value 10).
6. Alter the *Blackjack* game to immediately end if the player or dealer is dealt blackjack. Whoever has the blackjack is declared the winner and the other player is not allowed to draw. If both players are dealt blackjack, then it's a push.
7. Doubling down is the process of doubling your bet after the first two cards are dealt. If you choose to double down, then you can only draw one more card. Add this feature to the *Blackjack* game.
8. Splitting is the process of splitting your first two cards into two separate hands. Your bet applies to both hands and each hand competes against the dealer's hand. Add this feature to the *Blackjack* game.

(continues)

CHALLENGES *(continued)*

9. Alter the *Blackjack* game to incorporate a MultiPage control with two pages on the *Blackjack* form. The first page of the MultiPage control should contain the existing *Blackjack* game table. The second page of the MultiPage control should contain a List Box control with two columns (set the `ColumnCount` property). Use the List Box control as a card counter. The first column should list the card type (Ace, King, Queen, and so on). The second column should list the number of cards that have been played from the deck for the card type listed in the adjacent row of the first column. Don't forget to reset the List Box when the deck is shuffled.

Error Handling, Debugging, and Basic File I/O

The ability to read and write data to a computer's disk drives is fundamental to most programming languages. This chapter examines some of the different tools available in VBA and Excel that allow a programmer to write code for viewing a computer's file structure, and to read and write text files. Additional tools required for error handling and debugging your VBA programs are also discussed.

Specifically, this chapter will cover:

- Error handling
- Debugging
- File dialogs
- Creating text files

Project: Word Find

The *Word Find* program uses a text file containing a list of words associated with various topics that can be updated by the user to create word search puzzles. The program can also print each puzzle for the user's enjoyment. Figure 7.1 shows the `Wordfind` worksheet that is used by the *Word Find* program.

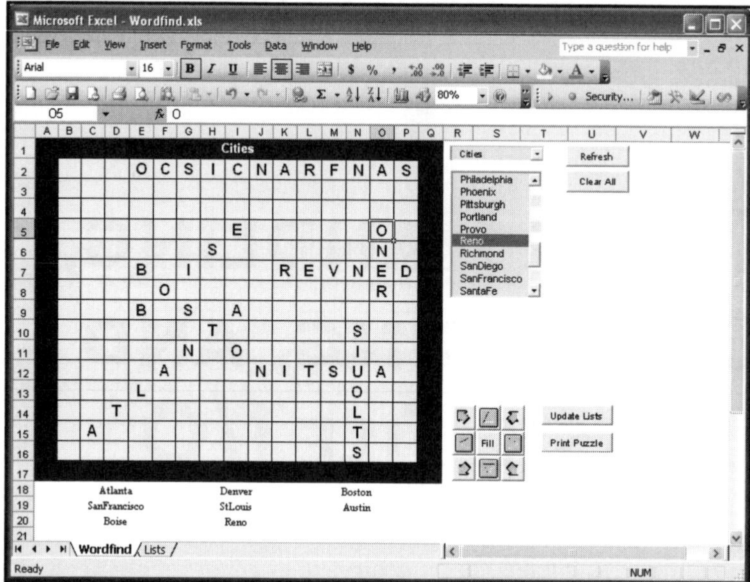

FIGURE 7.1

The `Wordfind` worksheet.

ERROR HANDLING

All programs contain errors (often called *bugs*). Syntax errors occur when the programmer violates the rules of the language (for example, misspelled keywords, missing components of a code structure, or improper declaration of a variable), preventing the program from compiling. Syntax errors are relatively easy to fix because the VBA debugger sends you right to the source of the problem. Logic errors occur when the code contains errors that result in improper program behavior (for example, an infinite loop or wrong variable initialization). Logic errors do not prevent the program from compiling and executing; therefore, logic errors can be difficult to find. With proper debugging, however, the number of errors in a program can be significantly reduced.

Besides syntax and logic errors, it is possible that a program's code may generate a runtime error as a result of invalid input. Examples might include a divide by zero error (as seen in Chapter 6) or a file not found error. Programmers must anticipate errors such as these because if they are left unchecked, these errors will cause the program to crash. Furthermore, errors of this type cannot be fixed by altering the logic of the program. In situations such as these, the program requires additional error handling code and procedures. Error handling code should be included whenever the program interacts with the user or other components of the computer. Validation procedures are examples of error handling procedures; I have already discussed adding them to your code (see Chapter 4). This section will focus on special statements and objects available in VBA for handling anticipated errors.

Using the On Error Statement

In the `MultiPage.xls` project from Chapter 6, the `Click()` event of the `cmdCalcStats` Command Button control contained the statement:

```
On Error Resume Next
```

The `On Error` statement enables error handling in a VBA program. The `On Error` statement must be followed with instructions to VBA for deciding a course of action when a runtime error is encountered. The course of action taken depends on the type of error that is anticipated.

The `On Error` statement must precede the code that is anticipated to generate the runtime error. The `On Error` statement is normally placed near the beginning of a procedure.

In the case of the `Click()` event procedure in Chapter 6, a runtime error was anticipated for the `AVERAGE()`, `MEDIAN()`, and `STDEVP()` worksheet functions when the user failed to select data, but clicked the Calculate button. Because the runtime error will only occur under special circumstances, it was handled by using the `Resume Next` clause. The `Resume Next` clause sends program execution to the next line of code following the line that generated the error. When the user notices that no statistics were calculated after clicking the Calculate button, then he or she should conclude that they need to select a range of cells on the worksheet. The `Resume Next` clause is the simplest solution for handling runtime errors and works well in the `MultiPage.xls` project; however, it may not always be the best solution.

When an anticipated error requires execution of a special block of code, use the `GoTo` statement after `On Error`.

```
On Error GoTo ErrorHandler
```

The term `ErrorHandler` refers to a line label used to direct program execution to the block of code specifically created for handling the runtime error. Line labels must start at the left-most position in the editor window and end with a colon. The error handling code follows the line label.

The use of the `GoTo` statement goes all the way back to the earliest versions of Basic and a few other programming languages. The `GoTo` statement is rarely seen anymore because when overused, the order of execution of programming statements can be very difficult to follow and results in what is termed "spaghetti code." Spaghetti code is very hard to debug and for that reason, the use of the `GoTo` statement in VBA should be limited to error handling routines.

An illustration of the error handling process appears in Figure 7.2.

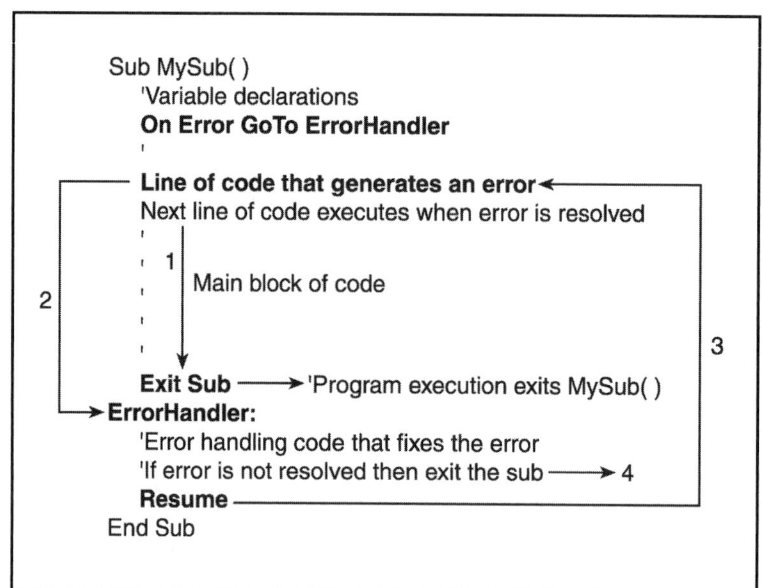

FIGURE 7.2

Order of program execution in a procedure with error handling.

Figure 7.2 shows the order of program execution in a sub procedure that contains error handling code. The order of program execution proceeds as follows:

1. If no error is generated, the main block of code executes but program execution exits the sub procedure before reaching the `ErrorHandler` line label.
2. An error is generated and code execution proceeds to the `ErrorHandler` line label.
3. The error is resolved in the `ErrorHandler` and code execution proceeds back to the original line of code that generated the error. Then the main block of code executes before program execution exits the sub procedure.
4. If the error is not resolved, then program execution should exit the sub without executing the main block of code.

Now consider the `Click()` event procedure of the Calculate button after I added a little more error handling code.

```
Private Sub cmdCalcStats_Click()
    Const NUMFORMAT = "#.00"

    On Error GoTo ErrorHandler
    lblCount.Caption = Application.WorksheetFunction.Count _
                      (Range(refStats.Text))
```

```
    lblSum.Caption = Application.WorksheetFunction.Sum _
                            (Range(refStats.Text))
    lblMin.Caption = Application.WorksheetFunction.Min _
                            (Range(refStats.Text))
    lblMax.Caption = Application.WorksheetFunction.Max _
                            (Range(refStats.Text))
    lblMedian.Caption = Application.WorksheetFunction.Median _
                            (Range(refStats.Text))
    lblAvg.Caption = Format(Application.WorksheetFunction.Average _
                            (Range(refStats.Text)), NUMFORMAT)
    lblStanDev.Caption = Format(Application.WorksheetFunction.StDevP _
                            (Range(refStats.Text)), NUMFORMAT)
    Exit Sub
ErrorHandler:
    MsgBox "An error was encountered while attempting to calculate the statistics. " _
            & vbCrLf & Err.Description & vbCrLf & _
            "Check for a valid range selection and try again." & vbCrLf, _
            vbCritical, "Error " & Err.Number
End Sub
```

After the constant declaration, the error handler is "turned on" with the `On Error` statement and a reference to the `ErrorHandler` line label. The error handling code starts with the line label, but is not a separate procedure. Instead, it is a block of code isolated by the line label; therefore, an `Exit Sub` statement is placed near the end of the procedure just before the line label to prevent the code in the error-handling block from being executed if no error is generated.

The error handling code follows the line label, and due to the structure of the sub procedure, will only be executed when a runtime error occurs. In this example, the error handling code is only one statement, albeit a long one. A message box with a description of the error is displayed to the user. The description is obtained from the `Description` property of the `Err` object. The `Err` object stores information about runtime errors and is intrinsic to VBA. The properties of the `Err` object are initialized when a runtime error occurs with an error handling routine enabled so you can access its properties in any error handling code block.

When possible, you should write code in your error handler that fixes the error and resumes program execution at the error's source using the `Resume` keyword. In this example, that is not possible because the error is generated by an invalid range selection. In this case, the best you can do is to anticipate the cause of the error and suggest a solution to the user.

Figure 7.3 shows the message box displayed by the error handler in the `Click()` event procedure of the Calculate button.

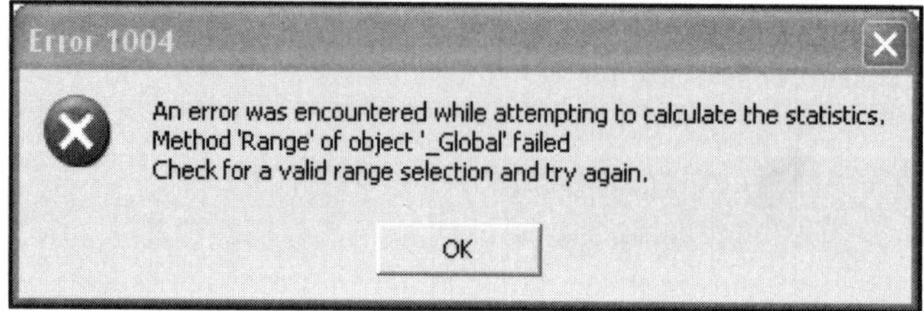

FIGURE 7.3
The message box displayed by the error handler in the *MultiPage.xls* project from Chapter 6.

More examples of error handling code blocks are discussed later in the chapter.

DEBUGGING

By now, you have certainly encountered numerous errors in your programs and probably struggled to correct some of these errors. Finding bugs in a program can be frustrating. Fortunately, VBA has several tools to help debug a program.

Break Mode

When your program generates a runtime error, a dialog box similar to the one shown in Figure 7.4 is displayed.

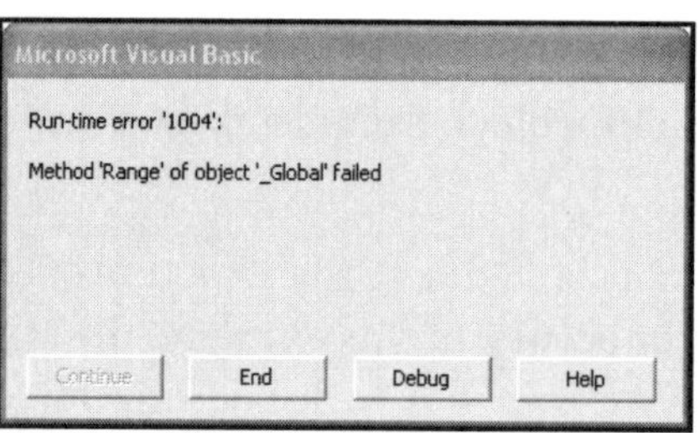

FIGURE 7.4
The runtime error dialog box.

Selecting the Debug option will load the VBA IDE and display the program in Break Mode. While in Break Mode, program execution is paused and can be stepped through one line at a time to closely examine factors such as order of code execution and the current values stored within variables. The line of code that generated the error will be highlighted as shown in Figure 7.5.

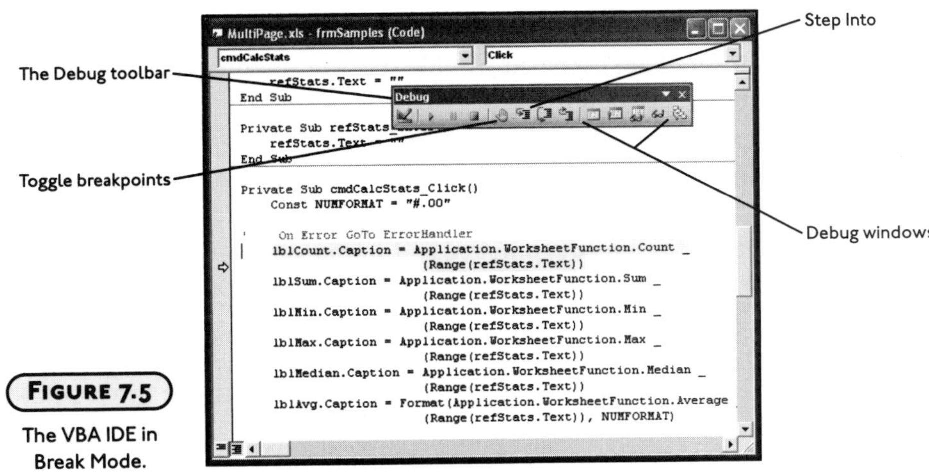

FIGURE 7.5

The VBA IDE in Break Mode.

To intentionally enter Break Mode, insert a breakpoint at the desired location in the program using the Debug menu item or Debug toolbar (select from the View menu) in the VBA IDE (refer to Figure 7.5). You can also toggle a breakpoint by clicking the left margin of the code window next to the line of code at which you want program execution to pause, or by pressing F9.

Insert break points at locations in code where bugs are suspected or known to exist and then run the program. Break Mode is entered when program execution proceeds to a line of code containing a breakpoint. At this time, you have the option of resetting the program, stepping through the program one line at a time, or continuing normal operation of the program. While in Break Mode, the value currently stored in a variable can be checked by holding the mouse cursor over the name of that variable. Logic errors are often caused by code that assigns the wrong value to a variable. Break Mode can help locate the code that creates these errors.

Another useful debugging method is stepping through code while in Break Mode. Use Step Into on the Debug toolbar, or press F8, to execute one line of code at a time starting from the location of the break. The order of program execution can be verified, and values stored within variables checked as code execution proceeds one line at a time.

The Immediate Window

Stepping through code one line at a time can be tedious if the error is not found quickly. The Immediate window allows you to test program variables and procedures under normal program execution. The Immediate window is displayed by selecting it from the View menu, the Debug toolbar (refer to Figure 7.5), or by pressing Ctrl + G in the IDE.

The Immediate window is often used to hold the value of a variable or variables written to it with debugging statements located at suspected trouble spots in the program. Debugging statements use the Assert() and Print() methods of the Debug object. The Assert() method can be used to break program execution based on a Boolean expression. The Print() method is used to write values to the Immediate window.

Debugging statements are not compiled and stored in the executable program file, so there is no harm in leaving them in your code.

The CalcScore() sub procedure in the *Blackjack* form module from Chapter 6 is listed below. You may remember that this procedure calculates the scores of the dealer's and player's hands. One of the trickier pieces of this procedure is the part that scores Aces as either one or eleven depending on the value of the hand. The procedure must score the Ace as eleven as long as the player's score does not exceed twenty-one. Several debugging statements have been added to the procedure to test its effectiveness.

In the CalcScore() sub procedure, the expression (numAces = 0) is used with the Assert() method of the Debug object to break program execution. The expression can be any expression that evaluates as true or false, as in this example, or any Boolean variable. The Assert() method breaks program execution when the Boolean expression evaluates as false. In this example, program execution breaks only when an Ace is dealt to either the dealer or player and their hand is scored. This allows you to step through each line of code that calculates the value of the hand based on the number of Aces dealt without having to waste time in Break Mode when no Ace has been dealt. Three statements use the Print() method of the Debug object to write the value of the variable score to the Immediate window before, during, and after the handling of the Aces. It is a good idea to include a string with the Print() method identifying the variable, especially if there are more debugging statements elsewhere in the program. After, or during program execution, the Immediate window and its contents can be viewed from the VBA IDE as shown in Figure 7.6.

```
Private Sub CalcScore(iPlayer As Integer)
'------------------------------
'Calculates the player's and dealer's score. Pass 0
'for the dealer and 1 for the player.
'------------------------------
    Dim I As Integer
    Dim numAces As Integer
    Dim score As Integer
    Const MAXHANDSIZE = 5
```

```
    '---------------------------
    'Calculates the score. Aces count one or eleven.
    '---------------------------
    For I = 0 To MAXHANDSIZE - 1
        score = score + scores(I, iPlayer)
        If scores(I, iPlayer) = 1 Then numAces = numAces + 1
    Next I
    Debug.Assert (numAces = 0)
    Debug.Print "Score Ace as 1: " & score
    If (numAces > 0) Then
        score = score + 10 * numAces
        Debug.Print "Score Ace as 11: " & score
        For I = 1 To numAces
            If (score > 21) Then score = score - 10
        Next I
    End If
    Debug.Print "Final Score: " & score
    If (iPlayer = 0) Then
        lblDlrScore.Caption = score
    Else
        lblPlyrScore.Caption = score
    End If
End Sub
```

You can also use the Immediate window to enter code statements while the program is in Break Mode. Statements that change the value of a variable, or the property of an ActiveX control, or call a procedure can be entered directly into the Immediate window. The statements take effect after the Enter key is pressed. Using the previous example, the value of the variable `score` can be changed while in Break Mode by entering `score = 5` (or any integer value) in the Immediate window. This is useful for re-directing program execution and testing the results without having to alter code.

The Watch Window

Besides the Immediate window, another useful tool for debugging VBA programs is the Watch window. The Watch window makes it possible to track the value of a variable or expression (property, function call, and so on) from anywhere in a program. Add a watch to an expression from the Debug menu or right click the expression and choose Add Watch from the shortcut menu. The resulting dialog box is shown in Figure 7.7.

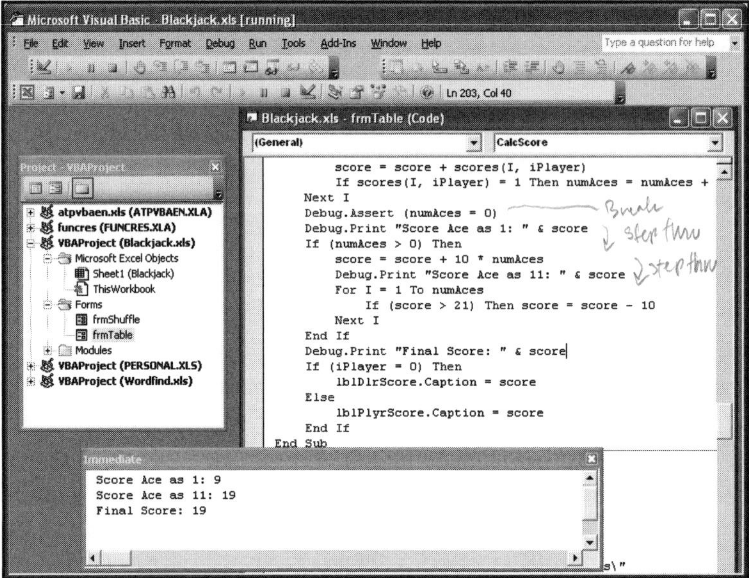

FIGURE 7.6

The Immediate window.

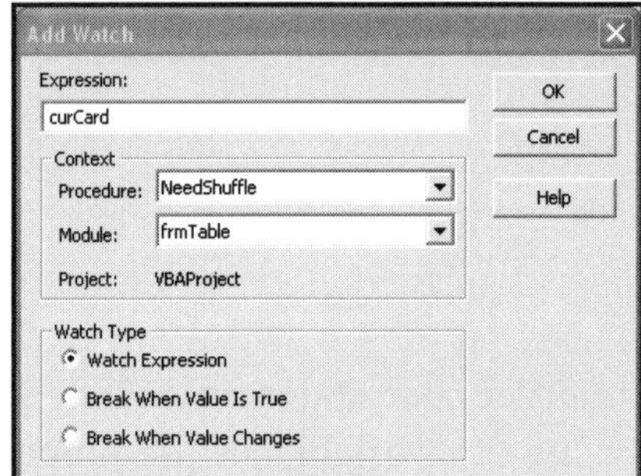

FIGURE 7.7

The Add Watch dialog box.

Choose either a specific procedure containing the expression you want to watch, or choose all procedures. Next, choose a specific module containing the expression you want to watch, or select all modules. Finally, select the type of Watch (Watch Expression, Break When Value Is True, or Break When Value Changes). The watch type selected will be displayed in the Watch window only when the program enters Break Mode. Therefore, if the Watch type Watch Expression is selected, a breakpoint will have to be inserted in the procedure(s) containing the expression before running the program. The other two watch types automatically pause the program at the specified location. A Watch window showing the value of an expression while the program is in Break Mode is shown in Figure 7.8.

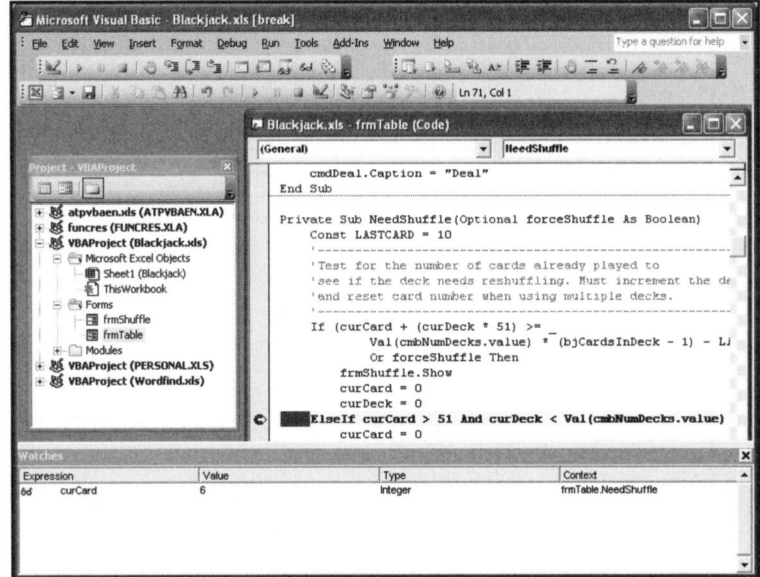

FIGURE 7.8

The Watch window.

The Locals Window

The Locals window (see Figure 7.9) displays the value of the declared variables local to the procedure in which program execution has been paused with a breakpoint. Module-level variables are also listed under the object `Me` in the Locals window. Display the Locals window by selecting it from the View menu or Debug toolbar.

When you suspect a procedure contains a logic error, insert a breakpoint in the procedure, run the program, and display the Locals window before stepping through the procedure's code. This is a handy tool for debugging a procedure as it allows you to view the values of all local variables while stepping through the code.

File Input and Output (I/O)

VBA includes several objects, methods, and functions that can be used for file I/O. You have probably surmised that one possibility for file I/O involves the `Workbook` object and its methods for saving and opening files; however, there are other tools available in VBA, the most relevant of which will be discussed in this chapter.

When a VBA application requires file I/O, it often involves a relatively small amount of data stored in program variables, and not in a worksheet or document. With Excel, the programmer has the choice of copying the data to a worksheet so the user can save the data in the usual way (File/Save menu item), or saving the content of the variables directly to a file. It is often

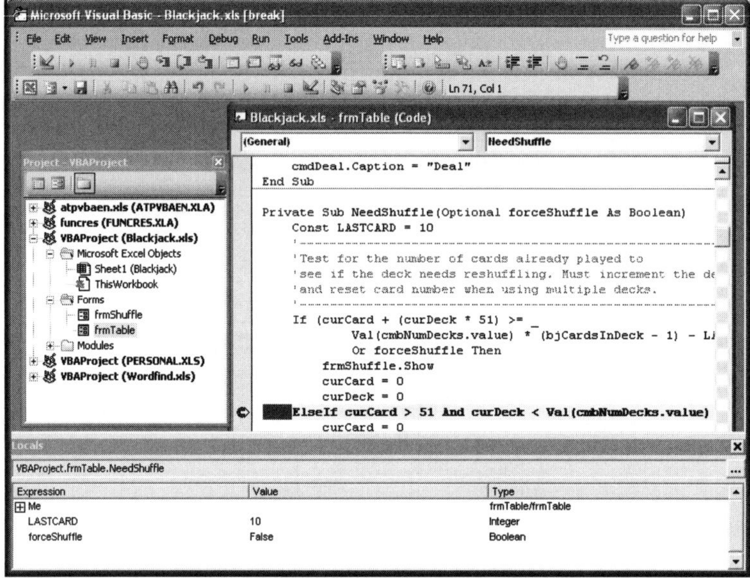

FIGURE 7.9

The Locals window.

more convenient to simply write the data directly to a file on the hard drive so the user does not have to be concerned with the task. In fact, it may be undesirable to give the user access to the data, as he or she might alter it before saving. In this case, reading and writing simple text files within the program code offers an attractive solution.

IN THE REAL WORLD

There are many types of files stored on a computer's hard drive including operating system (OS) files (for example, Windows or Macintosh files used to handle specific tasks performed by the OS), image files, and Excel files. Most of these files are created by specific applications and therefore are proprietary. Proprietary files should only be accessed by the applications from which they were created. In Windows, proprietary files have unique file extensions such as .doc, .xls, and .ppt to name just a few. The file extensions are used by the OS to identify the application that created the file.

A proprietary file (such as one created by Excel) contains not only the textual and numerical information entered by the user, but also content that the application uses to specify formatting options selected by the user (bold, font size and type, and so on) as well as any non-textual information entered by the user (for example, images and charts). The methods used to write all of this additional information to the file are specific to the application, and therefore can only be opened by the application that originally created the file.

File I/O Using Workbook and Worksheet Objects

The Workbook and Worksheet objects contain methods for opening, closing, and saving workbooks in the same manner a user might perform these operations from the Excel application. You can open and save workbook files using a variety of formats with VBA code. The same file formats may also be used to save individual worksheets within an existing workbook.

Opening and Saving Workbooks

You use the Open() method of the Workbooks collection object to open Excel-compatible files. The Open() method accepts numerous arguments, but the only required argument is the Filename. The syntax for the Open() method of the Workbooks collection object, including all arguments, follows:

```
Workbooks. Open(Filename, UpdateLinks, ReadOnly, Format, Password, WriteResPassword,
IgnoreReadOnlyRecommended, Origin, Delimiter, Editable, Notify, Converter, AddToMru,
Local, CorruptLoad)
```

You will never use most of these arguments, but those with unfamiliar names can be found in the online help. The following statement opens a workbook named MyWorkbook.xls located in the same directory as the active workbook. Note that the active workbook must be previously saved or the Path property of the Workbook object will not return a valid file path. Alternatively, you may use a string to specify the full path.

```
Dim filePath As String
filePath = ActiveWorkbook.Path
Workbooks.Open Filename:=filePath & "\MyWorkbook.xls"
```

To save a workbook from a VBA program, use either the Save() method of the Workbooks collection object or the SaveAs() method of the Workbook object. The Save() method does not accept arguments and will save a new workbook to the default directory (the directory last used or the directory specified in the General tab of Excel's Options dialog if a workbook has not been previously saved).

```
Workbook("MyWorkbook.xls).Save
```

The SaveAs() method accepts many of the same arguments as the Open() method of the Workbooks collection object. Most important are the Filename and FileFormat arguments used to specify the file's name and path, and the file type (.xls, .csv, .txt, and so on). The

`FileFormat` argument should be specified as one of VBA's defined `xlFileFormat` constants (look up `xlFileFormat` in the Object Browser to see a complete list). The syntax for the `SaveAs()` method of the `Workbook` object follows:

```
expression.SaveAs(Filename, Fileformat, Password, WriteResPassword,
ReadOnlyRecommended, CreateBackup, AccessMode, ConflictResolution, AddToMru,
TextCodepage, TextVisualLayout, Local)
```

The following line of code saves the active workbook to the default directory as an Excel 2003 file (`xlWorkbookNormal`).

```
ActiveWorkbook.SaveAs Filename:= "MyWorkbook.xls", FileFormat:=xlWorkbookNormal
```

You may also save data in a specific worksheet using the `SaveAs()` method of the `Worksheet` object. Again, the two main arguments are `Filename` and `FileFormat`.

```
expression.SaveAs(FileName, FileFormat, Password, WriteResPassword,
ReadOnlyRecommended, CreateBackup, AddToMru, TextCodepage, TextVisualLayout, Local)
```

You cannot use the `SaveAs()` method of the `Worksheet` object to save the entire workbook, but only data within a specific worksheet. Typically, you save the content of a single worksheet as some type of text file (comma delimited, tab delimited, .html, .xml, and so on). The following example saves the data in the active worksheet to a comma delimited text file named `MyData.csv`.

Text files only contain characters from the ANSI character set. The ANSI character set is comprised of 256 characters that represent the characters from your keyboard (alphabetical, numerical, punctuation, and so on).

```
ActiveSheet.SaveAs Filename:="MyData.csv", FileFormat:=xlCSV
```

Figure 7.10 shows an Excel worksheet with random numerical data that has been saved as a comma-delimited text file. Figure 7.11 shows the resultant file opened in WordPad.

Using VBA File I/O Methods

In addition to the `Open()`, `Save()`, and `SaveAs()` methods of the `Workbooks`, `Workbook`, and `Worksheet` objects, VBA and its associated object libraries include several I/O objects such as the `Dialogs`, `FileDialog`, `FileSystem`, and `FileSystemObject` objects, and other subordinate objects. Some of these objects are conceptually more difficult to use and therefore will not be discussed in this chapter; however, I will show you how to use one object from the Office library and VBA's `Open` statement for adding file I/O to your programs.

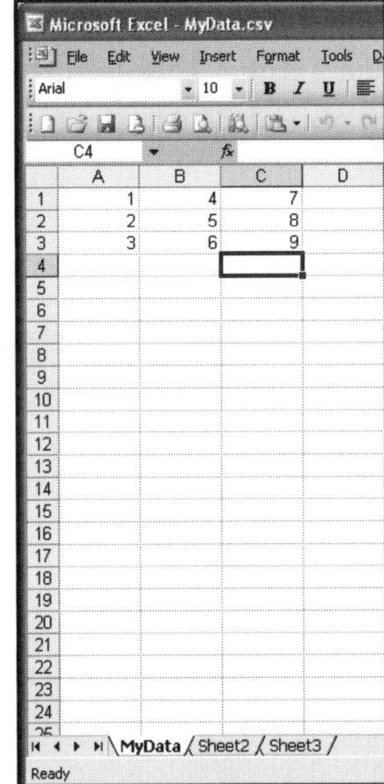

FIGURE 7.10

An Excel worksheet after saving as a text file (.csv extension).

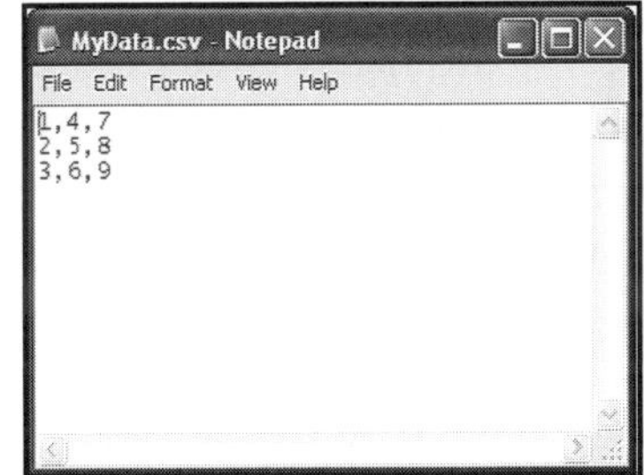

FIGURE 7.11

The text file that results from saving the worksheet in Figure 7.10.

The FileDialog Object

Included in the Office library of objects is the `FileDialog` object. The `FileDialog` object is essentially the standard dialog used in Office applications for opening and saving files. The dialog boxes from the `FileDialog` object allow users to specify the files and folders that a program should use and will return the paths of the selected files or folders. You can also use the `FileDialog` object to execute the associated action of the specified dialog box.

A reference must be set to the Microsoft Office object library before you can use the `FileDialog` object. From the VBA IDE, select Tools, References, and be sure the Check Box labeled Microsoft Office 11.0 Object Library is selected.

The FileDialog object contains two methods called Show() and Execute(). You use the Show() method to show one of four possible dialog boxes (see Table 7.1) depending on the constant passed to the FileDialog property of the Application object. The following statement shows the Open dialog.

```
Application.FileDialog(msoFileDialogOpen).Show
```

TABLE 7.1 DIALOG TYPES USED WITH THE FILEDIALOG OBJECT

Dialog Type	VBA Constant (FileDialogType)
Open	msoFileDialogOpen
Save	msoFileDialogSaveAs
File Picker	msoFileDialogFilePicker
Folder Picker	msoFileDialogFolderPicker

The Execute() method allows the user to carry out the specified action of the dialog box for files that are compatible with the Excel application (for example, files of type .xls, .xlt, .csv, and so on). For example, the Open dialog box allows the user to select one or more files to open when the Execute() method of the FileDialog object is invoked. When the following statement follows the Show() method for the Open dialog, the item(s) selected by the user are opened in Excel.

```
Application.FileDialog(msoFileDialogOpen).Execute
```

Be careful to set the properties of the FileDialog object appropriately for the desired action. For example, you cannot set the FilterIndex property of the FileDialog object when showing the Folder Picker dialog box because this dialog box shows only folders and does not allow file extension filters.

The FileDialogFilters and FileDialogSelectedItems Collection Objects

The FileDialog object has two subordinate collection objects—the FileDialogFilters and the FileDialogSelectedItems collection objects. The FileDialogFilters collection object contains a collection of FileDialogFilter objects that represent the file extensions used to filter what files are displayed in the dialog box (used with the Open and Save As dialog boxes). Use the

Filters property of the FileDialog object to return the FileDialogFilters collection and the Item property of the FileDialogFilters collection object to return a FileDialogFilter object. The Description and Extensions properties of the FileDialogFilter object return the description (for example, All Files) and the file extension used to filter the displayed files (for example, *.*).

I wrote the CheckFileFilters() sub procedure to generate a list of all possible file filters and their descriptions, then output the lists via message boxes. The procedure simply loops through each FileDialogFilter object in the FileDialogFilters collection and concatenates their Description and Extensions properties to separate string variables. Add the following procedure to any code module then run the program to generate message boxes similar to those shown in Figures 7.12 and 7.13.

```
Public Sub CheckFileFilters()
    Dim fileFilters As FileDialogFilters
    Dim fileFilter As FileDialogFilter
    Dim I As Integer
    Dim descrs As String
    Dim xtns As String

    Set fileFilters = Application.FileDialog(msoFileDialogOpen).Filters
    '------------------------
    'Loop through collection and build strings of
    'all extensions and descriptions.
    '------------------------
    For I = 1 To fileFilters.Count
        Set fileFilter = fileFilters.Item(I)
        descrs = descrs & fileFilter.Description & vbCrLf
        xtns = xtns & fileFilter.Extensions & vbCrLf
    Next I
    MsgBox descrs
    MsgBox xtns
End Sub
```

The FileDialogSelectedItems collection object contains the paths (as strings) to the files or folders selected by the user. Use the SelectedItems property of the FileDialog object to return the FileDialogSelectedItems collection. The GetSelectedItem() sub procedure first shows the Open dialog then loops through all items selected by the user in order to build a string containing their file paths. The file paths are then output in a message box. Note that the Item property of the FileDialogSelectedItems object returns a string.

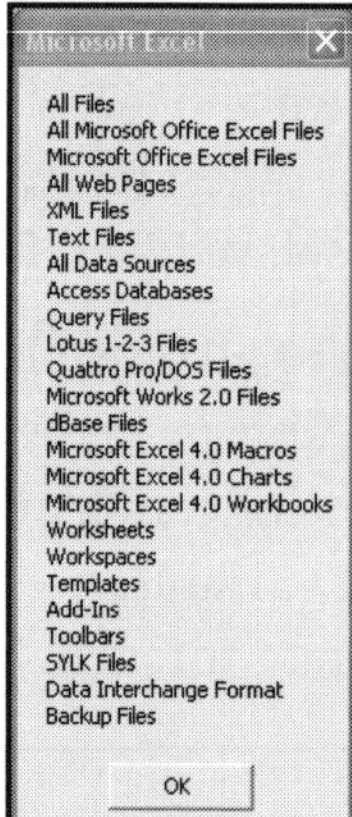

FIGURE 7.12

File filter descriptions for Excel.

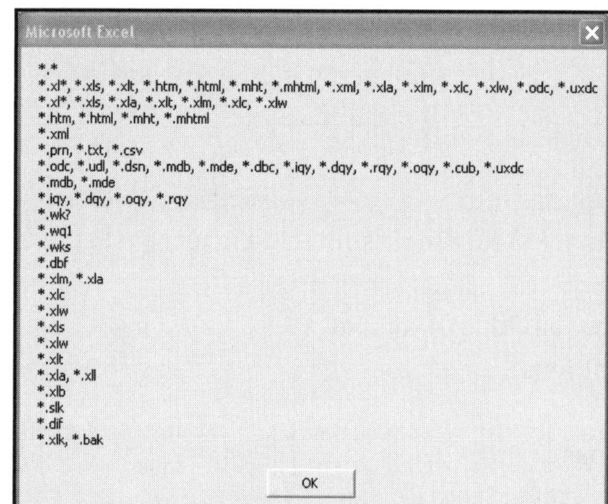

FIGURE 7.13

File filer extensions for Excel.

```
Public Sub GetSelectedItem()
    Dim selItems As FileDialogSelectedItems
    Dim I As Integer
    Dim paths As String

    '-----------------------------------------
    'Build a list of file paths to all files selected by user from Open dialog.
    '-----------------------------------------
    Application.FileDialog(msoFileDialogOpen).Show
    Set selItems = Application.FileDialog(msoFileDialogOpen).SelectedItems
    For I = 1 To selItems.Count
```

```
        paths = paths & selItems.Item(I) & vbCrLf
    Next I
    MsgBox paths
End Sub
```

You can use the Add() method of the FileDialogFilters collection object to create your own list of filters. The LoadImage() sub procedure shows the File Picker dialog box after clearing the FileDialogFilters collection and adding two new filters (*.*, and *.bmp). The Add() method requires a description and extension. An optional Position argument indicates the position of the added filter in the list.

The Show() method is called to display of the Open dialog after its properties are set. The Show() method of the FileDialog object returns -1 if the user presses the action button (Open in this example) and 0 if the action is cancelled. The FilterIndex property sets which filter is selected when the dialog is shown—essentially creating a default file filter. With the AllowMultiSelect property of the FileDialog object set to false, the user can only select one file. The path to this file is returned by the SelectedItems property of the FileDialog object which is used to load the selected image into an Image control named imgTest. You can test this procedure by adding it to the code module of a Worksheet object. Be sure to place an Image control on the worksheet and set its Name property before running the program.

```
Public Sub LoadImage()
    Dim fileDiag As FileDialog
    Dim imagePath As String

    Set fileDiag = Application.FileDialog(msoFileDialogFilePicker)
    With fileDiag
        .AllowMultiSelect = False
        .Filters.Clear
        .Filters.Add Description:="All files", Extensions:="*.*"
        .Filters.Add Description:="Image", Extensions:="*.bmp", Position:=1
        .FilterIndex = 1
        .InitialFileName = ""
        .Title = "Select BMP file"
        If .Show = -1 Then      'User pressed action button
            imagePath = .SelectedItems(1)
            imgTest.Picture = LoadPicture(imagePath)
        End If
    End With
End Sub
```

The path to the file selected by the user is returned from the FileDialogSelectedItems collection and stored in the string variable imagePath. If the Execute() method of the FileDialog object is omitted in the program, your program will need this path. Do not use the Execute() method of the FileDialog object when selecting files that are not compatible with Excel—doing so will either result in a runtime error or open a workbook containing incomprehensible data.

If the AllowMultiSelect property of the FileDialog object is true, the FileDialogSelectedItems collection will hold more than one file path. The ShowFileDialog() sub procedure loads the Open dialog box and allows the user to select multiple files. If the user clicks the Open button then the Execute() method attempts to open all selected files.

```
Public Sub ShowFileDialog()
    Dim fileDiag As FileDialog
    Const EXCELFILES = 2

    '---------------------
    'Configure and show the open dialog.
    'Open all files selected by the user.
    '---------------------
    Set fileDiag = Application.FileDialog(msoFileDialogOpen)
    With fileDiag       'Configure dialog box
        .AllowMultiSelect = True
        .FilterIndex = EXCELFILES
        .Title = "Select Excel File(s)"
        .InitialFileName = ""
        If .Show = -1 Then   'User clicked Open
            .Execute     'Open selected files
        End If
    End With
End Sub
```

The dialog box resulting from the ShowFileDialog() sub procedure is shown in Figure 7.14.

The FileSystem Object

The FileSystem object is a collection of methods that you can use to set and obtain information about files, directories, and drives. You can find the members of the FileSystem object listed in the Object Browser and in Table 7.2. You can use them as though they were just another group of VBA built-in functions. That is, you do not need to qualify the object when using these methods in your program.

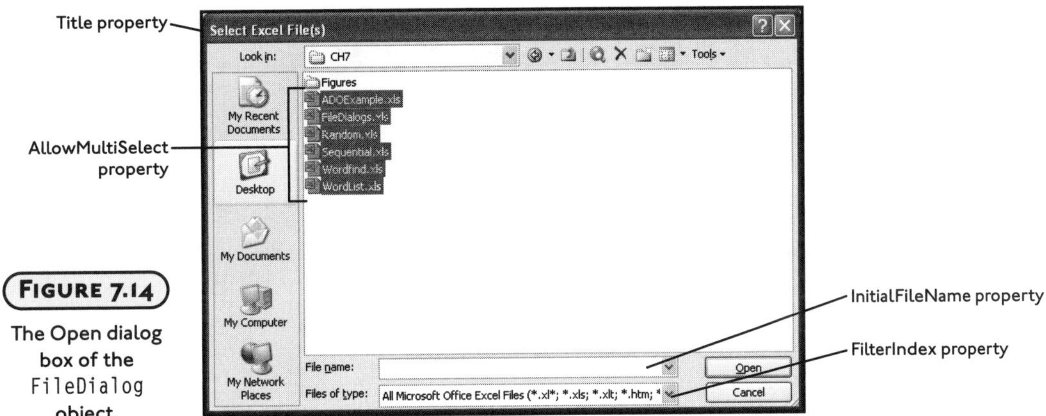

FIGURE 7.14

The Open dialog box of the `FileDialog` object.

The Open Statement

The `Open` statement is used to read or write data to a file. Table 7.3 summarizes the type of access, and modes or functions available for reading and writing data to a file with VBA.

There is also a Binary access type for reading and writing to any byte position in a file as might be done with an image; however, this technique is beyond the scope of this book.

The `Open` statement requires several arguments, including a string that designates the path to a specified file. If the file does not exist, then one will be created. The `Open` statement also requires an access mode (`Append`, `Binary`, `Input`, `Output`, or `Random`) and a file number. Optional parameters include an access parameter (`Read`, `Write`, or `Read Write`), lock (used to restrict operations on the file from other programs), and record length (specifies the length of the buffer or record).

```
Open "C:\Data\Test.txt" For Input As #1
```

The preceding line opens a file named `Test.txt` found at the designated path for input, and assigns the file to the file number 1. If the file is not found, then one will be created at the designated location with the name `Test.txt`.

You can open multiple files in your VBA programs, but they must be assigned unique file numbers.

Table 7.2 Members of the FileSystem Object

Member	Description
ChDir	Changes the current directory.
ChDrive	Changes the current drive.
CurDir	Returns the current directory path.
Dir	Returns the name of a file, directory, or folder that matches a pattern, file attribute, or the volume label of a drive.
EOF	End of file.
FileAttr	The mode used to open a file with the Open statement.
FileCopy	Copies a file from a source path to a destination path.
FileDateTime	Returns the date and time that a file was created or last modified.
FileLen	Returns the length of a file in bytes.
FreeFile	Returns an Integer representing the next file number available for use by the Open statement.
GetAttr	Returns an Integer representing the attributes of a file or directory.
Kill	Deletes a file or files.
Loc	Specifies the current read/write position within an open file.
LOF	Returns a Long integer specifying the length of an open file in bytes.
MkDir	Creates a new directory.
Reset	Closes all disk files opened using the Open statement.
RmDir	Deletes an empty directory.
Seek	Returns a Long integer specifying the current read/write position within an open file.
SetAttr	Sets attribute information for a file.

These methods are primarily designed to be used with the Open statement, but you may also find them useful with the other objects and methods discussed in this chapter.

Example	Return Value
`ChDir "C:\Documents and Settings" or ChDir ".."`	N/A
`ChDrive "D:"`	N/A
`MsgBox CurDir`	Outputs the current directory path in a message box.
`fileName = Dir("C:\test.txt", vbNormal)`	The file name if it exists. Otherwise an empty string.
`EOF(fileNum)`	A Boolean value indicating whether the end of an opened file (specified with a file number) has been reached.
`Mode = FileAttr(fileNum, 1)`	Returns a Long integer indicating the mode used to open a file (Input, Output, Random, and so on).
`FileCopy "C:\TestFile.txt", "D:\TestFile.txt"`	N/A
`fileDate = FileDateTime("C:\test.txt")`	For example, `1/23/2004 10:25:14 AM`
`fileSize = FileLen("C:\test.txt")`	For example, 4
`FileNumber = FreeFile`	For example, 2
`myAttr = GetAttr(CurDir)`	0=Normal, 1=Read-Only, 2=Hidden, 4=System, 16=Directory, 32=Archive
`Kill "C:\test.txt"`	N/A
`MyLocation = Loc(1)`	A Long integer
`FileLength = LOF(1)`	For example, 4
`MkDir "TestDir"`	N/A
`Reset`	N/A
`RmDir "TestDir"`	N/A
`Seek(1)`	If the file is opened in Random mode it returns the number of the next record, otherwise it returns the current byte position in the file.
`SetAttr "C:\test.txt", vbReadOnly`	N/A

Table 7.3 File Access Modes with VBA

Access Type	Writing Data	Reading Data
Sequential	Print#, Write#	Input#, Input
Random	Put	Get

Sequential Access Files

Writing information to a sequential access file is sort of like recording music to a cassette tape. The songs vary in length and are recorded one after the other. Because it is hard to know the location of each song on the tape, it is difficult to quickly access a particular song. When information is written to a sequential file, the individual pieces of data (usually stored in variables) vary in length and are written to the file one after the other. For example, a sequential file containing names and phone numbers may look something like what's shown here:

"John Smith", "111-2222"

"Joe James", "123-4567"

"Jane Johnson", "456-7890"

The names and phone numbers were all written to the file as strings so they are enclosed in quotes. Numerical values written to a sequential access file will not contain the quotes. The strings containing the names vary in length and will require different amounts of memory for storage. If access to a part of the sequential file is desired at a later time (say we want Jane Johnson's phone number), the entire file must be read into memory because it is not possible to know the location of the desired component within the file. After loading the file, the content must be searched for the desired value. This makes sequential access inefficient with very large files, because it will take too long to access the desired information. With smaller files, however, that do not take long to read, sequential access will work well. The `CreateSeqFile()` sub procedure writes textual information from the first three rows in columns A and B of a worksheet to a sequential access file.

```
Public Sub CreateSeqFile()
    Dim filePath As String
    Dim I As Integer
    filePath = ActiveWorkbook.Path & "\SeqPhone.txt"
    Open filePath For Output As #1
```

```
        For I = 1 To 3
            Write #1, Cells(I, "A").Value, Cells(I, "B").Value
        Next I
    Close #1
End Sub
```

The procedure above uses a `For/Next` loop to write the contents of the first three cells of columns A and B to a file called `SeqPhone.txt`. The I/O operation is terminated with the `Close` statement. The resulting file as viewed from Notepad is shown in Figure 7.15.

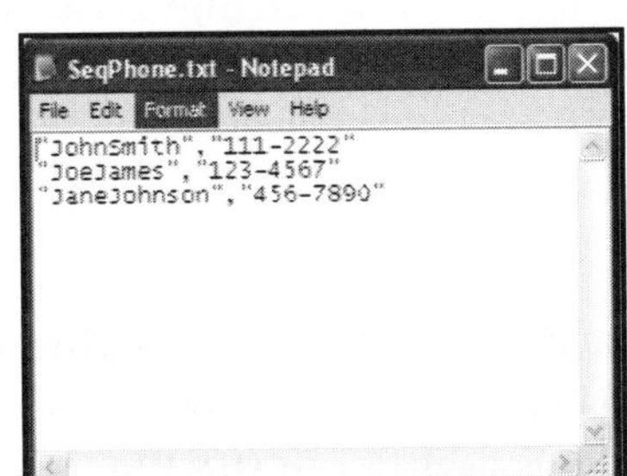

FIGURE 7.15

Using Notepad to view a sequential file created using VBA code.

Using `Write #` places quotes around each value written to the file. The file contains three lines of data because `Write #` adds a new line character to the end of the last value written to the file; because the `For/Next` loop iterates three times, the `Write #` statement was executed three times, resulting in three lines of data.

Because the structure of the file is known, it is a simple task to alter the `CreateSeqFile()` procedure to create a new procedure that reads the data.

```
Public Sub ReadSeqFile()
    Dim filePath As String
    Dim I As Integer
    Dim theName As String
    Dim theNumber As String
    I = 1
    filePath = ActiveWorkbook.Path & "\SeqPhone.txt"
    Open filePath For Input As #1
    Do While Not EOF(1)
        Input #1, theName, theNumber
        Cells(I, "A").Value = theName
        Cells(I, "B").Value = theNumber
        I = I + 1
```

```
    Loop
    Close #1
End Sub
```

I changed the Open statement in the ReadSeqFile() procedure to allow for data input, and I replaced Write # with Input #. I also replaced the For/Next loop with a Do-loop and used the EOF() function in the conditional to test for the end of the file. The EOF() function accepts the file number as an argument and returns true when the end of the file is reached. The loop, therefore, continues as long as the EOF() function returns false (Do While NOT False equates to Do While True). Variables must be used to hold the strings returned from the file. Two variables (theName and theNumber) are used in order to match the structure of the procedure that wrote the data to the file.

Random Access Files

Random access files allow the programmer to access specific values within the file without having to load the entire file into memory. This is accomplished by ensuring that the individual data elements are of the same length before writing to the file. Again, consider the example of a phone book. Instead of storing the information as variable-length strings, the name and phone number can be stored with fixed length strings. The combination of the two fixed length strings that follow require the same amount of memory for every line written to the file. This will make it easy to locate a particular line in the file when the data is input.

```
Dim theName As String*20
Dim theNumber As String*8
```

If the name to be stored is less than 20 characters, then spaces are added to match the defined length. If the string exceeds 20 characters, only the first 20 characters of the string are stored; therefore, it is important to define the length of the string so that it will be long enough to contain any possible value, yet not so long that too much memory is wasted by saving lots of spaces. The resulting data file might then look something like this:

“John Smith   ”, “111-2222”

“Joe James   ”, “123-4567”

“Jane Johnson   ”, “456-7890”

Each line in the file requires the same amount of memory to store and is referred to as a record. Records can be represented by one or more values of the same or different data type (string, integer, and so on). Because the length of each record is identical, finding a specific record in the file without loading the entire file into memory is relatively easy (as you will see shortly).

Rather than declare the individual elements of a record as separate variables, it is useful to define a custom data type that can be used in a variable declaration. The variable of the newly defined type can include all the desired elements of the record. To define a phone record for the previous example, a custom data type that includes both string elements must be declared in the general declarations section of a module.

With the new data type definition, any variable can now be declared in a procedure as type Phone as shown in the CreateRanAccessFile() sub procedure. Individual elements of the phoneRec variable are accessed using the dot operator. To take full advantage of the custom data type, I write the phoneRec variable to a file using random access.

```
Private Type Phone
    theName As String*20
    theNumber As String*8
End Type

Public Sub CreateRanAccessFile()
    Dim phoneRec As Phone
    Dim filePath As String
    Dim I As Integer, recNum As Integer

    recNum = 1
    filePath = ActiveWorkbook.Path & "\randomPhone.dat"
    Open filePath For Random As #1 Len = Len(phoneRec)
        For I = 1 To 3
            phoneRec.theName = Cells(I, "A").Value
            phoneRec.theNumber = Cells(I, "B").Value
            Put #1, recNum, phoneRec
            recNum = recNum + 1
        Next I
    Close #1
End Sub
```

The length of the record is specified by passing the variable phoneRec to the Len() function. The data is written to the file using the Put statement. (You should read a random access file with the Get statement.) An integer variable indicating the record number (recNum) must also be included with the custom variable in the Put statement so VBA knows where to insert the value within the file. The record number (indicated by the variable recNum in the CreateRanAccessFile() procedure) must begin with the value 1.

IN THE REAL WORLD

Many applications save data to a type of random access file that is more commonly referred to as a database. Database files such as those created by MS Access (.mdb extension) offer a lot more power to the programmer relative to the random access file created by VBA's `Open` statement. A single database file normally contains multiple tables of data that are linked together through related fields (columns). Furthermore, it is usually possible to use a database's programming engine to link your VBA program to a database file such that you can quickly retrieve and update very specific data.

With Excel, it is possible to link your VBA program to an Access database (and many others) even if the Access GUI has not been installed on your computer. Unfortunately, it would take at least an entire book to properly discuss database normalization, the Structured Query Language (SQL), and ActiveX Data Objects (ADO)—the topics required to understand and use database files in your VBA program.

CHAPTER PROJECT: WORD FIND

The *Word Find* project is an Excel VBA program that creates word search puzzles. Words for a puzzle are associated with a topic that the program uses to sort the data. The topics and words used in a puzzle are stored in a random access file. The file containing the words and topics is accessed and displayed by the program. New words and topics for puzzles can be added to the file by the user. A puzzle is created when the user selects individual words and places them within a fifteen by fifteen grid running in any direction. After placing the words, the empty spaces in the puzzle are randomly filled with letters before printing. The *Word Find* program is stored on the accompanying CD-ROM as `Wordfind.xls`.

Requirements for Word Find

The objectives for the *Word Find* project are to demonstrate some basic techniques for file I/O and error handling in a VBA program. To accomplish the task, I use an Excel worksheet as the grid for a word search puzzle and a VBA form for updating the data required by the program. The requirements for the program follow:

1. A VBA form (`UserForm` object) shall be used as the interface for updating the program's data (words and topics) stored in a random access file.
2. The form shall display all unique topics stored in the data file.
3. The form shall display all words stored in the data file that are associated with a user-selected topic.

Find

4. The form shall allow the user to add new records to the data file.
5. The form shall allow the user to update (edit) previously stored words in the data file for an existing topic. Note that the program will not allow for existing topics to be updated.
6. The form shall display new and updated records as they are created.
7. An Excel worksheet shall be used to create the word search puzzle.
8. The puzzle worksheet shall isolate an area of cells (fifteen by fifteen cells in size) for displaying a puzzle.
9. The puzzle worksheet shall isolate an area of cells for displaying the list of words that have been added to a puzzle.
10. The puzzle worksheet shall isolate an area of cells for displaying help/error messages to the user when creating a puzzle.
11. The puzzle worksheet shall isolate an area of cells for displaying a puzzle's title.
12. The puzzle worksheet shall display a list of unique topics from the data file for the user to choose from when creating a puzzle.
13. The puzzle worksheet shall display a list of words from the data file associated with the topic selected by the user.
14. The user shall be able to select a word from the displayed list of words on the puzzle worksheet and add it to the puzzle by indicating a starting position on the puzzle grid.
15. The user shall be able to select a direction for a word added to the puzzle from a series of buttons on the worksheet.
16. The program shall validate the user's selection for the location of a word to ensure the entire word fits within the defined area of the puzzle grid. There will be no validation to prevent a word from overwriting another word(s).
17. The user shall be able to clear the contents of the puzzle, the list of words in the puzzle, the list of topics, and the list of words associated with the selected topic from a button on the worksheet.
18. The user shall be able to finish a puzzle by adding randomly selected uppercase letters to the empty cells in the puzzle grid from a button on the worksheet.
19. The user shall be able to print the puzzle and the list of words contained in the puzzle from a button on the worksheet.
20. The user shall be able to display the form used to update the data in the data file from a button on the worksheet. Note that the user will not be able to edit the data in the file directly from the worksheet.

21. The user shall be able to refresh the list of topics, and list of words associated with a topic from a button on the worksheet.
22. The data for the program shall be stored in a random access file containing three fields of data per record. The first field contains the numbers used to identify specific records (rows) of data. The second field contains the topics, and the third field contains the words associated with the topics in the second field.
23. The data from the file shall be stored in a worksheet that is hidden from the user. The data from the file shall be written to the worksheet when the user elects to show the update form.
24. When the user chooses to edit an existing record or add a new record, the program shall write the new data to the text file and the hidden worksheet.

As with every program you write, you will edit the requirement list after you have designed it; sometimes even after you started writing the program because it is nearly impossible to think of everything from the beginning. I added and removed requirements from the previous list after careful consideration of the program's design and objectives.

Designing Word Find

The *Word Find* program's design features objects that are now familiar to you, including a VBA form and a worksheet. The form serves to allow the user to update the data file with new records as well as edit existing records. The worksheet serves as the interface for creating a word search puzzle. The program takes advantage of the grid-like nature of a worksheet to create the puzzle. Words are written to the puzzle using individual cells for holding the letters. After the puzzle is finished, it is a relatively simple task to print it for someone's enjoyment.

Designing the Form

The program is divided into two parts: the first part contains the form used to update the data file and the second part contains the worksheet used to create a puzzle. Figure 7.16 shows the form's design from the IDE.

Whenever a program is required to display a list, you should immediately think List Box or Combo Box control. I have added a Combo Box control to the form for displaying the list of topics and a List Box control for displaying the list of words associated with a selected topic. That is, when the user changes the selection in the Combo Box control the list of words in the List Box control will also change to match the topic.

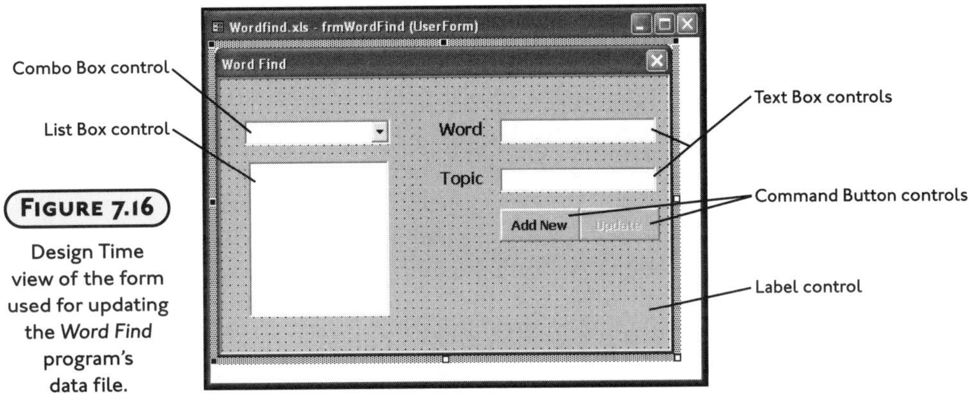

FIGURE 7.16

Design Time view of the form used for updating the *Word Find* program's data file.

Although I have not previously discussed the Text Box control, you should find it fairly easy to use. It is a simple control that serves to collect textual input from a user. As with all controls, you should edit the `Name` and appearance (size, font, and so on) properties of the Text Box control at Design Time. The value of the `Text` property stores whatever is currently entered in the Text Box, so this property is frequently accessed in your programs. Other properties of interest include: `MaxLength`, `MultiLine`, `PasswordChar`, `SpecialEffect`, `TextAlign`, and `WordWrap`. You should take the time to familiarize yourself with the Text Box control and some of its properties. The Text Box controls I added to the form serve to display the currently selected topic and word. I have used Text Box controls instead of Label controls because the user must be able to enter new values into these controls.

The purpose of the form is to allow the user to enter new records or edit existing records stored in the `Wordfind.txt` data file. I added the Text Box and Command Button controls to the form in order to achieve this purpose. To add a new record, the user can enter a new word in the appropriate text box control with an existing topic, or the user can enter a new topic before clicking the Add New button. To edit an existing record, the user must first select a word from the List Box to enable the Update button. Next, the user can edit the word and click Update. When the Update button is clicked, the existing record will be overwritten in the data file.

The data from the file must also be added to a hidden worksheet. I decided to use the worksheet because I wanted to display the data alphabetically sorted; thus taking advantage of Excel's ability to quickly sort data. It also makes sense to store the data somewhere it can be quickly and easily accessed, yet still protected. A worksheet that is hidden from the user works quite well, although further protections should probably be added (password protection of the worksheet). It is also important that the data in the hidden worksheet be updated as the file is updated by the user.

I have left a couple of potential problems in the form's design. It does not protect against adding identical records to the data file, does not allow records to be deleted, and it does not allow the user to edit the name of an existing topic (in case of a misspelling). I have left the challenge of solving these limitations to the reader along with several other enhancements to the program (see the Challenges at the end of the chapter).

Designing the Worksheet

A word search puzzle is created on a worksheet—the design of which is shown in Figure 7.17. A worksheet makes an ideal interface for this program since it is easy to write letters to the cells and print a portion of the worksheet (as you will see in the program code).

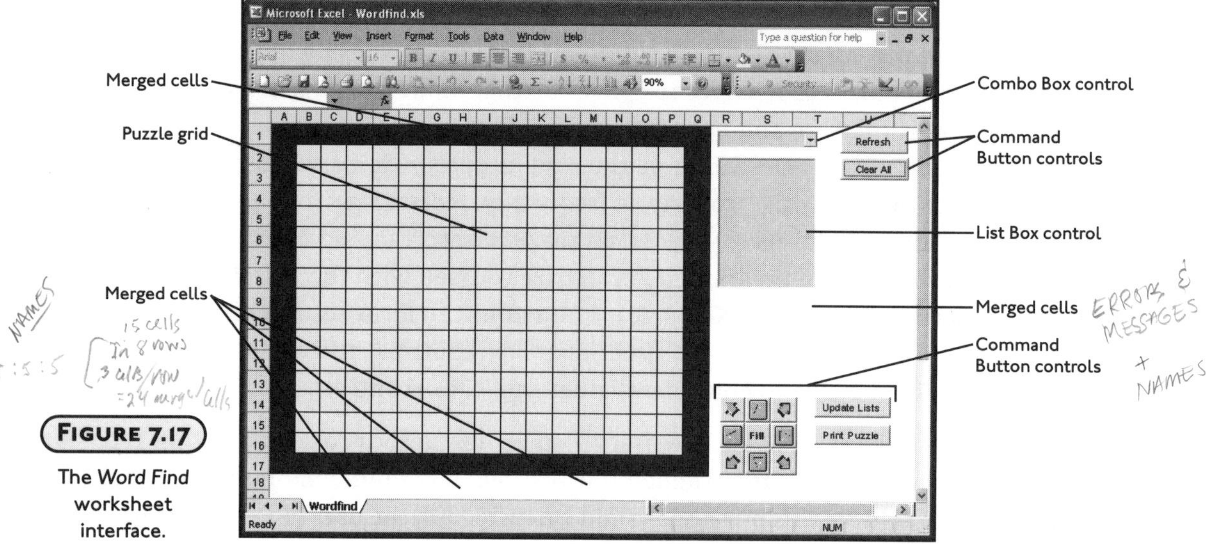

FIGURE 7.17

The Word Find worksheet interface.

As was done with the form, the worksheet contains a Combo Box and List Box control for displaying the topic and word lists, respectively. The data listed in the ActiveX controls on the puzzle worksheet will be read only from the hidden worksheet and not from the data file. Nothing is included directly on the worksheet that will allow the user to edit the data file. Instead, a Command Button control with the caption `Update Lists` is used to show the form that updates the data file. Other Command Button controls added to the worksheet include the following:

- `Clear All`: Clears data from the puzzle and ActiveX controls.
- `Refresh`: Refreshes the topic and word lists. This button is meant to be used after the user has updated the data using the form.

- `Print Puzzle`: Prints the puzzle.
- Pictures of arrows: Eight buttons for selecting the direction in which the program writes the word in the puzzle.
- `Fill`: Randomly fills the empty cells in the puzzle with uppercase letters.

In addition to the ActiveX controls, several areas of the worksheet are reserved for the puzzle, the puzzle title, the word list, and help messages. The puzzle grid is fifteen by fifteen cells and is formatted with borders and color. The range A1 : Q1 is merged and formatted with a light colored font so that the title of the puzzle (topic) is centered in the middle of the puzzle. The fifteen cells in the eight rows immediately below the puzzle are merged into three cells per row. This gives a total of twenty-four cells for holding the list of words that have been added to a puzzle. Finally, an area of cells just to the right of the puzzle are merged and formatted in a large font to hold error and help messages output by the program. All of these areas were assigned defined names (`Puzzle`, `Topic`, `WordList`, and `Output`) to make the code that accesses these ranges easier to read.

Program execution is meant to proceed as follows:

1. The user populates the Combo Box and List Box controls with topics and words by clicking the `Refresh` button.
2. The user selects a topic from the Combo Box control and a new list of words is displayed in the List Box.
3. The user selects a word from the list in the List Box.
4. The user selects a cell in the puzzle grid.
5. The user clicks a button indicating the direction in which to write the word and the word is added to the puzzle.
6. The user continues to add words to the puzzle until he or she is satisfied with the puzzle.
7. The user clicks the `Fill` button and the program fills empty cells in the puzzle grid.
8. The user clicks the `Print Puzzle` button and the puzzle and word list is printed.

Writing the Code for Word Find

As the interface for this program has two distinct parts, so will the code. The form and worksheet components can be written and tested as independent programs, then added together to complete this project. I will start with the code module for the `UserForm` object that updates the data file.

Writing the Code for the Userform Module

The program's data is stored in a random access file. The advantage to this type of file is that it can be quickly updated as long as your program correctly tracks the record number. In order to do this, a custom data type is required to ensure each record uses the same amount of memory. The custom data type named `PuzzleList` is built from three elements: a long integer and two strings. The long integer is an identification number (`IDNum`), and as you will see, I use it to make finding specific records easier. The two strings will hold the topics and words. The integer variable `recNum` is still required to serve as a place locator for I/O operations on a random access file. The value of the `recNum` variable will match that of the identification number which makes it easier to locate and update records in the data file. A variable array of type `PuzzleList` is declared at module level to be used in reading the data from the file and writing it out to the hidden worksheet.

```
Option Explicit
Private recNum As Integer
Private Type PuzzleList
    IDNum As Long
    topic As String * 30
    word As String * 15
End Type
Private curList() As PuzzleList
```

When the form is shown, its `Activate()` event procedure is triggered and its code calls the procedures that load the data from the file and writes it to the hidden worksheet. The data file's topics are retrieved from the worksheet by passing the dynamic array variable `topics` to the `GetUniqueTopics()` sub procedure. The name of the procedure, `GetUniqueTopics()`, implies its function. Remember that the data file, and thus the hidden worksheet, contains a topic for every word; therefore numerous repeat values for the topic exist. The array is passed by reference, so when it is re-dimensioned and filled with values in the `GetUniqueTopics()` sub procedure, it can be added to the Combo Box control via its `List` property (the `List` property of the Combo Box control is a variant array). The last line of code in the `Activate()` event procedure sets the topic that will be displayed in the Combo Box control. Be aware that setting the `Value` property of a Combo Box control triggers its `Change()` event.

```
Private Sub UserForm_Activate()
    Dim topics() As String

    '--------------------
    'Initialize worksheet and controls.
    '--------------------
```

```
    GetAllRecords
    WriteToWorksheet
    GetUniqueTopics topics
    cmbTopics.List = topics
    cmbTopics.Value = cmbTopics.List(0)
End Sub
```

The purpose of the `GetAllRecords()` sub procedure is to load the data from the file and store it in the module level variable array `curList`. Because the procedure involves file I/O, some validation and error handling code is included.

To avoid file I/O errors that may crash the program, first the path to the `Workdfind.txt` file must be validated and appropriate action taken if the file is not found. The `Dir()` function serves to validate the file path. The `Dir()` function is a member of the `FileSystem` object, but can be used without its object qualifier. In the `GetAllRecords()` sub procedure, the `Dir()` function returns the string `"WordFind.txt"` if this file is found at the specified path. If the file does not exist at the specified path then the `Dir()` function returns a zero-length string (`""`) and the `GetFile()` function is called to display a file dialog and give the user a chance to find and select the file to open. If the user finds the file and selects OK, then its path is returned to the variable `filePath`. If the file's path is not found and the user selects Cancel, then code execution continues.

The second step in avoiding a program crash from a file I/O error is adding an error handler. Although it is difficult to foresee errors other than an invalid path and/or file name, certainly more possibilities for file I/O errors exist (for example, a corrupt file); therefore, the error handler is added to display a message box indicating the nature of the error and end the program. The error handler is also called if the file path is invalid and the user chooses to cancel the file dialog used to find the file (this returns an empty string for the file path). I handle the error this way because of the difficulty in predicting what error might occur. All I know is that the `Open` statement has failed, so the program must end. Most importantly, the error handler prevents the program from crashing and starting the debugger.

Normally, I would place the call to the `GetFile()` sub procedure in the error handler, but the `Open` statement does not fail if a valid path is used and the file is not found at this location. Instead a new file is created and that's not the required action.

```
Private Sub GetAllRecords()
    Dim filePath As String
    Dim curRec As PuzzleList
```

```
    '------------------------------
    'Load all records from random access text file into
    'variable array of custom data type.
    '------------------------------
    On Error GoTo FileIOError
    filePath = ActiveWorkbook.Path & "\Wordfind.txt"

    '------------
    'Test for valid path.
    '------------
    If Dir(filePath) <> "Wordfind.txt" Then
        filePath = GetFile
    End If

    '----------------------
    'Open the file and fill records into custom
    'variable array.
    '----------------------
    recNum = 1
    Open filePath For Random Access Read As #1 Len = Len(curRec)
    Do While Not EOF(1)
        Get #1, recNum, curRec
        ReDim Preserve curList(recNum - 1)
        curList(recNum - 1).IDNum = curRec.IDNum
        curList(recNum - 1).word = curRec.word
        curList(recNum - 1).topic = curRec.topic
        recNum = recNum + 1
    Loop
    Close #1
    recNum = recNum - 1
    Exit Sub

'----------------------
'Use error handler for unforeseen errors.
'----------------------
FileIOError:
        MsgBox "The program has encountered an error trying to " & _
            "access the file Wordfind.txt. " & vbCrLf & Err.Description, _
```

```
            vbCritical, "Error " & Err.Number
        End
End Sub
```

The `GetFile()` sub procedure is only called from the `GetAllRecords()` sub procedure when the data file is not found at the specified path. The procedure shows a `FileDialog` object to allow the user to search the computer's file structure in order to locate the file. If the user locates the file and clicks the OK button, then the file's path is returned to the calling function.

```
Private Function GetFile() As String
    Dim fileDiag As FileDialog

    '--------------------
    'Configure and show the open dialog.
    'Return path to calling function.
    '--------------------
    Set fileDiag = Application.FileDialog(msoFileDialogFilePicker)
    With fileDiag      'Configure dialog box
        .Filters.Clear
        .Filters.Add Description:="All files", Extensions:="*.*"
        .Filters.Add Description:="Text", Extensions:="*.txt", Position:=1
        .AllowMultiSelect = False
        .FilterIndex = 1
        .Title = "Select Wordfind.txt File"
        .InitialFileName = ""
        If .Show = -1 Then   'User clicked Open
            GetFile = .SelectedItems(1)   'Return path to selected file
        End If
    End With
End Function
```

The data is written to a hidden worksheet named `Lists` that is in the same workbook as the `Wordfind` puzzle worksheet. After the sheet is cleared, the topics, words, and identification numbers are copied to the first three columns of the `Lists` worksheet from the module level variable array `curList` (this variable was initialized in the `GetAllRecords()` sub procedure) using a `For/Next` loop. I qualify the `Lists` worksheet with an object variable (`ws`) because it is never the active worksheet.

The last statement in the procedure sorts the data alphabetically, first by topic and then by word. This is the major reason I write the data to the worksheet—to take advantage of its fast sorting capabilities so the data is listed alphabetically in the ActiveX controls. Furthermore, when the topics are sorted alphabetically, it's easier to pick out the unique values from the list. Note that I passed the `Sort()` method of the `Range` object several arguments. They are all optional, but at the very least, `Key1` and `Key2` must be included in order to specify the primary and secondary keys on which to sort, which in this case, are the topic and word, respectively. I also included the `MatchCase` argument to specify a case-insensitive sort. You can also pass the `Sort()` method arguments that specify the sort order for each key (`Order1`, `Order2`), whether or not to ignore a header row (`Header`), whether to sort by rows or columns (`Orientation`), and whether or not to treat numbers as text for each key (`DataOption1`, `DataOption2`).

Excel worksheets are hidden and unhidden by selecting Format, Sheet, Hide/Unhide in the application window.

```
Private Sub WriteToWorksheet()
    Dim lastRow As Integer
    Dim ws As Worksheet
    Dim I As Integer

    Set ws = Worksheets("Lists")

    '------------
    'Clear the worksheet
    '------------
    lastRow = ws.UsedRange.Rows.Count
    ws.Range("A2:C" & lastRow).ClearContents

    '----------------
    'Write records to worksheet
    '----------------
    For I = 2 To recNum
        ws.Cells(I, "A").Value = Trim(curList(I - 2).topic)
        ws.Cells(I, "B").Value = Trim(curList(I - 2).word)
        ws.Cells(I, "C").Value = Trim(curList(I - 2).IDNum)
    Next I

    '---------
    'Sort records.
    '---------
```

```
    ws.Range("A2:C" & recNum).Sort Key1:=ws.Range("A2"), Key2:=ws.Range("B2"), _
        MatchCase:=False

End Sub
```

When the user selects a new topic, the `Change()` event of the Combo box is triggered and the List Box is updated with the words associated with the selected topic. This event is also triggered from the `Activate()` event of the `UserForm` object when the `List` property of the Combo Box is assigned the values in the variable array `topics`. The words are added to the List Box by the `GetWords()` sub procedure which reads the values from the hidden worksheet.

```
Private Sub cmbTopics_Change()
    txtTopic.Text = cmbTopics.Text
    txtWord.Text = ""
    cmdUpdate.Enabled = False
    GetWords
End Sub

Private Sub GetWords()
    Dim I As Integer
    Dim ws As Worksheet

    '----------------------
    'Add word list to list box associated with
    'topic on combo box.
    '----------------------
    lstWords.Clear
    Set ws = Worksheets("Lists")
    For I = 2 To ws.UsedRange.Rows.Count
        If ws.Cells(I, "A").Value = cmbTopics.Value Then
            lstWords.AddItem ws.Cells(I, "B").Value
        End If
    Next I
End Sub
```

The `Click()` event of the List Box is triggered whenever the user selects a new value from its list. After the selected word is copied to the Text Box control, the ID number associated with the selected word is retrieved using the `GetIDNum()` function. The ID number is copied to a Label control on the form. I originally added the Label control to the form to test and help debug the program. It serves no purpose to allow the user to see this value; however, the

Label control serves as a convenient location for storing the number of the record currently displayed on the form. The record number is required for updating the file so it can simply be read from the Label control when the user selects the Update button. If you like, you can set the `Visible` property of the Label control to false to prevent the user from seeing the record number. Figure 7.18 shows an example of how the form appears when a word has been selected from the List Box control.

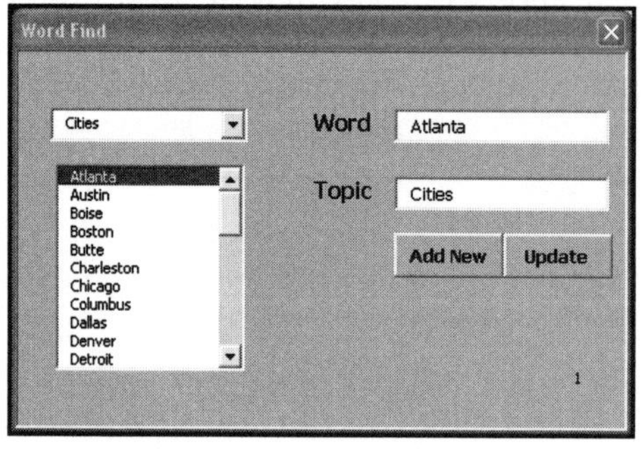

FIGURE 7.18

The update form from the *Word Find* program displaying a user-selection.

```
Private Sub lstWords_Click()
    txtWord.Text = lstWords.Text
    lblIDNum.Caption = GetIDNum
    cmdUpdate.Enabled = True
End Sub

Private Function GetIDNum() As Long
    Dim ws As Worksheet
    Dim c1 As Range, c2 As Range

    '-------------------------------
    'Loop through columns A and B in Lists worksheet to find
    'the correct topic and word and then return ID number.
    '-------------------------------
    Set ws = Worksheets("Lists")
    For Each c2 In ws.Range("A2:A" & ws.UsedRange.Rows.Count)
        If c2.Value = cmbTopics.Value Then
            For Each c1 In ws.Range("B2:B" & ws.UsedRange.Rows.Count)
                If c1.Value = lstWords.Text Then
                    GetIDNum = ws.Range("C" & c1.Row).Value
                    Exit Function
                End If
```

```
            Next
        End If
    Next

End Function
```

To add a new record to the data file, the user must simply enter values for the topic and word before clicking the Add New button. Calls to the `AddRecToWorksheet()`, `AddToControls()`, and `AddToFile()` sub procedures update the hidden `Lists` worksheet and the ActiveX controls, and add a new record to the data file. Note that a new ID number must be assigned to the new record. The code in these procedures should be familiar to you.

```
Private Sub cmdAddNew_Click()

    '------------------------
    'If nothing in text boxes then exit the sub.
    '------------------------
    If txtWord.Text = "" Or txtTopic.Text = "" Then
        MsgBox "You must enter a topic and word before updating the list.", _
                vbOKOnly, "No Entry"
        txtWord.SetFocus
        Exit Sub
    End If

    '------------------------------
    'Add the new record to the Lists worksheet, the file,
    'the List box, and the combo box.
    '------------------------------
    AddRecToWorksheet
    AddToControls
    AddToFile

    txtWord.Text = ""
    recNum = recNum + 1
End Sub

Private Sub AddRecToWorksheet()
    Dim ws As Worksheet
```

```
    '----------------------------------
    'Update the "Lists" worksheet with the new record.
    '----------------------------------
    Set ws = Worksheets("Lists")
    ws.Cells(recNum + 1, "A").Value = txtTopic.Text
    ws.Cells(recNum + 1, "B").Value = txtWord.Text
    ws.Cells(recNum + 1, "C").Value = recNum

    ws.Range("A2:C" & recNum + 1).Sort Key1:=ws.Range("A2"), _
        Key2:=ws.Range("B2"), _
        Order1:=xlAscending, Header:=xlNo, MatchCase:=False, _
        Orientation:=xlSortColumns, DataOption1:=xlSortNormal
End Sub

Private Sub AddToControls()
    Dim I As Integer

    '----------------------------
    'Update the controls on the Userform.
    'Update topic only if its new.
    '----------------------------
    lblIDNum.Caption = recNum
    lstWords.AddItem txtWord.Text
    For I = 0 To cmbTopics.ListCount - 1
        If cmbTopics.List(I) = txtTopic.Text Then
            Exit Sub    'The topic is not new, so exit sub.
        End If
    Next I
    cmbTopics.AddItem txtTopic.Text
End Sub

Private Sub AddToFile()
    Dim filePath As String
    Dim curRec As PuzzleList

    On Error GoTo FileIOError
```

```
    '------------
    'Test for valid path.
    '------------
    filePath = ActiveWorkbook.Path & "\Wordfind.txt"
    If Dir(filePath) <> "Wordfind.txt" Then
        filePath = GetFile
    End If

    curRec.topic = txtTopic.Text
    curRec.word = txtWord.Text
    curRec.IDNum = recNum

    '------------------------------
    'Add the new record to the random access text file.
    '------------------------------
    Open filePath For Random Access Write As #1 Len = Len(curRec)
    Put #1, recNum, curRec
    Close #1
    Exit Sub

'----------------------
'Use error handler for unforseen errors.
'----------------------
FileIOError:
        MsgBox Err.Description, vbCritical, "Error " & Err.Number
        End
End Sub
```

Updating the data file is a bit trickier. Care has to be taken to ensure the correct record in the file is overwritten. This is where the Label control becomes so convenient because its `Caption` property holds the number of the currently displayed record. A record is updated when the user clicks the Update button, presumably after editing an existing word from the list. The `Click()` event procedure of the Update button updates the `Lists` worksheet, the ActiveX controls, and the data file with calls to `UpdateWorksheet()`, `UpdateControls()`, and `UpdateFile()`, respectively. Note that the topic is validated before the record is updated because the program requirements specified that no updates to the topics are allowed.

```
Private Sub cmdUpdate_Click()
    Dim I As Integer
```

```
    Dim validTopic As Boolean

    For I = 0 To cmbTopics.ListCount - 1
        If cmbTopics.List(I) = txtTopic.Text Then
            validTopic = True
            Exit For
        End If
    Next I
    If Not validTopic Then
        MsgBox "You must use a current topic before updating a record.", _
            vbOKOnly, "No Valid Topic"
        Exit Sub
    End If

    '-----------------------------
    'Update record in worksheet, controls, and text file.
    'Only allow updates to the word and not the topic.
    '-----------------------------
    UpdateWorksheet
    UpdateControls
    UpdateFile

    cmdUpdate.Enabled = False
End Sub

Private Sub UpdateWorksheet()
    Dim ws As Worksheet
    Dim updateRow As Long

    Set ws = Worksheets("Lists")
    updateRow = ws.Range("C2:C" & ws.UsedRange.Rows.Count).Find(lblIDNum).Row
    ws.Range("B" & updateRow).Value = txtWord.Text
End Sub

Private Sub UpdateControls()
    '-----------------------
    'Update the list box containing the words.
    '-----------------------
    lstWords.List(lstWords.ListIndex) = txtWord.Text
End Sub
```

```
Private Sub UpdateFile()
    Dim filePath As String
    Dim curRec As PuzzleList

    On Error GoTo FileIOError
    filePath = ActiveWorkbook.Path & "\Wordfind.txt"

    '------------
    'Test for valid path.
    '------------
    If Dir(filePath) <> "Wordfind.txt" Then
        filePath = GetFile
    End If

    '------------
    'Update current record.
    '-------------
    curRec.IDNum = lblIDNum.Caption
    curRec.topic = txtTopic.Text
    curRec.word = txtWord.Text
    Open filePath For Random Access Write As #1 Len = Len(curRec)
    Put #1, Val(lblIDNum.Caption), curRec
    Close #1

    Exit Sub
'---------------------
'Use error handler for unforeseen errors.
'---------------------
FileIOError:
        MsgBox Err.Description, vbCritical, "Error " & Err.Number
        End
End Sub
```

The last procedure listed in the code module for the `UserForm` object is the `QueryClose()` event procedure that is simply used to hide the form.

```
Private Sub UserForm_QueryClose(Cancel As Integer, CloseMode As Integer)
    frmWordFind.Hide
End Sub
```

Because the `GetUniqueTopics()` sub procedure is called from the code modules for the `UserForm` and the `Worksheet` objects, I entered it into a standard code module and gave it public scope. It is called from the `Activate()` event of the `UserForm` object in order to retrieve the unique values for the topics listed in the `Lists` worksheet. The variable array `topics` is passed by reference and filled with the unique topics from column A of the worksheet.

```
Public Sub GetUniqueTopics(topics() As String)
    Dim c As Range, cRange As Range
    Dim ws As Worksheet
    Dim lastRow As Integer
    Dim curValue As String
    Dim I As Integer

    '---------------------------
    'Set object variables. The range should only be
    'set to the used portion of column A.
    '---------------------------
    Set ws = Worksheets("Lists")
    lastRow = ws.UsedRange.Rows.Count
    Set cRange = ws.Range("A2:A" & lastRow)

    '------------------------------
    'Loop through column A in Lists worksheet and find
    'all unique topics.
    '------------------------------
    For Each c In cRange
        If c.Value <> curValue Then
            ReDim Preserve topics(I)
            curValue = c.Value
            topics(I) = c.Value
            I = I + 1
        End If
    Next
End Sub
```

Writing the Code for the Worksheet Module

The remaining code is entered into the code module for the `Worksheet` object and controls the creation of a word search puzzle. This part of the program only reads data from the hidden worksheet (`Lists`) so it does not require any file I/O. The code for the `Worksheet` object module is listed next.

In the same manner as the `Activate()` event of the `UserForm` object, the `Click()` event of the `Refresh` button (`Name` property `cmdRefresh`) serves to fill the Combo Box and List Box controls with the unique topics and words from the `Lists` worksheet. To clear the worksheet of data requires triggering the `Click()` event of the Clear All button (`cmdClear`). The named ranges on the worksheet make the program more readable by identifying what ranges must be cleared of data. Note that the `ClearContents()` method of the `Range` object fails if the range contains merged cells; therefore, the `Value` property of the ranges defined by the names `Output` and `Topic` are initialized to a zero-length string in order to clear their content.

```
Option Explicit

Private Sub cmdRefresh_Click()
    Dim topics() As String

    '----------------------
    'Get unique topics and add to combo box.
    '----------------------
    GetUniqueTopics topics
    cmbTopics.List = topics
    cmbTopics.Value = cmbTopics.List(0)
End Sub

Private Sub cmdClear_Click()

    '--------------------------
    'Clear the puzzle board and ActiveX controls.
    '--------------------------
    Range("WordList").ClearContents
    Range("Puzzle").ClearContents
    Range("Output").Value = ""
    Range("Topic").Value = ""
    cmbTopics.Clear
    lstWords.Clear
End Sub
```

The Change() event of the Combo Box control and the GetWords() sub procedure fill the List Box control with the words associated with the selected topic. The selected topic serves as a title for the puzzle. After the words are added to the List Box, the user may select one item from the list (MultiSelect property fmMultiSelectSingle). This triggers the Click() event procedure of the List Box control which contains a single statement that outputs a string to the worksheet range named Output telling the user what to do next.

```
Private Sub cmbTopics_Change()
    '------------------------------
    'Get words associated with topic and add to list box.
    '------------------------------
    GetWords
    Range("Topic").Value = cmbTopics.Value     'Add a title to the puzzle.
End Sub

Private Sub GetWords()
    Dim c As Range, cRange As Range
    Dim ws As Worksheet
    Dim lastRow As Integer

    '--------------------------
    'Set object variables. The range should only be
    'set to the used portion of column A.
    '--------------------------
    Set ws = Worksheets("Lists")
    lastRow = ws.UsedRange.Rows.Count
    Set cRange = Worksheets("Lists").Range("A2:A" & lastRow)

    '----------------------------
    'Loop through column A in Lists worksheet and find
    'all unique topics. Then add word from column B to List box.
    '----------------------------
    lstWords.Clear
    For Each c In cRange
        If c.Value = cmbTopics.Value Then
            lstWords.AddItem ws.Range("B" & c.Row).Value
        End If
    Next
    lstWords.AddItem ""
End Sub
```

```
Private Sub lstWords_Click()
    Range("Output").Value = "Select a location in the puzzle grid and " _
            & "click on an arrow to specify the words direction."
End Sub
```

The Click() event procedure of the Command Button controls containing an image of an arrow (I used the Picture property to load the images at Design Time) sends program execution to the PlaceWord() sub procedure. The PlaceWord() sub procedure accepts a string argument that indicates the direction ("N", "NE", "E", "SE", "S", "SW", "W", and "NW") in which to write the word in the puzzle. There are a total of eight Click() event procedures that call the PlaceWord() sub procedure.

```
Private Sub cmdEast_Click()
    PlaceWord ("E")
End Sub
Private Sub cmdNE_Click()
    PlaceWord ("NE")
End Sub
Private Sub cmdNorth_Click()
    PlaceWord ("N")
End Sub
Private Sub cmdNW_Click()
    PlaceWord ("NW")
End Sub
Private Sub cmdSE_Click()
    PlaceWord ("SE")
End Sub
Private Sub cmdSouth_Click()
    PlaceWord ("S")
End Sub
Private Sub cmdSW_Click()
    PlaceWord ("SW")
End Sub
Private Sub cmdWest_Click()
    PlaceWord ("W")
End Sub
```

The idea of adding a word to a puzzle in one of eight different directions is conceptually pretty simple. The practical solution to the problem is a bit more difficult. You should recognize that in order to copy each letter of the word to a worksheet cell, you must loop through the string value of the word one letter per iteration. Next, while proceeding through each letter in the string variable, you must increment or decrement a row and/or column index (depends on the specified direction) in order to locate the next cell before copying a letter to that cell.

The `PlaceWord()` sub procedure writes the selected word in the List Box control to the specified cells on the worksheet in its puzzle area. For example, if the user clicks on the Command Button control named `cmdSE` (bottom right button in the 3 × 3 grid of buttons), then the selected word will be written on a diagonal proceeding down and to the right on the puzzle grid, as shown with the word `"BOSTON"` in Figure 7.19.

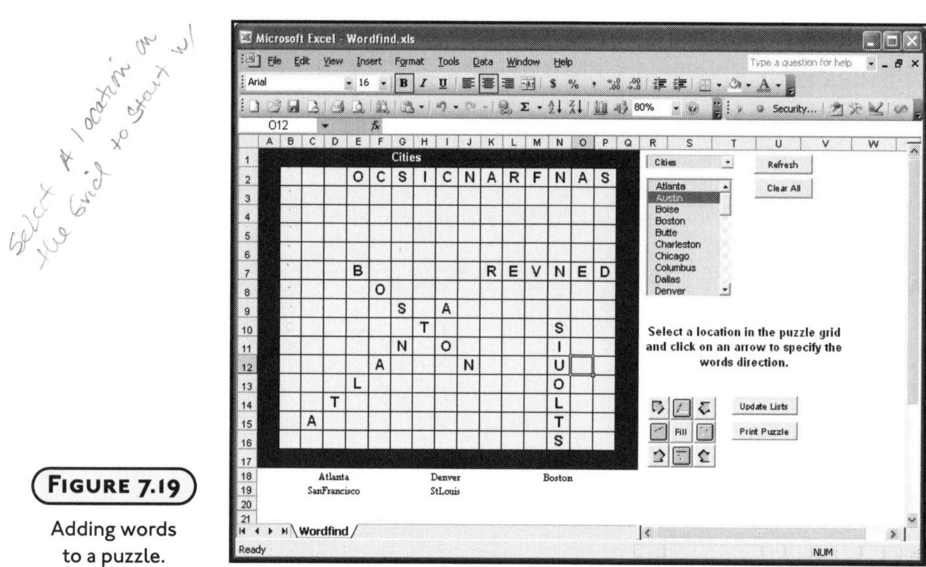

FIGURE 7.19

Adding words to a puzzle.

An error handler is required in the `PlaceWord()` sub procedure to ensure that the user has selected a word from the List Box control before trying to add it to the puzzle. VBA generates an error if you try to access the `ListIndex` property of the List Box control when no item(s) is selected.

The user's selection is validated with a call to the `SelectionValid()` function procedure before it is written to the puzzle with a call to the `WriteWord()` sub procedure. The constants `INC`, `DEC`, and `NOCHANGE` are passed to the `WriteWord()` sub procedure and specify whether to increment, decrement, or do not change the value of the row and column indices while adding the word to the puzzle one letter at a time. For example, if the word is supposed to go straight left to right (`wordDirection = "E"`), then the column index of the cell must be incremented by one and the row index of the cell must remain unchanged while the word is added to the puzzle letter by letter.

```
Private Sub PlaceWord(wordDirection As String)
    Const INC = 1, DEC = -1, NOCHANGE = 0

    On Error GoTo ErrorHandler

    If Not SelectionValid(wordDirection) Then
        Exit Sub
    End If
    Range("Output").Value = ""

    '---------------
    'Write word to puzzle grid.
    '---------------
    Select Case wordDirection
        Case Is = "NW"
            WriteWord DEC, DEC
        Case Is = "N"
            WriteWord DEC, NOCHANGE
        Case Is = "NE"
            WriteWord DEC, INC
        Case Is = "E"
            WriteWord NOCHANGE, INC
        Case "SE"
            WriteWord INC, INC
        Case "S"
            WriteWord INC, NOCHANGE
        Case "SW"
            WriteWord INC, DEC
        Case "W"
            WriteWord NOCHANGE, DEC
    End Select
    WordToList  'Add word to the list below puzzle.
    Range("Output").Value = ""

    Exit Sub
ErrorHandler:
    Range("Output").Value = "Please select a word from the list!"
End Sub
```

The SelectionValid() and CountCells() function procedures work together to validate the user's selection on the puzzle grid for adding a word. The selection is validated to ensure that the user has selected only one cell, that this cell is within the puzzle grid, and that the entire length of the word fits in the puzzle grid. The CountCells() function procedure helps with the latter task.

```
Private Function SelectionValid(wordDirection As String) As Boolean
    Dim wordLength As Integer

    '------------------
    'Test that user selected one cell.
    '------------------
    If Selection.Count <> 1 Then
        SelectionValid = False
        Range("Output").Value = "You must select ONE cell in the puzzle grid."
        Exit Function
    End If

    '---------------------
    'Start cell must be in the puzzle range.
    '---------------------
    If (Selection.Row < 2 Or Selection.Row > 16) Or _
            (Selection.Column < 2 Or Selection.Column > 16) Then
        SelectionValid = False
        Range("Output").Value = "Your selection must be in the puzzle grid."
        Exit Function
    End If

    '----------------------
    'The word should fit within puzzle range.
    '----------------------
    wordLength = Len(lstWords.List(lstWords.ListIndex))
    If wordLength > CountCells(wordDirection) Then
        Range("Output").Value = "The selection does not fit in the target area."
        SelectionValid = False
        Exit Function
    End If
    SelectionValid = True
End Function
```

The `CountCell()` function procedure first calculates the number of available cells going up, down, left, and right from the user's selection on the puzzle grid. Next, a `Select/Case` structure chooses the number of available cells from these four possible values based on the word's direction. The function returns the maximum allowed number of cells that can be used to add a word to the puzzle in the desired direction. The `SelectionValid()` function procedure compares this returned value to the length of the word selected by the user in order to validate that word.

```
Private Function CountCells(wordDirection As String) As Integer
    Dim numCellsUp As Integer, numCellsDown As Integer
    Dim numCellsLeft As Integer, numCellsRight As Integer

    numCellsUp = Selection.Row - 1
    numCellsDown = 17 - Selection.Row
    numCellsLeft = Selection.Column - 1
    numCellsRight = 17 - Selection.Column

    '--------------------------------
    'Determine the number of available cells in the puzzle grid
    'for given word direction. Ignore placement of other words.
    '--------------------------------
    Select Case wordDirection
        Case Is = "NW"
            CountCells = Application.WorksheetFunction.Min( _
                         numCellsUp, numCellsLeft)
        Case Is = "N"
            CountCells = numCellsUp
        Case Is = "NE"
            CountCells = Application.WorksheetFunction.Min( _
                         numCellsUp, numCellsRight)
        Case Is = "E"
            CountCells = numCellsRight
        Case "SE"
            CountCells = Application.WorksheetFunction.Min( _
                         numCellsDown, numCellsRight)
        Case "S"
            CountCells = numCellsDown
```

```
        Case "SW"
            CountCells = Application.WorksheetFunction.Min( _
                         numCellsDown, numCellsLeft)
        Case "W"
            CountCells = numCellsLeft
    End Select
End Function
```

The WriteWord() sub procedure adds the word to the puzzle one letter at a time. The word is first converted to all uppercase letters using the UCase() function before a Do-Loop iterates through the word letter by letter. Each letter is written to the appropriate cell based on the values of the vertical and horizontal arguments. These arguments were passed in from the PlaceWord() sub procedure as the INC, DEC, and NOCHANGE constants. That is, the values of the vertical and horizontal arguments will either be 1, -1, or 0. These values are used to increment, decrement, or leave unchanged the row and column indices passed to the Cells property of the Worksheet object.

```
Private Sub WriteWord(vertical As Integer, horizontal As Integer)
    Dim curWord As String, wordLength As Integer
    Dim I As Integer
    Dim cellRow As Integer, cellCol As Integer

    '-------------
    'Initialize variables.
    '-------------
    curWord = UCase(lstWords.Value)
    wordLength = Len(curWord)
    cellRow = Selection.Row
    cellCol = Selection.Column

    '-------------------------------
    'Write the word to the puzzle grid in indicated direction.
    '-------------------------------
    Do
        Cells(cellRow, cellCol).Value = Mid(curWord, I + 1, 1)
        I = I + 1
        cellRow = cellRow + vertical
        cellCol = cellCol + horizontal
    Loop While (I < wordLength)
End Sub
```

After a word has been successfully added to the puzzle, the WordToList() sub procedure adds the word to the next cell in a series of cells below the puzzle grid. These cells are a merged set of five cells across one row. For example, the range B18 : F18 is merged into one cell as is G18 : K18, L18 : P18, B19 : F19, and so on. Because merged cells are accessed using the row and column index of the upper most left cell in the range, the merged cells of interest are those with column index values of 2, 7, and 12. Even though I use a For/Each loop to iterate through the defined range of merged cells, I must qualify the cell in a conditional statement using a column index because the loop still accesses every cell in the merged range and I only want it to access every fifth cell.

```
Private Sub WordToList()
    Dim c As Range

    '--------------------------
    'Add the word to the list below the puzzle grid.
    'Cells are merged across five columns.
    '--------------------------
    For Each c In Range("WordList")
        If c.Value = "" And (c.Column = 2 Or c.Column = 7 Or _
        c.Column = 12) Then
            c.Value = lstWords.Value
            Exit Sub
        End If
    Next
End Sub
```

The Click() event procedure of the Fill button (cmdFill) fills the empty cells in the puzzle grid with randomly chosen uppercase letters. To generate random uppercase letters, I generate random numbers between 65 and 90 and convert them to their ASCII character using the Chr() function. (The ASCII characters A through Z are represented by decimal values 65 through 90.) A For/Each loop searches the puzzle grid for empty cells and adds a letter to each. Figure 7.20 shows an example of a completed puzzle that is ready for printing.

```
Private Sub cmdFill_Click()
    Dim c As Range
    Dim ranNum As Integer

    '---------------------
    'Output random uppercase characters to
    'empty cells in puzzle grid.
    '---------------------
```

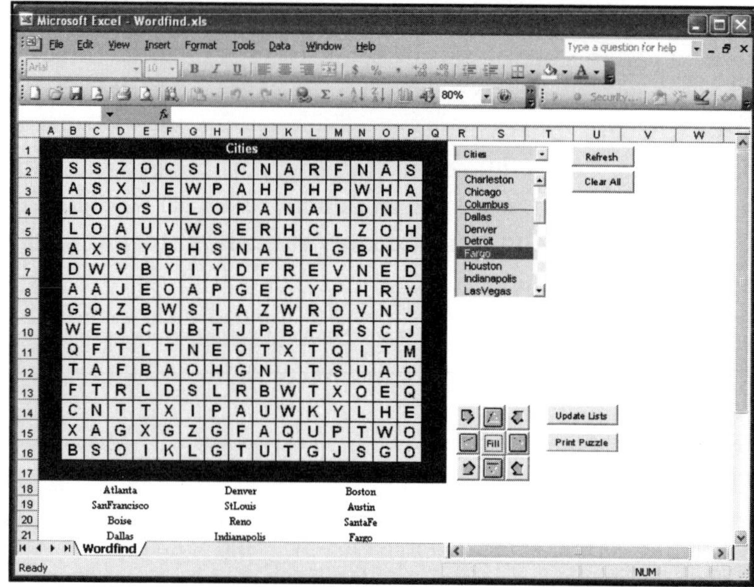

FIGURE 7.20

A completed word search puzzle.

```
    Randomize
    For Each c In Range("Puzzle")
        ranNum = Int(26 * Rnd + 65)
        If c.Value = "" Then c.Value = Chr(ranNum)
    Next
    Range("Output").Value = ""
End Sub
```

The data update form is shown modally when the user clicks the Update Lists button (`cmdUpdateLists`).

```
Private Sub cmdUpdateLists_Click()
    frmWordFind.Show vbModal
End Sub
```

The last procedure listed is the `Click()` event of the `Print` button (`cmdPrint`). This procedure first removes the borders and background color from the area of cells that define the puzzle so they won't show on the printout. Next, the `PrintArea` property of a `PageSetup` object is set to the string representing the range that defines the puzzle grid and the list of words below it. I defined the range A1:Q25 in the `Wordfind` worksheet to the name `"Print_Area"`. The

PrintOut() method of the Worksheet object prints the defined area. Finally, the original borders and color are added back to the puzzle area of the worksheet. An error handler is included to display any runtime errors generated by trying to print the puzzle (for example, No printer available).

```
Private Sub cmdPrint_Click()
    On Error GoTo ErrorHandler

    '-------------------------
    'Format puzzle with no borders or color.
    '-------------------------
    Range("Puzzle").Select
    Selection.Borders(xlEdgeLeft).LineStyle = xlNone
    Selection.Borders(xlEdgeTop).LineStyle = xlNone
    Selection.Borders(xlEdgeBottom).LineStyle = xlNone
    Selection.Borders(xlEdgeRight).LineStyle = xlNone
    Selection.Borders(xlInsideVertical).LineStyle = xlNone
    Selection.Borders(xlInsideHorizontal).LineStyle = xlNone
    Selection.Interior.ColorIndex = xlNone

    '---------------------------
    'Print the puzzle and word list below it.
    '---------------------------
    ActiveSheet.PageSetup.PrintArea = "Print_Area"
    ActiveSheet.PrintOut Copies:=1
    '---------------------------
    'Reset the borders and color on the puzzle.
    '---------------------------
    Selection.Borders(xlEdgeLeft).LineStyle = xlContinuous
    Selection.Borders(xlEdgeTop).LineStyle = xlContinuous
    Selection.Borders(xlEdgeBottom).LineStyle = xlContinuous
    Selection.Borders(xlEdgeRight).LineStyle = xlContinuous
    Selection.Borders(xlInsideVertical).LineStyle = xlContinuous
    Selection.Borders(xlInsideHorizontal).LineStyle = xlContinuous
    Selection.Interior.ColorIndex = 34
    Exit Sub
```

```
    '--------------------
    'Output unforeseen errors with printing.
    '--------------------
ErrorHandler:
    MsgBox Err.Description, vbCritical, "Error"
    End
End Sub
```

This concludes the *Word Find* program. If you know someone who likes word search puzzles, you can now create a few for him or her. Add the features described in the Challenges section at the end of the chapter to more easily create puzzles with this program.

Chapter Summary

In this chapter, you learned how to create and access text files using sequential and random methods. VBA includes a number of additional methods for file I/O not covered in this chapter; however, learning how to read and write text files is a good first step and often comes in handy with applications that only require access to small amounts of data. You also learned how to create error-handling routines in VBA procedures that prevent the program from crashing because of a runtime error. Finally, you learned how to use some of the debugging tools available from the VBA IDE to help write near error-free code.

This chapter introduced the last of the fundamental programming concepts covered in this book. The remaining chapters are concerned with programming specific objects in the Excel object model.

CHALLENGES

1. Load the `Wordfind.xls` project and open the IDE. Find the `PlaceWord()` sub procedure and set a breakpoint on the statement `If Not SelectionValid(wordDirection) Then`. Return to Excel and run the program by clicking the Clear All button. Do not click refresh! Next, select a cell in the puzzle grid and click on an arrow button. When the debugger is invoked follow the order of program execution to see which statement generates the runtime error and triggers the code in the error handler.
2. Load the `Wordfind.xls` project and open the IDE. Set a break point to the statement that starts the `For/Each` loop in the `GetWords()` sub procedure listed in the code module for the `Wordfind` worksheet. Inside the `For/Each` loop, add a `Debug.Print` statement that outputs the value of the iterative cell to the Immediate window. Run the program to initiate debug mode and step through the program code while viewing the content of the Immediate window.
3. Clear the content of the `Wordfind` worksheet by clicking the Clear All button. Proceed to the IDE and replace the `Debug.Print` statement in Challenge 2 with the `Debug.Assert` statement: `Debug.Assert c.Value = cmbTopics.Value`. Next, proceed to the `Wordfind` worksheet and click the `Refresh` button. After the program enters debug mode view the worksheet again to see if the content of the ActiveX controls has changed.
4. Write two VBA programs that save the content of the first 10 rows and columns in a worksheet to a tab-delimited text file. First use the `SaveAs()` method of the `Worksheet` object, then try using the `Open` statement to create a sequential access file. Be sure to include an error handler in the procedure that writes the data to the file.
5. Write two VBA programs that read the content of the text file created in Challenge 4. Use the `Open()` method of the `Workbooks` collection object and the `Open` statement.
6. Write a VBA program that saves the content of the first 3 rows and columns in a worksheet to a random access file. Write another program that reads the file into a worksheet.
7. Write a VBA program containing a UserForm with an Image control and a Command Button control such that the click of the Command Button control allows the user to select an image for loading into the Image control.
8. Edit the form module's code and/or design in the *Word Find* program to prevent the user from adding identical records to the data file.

(continues)

CHALLENGES (*CONTINUED*)

9. Edit the form module's code in the *Word Find* program to allow the user to update existing topics in the data file.
10. Edit the form module's code in the *Word Find* program to allow users to delete selected records from the data file.
11. Edit the error handler in the `GetAllRecords()` sub procedure of the form module in the *Word Find* program such that it creates a new data file when a runtime error occurs. Be sure to fix any errors in other procedures that may result from the creation of an empty data file.
12. Enhance the *Word Find* program to include validation procedures that prevent the user from overwriting words previously added to a puzzle.
13. Enhance the *Word Find* program to include the ability to save and reload puzzles. Do not save the entire worksheet; instead, save the content of the puzzle and word list to a text file (give the file a custom extension such as .puz). Then write a procedure to read the text file into the `Wordfind` worksheet. Be sure to include a `FileDialog` object to allow the user to select a saved puzzle.
14. Enhance the *Word Find* program to include the ability to automatically generate puzzles based on the user's selection of a topic. The program should randomly select twenty-four words (or as many words that are in the list for that topic) from the list and add them to the puzzle without overwriting each other. Alternatively, the program can add just those words selected by the user from the List Box control. Be sure to change the `MultiSelect` property of the List Box control to allow for multiple selections.

Using XML with Excel-VBA Projects

If you have any experience with the World Wide Web, whether it's developing Web sites or just browsing, then I am sure you have heard of XML (e**X**tensible **M**arkup **L**anguage). Although not a new technology, it has only been in recent years that XML has generated a lot of interest. This is partially evident by Microsoft's decision to add XML support to some of its Office programs (including Excel) starting with version 10.0 (XP) and extending that support in version 11.0 (2003). I expect the level of XML support to increase in subsequent versions of Office applications. In this chapter I will discuss the following topics:

- Basic XML syntax
- Opening and saving XML files with Excel
- Importing and exporting XML documents with VBA
- The `XmlMap` Object
- The `ListObject` Object

Project: Revisiting the Math Game

In Chapter 4 I introduced you to the *Math Game* program which used a worksheet interface to quiz a student's elementary math skills. In this chapter, I will discuss enhancements to the *Math Game* program that rely on data from XML files. Enhancements to the *Math Game* program include the following:

- The ability to use prewritten tests read from an XML file instead of generating problems for a test randomly.

- The ability to track students' test scores and automatically increase the difficulty level of their next test based on the results of their last test.
- The ability to save students' scores to an XML file.

The *Math Game* program relies on XML files serving as a database that store the tests, student information, and test scores. The main interface for the program is similar to the one from Chapter 4 and is shown in its revised form in Figure 8.1. Worksheets have been added to the program interface to allow a user (i.e., teacher) to quickly write and save exams, update student lists, and view test results.

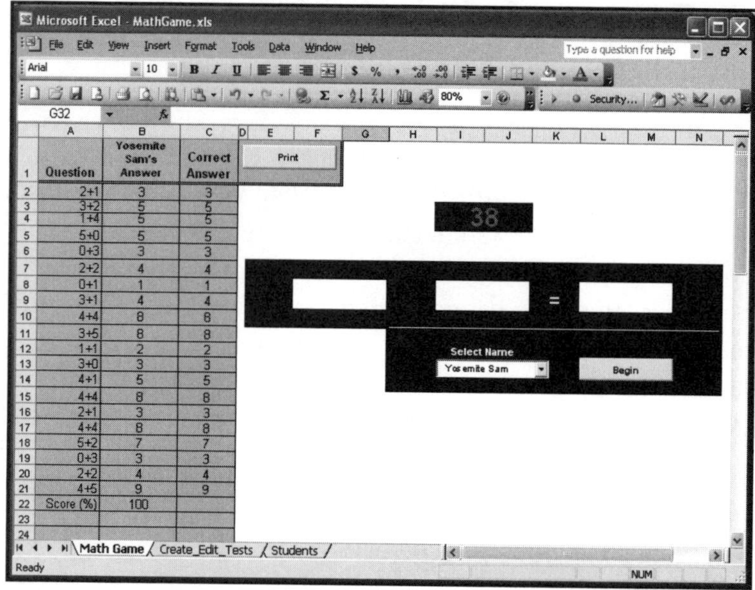

FIGURE 8.1

The Math Game.

INTRODUCTION TO XML

You may already be familiar with the **H**yper**T**ext **M**arkup **L**anguage (HTML) which is used by Web developers to instruct browsers on how to display Web pages. For example, when the following HTML code is saved as a text file with an .html (or .htm) extension, any Web browser can recognize the file and display its markup. In this case, a browser displays the message HELLO WORLD! on a white background as shown in Figure 8.2.

```
<HTML>
    <HEAD>
        <TITLE>Basic HTML Document</TITLE>
    </HEAD>
```

```
    <BODY BGCOLOR=WHITE>
        <P>HELLO WORLD!</P>
    </BODY>
</HTML>
```

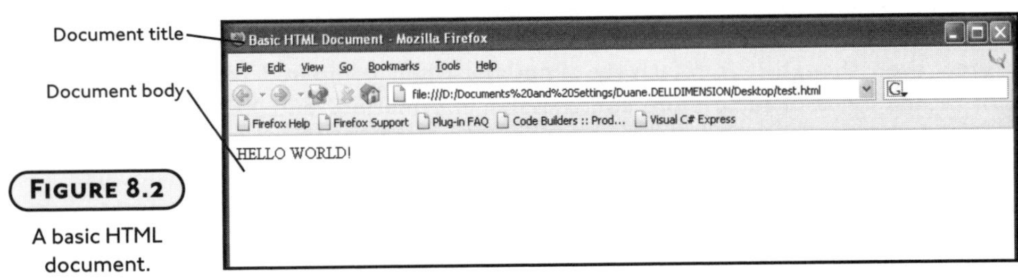

FIGURE 8.2

A basic HTML document.

HTML uses predefined *tags* enclosed in angle brackets (< >) to identify different formatting elements of a document. You don't really have to know HTML to identify the purpose of the tags in the previous document. For example, `<TITLE> </TITLE>` defines the title of the document and `<BODY> </BODY>` defines that part of the document displayed in the browser window (see Figure 8.2). You will note that the tags do not appear in the Web browser window. Of course, that is the purpose of HTML—to use tags to mark up how a document should appear in a browser window without showing the markup language.

In addition to the few tags I've shown here, there are many more HTML tags for marking up how a Web document is displayed; however, it's not this book's purpose to teach you HTML. Instead, I suggest consulting some of the numerous Web tutorials or available books if you are interested in learning HTML.

XML is another markup language with similarities to HTML, but with an entirely different purpose. In the next few sections, I will define and describe what it takes to create a basic XML document.

What Is XML?

XML is a text-based markup language designed to describe a document's data, not its appearance. HTML is great for displaying data, but it is difficult and awkward to use for describing data. XML serves to separate the two processes making it easier to do both. Because HTML displays data and XML describes data, the two technologies are complimentary, not competitive.

In the Real World

In the highly competitive world of computer technology it is a rare occurrence when everyone agrees on a standard. The XML standard (defined by the World Wide Web Consortium—see http://www.w3c.org) has been widely adopted and continues to grow in terms of its use and available support tools (editors, code libraries, samples, and so on). The popularity of XML continues to grow even though it is relatively simplistic when compared to other data-communication technologies used to store and transfer information. Will XML eventually replace some of these more advanced and efficient technologies? Only time will tell, but the idea of using a free technology that doesn't require the installation of special software drivers, or the purchase of special licenses, is intriguing.

When you create a new XML document, **you** define the tags; therefore, you are essentially defining a new language. This is an area where XML differs significantly from HTML. Yes, both markup languages use tags, but with HTML, all tags are predefined by a standard.

Even though you define the tags, there are a few rules you must follow when creating an XML document. The standards that define XML syntax (discussed later) must be followed, and if you intend to allow other applications to use your language, you must create another document called a schema that defines the tags in your document. All of this results in XML documents that store your data as text files for use in Web browsers and other applications.

XML is becoming very popular for several reasons. Foremost, XML is free, so you do not have to pay any proprietary fees in order to use it. With regard to Web development, XML files are text files and the Web is very good at exchanging data stored in text files. XML finally gives Web developers a consistent (and best of all free) medium in which to share data, but the Web is not the only medium for which XML is well-suited. Application development often requires the use of text files and/or database files for storing and sharing critical data. XML allows for the use of a consistent medium for data I/O without having to install and configure additional drivers or pay for proprietary software. Finally, because XML documents are text documents, they can easily be shared between applications across any platform.

An XML Sample

In the *Math Game* program, I create an XML language that describes an elementary math test. The following XML code describes a test for the *Math Game* program. The code is only a portion of the document, but the omitted portion is repetitive.

```
<?xml version="1.0" encoding="UTF-8">
<test>
    <problem>
        <number>1</number>
        <left_operand>2</left_operand>
        <operator>+</operator>
        <right_operand>1</right_operand>
        <answer>3</answer>
    </problem>
    <problem>
        <number>2</number>
        <left_operand>3</left_operand>
        <operator>+</operator>
        <right_operand>2</right_operand>
        <answer>5</answer>
    </problem>
</test>
```

You should be able to recognize that this defines the structure of an elementary math test. The first line of the code is an XML declaration and defines the XML version and character encoding used in the document. In this example, the document conforms to the 1.0 specification of XML (see http://www.w3c.org) and uses the Unicode text formatting character set (UTF-8).

```
<?xml version="1.0" encoding="UTF-8">
```

Most XML files begin with a similar line and Excel requires this line, or it won't recognize the file as XML and will try to open it as an ordinary text file.

I invented all other tags (<test>, <problem>, <number>, <left_operand>, <operator>, <right_operand>, and <answer>) used in the document, and examination of the XML document's structure shows a repetitive pattern. The document consists of a set of two <problem> </problem> tags nested within the root tag <test> </test>. There are also several tags describing the problem number, operands, operator, and answer nested within each <problem> </problem> tag; thus, there is a hierarchy to the document's structure that follows from <test> to <problem> to all remaining elements.

A test with only two problems doesn't really test a student's ability. In reality, the XML document would contain several more <problem> tags, but I've left them out for brevity.

XML Syntax

I've already discussed how XML allows you to create your own language by defining your own set of tags to use in a document; however, you still have to follow a standard set of rules when creating your own XML language. Unlike HTML, the syntax requirements of XML are strict, but there aren't very many rules and they are easy to learn.

XML Documents Must Have a Root Element

Every XML document you write must contain a pair of tags that define a root element. In the previous example, the tags `<test> </test>` define the document's root element (I use the words *tag* and *element* interchangeably). All other tags must be nested within this element. Nested elements are referred to as child elements. There are also sub-child elements and parent elements, but this is just jargon for describing a document's hierarchy. For example, the root element `<test>` is a parent to the child element `<problem>`. Furthermore, `<problem>` is a parent element to the child elements `<number>`, `<left_operand>`, `<operator>`, `<right_operand>`, and `<answer>` which are also sub-child elements to `<test>`.

XML Elements Must Have a Closing Tag

In HTML, you can get away with omitting the closing tag for many of its elements. For example, you can omit the closing tags `</P>` and `</LI>` for closing paragraphs and list elements, respectively.

```
<P>This is my paragraph.
<LI>This is an item in my list.
```

In XML, all elements **must** have a closing tag. To distinguish a closing tag from an opening tag, you use a forward slash (/) inside the angle bracket of the second tag, as follows:

```
<p>This is my paragraph.</p>
<li>This is an item in my list.</li>
<name>Fred Flintstone</name>
```

In cases where tags do not have an ending tag (such as the `<img>` tag in HTML, used to define an image), you may use a single tag in XML, but you must also include a forward slash just before the closing angle bracket, as follows:

```
<img src="aPicture.jpg" />
```

You may have noticed that the opening declaration in the XML test document does not have a closing tag. This is because the declaration is not an XML element, and is technically not even part of the XML document. The declaration begins with <? and ends with ?> to indicate that this is a special header line and not part of the document itself. There is, therefore, no violation of XML syntax.

XML Tags Are Case-Sensitive

In HTML, you are allowed to mix uppercase or lowercase characters. For example, HTML doesn't care if you open the body of a document with `<BODY>` and close it with `</body>`.

In XML, opening and closing tags must be written in the same case. The tag pair `<TEST> </test>` is illegal in XML and must be written as `<test> </test>` or `<TEST> </TEST>` or some other combination where the case of each letter in the opening and closing tags match exactly.

Although not required by XML, it is a convention to use all lowercase characters in your XML tags. To distinguish separate words in a single tag, you may use mixed case or an underscore, such as `<firstName>` or `<first_name>`. At the very least, you should use descriptive names for your tags as it helps self-document your XML code.

XML Tags Must Be Properly Nested

In HTML, some tags can be improperly nested but still yield the desired result. The following HTML statement improperly nests the bold (`<B>`) and italic (`<I>`) tags.

```
<B>This sentence is in bold font and the last word is also in <I>italic</B></I>
```

In XML, the statement must be written with properly nested tags.

```
<b>This sentence is in bold font and the last word is also in <i>italic</i></b>
```

To help document your XML code, you can include comments in the same manner that they are used in HTML.

```
<--This is a comment. -->
```

XML Attributes Must Be Enclosed in Quotes

In XML, tags may have attributes assigned as name/value pairs. For example, in the XML document describing a test for the *Math Game*, I could extend the definition of the `<test>` tag to include a test identification number for the purpose of describing the level of difficulty.

```
<test testID="1A">
```

In this example, testID is an attribute of the tag <test> and it must be assigned a value using quotes.

Use child elements instead of attributes as much as possible in your XML documents. There are no rules in XML that state when to use attributes or child elements; however, it is usually easier to include a child element instead of an attribute. For example, instead of using the testID attribute, you could just as easily include it as a child element of <test>.

```
<test>
    <testID>1A</testID>
    <!--and so on-->
```

XML Element Names

I've already discussed some aspects of naming your XML element tags, such as their case-sensitivity and the convention to use all lowercase characters. There are a few more rules and conventions regarding element names. Rules that you must follow include:

- Names may contain letters, numbers, and other characters.
- Names must not start with a number or punctuation character.
- Names must not start with XML (or any other form of these letters in a different case).
- Names must not contain spaces.

Remember to use descriptive names for your tags, but avoid the following:

- Overly long names. Names should be descriptive and as short as possible. For example, don't use the_students_first_name when first_name is sufficient.
- Using the dash (-), colon (:) or period (.) in a name. Depending on the software that reads your XML document, you could get into some trouble using these characters as the program may try to subtract something, or try to invoke a property or method of an unknown object. The colon is reserved for something called namespaces (not discussed) and should never be used in an element's name.
- Unusual characters that may not be supported on all platforms. Characters with umlauts, accents, and so forth are legal in XML, but if they are not supported by the software using your XML document, the program may crash.

XML Schemas

XML schemas are text-based documents written in the XML schema language that describe the structure of your XML document(s). An XML schema is, in effect, the definition of your language. In order for other people to use your language in their application they need the definitions described in the schema. Other applications need this definition in order to understand the elements' meaning in your XML document; otherwise, the language cannot be understood except by your own applications—because, of course, you know the meaning of your own language. The following schema defines the elements of the XML document that describes a test for the *Math Game* program.

```
<xsd:schema xmlns:xsd="http://www.w3.org/2001/XMLSchema">
   <xsd:element nillable="true" name="test">
      <xsd:complexType>
         <xsd:sequence minOccurs="0">
            <xsd:element minOccurs="0" maxOccurs="unbounded" nillable="true"
name="problem" form="unqualified">
               <xsd:complexType>
                  <xsd:sequence minOccurs="0">
                     <xsd:element minOccurs="0" nillable="true" type="xsd:integer"
name="number" form="unqualified">
                     </xsd:element>
                     <xsd:element minOccurs="0" nillable="true" type="xsd:integer"
name="left_operand" form="unqualified">
                     </xsd:element>
                     <xsd:element minOccurs="0" nillable="true" type="xsd:string"
name="operator" form="unqualified">
                     </xsd:element>
                     <xsd:element minOccurs="0" nillable="true" type="xsd:integer"
name="right_operand" form="unqualified">
                     </xsd:element>
                     <xsd:element minOccurs="0" nillable="true" type="xsd:integer"
name="answer" form="unqualified">
                     </xsd:element>
                  </xsd:sequence>
               </xsd:complexType>
            </xsd:element>
         </xsd:sequence>
      </xsd:complexType>
   </xsd:element>
</xsd:schema>
```

If you glance through this code, you may recognize that it's defining data types and properties for the elements in the XML document describing a test. Unfortunately, learning how to write XML schemas is beyond the scope of this book; however, at this point, it really doesn't matter because Excel will generate schemas for you if you don't define them yourself. In the *Math Game* program, you will never have to work with a schema even though they are present and working in the background.

XML Validation

Validation is the process of testing XML documents and schemas to ensure that they follow the rules of the language. After writing an XML document, you should check to ensure that it is well-formed; that is, the document must adhere to the syntax rules I've already discussed. The process of testing a document's form is analogous to compiling a VBA program. When your VBA program contains syntax errors, you receive a compile error and the debugger is invoked. When your XML document is not well-formed, a good XML editor will display an error message and highlight the section of the document containing the error.

Although you can use simple text editors such as Notepad for creating XML documents, these editors cannot validate your code. Instead, I recommend you find a dedicated XML editor if you intend to spend any time developing applications that rely on XML documents. Alternatively, you can find XML validation tools on the internet. One such validation tool can be found at http://www.w3schools.com/dom/dom_validate.asp.

XML and Excel

Microsoft first added minimal XML support to Office 2000 (so little support that I don't really count it) and Excel with the ability to embed XML in spreadsheets saved as HTML documents. Support for XML has since been extended in Office XP and 2003 where users can save a spreadsheet as an XML document using either a custom or an Excel-spreadsheet schema. You can also open XML documents as new spreadsheets or import the data from an XML document into an existing worksheet.

Many of the features I am about to show, both from the Excel application and VBA, are supported only in Excel 2003.

Opening and Importing XML Documents into an Excel Worksheet

To open an XML document from the Excel application, select File, Open and then choose the desired XML file (.xml file extension) from the Open dialog box. After selecting a file, you will be asked if you want to open the file as an XML list, read-only workbook, or to use the XML Source Task Pane (see Figure 8.3). Typically, you load the data into a worksheet as an Excel list in order to take advantage of the data management features a list provides.

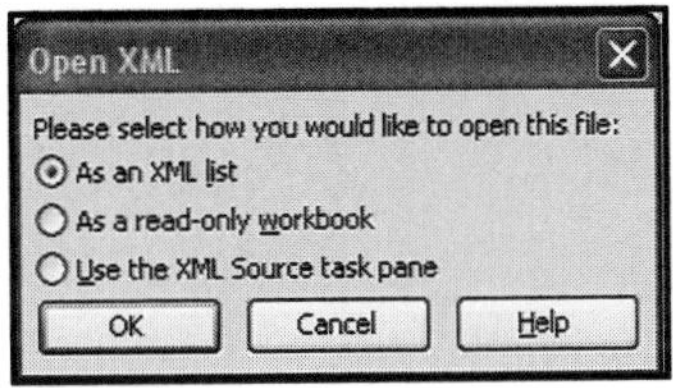

FIGURE 8.3

Selecting the data format when opening an XML file.

If the XML file does not reference an existing schema document (.xsd file extension), Excel will automatically create one (you may be notified of this fact as shown in Figure 8.4) and store it internally with the workbook. You don't have to see the schema, or know how it describes your XML document, but you should know that it's there working in the background defining your data elements for Excel.

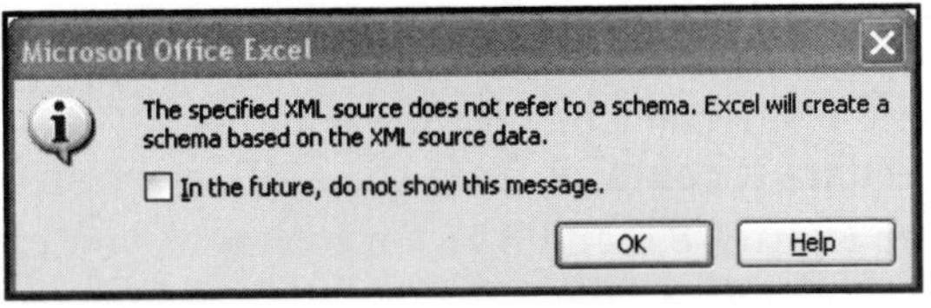

FIGURE 8.4

Opening an XML file with no referenced schema.

When you open an XML file as a list, Excel adds the data to a worksheet and creates a list (normally created from the Data menu). An Excel list provides additional features and formatting that makes it easy to identify and modify the list. Figure 8.5 shows data from an XML document that describes a list of words and topics (something you might use in the project for Chapter 7). The list is highlighted with a blue border, and a filter (normally selected from the Data menu) is automatically applied. In addition, an asterisk marks the next available row for inserting data into the list. The following XML code defines the basic structure of the XML file opened in Figure 8.5—the data was omitted for brevity.

```
<?xml version="1.0" encoding="UTF-8"?>
<word_find>
     <topic_word_pair>
          <topic></topic>
          <word></word>
     </topic_word_pair>
     <!--repeat topic_word_pair element-->
</word_find>
```

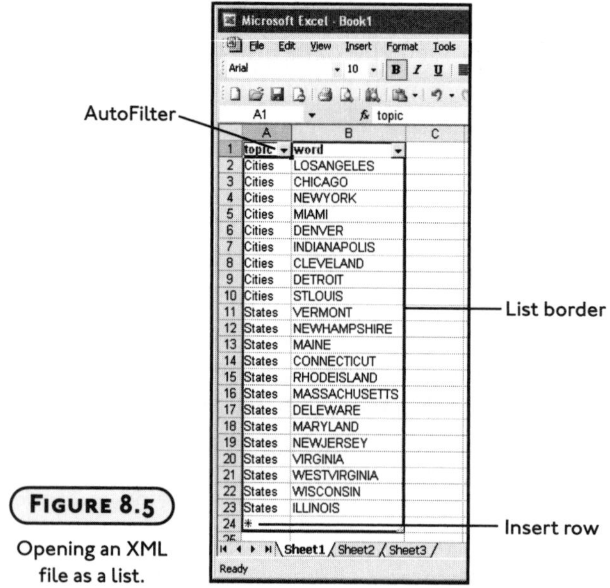

FIGURE 8.5

Opening an XML file as a list.

You can manage the list and the data it contains from the XML selection on the Data menu and/or the Source Task Pane (see Figures 8.6 and 8.7). For example, you can export changes to the list to the XML file, refresh the data in the list, edit the properties of the XML map, and more. As you will see shortly, Excel provides several objects that allow your VBA programs to accomplish these same tasks.

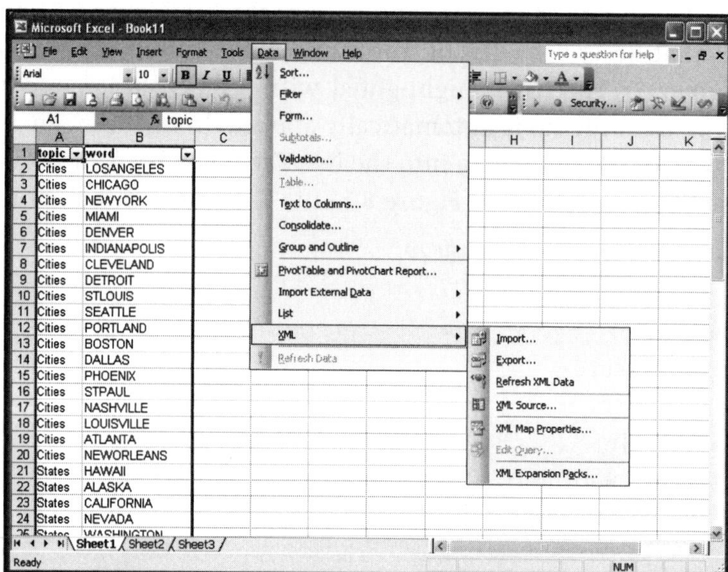

FIGURE 8.6

The XML menu selection in Excel.

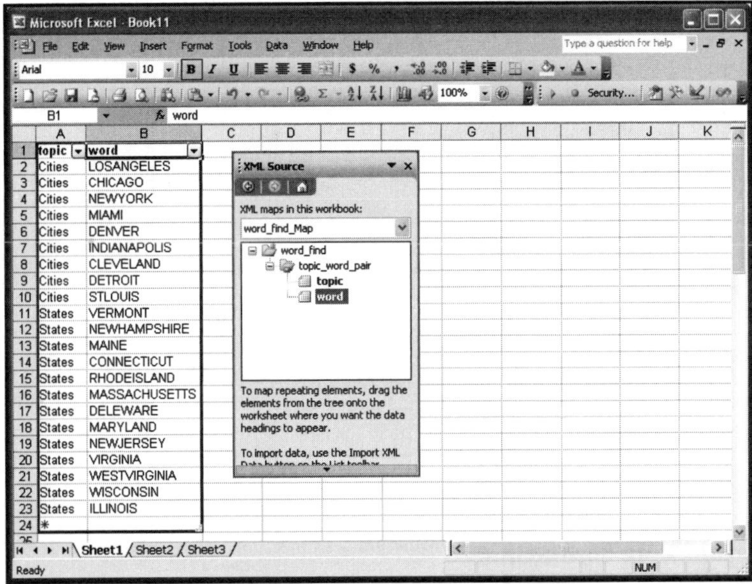

FIGURE 8.7

The XML Source Task Pane.

Excel also uses the provided (or created) XML schema to create an XML map that serves to map the elements in the XML file to specific ranges in the worksheet. The map, shown in the Source Task Pane in Figure 8.7, was created automatically when I opened the XML file. The `topic` element is mapped to the range `A1:A23` in the worksheet and `word` is mapped to `B1:B23`. The map tells Excel how changes to the list must be saved in the XML file such that it preserves its original structure.

You can also import data from an XML file into any existing worksheet by selecting Data, XML, Import (see Figure 8.6) from the application window. Again, a schema will be automatically created (if one is not referenced) and you will be prompted to select a range in the worksheet telling where you want the data inserted.

Saving Worksheets to XML Files

Saving existing data from a worksheet to an XML file is easy. Select File, Save As from the application window and choose one of two possibilities for XML file types from the Save As dialog box as shown in Figure 8.8.

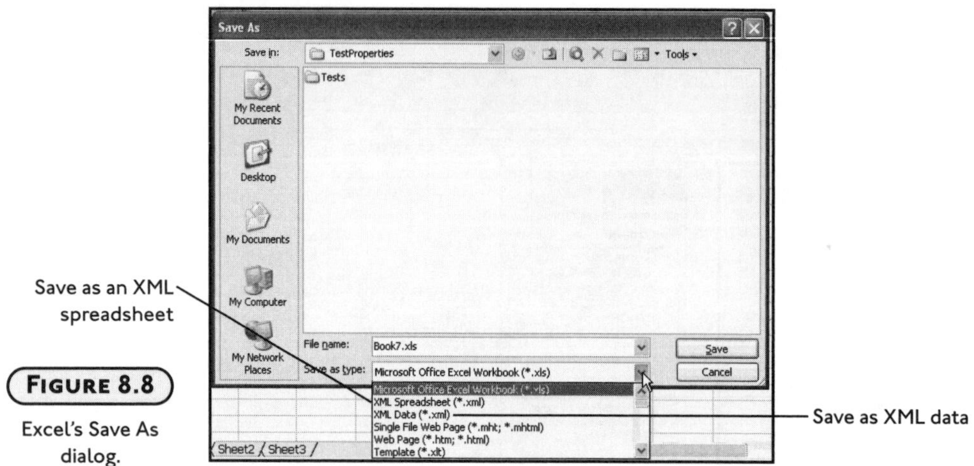

FIGURE 8.8

Excel's Save As dialog.

Saving Data as an XML Spreadsheet

If you choose to save the data as an XML spreadsheet, Excel will use its own schema to define the document. As you might expect, the XML required to define a spreadsheet is quite long, but you don't have to worry about that because Excel creates it for you. The root tag is `<Workbook>` and it will contain nested `<Worksheet>` tags for every worksheet in a workbook. In addition to the `<Worksheet>` tags, there are several other tags that describe the formatting and objects in the workbook. The following code shows the basic format of a document saved using the Excel-XML structure (data and attributes have been deleted for brevity and clarity).

```
<Workbook>
  <DocumentProperties/>
  <OfficeDocumentSettings/>
  <ExcelWorkbook/>
  <Styles>
    <Style/>
  </Styles>
  <Names>
    <NamedRange"/>
  </Names>
  <Worksheet>
    <Table>
      <Column>
      <Row>
        <Cell>
          <Data/>
```

```
        </Cell>
      </Row>
    </Table>
    <WorksheetOptions/>
  </Worksheet>
</Workbook>
```

The document resulting from saving a workbook with the Excel-XML structure is just a text file; however, it is also an XML file defined using the Excel-XML schema. As a well-formed and schema-defined XML document, it can be opened by other applications that support XML such that the formatting and other elements of the spreadsheet (for example, formulas) are preserved. Unfortunately, Excel cannot save objects such as autoshapes and charts in an Excel workbook to an XML document.

Saving a Worksheet as XML Data

Saving data in a worksheet to an XML document without following the Excel-XML schema is a bit more complicated. In fact, you can't save worksheet data to a new XML file using the file type *XML Data* (see Figure 8.8) unless it has first been mapped to an existing schema. The easiest way to save data to a new XML file without using the Excel-XML format is to first open or import an existing XML file with the desired structure as a list into a worksheet. The XML file doesn't even need data, just the required tags. After opening the XML file and editing the data in Excel, you can simply save it as a new XML file using the map created by Excel when you first opened or imported the file.

XML and VBA

The XML object model may still be evolving, but the Excel 2003 object model is reasonably robust with regard to XML support. There are several methods of the `Workbook` object that can be used to import and export XML data. Furthermore, the `XmlMaps` object has been added to the object hierarchy to provide more methods for data management.

Saving and Opening XML Documents

To save a workbook as an XML document use the `SaveAs()` method of the `Workbook` object. The following example saves the workbook as an XML document with the name `myFile.xml` using two named arguments (`Filename` and `FileFormat`) with the `SaveAs()` method.

```
ActiveWorkbook.SaveAs Filename:= "myFile.xml", FileFormat:=xlXMLSpreadsheet
```

The constant `xlXMLSpreadsheet` assigned to the `FileFormat` argument specifies the Excel-XML format.

To open an XML document previously saved with the Excel-XML structure use either the `Open()` or `OpenXML()` methods of the `Workbooks` collection object.

```
Workbooks.Open Filename:= "myFile.xml"
```

If the structure of the XML document is Excel-XML, then the opened file will conform to that of a normal Excel spreadsheet; however, if the file is just a well-formed XML document (not structured as Excel-XML), then Excel will open it as tabular data. Figure 8.9 shows the result of opening the `words.xml` file with the `Open()` method of the `Workbooks` collection object. The `words.xml` file had not been previously saved using the Excel-XML structure.

FIGURE 8.9

An XML file opened in tabular form.

The `OpenXML()` method of the `Workbooks` collection object includes an optional argument (`LoadOption`) that allows you to choose how to open the XML file. VBA-defined constants you can use with the `LoadOption` argument include: `xlXmlLoadImportToList`, `xlXmlLoadOpenXml`, `xlXmlLoadMapXml`, and `xlXmlLoadPromptUser`. To import the document as a list, use `xlXmlLoadImportToList`; otherwise `xlXmlLoadOpenXml` will open the document in tabular form. Using the constant `xlXmlLoadMapXml` will display the schema-map of the XML document file in the XML Source Task Pane, but will not import any data into the worksheet. Finally, the constant `xlXmlLoadPromptUser` displays a prompt (see Figure 8.3) to the user so he or she can choose how to open the file.

```
Workbooks.OpenXML Filename:= "myFile.xml", LoadOption:=xlXmlLoadImportToList
```

The XmlMap Object

When you open an XML file, either programmatically or through the application interface, Excel automatically creates an XML map. An XML map is represented in VBA by the XmlMap object. An XML map serves to map the elements and attributes of an XML file to worksheet ranges. For example, the XML map named word_find_Map in Figure 8.7 maps the range A1:A23 to the <topic> element in the words.xml document and the range B1:B23 to the <word> element.

Each XmlMap object is contained in an XmlMaps collection object which is returned from the Workbook object via the XmlMaps property. The following code loops through the XmlMaps collection in the active workbook and prints the names of all XmlMap objects in the active workbook to the Immediate window.

```
Dim maps As XmlMaps
Dim myMap As xmlMap
Set maps = ActiveWorkbook.XmlMaps
For Each myMap In maps
     Debug.Print myMap.Name
Next
```

The XmlMap object includes four methods for importing and exporting data between an XML file or string variable, and worksheet ranges mapped to the object. Use the Import() and Export() methods of the XmlMap object to import and export data between an XML file and mapped ranges on a worksheet. The following example first imports data from the XML file called words.xml using an existing XmlMap object in the active workbook and then exports the same data to the file words2.xml. The file words2.xml is created if it doesn't already exist.

```
Dim filePath As String, filePath2 As String

filePath = ActiveWorkbook.Path & "\words.xml"
filePath2 = ActiveWorkbook.Path & "\words2.xml"
ActiveWorkbook.XmlMaps(1).Import URL:=filePath, Overwrite:=True
ActiveWorkbook.XmlMaps(1).Export URL:=filePath2, Overwrite:=True
```

The URL argument of the Import() and Export() methods is a string that specifies a file's path. When the Overwrite argument is true, the data is overwritten in the worksheet cells or the file, depending if you are importing or exporting data, respectively. At least one XmlMap object (note the index value used with the XmlMaps property) must already exist in the active workbook, or the previous code listing will fail to execute. Furthermore, the XmlMap object should be compatible with the structure of the XML file words.xml, or the data will not be properly mapped to the appropriate ranges in the worksheet. Presumably, you can create the XmlMap object from a compatible file by opening it in the Excel application prior to invoking these methods, so this shouldn't present a problem.

To copy data between a string variable and a mapped range on a worksheet, use the ImportXml() and ExportXml() methods of the XmlMap object. The following example exports data mapped with the XmlMap object named word_find_Map to the string variable xmlStr. The ExportXml() method returns an XlXmlExportResult constant (xlXmlExportSuccess or xlXmlExportValidationFailed) indicating the result of the data export. The names of the constants are self-explanatory.

```
Dim xmlStr As String
If ActiveWorkbook.XmlMaps("word_find_Map").ExportXml(Data:=xmlStr) <>
xlXmlExportSuccess Then
        MsgBox "Export failed"
End If
```

Similarly, to copy data from the string variable xmlStr to the cells mapped by the XmlMap object named word_find_Map, I use the ImportXml() method of the XmlMap object. The content of the variable xmlStr must be structured as a well-formed XML document.

```
If ActiveWorkbook.XmlMaps("word_find_Map").ImportXml(xmlData:=xmlStr) <>
xlXmlImportSuccess Then
     MsgBox "Import failed"
End If
```

The ImportXML() method returns an XlXmlImportResult constant that I have used to test for a successful import (the remaining two constants are xlXmlImportElementsTruncated and xlXmlImportValidationFailed).

There are several properties associated with the XmlMap object. Most notable are the Name, DataBinding, IsExportable, RootElementName, and Schemas properties. The DataBinding property returns an XmlDataBinding object. The XmlDataBinding object represents the connection between the data source (XML file) and the XmlMap object. The Refresh() method of the XmlDataBinding object quickly refreshes the mapped cells with the data from the XML file.

```
ActiveWorkbook.XmlMaps("word_find_Map").DataBinding.Refresh
```

The IsExportable property of the XmlMap object returns a Boolean value indicating whether or not Excel can export the mapped data. Potential reasons that an export would fail include: file path error, improper mappings, or incompatibilities with the schema.

The Schemas property returns an XMLSchemas collection object contained by an XmlMap object. Typically, there is only one XmlSchema object per XmlMap object; so specifying an index value of 1 with the Schemas property returns the desired XmlSchema object. The XmlSchema object represents the schema that defines the mapped XML document.

The following code listing first exports mapped data to a file called words3.xml before outputting the value of a few properties of an XmlMap object to the Immediate window. The XmlMap object was created from the words.xml file whose structure was listed earlier in this chapter.

```
Dim myMap As XmlMap
Dim filePath As String

filePath = ActiveWorkbook.Path & "\ words3.xml"
Set myMap = ActiveWorkbook.XmlMaps("word_find_Map")
With myMap
    If .IsExportable Then
        .Export URL:=filePath, Overwrite:=True
    Else
        MsgBox "Not exportable"
    End If
    Debug.Print .Name
    Debug.Print .RootElementName
    Debug.Print .Schemas(1).XML
End With
```

The XML property of the XmlSchema object (returned by the Schemas property of the XmlMap object) returns a string representing the schema used in the mapping; thus, it is an excellent method for collecting a schema for an existing XML file. Unfortunately, the XML property returns the string without white space so you have to add the line feeds and indentation to make the text well-formed.

Other methods of the Workbook object you can use to save or import XML data include: SaveAsXmlData(), XmlImport(), and XmlImportXml(). The SaveAsXmlData() method exports mapped data to an XML document file. It requires two arguments—Filename and Map—that are used to specify a name for the XML file and the XmlMap object representing the mapped data.

```
Dim myMap As XmlMap
Dim filePath As String
Set myMap = ActiveWorkbook.XmlMaps(1)
filePath = ActiveWorkbook.Path & "\test.xml"
ActiveWorkbook.SaveAsXMLData Filename:=filePath, Map:=myMap
```

The `XmlImport()` and `XmlImportXml()` methods import data from an XML file and data stream (string variable), respectively. Both methods require a data source (XML file or string variable) and an `XmlMap` object. The arguments `Overwrite` and `Destination` are optional, but `Destination` must be omitted if the `XmlMap` object has already been loaded into the workbook. This makes sense because once an `XmlMap` object has been created, the data is mapped to specific ranges in the worksheet and cannot be changed. The following code imports XML data from the file `sample.xml` to a mapped range on the active worksheet using an existing `XmlMap` object (`sample_Map`).

```
Dim myMap As XmlMap
Dim filePath As String

filePath = ActiveWorkbook.Path & "\sample.xml"
Set myMap = ActiveWorkbook.XmlMaps("sample_Map")
ActiveWorkbook.XmlImport URL:=filePath, ImportMap:=myMap, Overwrite:=True
```

The `XmlImport()` method imports data from an XML file whereas the `XmlImportXml()` method imports XML data from a string variable. The data stored in the string variable (`xmlStr` in the following example) must be that of a well-formed XML document and is assigned to the `Data` argument of the `XmlImportXml()` method.

```
ActiveWorkbook.XmlImportXml Data:=xmlStr, ImportMap:=myMap2, Overwrite:=True
```

The ListObject Object

As discussed earlier, when you import XML data into a worksheet you have the choice to insert the data as an Excel list. When adding XML data to a list, Excel creates a `ListObject` object to represent the list. The `ListObject` object is subordinate to the `Worksheet` object; therefore, all `ListObject` objects added to a worksheet are returned as a collection via the `ListObjects` properties of the `Worksheet` object. Individual `ListObject` objects can be accessed from the `ListObjects` collection.

```
Dim lstObjects as ListObjects
Dim lstObject As ListObject
Set lstObjects = ActiveSheet.ListObjects
Set lstObject = lstObjects(1)
```

Each XML data set that has been mapped to a list is represented by a `ListObject` object. The `ListObject` object provides an easy path to the range of cells mapped to an XML document. Use the `Range` property of the `ListObject` object to return the `Range` object representing these mapped cells. To return the range representing the insert row for a list (that's the row with the asterisk, see Figure 8.5), use the `InsertRowRange` property. Please note that the active cell(s) must be within the `ListObject` object's range or the `InsertRowRange` property will fail.

```
Dim lstObject As ListObject
Dim insertRow As Range

Set lstObject = ActiveSheet.ListObjects(1)
'----------------------
'If list is not active then activate its range.
'----------------------
If Not lstObject.Active Then
    lstObject.Range.Activate
End If
Set insertRow = lstObject.InsertRowRange
```

To ensure the `ListObject` object's range is active, the Boolean value returned by the `Active` property of the `ListObject` object is tested in a conditional statement. The `ListObject` object's range is activated with the `Activate()` method of the `Range` object. This allows you to set the `Range` object returned by the `InsertRowRange` property of the `ListObject` object. It is now a simple matter to add new data to the list. For example, if the data is mapped to two columns that include a name and number, you can add new data as follows:

```
insertRow.Cells(1, 1).Value = "Duane Birnbaum"
insertRow.Cells(1, 2).Value = 5
```

Here I use the `Cells` property of the `Range` object to return the first cell in the first two columns of the range represented by the variable `insertRow`.

If the data in an Excel list has been mapped to XML data, you can access the resulting `XmlMap` object via the `XmlMap` property of the `ListObject` object.

```
Dim myMap As XmlMap
Set myMap = ActiveSheet.ListObjects(1).XmlMap
```

Now you can invoke all the properties and methods of the `XmlMap` object that were discussed earlier.

Chapter Project: The Math Game

The *Math Game* program from Chapter 4 was fairly simple with randomly generated problems that were stored in memory, and then written to a worksheet at the end of the game—potentially the only data saved by the program (but only if the user so desired). The new version of the *Math Game* automatically stores the program's data (tests, student names, and test results) in XML files. I added worksheet interfaces for writing tests, maintaining student lists, and viewing test results. The program illustrates the use of basic XML files as a database for an application and how these files are accessed using Excel-VBA.

Requirements for the Math Game Program

The original interface to the *Math Game* program required a single worksheet that presented randomly generated math problems, timed the game, and scored the results when the time allotted reached zero. The student taking the test was allowed to choose the mathematical operation. I've kept that interface pretty much intact; removing the Option Button controls that allowed the student to choose the mathematical operator for the problems, and adding one Combo Box control that displays the list of students stored in an XML file. The only other requirements for the `Math Game` worksheet interface are that the student must sign in via a Combo Box control before starting a test, and the student may print the results of his or her test by clicking on a Command Button control placed on the worksheet. The remaining requirements for the `Math Game` worksheet interface are listed in Chapter 4 so I will not repeat them here.

The new features to the *Math Game* program require two additional worksheets; one for writing exams, and the other for maintaining the list of students and viewing test results. The following lists the requirements of the part of the program interface involving these two worksheets.

1. The user shall be allowed to write a new test by entering the problems in a worksheet and then save the test to an XML file.
2. The difficulty level and length of time allowed to complete a test (test properties) shall also be stored in an XML file.
3. The user shall be allowed to edit existing tests from the same worksheet interface. This means that the program must be able to import data from an XML file representing a test.
4. The worksheet interface used to create or edit tests shall be previously formatted with two XML maps and Excel lists that map the problems and properties of a test to the appropriate XML files.
5. Test files shall be named by concatenating a filename and difficulty level input by the user.
6. When a student signs in to take a test, the XML test file of the appropriate level shall be loaded into the test worksheet.

7. While taking a test, problems shall be read from the test worksheet and displayed on the `Math Game` worksheet.
8. When a student finishes a test, the test is scored and the result recorded. When a student fails to finish a test within the allotted time, unanswered problems shall be included in the result as incorrect answers.
9. Students and their current testing level shall be entered in an Excel list whose ranges are mapped to an XML file.
10. Updates to the list of students shall be allowed; that is, the program must be able to export the data mapped to the student's XML file.
11. The list of students shall provide the data source for the Combo Box control on the `Math Game` worksheet.
12. The user shall be allowed to view the test results for all students.
13. The results worksheet shall be formatted with an XML map and Excel list to link the data in the worksheet to the file containing the results.
14. The results worksheet and the XML file containing the results shall be updated at the completion of each test.
15. The user shall be able to clear the worksheet and XML file of all test results.

Designing the Math Game

As far as a student is concerned, the program interface doesn't change much from the one in the Chapter 4 program. The `Math Game` worksheet still contains the test problems, the timer, and the scored results. The number and type of ActiveX controls is the part that's different. Additional worksheets contained in the project are not meant to be viewed by a student, so hiding them would be a good idea.

The other two worksheets must contain lists of test problems, students, and results. I will use a single worksheet for creating the list of problems that make up a test (`Create_Edit_Tests`) and another worksheet will contain the list of students and their test results (`Students`). I will create each XML map and corresponding data list prior to writing any code, but after I have designed and written the XML files. This must be the case because I can't create an XML map in a worksheet without an XML file.

Taking a Test

The interface used to take a test is shown in Figure 8.10. I removed the Option Button controls from the Chapter 4 program and added a Combo Box and a Command Button control; otherwise, the interface is the same. I set the `Style` property of the ComboBox control to fmStyleDropDownList so the student cannot enter a new name but only choose existing names from the list. As usual, I also edited the Name property and a few appearance properties of the ActiveX controls at design time.

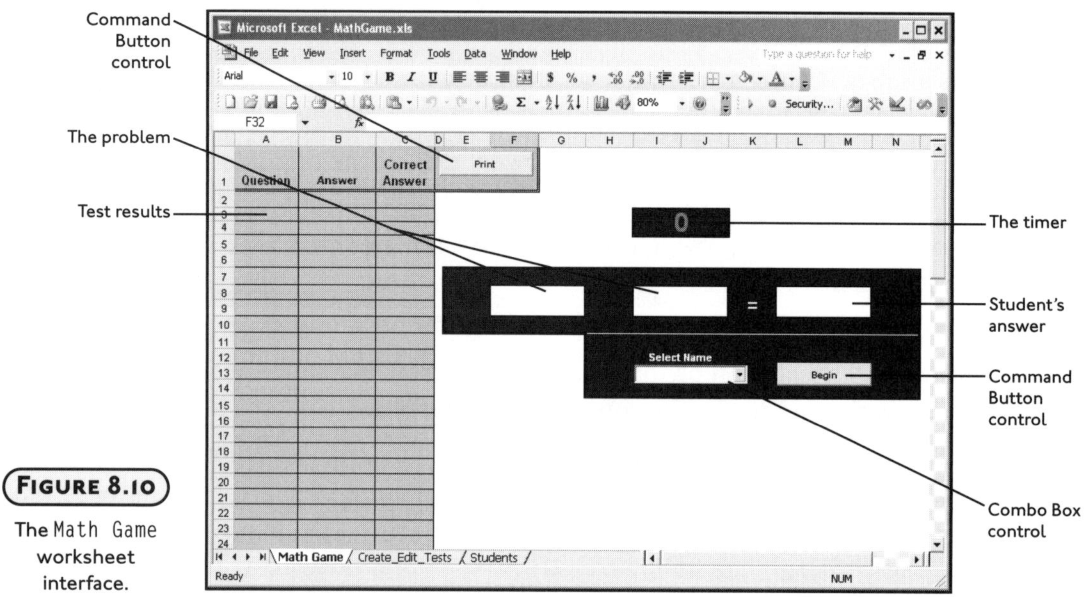

FIGURE 8.10

The Math Game worksheet interface.

The process of taking a test is uncomplicated and nearly identical to the Chapter 4 program. After a student selects his or her name from the Combo Box control, the Command Button control labeled Begin is enabled and must be used to start the test. The appropriate test is loaded into the Create_Edit_Tests worksheet to provide the source for the test questions. Problems are presented one at a time and the student must enter an answer to each problem before continuing. The answer cell remains selected at all times during a test. When the student finishes the test, or the allotted time runs out, the test is scored and written to the worksheet. The length of time allotted for a test is also read from the Create_Edit_Tests worksheet. After completing a test, a student can print the range of cells containing the problems, answers, and score (columns A through C) with a click of the Command Button control labeled Print.

Creating Tests

Tests are written from a separate worksheet interface. Figure 8.11 shows the Create_Edit_Tests worksheet with problems from an existing test imported into its data list.

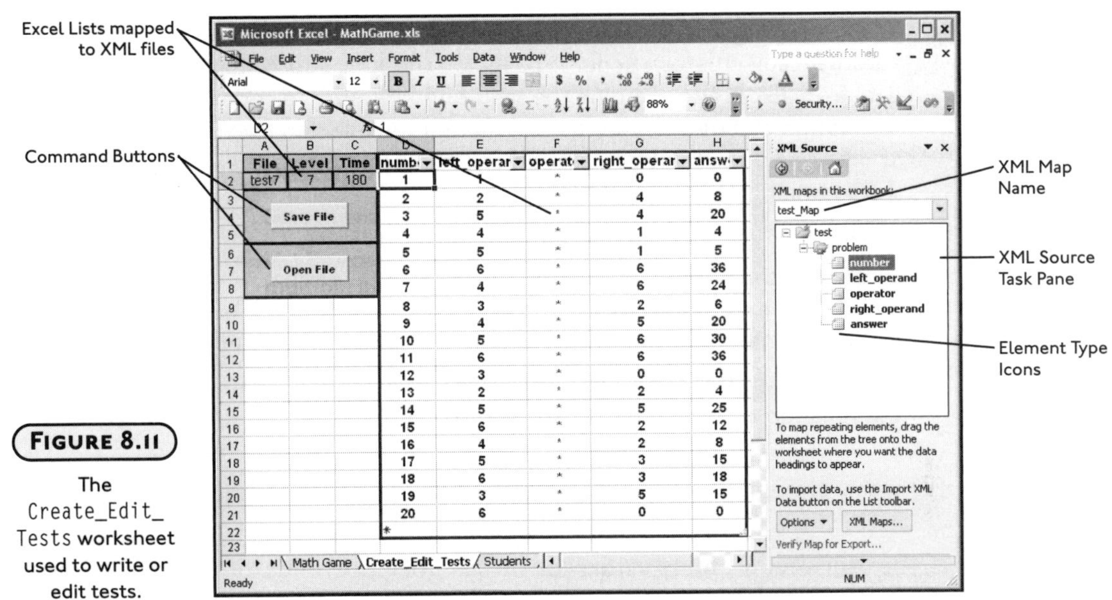

FIGURE 8.11 The `Create_Edit_Tests` worksheet used to write or edit tests.

The data in the worksheet is formatted as an Excel list and is mapped to two XML files. The range A2:C2 is mapped to an XML file with the following structure:

```
<?xml version="1.0" encoding="UTF-8"?>
<test_properties fileID="">
     <level></level>
     <time></time>
</test_properties>
```

The elements `<level>` and `<time>` are mapped to cells B2 and C2 respectively, and the `fileID` attribute of the `<test_properties>` element is mapped to cell A2. I initially created the map by importing the file as an XML list when it was void of data; although, it doesn't matter if there is data in the XML file because it's the document structure that's important. The name of the map is `test_properties_Map`. Excel creates the initial value for a map's name by concatenating the root element name with the word `Map`. You can change it by selecting Data, XML, XML Map Properties in the Excel application window.

The `<level>` and `<time>` elements are non-repeating child elements of `<test_properties>` so each test will have an associated test properties file. These files are named by concatenating the `fileID` attribute in cell A2 with the character `p` followed by the `xml` file extension.

When opening an XML file in Excel that does not reference a schema, Excel automatically creates a schema based on the XML source data. If you resave the data from Excel and examine the resulting XML source code in a text editor, you will notice two new declarations. The first new declaration is referred to as the `standalone` document declaration and can be found in the XML declaration at the beginning of the document.

```
<?xml version="1.0" encoding="UTF-8" standalone="yes"?>
```

Excel adds the `standalone` document declaration so that it knows the XML document has external markup declarations (the schema created by Excel), but these external declarations do not affect the document's content.

In addition to the `standalone` document declaration, Excel adds a reference to the location of the schema reserved for an Excel workbook. The reference is added as an attribute to the root element of the XML document.

```
<root_element_name xmlns:xsi="http://www.w3.org/2001/XMLSchema-instance">
```

To create a test, the user simply enters values for the number, operands, operator, and answer into the corresponding columns in the worksheet. In order to save time, the user may use formulas (if desired) to calculate answers or generate operands. The problems contained in the data list (cells `D2:H22` in Figure 8.11) are mapped to a second XML file. The data list can be extended to any number of rows. The name of the XML map is `test_Map` (see Figure 8.11) and the XML document structure is listed again in the following:

```
<?xml version="1.0" encoding="UTF-8"?>
<test>
      <problem>
            <number></number>
            <left_operand></left_operand>
            <operator></operator>
            <right_operand></right_operand>
            <answer></answer>
      </problem>
      <!--repeating <problem> elements-->
</test>
```

The structure of the XML test file contains the root element `<test>` with a series of child elements (`<problem>`) that represent the test problems. Each `<problem>` element contains the child elements that define a problem (`<number>`, `<left_operand>`, `<operator>`, `<right_operand>`, and `<answer>`).

When this file is opened as an XML list, the data elements are loaded into adjacent columns in the worksheet. Element types (child, parent, attribute, and so on) can be identified from the icon displayed in the XML Source Task Pane. In order for Excel to recognize a repeating parent element such as `<problem>`, I had to include at least two of these elements in the original file that I opened with Excel when creating the XML list and map.

I will use the `fileID` attribute of the `<test_properties>` element to specify the file name of a test file; therefore, each test is associated with two XML files (for example, `test7p.xml` and `test7.xml`). The program only needs one of these files to open an existing test because a test file's name is stored in the `fileID` attribute of the test properties file; thus, when the user chooses to open a test file, they must be shown a selection of test property files and not the test files themselves.

You may be wondering why I used two XML files to describe a single test. An easier approach might combine the two structures into a single XML document similar to the following:

```
<?xml version="1.0" encoding="UTF-8"?>
<test fileID="">
    <level></level>
    <time></time>
    <problem>
        <number></number>
        <left_operand></left_operand>
        <operator></operator>
        <right_operand></right_operand>
        <answer></answer>
    </problem>
    <!--repeating <problem> elements-->
</test>
```

The problem with this structure is that the `<level>` and `<time>` elements, and the `fileID` attribute are associated with every `<problem>` element in the file; so when Excel imports the data into a worksheet, it will repeat the values for the `fileID` attribute, and `<level>` and `<time>` elements. This causes a data redundancy and the resulting map is said to be *denormalized*. Excel cannot export data from a denormalized map to an XML file.

Maintaining Student Lists and Viewing Test Results

The last part of the *Math Game* program is the worksheet used to edit the student list and view their test results. The worksheet interface is shown in Figure 8.12.

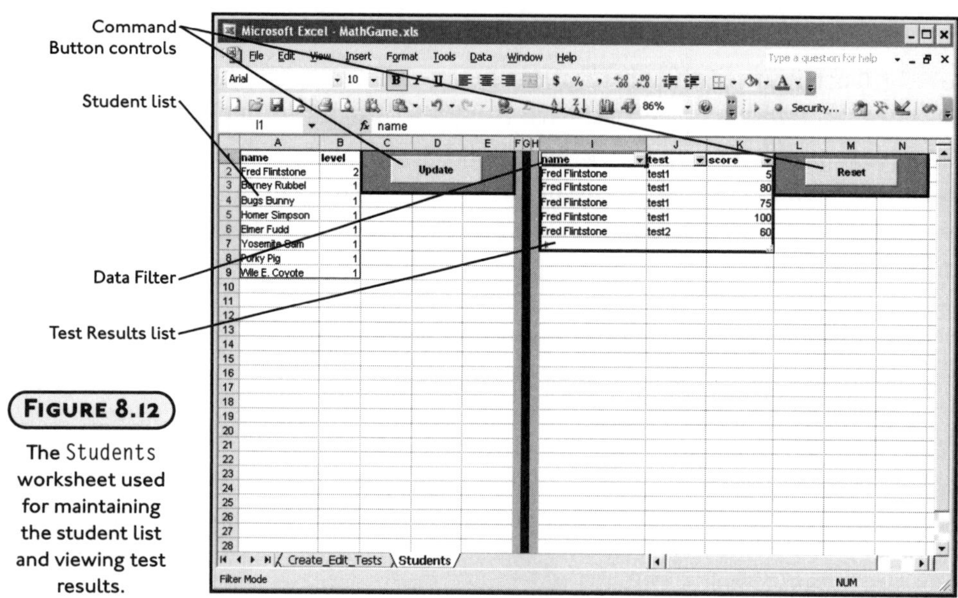

FIGURE 8.12

The Students worksheet used for maintaining the student list and viewing test results.

Because these are relatively small lists, I included both of them in one worksheet. The XML document structure describing the students is as follows:

```
<?xml version="1.0" encoding="UTF-8"?>
<students>
      <student>
            <name> </name>
            <level></level>
      </student>
      <!--repeating <student> elements-->
</students>
```

The file's data consists of the student's name and current testing level. The data in the `<level>` element will have to be updated whenever a student passes a test. A single file called `students.xml` stores all data describing the students. The data in the file is mapped to the first two columns in the worksheet using the XML map named `students_Map`.

Test results are also stored in a single XML file called `results.xml` (listed next) mapped to the data in columns I through K via the XML map named `results_Map`. Because the file stores all test results, the program will have to add one more `<student>` element with each completed test. The `<name>` element is the name of the student; the `<test>` element, the name of the test; and the `<score>` element, the test result expressed as percent correct.

```
<?xml version="1.0" encoding="UTF-8"?>
<results>
     <student>
          <name> </name>
          <test> </test>
          <score></score>
     </student>
     <!--repeating <student> elements-->
</results>
```

One of the advantages to using an Excel list to view the results is the applied filter can be used to quickly view individual students or all student results (or a custom filter if desired).

Coding the Math Game Program

Much of the code for the *Math Game* involves objects and methods discussed in previous chapters. At this point you are familiar with many of the structures and common objects used in Excel-VBA programs. New topics will usually come in the form of a new object and its associated methods and subordinate objects. Now, the greatest challenge for you is designing programs and developing algorithms.

Since I am using three worksheets for the program interface, I will try to isolate the code that serves each interface to their respective code modules; however, there are occasions when it is easier to add procedures to a standard module so they can be shared by multiple interfaces.

Writing Tests

The code module for the worksheet used to create or edit tests must contain procedures that import and export data between the mapped ranges in the worksheet and the two XML files that describe a test document's properties and its problems.

The first procedure listed is the `Click()` event of the Command Button control labeled `Save File` (see Figure 8.11). This procedure exports the data entered in the lists to two separate XML files (the test and test properties files). Both file names are obtained from cell `A2` in the worksheet. The test properties file name is appended with a `p` just before the `xml` file extension.

When a worksheet already contains an Excel list mapped to an XML document file, you can use the `XmlMap` object to export the current data from the list to the file. This is exactly what I've done here. I set the `XmlMap` object variable to its corresponding XML map in the worksheet using the name defined when the XML document was first imported into the worksheet. The names of the XML maps can be found in the XML Source Task Pane (select Data, XML, XML Source). After testing to see if the map is exportable (`IsExportable` property), I invoked the `Export()` method of the `XmlMap` object to export the data from the list to the file specified in the `URL` argument. With the `Overwrite` argument set to true, an existing file is replaced with the current data; however, if the file doesn't exist, then a new one is created. This means this event procedure can be used to save new test files or save edits to existing test files.

Finally, because the event procedure involves file I/O, I have added a basic error handler to output the nature of the error to the user via a message box before ending the program.

```
Option Explicit
Private Sub cmdFileSave_Click()
    Dim mapProperties As XmlMap, mapTests As XmlMap
    Dim pathProperties As String, pathTests As String

    On Error GoTo ExportError
    '------------------------------------
    'Save the new exam as an xml file (one for test properties
    'and one for test).
    '------------------------------------
    pathProperties = ActiveWorkbook.Path & "\TestProperties\" & Range("A2").Value & "p.xml"
    pathTests = ActiveWorkbook.Path & "\Tests\" & Range("A2").Value & ".xml"
    Set mapProperties = ActiveWorkbook.XmlMaps("test_properties_Map")
    Set mapTests = ActiveWorkbook.XmlMaps("test_Map")

    If mapProperties.IsExportable Then
        mapProperties.Export URL:=pathProperties, Overwrite:=True
    Else
        MsgBox "XML map is not exportable!", vbOKOnly, "XML Map"
    End If
    If mapTests.IsExportable Then
        mapTests.Export URL:=pathTests, Overwrite:=True
    Else
        MsgBox "XML map is not exportable!", vbOKOnly, "XML Map"
    End If
    Exit Sub
```

```
ExportError:
    MsgBox "Test file not saved." & Err.Description, vbOKOnly, _
        "File Save Error: " & Err.Number
    End
End Sub
```

When the user decides to edit an existing test file, a click of the Command Button labeled `Open File` sends program execution to its `Click()` event procedure. I have used this procedure to display a file open dialog containing a list of test property files from which the user must choose one. The data in the selected file, along with the data in its test file counterpart, are then imported into the worksheet. For example, if the user selects the file `test1p.xml`, its data is imported into the mapped range `A2:C2` and the value of its `fileID` attribute specifies the test file to import into the `test_Map` range. I have written two custom procedures (`GetXMLFile()` and `OpenXMLFile()`) to handle these tasks.

```
Private Sub cmdFileOpen_Click()
    Dim fileName As String

    '-------------------
    'Import xml files to worksheet.
    '-------------------
    fileName = GetXmlFile
    If fileName <> "" Then
        OpenXMLFile fileName
    End If
End Sub
```

The `GetXMLFile()` function procedure uses a `FileDialog` object (refer to Chapter 7) to display an Open dialog box. I set the file path to the `TestProperties` directory that contains the test property XML files and added a `FileDialogFilters` object to ensure the dialog box lists only XML files. The selected file is returned to the calling procedure as a string where it is passed to the `OpenXMLFile()` procedure. The Open dialog is shown in Figure 8.13.

```
Private Function GetXmlFile() As String
    Dim fileDiag As FileDialog
    Dim fPath As String

    fPath = ActiveWorkbook.path & "\TestProperties\"
```

```
    '---------------------
    'Configure and show the open dialog.
    'Open the file selected by the user.
    '---------------------
    Set fileDiag = Application.FileDialog(msoFileDialogOpen)
    With fileDiag     'Configure dialog box
        .Filters.Clear
        .Filters.Add Description:="XML", Extensions:="*.xml", Position:=1
        .FilterIndex = 1
        .AllowMultiSelect = False
        .Title = "Select XMl Test File"
        .InitialFileName = fPath
        If .Show = -1 Then   'User clicked Open
            GetXmlFile = .SelectedItems.Item(1)
        End If
    End With
End Function
```

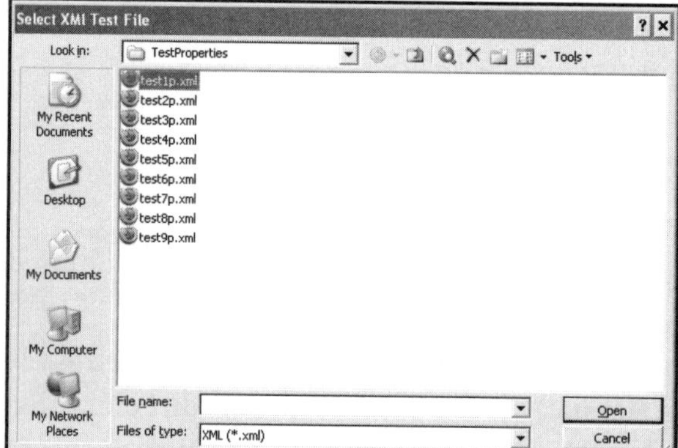

FIGURE 8.13

The Open dialog for selecting existing test files.

I added the `OpenXMLFile()` procedure to a standard code module and gave it public scope because it has to be called from other object code modules in the program. The procedure first uses the string from the `fileName` argument to import the test properties data from the XML file to the cells in the list. The `XmlImport()` method of the `Workbook` object imports the data from the XML document file. It is worth reiterating that the XML document file structure must match the existing XML map structure in the workbook. If the two structures do not match, Excel ignores the command.

```
Public Sub OpenXMLFile(fileName As String)
    Dim ws As Worksheet

    On Error GoTo ImportError

    '------------------------
    'Open the test properties and test XML files.
    '------------------------
    Set ws = Worksheets("Create_Edit_Tests")
    ActiveWorkbook.XmlImport URL:=fileName, _
        ImportMap:=ActiveWorkbook.XmlMaps("test_properties_Map"), _
        Overwrite:=True
    ws.Columns("A:C").ColumnWidth = 7
    ActiveWorkbook.XmlImport URL:=ActiveWorkbook.path & _
        "\Tests\" & ws.Range("A2").Value & _
        ".xml", ImportMap:=ActiveWorkbook.XmlMaps("test_Map"), _
        Overwrite:=True
    Exit Sub

ImportError:
    MsgBox "Could not import XML file." & Err.Description, _
        vbOKOnly, "File Import Error: " & Err.Number
    End
End Sub
```

Maintaining the Student List and Viewing Results

After a test is completed and scored, the results are added to the `Students` worksheet and the XML file is automatically updated (discussed later). Results can be viewed from the `Students` worksheet, where the XML list that holds all test results has been created in columns I through K. Although there is no need to allow the user to export the results, they are allowed to clear the data from the XML file.

Users may clear the list in the worksheet manually or by clicking the Command Button control labeled `Reset`. This triggers the `Click()` event procedure that follows. To clear the list, I first activate its range of cells before using the `InsertRowRange` property of the `ListObject` object to determine the next available row in the list. The list's range must be active or the `InsertRowRange` property fails—generating a runtime error. Data in the list is deleted using the `Delete()` method of the `Range` object and shifting cells up. Note that I do not update the XML document file after clearing the range. It's not necessary since it will be updated with the next completed test.

```
Option Explicit

Private Sub cmdResetResults_Click()
    Dim insertRow As Integer
    Dim lsObj As ListObject

    '---------
    'Clear the list.
    '---------
    Set lsObj = ActiveSheet.ListObjects("Results")
    If Not lsObj.Active Then
        lsObj.Range.Activate
    End If
    insertRow = lsObj.InsertRowRange.Row
    Range("I1").Select
    If insertRow <= 2 Then Exit Sub
    Range("I2:K" & insertRow - 1).Delete xlShiftUp
End Sub
```

Students are added to or removed from the data base by editing the corresponding XML document (`students.xml`) via the `Students` worksheet. When the `Click()` event procedure of the Command Button control labeled `Update` is triggered, the data in the list overwrites the data in the XML document file. Again, I have used the `Export()` method of the `XmlMap` object to update an XML file. The `UpdateStudentXml()` sub procedure was also entered into a standard code module because it is called from more than one object module.

```
Private Sub cmdUpdate_Click()
    UpdateStudentXml True
End Sub

Public Sub UpdateStudentXml(Optional UpdateCmbList As Boolean)
    Dim mapStudents As xmlMap
    Dim pathStudents As String

    On Error GoTo UpdateError
    '-------------
    'Update student XML file.
    '-------------
    pathStudents = ActiveWorkbook.path & "\Students\students.xml"
    Set mapStudents = ActiveWorkbook.XmlMaps("students_Map")
    If mapStudents.IsExportable Then
```

```
        mapStudents.Export URL:=pathStudents, Overwrite:=True
    Else
        MsgBox "XML map is not exportable!", vbOKOnly, "XML Map"
    End If

    '-----------------------------
    'Update combo box if this procedure was called from
    'Update button on sheet 3.
    '-----------------------------
    If UpdateCmbList Then ListStudents
    Exit Sub

UpdateError:
    MsgBox "Student list not updated." & Err.Description, _
        vbOKOnly, "File Save Error: " & Err.Number
    End
End Sub
```

The ListStudents() sub procedure is called from UpdateStudentXml() and the Open() event procedure of the Workbook object. The procedure serves to update the list of students listed in the Combo Box control on the Math Game worksheet. Notice that I use the ListObject object to retrieve the student names. This is another advantage of Excel lists—the Range property of the ListObject object makes it easy to access the content of the list, so you don't have to search through the rows to find the last item. It is also worth noting that in order to access the Combo Box control, I had to qualify the worksheet name in the object path because the ListStudents() sub procedure is not in the same code module as the control.

```
Public Sub ListStudents()
    Dim studList As ListObject
    Dim student As Range
    Dim I As Integer

    '------------------
    'Add student list to combo box.
    '------------------
    MathGameSheet.cmbStudents.Clear
    Set studList = Worksheets("Students").ListObjects("Students")
    For I = 2 To studList.Range.Rows.Count
        MathGameSheet.cmbStudents.AddItem studList.Range.Cells(I, 1).Value
    Next I
End Sub
```

Taking a Test

A majority of the code for the *Math Game* program is still located in the same worksheet module as the original program from Chapter 4. Once the test begins, the algorithm is pretty much the same, but instead of generating problems randomly, they are read from the `Create_Edit_Tests` worksheet. Since the algorithm and much of the code is nearly the same as the program from Chapter 4, I will limit the discussion to the new sections of the program.

Before a test begins, a student must sign in by selecting their name from the Combo Box control which triggers its `Change()` event.

```
Option Explicit

Private curQuestion As Integer
Private numQuestions As Integer
Private curDate As Date
Private gameRunning As Boolean
Private curStudent As String
```

I use the `Change()` event procedure to initialize variables and the appearance of the worksheet, after which the appropriate test for the student (according to their level) is loaded into the `Create_Edit_Tests` worksheet.

```
Private Sub cmbStudents_Change()
    Dim fileName As String
    Dim studLevel As Integer
    Dim studRange As Range

    If gameRunning Then Exit Sub
    ClearBoard
    With Range("A2:C" & UsedRange.Rows.Count)
        .ClearContents
        .Font.Color = vbBlack
    End With
    Range("B1").Value = cmbStudents.Value & "'s" & " Answer"
    curStudent = cmbStudents.Value

    '-----------------------------
    'Determine the test level for the selected student.
    '-----------------------------
    Set studRange = Worksheets("Students").ListObjects("Students").Range
```

```
    studLevel = studRange(studRange.Find(What:=curStudent).Row, 2).Value

    '-----------------------------------
    'Load a new exam when the student name is changed in combo box.
    '-----------------------------------
    fileName = ActiveWorkbook.path & "\TestProperties\test" & studLevel & "p.xml"
    cmdBegin.Enabled = True
    OpenXMLFile fileName
End Sub

Private Sub ClearBoard()
    '-----------------------------------
    'Clears the operands and the answer from the worksheet cells.
    '-----------------------------------
    Range("LeftOperand").Value = ""
    Range("RightOperand").Value = ""
    Range("Answer").Value = ""
End Sub
```

The test begins with the triggering of the `Click()` event of the Command Button control labeled `Begin`. The questions are read from the `Create_Edit_Tests` worksheet. (Recall that the appropriate test is loaded into this worksheet after the user signs in.)

Instead of using index numbers with the `ListObjects` collection object, I prefer to use specific names for each `ListObject`; however, Excel assigns the names `List1`, `List2`, and so on to each list as it is created. Therefore, to change a name to something meaningful, I select the worksheet containing the list(s) I want to name and then write a VBA procedure similar to the following:

```
Sub ChangeLOName()
    Dim lo As ListObject
    For Each lo In ActiveSheet.ListObjects
        If lo.Name = "List1" Then
            lo.Name = "Problems"
        End If
    Next
End Sub
```

This gives a meaningful name to the `ListObject` object that I can reference in my program to make it more self-documenting.

Setting the MoveAfterReturn property of the Application object to false ensures that the answer cell (merged range L8:M9) remains selected as the student enters his or her answers. Setting the Calculation property to manual prevents interference from Excel attempting to calculate the worksheet while the timer counts down. This isn't really necessary, but if you don't turn off the automatic calculation in a situation like this, you will probably see considerable screen flicker while the program executes.

Problems are written to the worksheet with a call to the GetProblem() sub procedure which reads individual problems from the Create_Edit_Tests worksheet and writes it to the appropriate cells on the Math Game worksheet. Next, the timer is started with a call to the MathGame() sub procedure.

```
Private Sub cmdBegin_Click()
    Dim qNumbers As Range

    Set qNumbers = Worksheets("Create_Edit_Tests").ListObjects("Problems").Range
    '-------------------
    'Initialize variables and controls.
    '-------------------
    cmdBegin.Enabled = False
    gameRunning = True
    curQuestion = 1
    numQuestions = qNumbers.Cells(qNumbers.Rows.Count, 1).Value
    Range("Answer").Select
    Application.MoveAfterReturn = False
    Application.Calculation = xlCalculationManual

    '-------------
    'Get the first question.
    '-------------
    GetProblem

    '---------------------
    'Mark the start time and start the clock.
    '---------------------
    curDate = Now
    MathGame
End Sub
```

```
Private Sub GetProblem()
    Dim ws As Worksheet

    '-------------------------------
    'Reads the problem from the test worksheet and writes
    'it to the cells in the Math Game worksheet.
    '-------------------------------
    Set ws = Worksheets("Create_Edit_Tests")

    Range("LeftOperand").Value = ws.ListObjects("Problems").Range.Cells(curQuestion _
+ 1, 2).Value
    Range("Operator").Value = ws.ListObjects("Problems").Range.Cells(curQuestion _
+ 1, 3).Value
    Range("RightOperand").Value = ws.ListObjects("Problems").Range.Cells(curQuestion _
+ 1, 4).Value
    curQuestion = curQuestion + 1
End Sub
```

The `MathGame()` procedure contains the call to the `OnTime()` method of the `Application` object and sets the schedule for this procedure to be called every second. The allotted time for a test is read from the `Create_Edit_Tests` worksheet. The `OnTime()` method is cancelled when the timer reaches zero or the student answers every test question. After the test is over, the results are scored, variables and properties are reset, and the student's level is increased by one if they score 100%.

```
Private Sub MathGame()
'Manages the clock while testing. Calls scoring procedures when test is over.
    Dim numSeconds As Integer
    Dim nextTime As Date
    Dim timeAllowed As Integer
    Dim newLevel As Boolean

    On Error GoTo TimingError
    timeAllowed = Worksheets("Create_Edit_Tests").Range("C2").Value
    numSeconds = DateDiff("s", curDate, Now)

    '----------
    'Start the clock.
    '----------
```

```
    Range("Clock").Value = timeAllowed - numSeconds
    nextTime = Now + TimeValue("00:00:01")
    Application.OnTime EarliestTime:=nextTime, _
Procedure:="MathGameSheet.MathGame", Schedule:=True

    '-----------------------------------
    'Disable timer when it reaches zero, score results, and clean up
    'worksheet controls/cells.
    '-----------------------------------
    If (timeAllowed - numSeconds <= 0) Or (curQuestion >= (numQuestions + 2)) Then
        Application.OnTime EarliestTime:=nextTime, _
Procedure:="MathGameSheet.MathGame", Schedule:=False
        cmbStudents.Value = ""
        ClearBoard
        If curQuestion < numQuestions Then
            WriteRemainingProblems
        End If
        newLevel = ScoreAnswers
        StoreResults
        If newLevel Then IncrementStudentLevel
        Application.MoveAfterReturn = True
        Application.Calculation = xlCalculationAutomatic
        gameRunning = False
    End If
    Exit Sub

TimingError:
    MsgBox "An error occurred with the game timer." & vbCrLf & Err.Description _
        , vbOKOnly, "Timer Error: " & Err.Number
    End
End Sub
```

Student answers to questions are captured from the `Change()` event of the `Worksheet` object which is triggered when an answer is entered (student presses the Enter key on the keyboard). After the answer is collected, the next question is written to the `Math Game` worksheet with another call to the `GetProblem()` sub procedure. Problems and the student's answer are written to the report area of the worksheet before the answer is cleared from the problem area.

```
Private Sub Worksheet_Change(ByVal Target As Range)

    '-------------------------------
    'Copies question and answer entered by the user to the
    'report area and gets the next question.
    '-------------------------------
    If (Target.Address = "$L$8") And (Range("Answer").Value <> "") And gameRunning _
Then
        Range("A" & curQuestion).Value = Range("LeftOperand").Value & _
            Range("Operator").Value & Range("RightOperand").Value
        Range("B" & curQuestion).Value = Range("Answer").Value
        GetProblem
        Range("Answer").Value = ""
    End If
End Sub
```

If the student fails to finish the test, the remaining unanswered questions are written to the report area of the `Math Game` worksheet with a call to the `WriteRemainingProblems()` sub procedure. This procedure is called from the `MathGame()` sub procedure listed earlier.

```
Private Sub WriteRemainingProblems()
    Dim qRange As Range
    Dim c As Range

    '------------------------------------
    'Writes questions not answered by student to the report area.
    '------------------------------------
    Set qRange = Worksheets("Create_Edit_Tests").ListObjects("Problems").Range
    For Each c In Range("A" & curQuestion & ":A" & numQuestions + 1)
        c.Value = qRange.Cells(curQuestion, 2).Value
        c.Value = c.Value & qRange.Cells(curQuestion, 3).Value
        c.Value = c.Value & qRange.Cells(curQuestion, 4).Value
        curQuestion = curQuestion + 1
    Next
End Sub
```

You may recall that in the *Math Game* program from Chapter 4, I used arrays to hold the problems and answers as they were generated by the program. That's no longer necessary since the problems are listed in a worksheet. This makes scoring a student's test a little easier since all I have to do is read an answer from the Create_Edit_Tests worksheet and compare it to the student's answer listed in column B of the Math Game worksheet. Note that the ScoreAnswers() function procedure returns a Boolean value to the calling procedure indicating whether or not the student scored 100 percent on the test.

```
Private Function ScoreAnswers() As Boolean
    Dim I As Integer
    Dim numWrong As Integer
    Dim ws As Worksheet
    Dim c As Range

    '-------------------------------------------------
    'After the test is over, the user's answers are scored and the
    'results written to the worksheet.
    '-------------------------------------------------
    Set ws = Worksheets("Create_Edit_Tests")
    I = 1
    For Each c In Range("C2:C" & curQuestion - 1)
        c.Value = ws.ListObjects("Problems").Range.Cells(I + 1, 5).Value
        If (c.Value <> Range("B" & c.Row).Value) Or (Range("B" & c.Row).Value = "") Then
            Range("B" & c.Row).Font.Color = RGB(255, 0, 0)
            numWrong = numWrong + 1
        Else
            Range("B" & c.Row).Font.Color = RGB(0, 0, 0)
        End If
        I = I + 1
    Next

    '----------------------------------
    'Compute % correct and write to the worksheet.
    '----------------------------------
    Cells(I + 1, "A").Value = "Score (%)"
    Cells(I + 1, "B").Font.Color = RGB(0, 0, 0)
    Cells(I + 1, "B").Formula = "=" & (I - 1 - numWrong) / (I - 1) & "*100"
    If Cells(I + 1, "B").Value = 100 Then ScoreAnswers = True
End Function
```

The StoreResults() sub procedure writes individual test results to the Students worksheet and the XML document file (results.xml). First, the appropriate ListObject object is made active before the student's name and score is added to the end of its list (determined using the InsertRowRange property). Note that I turned off the screen updating because I don't want to show the Students worksheet.

Since the XmlMap object already exists, it's a simple task to export the new results to the XML document file.

```
Private Sub StoreResults()
    Dim studList As ListObject
    Dim wsTest As Worksheet, wsStud As Worksheet, wsGame As Worksheet
    Dim mapResults As xmlMap
    Dim pathResults As String
    Dim nextRow As Integer

    On Error GoTo StoreError

    '--------------------
    'Stores results of exam to XML file.
    '--------------------
    Set wsTest = Worksheets("Create_Edit_Tests")
    Set wsStud = Worksheets("Students")
    Set wsGame = Worksheets("Math Game")
    Set studList = wsStud.ListObjects("Results")
    If Not studList.Active Then
        Application.ScreenUpdating = False
        wsStud.Activate
        studList.Range.Activate
        nextRow = studList.InsertRowRange.Row
        wsGame.Activate
    End If
    studList.Range.Cells(nextRow, 1).Value = curStudent
    studList.Range.Cells(nextRow, 2) = wsTest.Range("A2").Value
    studList.Range.Cells(nextRow, 3) = Cells(Range("A:A").Find(What:="Score").Row, 2). _
Value

    Set mapResults = ActiveWorkbook.XmlMaps("results_Map")
    pathResults = ActiveWorkbook.path & "\TestResults\results.xml"
    If mapResults.IsExportable Then
        mapResults.Export URL:=pathResults, Overwrite:=True
```

```
    Else
        MsgBox "XML map is not exportable!", vbOKOnly, "XML Map"
    End If
    Exit Sub

StoreError:
    MsgBox "An error occurred while attempting to store the results." _
        & vbCrLf & Err.Description, vbOKOnly, "Store Error: " & Err.Number

End Sub
```

When a student scores 100 percent on a test, their level is increased by one so that the next time they sign in they are given the next test in the sequence. The IncrementStudentLevel() sub procedure (called from the MathGame() sub procedure if the student scored 100 percent) increments a student's level in the appropriate list in the Students worksheet and then updates the XML document file (students.xml) with a called to the UpdateStudentXml() sub procedure located in a standard module (listed earlier). The next test associated with the student's new level is then loaded in the worksheet.

```
Private Sub IncrementStudentLevel()
    Dim studList As ListObject
    Dim studLevel As Range
    Dim ws As Worksheet
    Dim fileName As String

    On Error GoTo FileError
    Set ws = Worksheets("Students")
    '--------------------
    'Increment the value in the worksheet.
    '--------------------
    Set studList = ws.ListObjects("Students")
    Set studLevel = ws.Cells(studList.Range.Find(What:=curStudent).Row, 2)
    studLevel.Value = studLevel.Value + 1

    '----------------------
    'Save the xml file and load the new test.
    '----------------------
    UpdateStudentXml False
    fileName = ActiveWorkbook.path & "\TestProperties\test" & studLevel.Value & "p.xml"
```

```
    OpenXMLFile fileName
    Exit Sub

FileError:
    MsgBox "The student's level was not increased." _
        & vbCrLf & Err.Description, vbOKOnly, "IncrementStudentLevel: " & Err.Number
End Sub
```

The last procedure listed is the `Click()` event of the Command Button control labeled `Print`. This procedure prints the report area of the `Math Game` worksheet (columns A through C) using the `PrintOut()` method of the `Range` object.

```
Private Sub cmdPrint_Click()
    Dim pRange As Range
    Dim lastRow As Integer

    '------------------
    'Print the results of the test.
    '------------------
    On Error GoTo PrintError
    lastRow = Range("A:A").Find(What:="", After:=Range("A1")).Row - 1
    Set pRange = Range("A1:C" & lastRow)
    pRange.PrintOut
    Exit Sub

PrintError:
    MsgBox Err.Description, vbOKOnly, "Printing Error " & Err.Number
    End
End Sub
```

That concludes the revised version of the *Math Game* program. As usual, I left considerable room for improvement; some of these improvements are suggested as exercises in the Challenges section at the end of the chapter.

Chapter Summary

In this chapter, you were introduced to XML by learning its purpose, definition, and basic syntax. You also learned how to open and save XML documents from the Excel application window and the advantages of adding the data to an Excel list. Finally, you learned how to use several new objects in the Excel object model designed to support XML. This included the XmlMap object and the ListObject object and some of their associated and/or subordinate objects. For the chapter project, you revisited the *Math Game* by adding XML support such that the program's data was stored in XML document files.

Challenges

1. **Open your favorite text editor, then enter and save the following with an .xml file extension.**

```
<?xml version="1.0" encoding="UTF-8"?>
<myData>
    <myElement>
        <ranData1>A</ranData1>
        <ranData2>1</ranData2>
    </myElement>
    <myElement>
        <ranData1>B</ranData1>
        <ranData2>2</ranData2>
    </myElement>
</myData>
```

2. **Open your xml file in Excel as an XML list. From the Source Task Pane (select Data, XML, XML Source) select the different elements in the XML map and note what is selected in the worksheet. Add a couple more rows of data to the list by first selecting the insert row (the row marked with an asterisk *) and entering random values. With the list selected, export the data to the same XML file by selecting Data, XML, Export. Finally, re-open the file in a text editor and note the change from the original.**
3. **Clear the data from the XML list in Challenge 2 then refresh the list by selecting Data, XML, Refresh XML Data.**
4. **Write a VBA procedure that exports the data from your XML list created in Challenge 2 to a new XML file.**
5. **Write a VBA procedure that refreshes the data in your XML list created in Challenge 2.**
6. **Write a VBA procedure that outputs the schema text associated with the XML map created in Challenge 2 to a text file. Hint: use the XML property of the XmlSchema object to retrieve the schema text. Next, use the Open statement (see Chapter 7) to save the schema text.**

(continues)

Challenges *(continued)*

7. Revise the *Math Game* program to allow students to skip problems. While taking a test, the program should repeat skipped problems after the student has answered the last problem.

8. Revise the *Math Game* program to force students to sign in to take a test using a password. Passwords should be saved in the `students.xml` document file.

9. Revise the *Math Game* program to store the complete results of each exam. This includes the answers entered by the student and the length of time taken to finish.

10. Revise the *Math Game* program to allow a user to quickly view basic statistics regarding test results. For example, the program should calculate the average score on a particular test, the average number of attempts per test, and so on.

Excel Charts

Charts are valuable tools for data analysis and presentation in Excel or any other spreadsheet application. Unfortunately, the learning curve for creating charts is typically a bit longer and steeper than for other spreadsheet components. This is also true with regard to programming charts in Excel because the `Chart` object is a rather substantial component of the Excel object model. Before attempting to program with Excel's `Chart` object, a good understanding of the common chart types and their components is required.

This chapter discusses the following topics:

- The `Chart` object
- Accessing charts
- Chart sheets and embedded charts
- Manipulating charts
- Creating charts
- Chart events

Project: The Alienated Game

The *Alienated Game* is similar to a number of games that can be found on the Internet. The game is played with a bubble chart and interacts with the user via the mouse. The object of the game is to swap two images to create a group of three or more aliens in a row or column (please forgive the images of the aliens—I'm artistically challenged). The *Alienated Game* I created for Excel is shown in Figure 9.1.

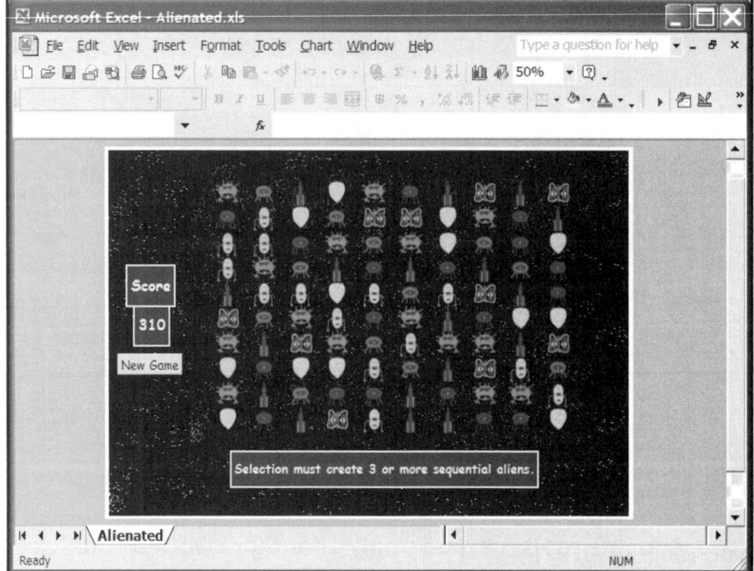

FIGURE 9.1

The *Alienated* Game.

The Chart Object

A graphical representation of the `Charts` collection object and `Chart` object are shown in Figure 9.2. The figure shows the objects and collections that are subordinate to the `Chart` object. Many of these components also have numerous subordinate objects, so Figure 9.2 does not illustrate the breadth of the `Chart` object. You should not be intimidated, though, because programming the `Chart` object involves many of the same techniques that have been discussed throughout this book. The goal of this chapter is to point out major components and some of the unique properties involved with programming the `Chart` object.

In the Real World

Charts are used in spreadsheet applications as a tool for interpreting data. The analysis may be as simple as a visual inspection of the charted numerical data or as complex as a multidimensional curve-fit to the data.

Complex data analyses involving searches for parameter minima through multidimensional space often required customized software that ran on mainframe (or larger) computers. With the incredible advances in computer technology in recent years, the same analysis can now often be done on a desktop computer using ordinary software such as Excel.

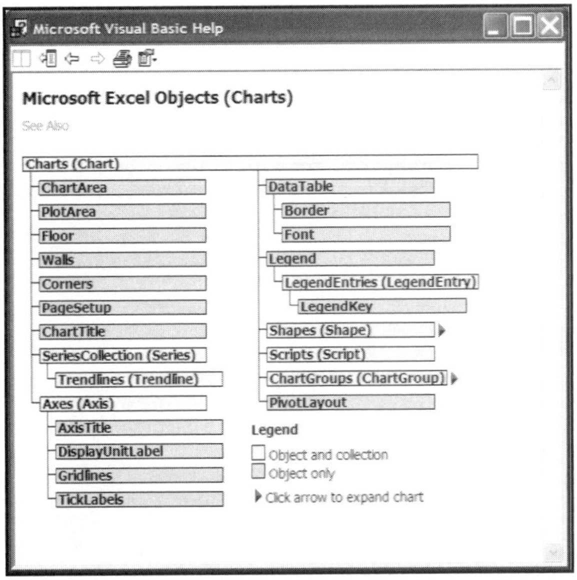

FIGURE 9.2

The `Charts` collection object and subordinate objects in the Excel object model.

Accessing Existing Charts

When creating a chart in Excel, you have the choice of embedding the chart in an existing worksheet or creating a new worksheet to hold the chart. When a chart is created and placed in a new worksheet, it is referred to as a *chart sheet*. Chart sheets are special because their only function is to display a chart; they cannot be used for holding any other data. Worksheets and chart sheets serve as containers for embedded charts. There are no limits (other than system memory) to the number of embedded charts a worksheet or chart sheet can hold. Using VBA to programmatically control chart sheets and embedded charts involves the use of different objects that, at first, can be a little confusing; however, when the object model is followed, the differences make sense.

Chart Sheets

In Chapter 5, you learned that a collection of `Worksheet` objects were members of the `Worksheets` collection object. Chart sheets (see Figure 9.3), on the other hand, are not included with this collection. This makes sense because a chart sheet is not a spreadsheet and should not be contained in a collection object called `Worksheets`. Instead, chart sheets are members of two different collection objects: the `Sheets` and `Charts` collection objects. The `Sheets` collection object has broader scope, including both `Worksheet` objects and `Chart` objects (as chart sheets). This is somewhat unusual because chart sheets and worksheets are really two different beasts, and collection objects generally hold objects of only one type. As you might expect, however, VBA does provide a collection object that contains only chart sheets—the

Charts collection object. As an example, consider a workbook that contains multiple worksheets and chart sheets. All Chart objects can be returned to your program in a Charts collection via the Charts property of the Workbook object.

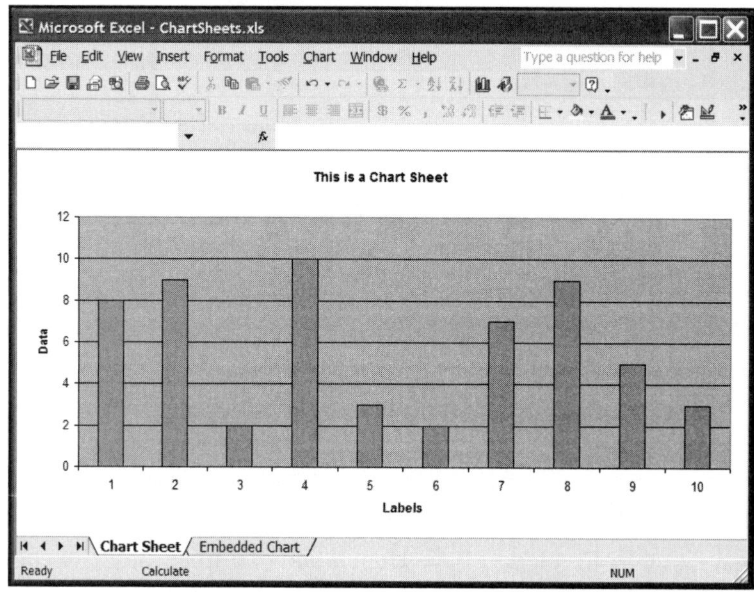

FIGURE 9.3

A chart sheet.

```
ActiveWorkbook.Charts
```

It is important to point out that the Charts collection object returned by the Charts property returns only the chart sheets in the specified workbook. To access an individual chart sheet, specify an index (or object name as a string) with the Charts property.

```
ActiveWorkbook.Charts(1)
```

or

```
ActiveWorkbook.Charts("MyChart")
```

Consider the GetChartSheets() sub procedure. This procedure uses a For/Each loop to iterate through a Sheets collection in an attempt to return only those sheets from the active workbook that are chart sheets. This procedure will execute successfully if the active workbook only contains chart sheets—something that you will probably never create. The problem with the GetChartSheets() sub procedure is that any worksheets contained in the active workbook will also be returned in the Sheets collection; therefore, a runtime error is generated (type mismatch) when the current iteration of the loop tries to access a Worksheet object with the variable that was declared as a Chart object (chSheet).

```
Public Sub GetChartSheets()
    Dim chSheet As Chart
    For Each chSheet In ActiveWorkbook.Sheets
        Debug.Print chSheet.Name
    Next
End Sub
```

To fix the `GetChartSheets()` sub procedure use the `Charts` property of the `Workbook` object to return all `Chart` objects (as chart sheets) from the active workbook.

```
Public Sub GetChartSheets()
    Dim chSheet As Chart
    For Each chSheet In ActiveWorkbook.Charts
        Debug.Print chSheet.Name
    Next
End Sub
```

It may seem confusing to use the `Charts` property to return a collection of chart sheets, and not all charts (including embedded charts) from the workbook. An embedded chart is a chart that has been placed on a worksheet (see Figure 9.4), or a chart sheet (see Figure 9.5). When you think about it, embedded charts are subordinate to a `Worksheet` object or `Chart` object (when it references a chart sheet); so it makes sense that you cannot access embedded charts from a property of the `Workbook` object.

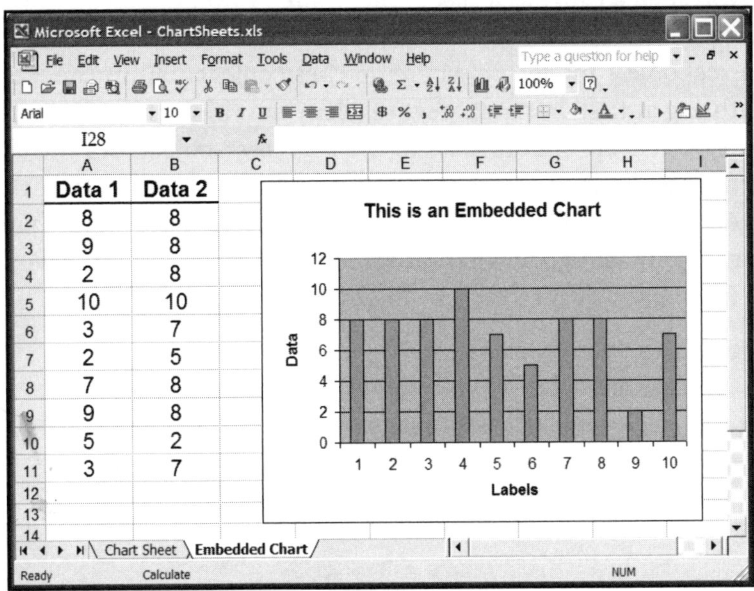

FIGURE 9.4

An embedded chart placed on a worksheet.

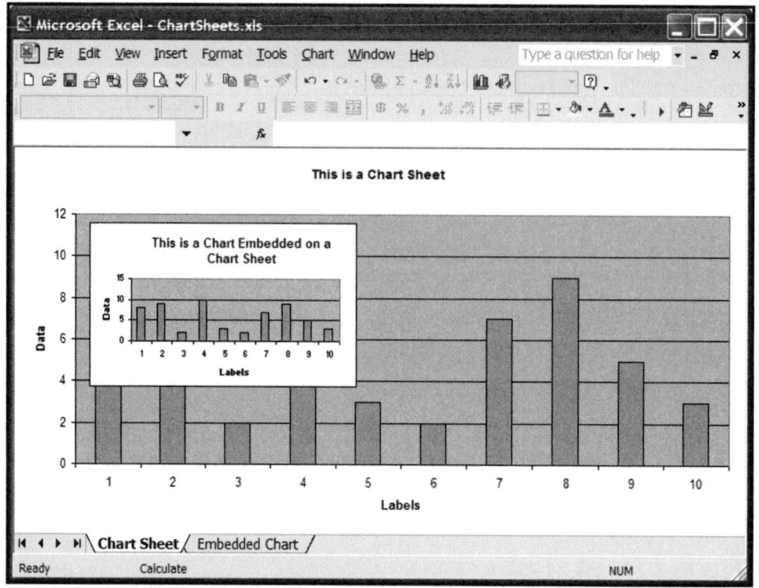

FIGURE 9.5

An embedded chart placed on a chart sheet.

Embedded Charts

To access embedded charts, use the `ChartObjects` collection and `ChartObject` objects. A `ChartObjects` collection object contains all `ChartObject` objects on a worksheet or chart sheet. A `ChartObject` object is a container for a single `Chart` object, but not if this `Chart` object represents a chart sheet. If there was such a thing as a `Sheet` object, then I would tell you the `ChartObjects` and `ChartObject` objects are subordinate objects of the `Sheet` object; however, there is no `Sheet` object in the Excel object model. So where do these objects fall in the hierarchy? As I said before, it's confusing at first, but makes sense when you think about it—but the `ChartObjects` and `ChartObject` objects are subordinate to the `Worksheet` object and the `Chart` object. They are only subordinate, however, to the `Chart` object when the `Chart` object represents a chart sheet. Confusion between the `ChartObject` object and the `Chart` object will be a common source of error in your VBA code when programming charts. The following example helps clarify how to use these objects to access an embedded chart.

```
Public Sub GetEmbeddedChartObjects()
    Dim chObj As ChartObject

    For Each chObj In ActiveSheet.ChartObjects
        Debug.Print chObj.Chart.Name
    Next
End Sub
```

The `GetEmbeddedChartObjects()` sub procedure loops through all `ChartObject` objects on the active sheet (chart sheet or worksheet) using a `For/Each` loop. A `Chart` object is returned via the `Chart` property of the `ChartObject` object and the value of the `Chart` object's `Name` property is output to the Immediate window. Please note that to access the actual `Chart` object and not just the container object, the `Chart` property of the `ChartObject` object must be used (`chObj.Chart`). Without the `Chart` property (for example, `chObj.Name`), the preceding procedure would output the value of the `Name` property of a `ChartObject` object, which is not the same as the `Name` property of the `Chart` object. The point of this is to illustrate that the path to a `Chart` object contained in an embedded chart is:

```
Application
     Workbook
          Worksheet or Chart (as a chart sheet)
             ChartObject
                   Chart.
```

You now know how to access `Chart` objects associated with chart sheets and embedded charts using the VBA objects summarized in Table 9.1. Next, I will discuss some of the methods and properties you can use to manipulate these charts.

TABLE 9.1 VBA OBJECTS USED TO ACCESS EXCEL CHARTS

Object	Function
`Sheets` collection	A collection of all sheets in the specified workbook, including chart sheets as `Chart` objects and `Worksheet` objects.
`Charts` collection	A collection of all chart sheets in the specified workbook as `Chart` objects.
`Chart`	Represents a single `Chart` object (embedded or as a chart sheet).
`ChartObjects` collection	A collection of all `ChartObject` objects on a specified worksheet or chart sheet.
`ChartObject`	Represents the container object for an embedded `Chart` object.

Manipulating Charts

You can create several different types of charts in Excel, including the common column and pie charts and the not-so-common doughnut and radar charts. Table 9.2 summarizes the more commonly used chart types available in Excel and their function.

TABLE 9.2 COMMON EXCEL CHART TYPES

Chart Type	Function
Column	Compares categorized values by charting the data as vertical columns running from 0 to the charted value. There is one column for each value and all columns in the same category have the same color.
Bar	The same as a column chart, except that the columns now run in a horizontal direction and are called `bars`.
Line	Similar to column and bar charts, except that the values are charted as points connected by a line.
Pie	Charts each value in a data series as its percent contribution to the whole.
Area	Combines a line chart with a pie chart. Shows the contribution to the whole for several data series over time or categories.
Scatter	Plots *x,y* coordinate pairs as a series of points.
Bubble	Same as a scatter, except that a third variable is included and represented by the size of the data marker.

There are several objects subordinate to the `Chart` object that represent various components of an Excel chart. The properties and methods of all these objects can be used in your VBA code to alter the appearance and behavior of an Excel chart. Some of the objects that are common to most charts are shown in Figure 9.6 and the Excel application file `ChartDemos.xls` (found on the book's CD-ROM) contains several examples of manipulating charts using VBA programs. One worksheet from this file (named `Chart Type`) is shown in Figure 9.7.

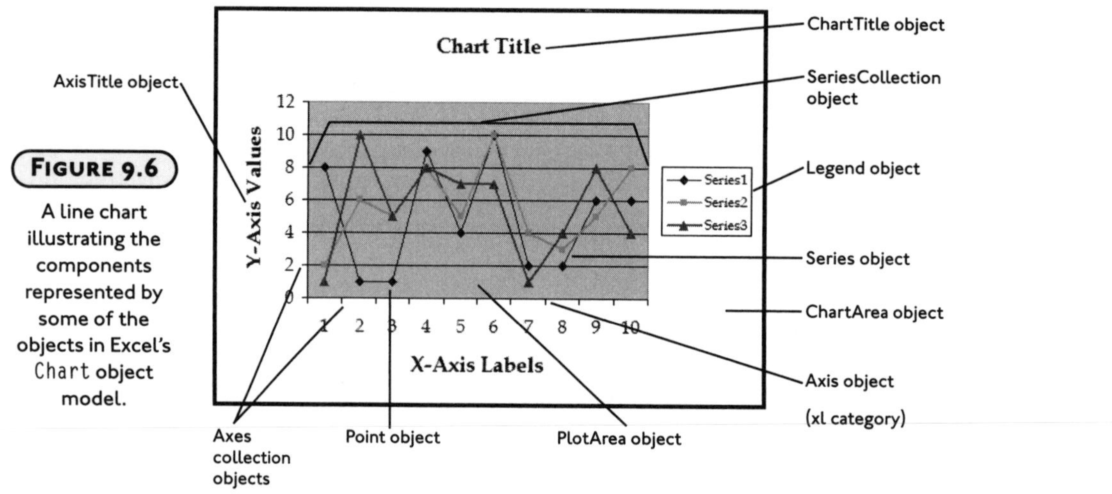

FIGURE 9.6

A line chart illustrating the components represented by some of the objects in Excel's `Chart` object model.

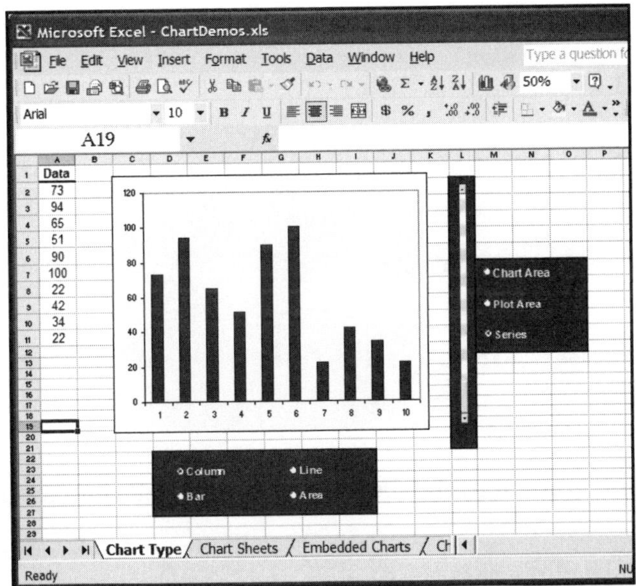

FIGURE 9.7

The Chart Type worksheet with a column chart.

The `Chart Type` worksheet contains a column of arbitrary data charted in a column chart. Several ActiveX controls are used to change the properties of the embedded chart. Option Button controls are used to select one of four chart types (Column, Bar, Area, or Line). Another set of Option Button controls and a Scroll Bar control are used to change the color of the chart area, plot area, and data series.

To learn how to manipulate properties of a chart using VBA, record a macro while changing the desired properties from the Excel application.

To change the type of chart, the integer constant representing the chart type is passed to the sub procedure `SetChartType()` where the `ChartType` property of the `Chart` object is set. I found the constants used to specify the chart type in the online help by looking up the `ChartType` property. I found the `ChartType` property in the list of `Chart` object members in Object Browser.

```
Private Sub optArea_Click()
    SetChartType (xlArea)
End Sub
Private Sub optBar_Click()
    SetChartType (xlBarClustered)
End Sub
```

```
Private Sub optColumn_Click()
    SetChartType (xlColumnClustered)
End Sub
Private Sub optLine_Click()
    SetChartType (xlLine)
End Sub

Private Sub SetChartType(myType As Integer)
    Dim myChart As Chart

    Set myChart = ActiveSheet.ChartObjects(1).Chart
    myChart.ChartType = myType
End Sub
```

For example, selecting the Option Button labeled `Bar` in Figure 9.7 changes the chart type to a bar chart.

The path to the chart traverses the `Worksheet` object, the `ChartObjects` collection object, and the `ChartObject` object before finally reaching the destination `Chart` object. An index value of one is used to return the specific `ChartObject` object from the `ChartObjects` collection object. This works because there is only one chart embedded on the worksheet. If subsequent charts are added to the worksheet, their index values will proceed in the order they are added (2, 3, 4, and so on). As with any collection object, be careful when using index values to return specific objects to ensure that the desired object is returned.

Option Buttons and a Scroll Bar are used to set the color of various components of the chart. The action occurs in the sub procedure `ChangeColor()` which is called when the `Change()` event of the Scroll Bar control or the `Click()` event of one of the Option Button controls is triggered by the user.

```
Private Sub optChartArea_Click()
    ChangeColor
End Sub
Private Sub optPlotArea_Click()
    ChangeColor
End Sub
Private Sub optSeries_Click()
    ChangeColor
End Sub
Private Sub scrColor_Change()
    ChangeColor
End Sub
```

In the `ChangeColor()` sub procedure, a reference to the chart is set with the variable `myChart` using the same object path in the `SetChartType()` sub procedure. A simple test for the value of the Option Button controls (`optChartArea`, `optPlotArea`, and `optSeries`) sets the variable used as the conditional in a `Select/Case` decision structure. In the `Select/Case` structure, the `ColorIndex` property of the `ChartArea`, `PlotArea`, and `Series` objects is assigned to the `Value` property of the Scroll Bar control (`scrColor`). The `ChartArea` object generally represents the background, axes, titles and legend in a chart; but this depends on the chart type. The `PlotArea` object represents the area on a chart where the data is plotted (data markers, data labels, gridlines, and so on). The `Series` object represents an individual data series and is returned from the `SeriesCollection` collection object.

```
Private Sub ChangeColor()
    Dim component As Integer
    Dim myChart As Chart

    Set myChart = ActiveSheet.ChartObjects(1).Chart
    If optChartArea.Value = True Then component = 1
    If optPlotArea.Value = True Then component = 2
    If optSeries.Value = True Then component = 3
    Select Case component
        Case 1
            myChart.ChartArea.Interior.ColorIndex = scrColor.Value
        Case 2
            myChart.PlotArea.Interior.ColorIndex = scrColor.Value
        Case 3
            If optLine.Value <> True Then
                myChart.SeriesCollection(1).Interior.ColorIndex = scrColor.Value
            End If
        Case Else
            MsgBox ("Please select a chart component")
    End Select
End Sub
```

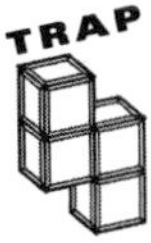

The available objects and properties of a `Chart` object will vary somewhat with chart type; therefore, it is very important that you have a good understanding of the type of chart you are trying to manipulate.

For example, unlike the area, column, and bar charts, a line chart does not have an `Interior` object subordinate to its `Series` object. As a result, you cannot set the `ColorIndex` property of the `Interior` object of the `Series` object for a line chart. Attempting to do so will result in a runtime error.

Although the Chart Type worksheet illustrates the manipulation of a few properties of the Chart object, it is not a practical example of a good VBA application because it is just as easy for the user to manipulate these properties from the Excel application.

Typically, properties of a Chart object are set from VBA code when the chart must be added to the workbook or worksheet programmatically.

See the PieClock.xls workbook for another example of chart manipulation where an analog clock is simulated using a pie chart.

Creating Charts

To write a VBA procedure that creates a chart, you must decide whether to create a chart sheet or embed the chart in an existing worksheet. The difference between creating a chart sheet and embedding a chart is subtle; it is presented in the code listings that follow. These procedures can also be found in the ChartDemo.xls file and activated from the worksheet named Embedded Charts.

Creating a Chart Sheet

The sub procedure AddChartSheet() creates a new chart sheet and a column chart of sample data selected from a worksheet by the user.

The worksheet range that contains the data is selected via a custom dialog box using methods discussed in Chapter 6. The Add() method of the Charts collection object is used to create a column chart on a new chart sheet. Remember, the Charts collection object represents a collection of chart sheets in a workbook (refer to Table 9.1). After the chart sheet is added, the chart it contains is automatically active because it is the only component of the sheet. Next, a With/End With structure is used to modify the properties of the Chart object. Many of these subordinate objects and properties have common sense names, so their function is intuitive.

```
Public Sub AddChartSheet()
    Dim dataRange As Range
    Set dataRange = Range(frmDataRange.txtDataRange.Text)
    frmDataRange.Hide

    Charts.Add
    With ActiveChart
        .ChartType = xlColumnClustered
        .HasLegend = True
        .Legend.Position = xlRight
```

```
        .Axes(xlCategory).MinorTickMark = xlOutside
        .Axes(xlValue).MinorTickMark = xlOutside

        '-------------------------------
        'Use Excel worksheet function to set the maximum scale on
        'the value axis.
        '-------------------------------
        .Axes(xlValue).MaximumScale = Application.WorksheetFunction. _
                   RoundUp(Application.WorksheetFunction. _
                   Max(dataRange), -1)
        .Axes(xlCategory).HasTitle = True
        .Axes(xlCategory).AxisTitle.Characters.Text = "X-axis Labels"
        .Axes(xlValue).HasTitle = True
        .Axes(xlValue).AxisTitle.Characters.Text = "Y-axis"

        .SeriesCollection(1).Name = "Sample Data"
        .SeriesCollection(1).Values = dataRange
    End With
End Sub
```

In the `AddChartSheet()` sub procedure, a specific `Axis` object is returned from the `Axes` collection object by passing a defined constant with the `Axes()` method. The `Axes()` method returns an `Axis` object and takes up to two parameters: one for the axis type (`xlCategory`, `xlSeries`, or `xlValue`), and another for the axis group (`xlPrimary` or `xlSecondary`). The axis type `xlCategory` represents the *x*-axis on the chart, and `xlValue` represents the *y*-axis. The axis type `xlSeries` applies only to 3D charts and represents the *z*-axis. The axis group is either `xlPrimary` (default) or `xlSecondary` (applies to charts containing multiple `Series` objects).

The rest of the objects and properties set via the `Axis` object are fairly straightforward and include setting tick marks and chart labels. The upper limit of the *y*-axis scale is set using Excel worksheet functions that return the maximum value from the variable `dataRange` (defined at the beginning of the procedure) rounded up to single-digit precision.

The data is finally added to the chart by setting the `Values` property of the `Series` object (returned from the `SeriesCollection` collection object) with the range variable `dataRange`.

Figure 9.8 shows the components specifically added to the chart by the preceding code. The chart also contains components created from default properties of the various chart related objects. For example, the gridlines in the figure are the major gridlines on the *y*-axis and are displayed by default. To prevent them from being displayed, I could have added a statement such as `ActiveChart.Axes(xlValue).MajorGridlines = False`.

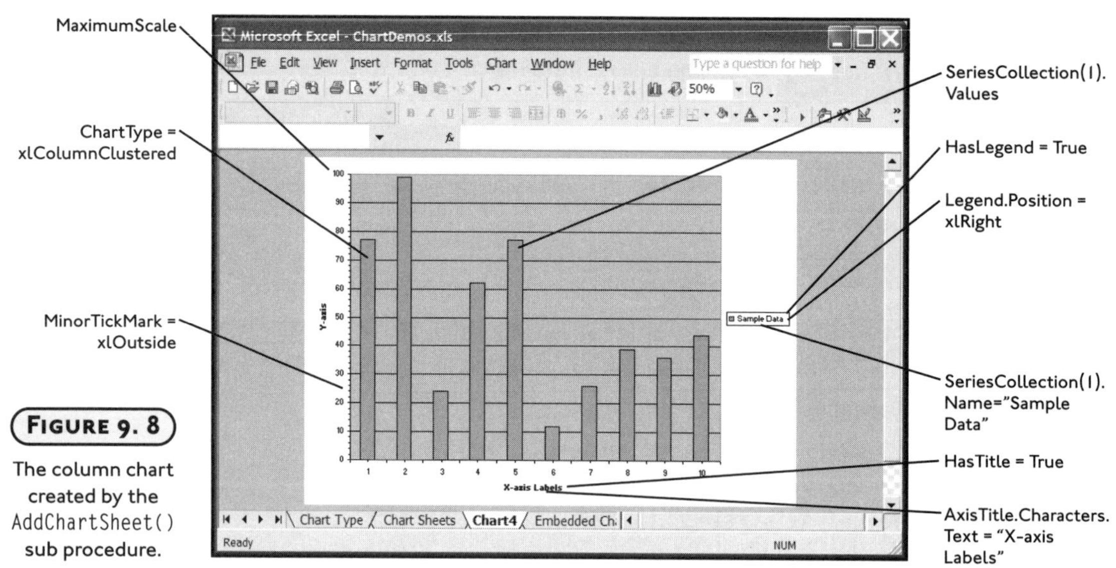

FIGURE 9.8

The column chart created by the `AddChartSheet()` sub procedure.

Creating an Embedded Chart

To add an embedded chart to a worksheet, use the `Add()` method of the `ChartObects` collection object. The `AddEmbeddedChart()` sub procedure creates the same column chart as the `AddChartSheet()` sub procedure listed in the previous section; however, it embeds the chart on an existing worksheet named `Embedded Charts`.

```
Public Sub AddEmbeddedChart()
    Dim dataRange As Range

    Set dataRange = Range(frmDataRange.txtDataRange.Text)
    frmDataRange.Hide

    Sheets("Create Chart").ChartObjects.Add Left:=200, _
                          Top:=50, Width:=500, Height:=350
    Sheets("Create Chart").ChartObjects(1).Activate
    With ActiveChart
        .ChartType = xlColumnClustered
        .SeriesCollection.NewSeries
        .HasLegend = True
        .Legend.Position = xlRight
        .Axes(xlCategory).MinorTickMark = xlOutside
        .Axes(xlValue).MinorTickMark = xlOutside
```

```
        .Axes(xlValue).MaximumScale = Application.WorksheetFunction.RoundUp( _
                             Application.WorksheetFunction.Max(dataRange), -1)
        .Axes(xlCategory, xlPrimary).HasTitle = True
        .Axes(xlCategory, xlPrimary).AxisTitle.Characters.Text = _
                             "X-axis Labels"
        .Axes(xlValue, xlPrimary).HasTitle = True
        .Axes(xlValue, xlPrimary).AxisTitle.Characters.Text = "Y-axis"
        .SeriesCollection(1).Name = "Sample Data"
        .SeriesCollection(1).Values = dataRange
    End With
End Sub
```

When adding an embedded chart, the `Add()` method of the `ChartObjects` collection object accepts four parameters that define the position of the upper-left corner of the chart on the worksheet, as well as the chart width and height. The position properties of the `Add()` method (`Left` and `Top`) are relative to the upper-left corner of cell A1 and are in units of points. The `Activate` method of the `ChartObject` object is equivalent to selecting the chart because only one `Chart` object is contained in a `ChartObject` object.

Before setting the properties of the `Chart` object, the chart must contain at least one `Series` object. Thus, the `NewSeries` method is used to add an empty `Series` object to the chart. This is another difference from adding chart sheets, where a `Series` object is automatically added on creation of the chart sheet. The properties of the `Chart` object are then set in the same manner as was done with the chart sheet.

The preceding examples demonstrate only a small fraction of the objects, properties, and methods available in a `Chart` object. Don't be intimidated by the breadth of the `Chart` object and its components! Always remember that a large problem can be broken into many smaller, more manageable problems. Once you learn how to access a chart, setting the properties of any of its component objects is basically the same. The hard part is learning what objects are available to the specific chart being manipulated. The number of component objects in a `Chart` object varies with the chart type (column, bar, scatter, and so on) and with the subcategory of chart type (clustered, stacked, 3D, and so on). For example, a 3D column chart has `Wall`, `Floor`, and `Corners` objects, but a clustered column chart does not have these objects.

To learn the differences between chart types or to just learn what is available for a specific chart type, use recorded macros. First, create the chart from the Excel application then alter its appearance with the macro recorder turned on. Be careful to record only a small number of actions, say two to three at one time, because the macro recorder adds a lot of unnecessary code (setting default values). Keep in mind that as you select a component of the chart with the mouse, you are really selecting a component object of the `Chart` object. The dialog box that appears when the component object is double-clicked or selected from the chart menu sets the properties of that object. For example, the Format Axis dialog box shown in Figure 9.9 appears when the user double-clicks on a chart axis.

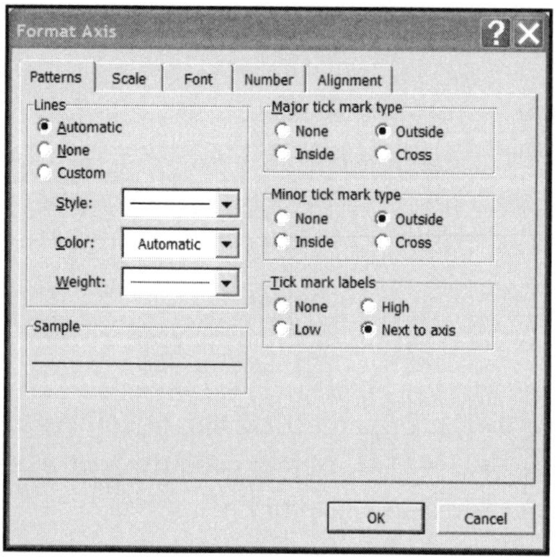

FIGURE 9.9

The Format Axis dialog box.

Figure 9.9 shows some of the properties of the `Axis` object. If the macro recorder is on while these properties are altered, the VBA code used to set these properties will be recorded when OK is clicked in the dialog box. After recording a small macro, proceed to the VBA IDE to examine the recorded code. If any of the code needs clarification, select the unknown keyword and press F1 to retrieve its documentation from the online help. This is an extremely helpful tool for learning how to program specific Excel components and the advantage should be exploited.

Chart Events

The `Chart` object has several events that are triggered by various user actions. Some of the events are familiar—like `Activate()`, `MouseDown()`, and `MouseUp()`—but a few are unique to the `Chart` object. Table 9.3 summarizes the less familiar events associated with the `Chart` object.

`Chart` object events are not automatically enabled with embedded charts. Although `Chart` object events can be enabled for embedded charts, the methods involved are beyond the scope of this book.

Table 9.3 Chart Object Events

Event	Trigger
`Calculate`	When new or changed data is charted
`DragOver`	When a range of cells is dragged over a chart
`DragPlot`	When a range of cells is dragged and dropped on a chart
`Resize`	When the chart is resized
`Select`	When a chart element is selected
`SeriesChange`	When the value of a charted data point changes

Chart Sheets

Chart events are automatically enabled with chart sheets. To catch events triggered by the user in a chart sheet, add code to an event procedure contained in the module associated with the chart sheet. The code window can be opened in the same manner as with a worksheet. Figure 9.10 shows the code window of a chart sheet selected from the project explorer. The active project displayed in Figure 9.10 is an Excel workbook containing several chart sheets.

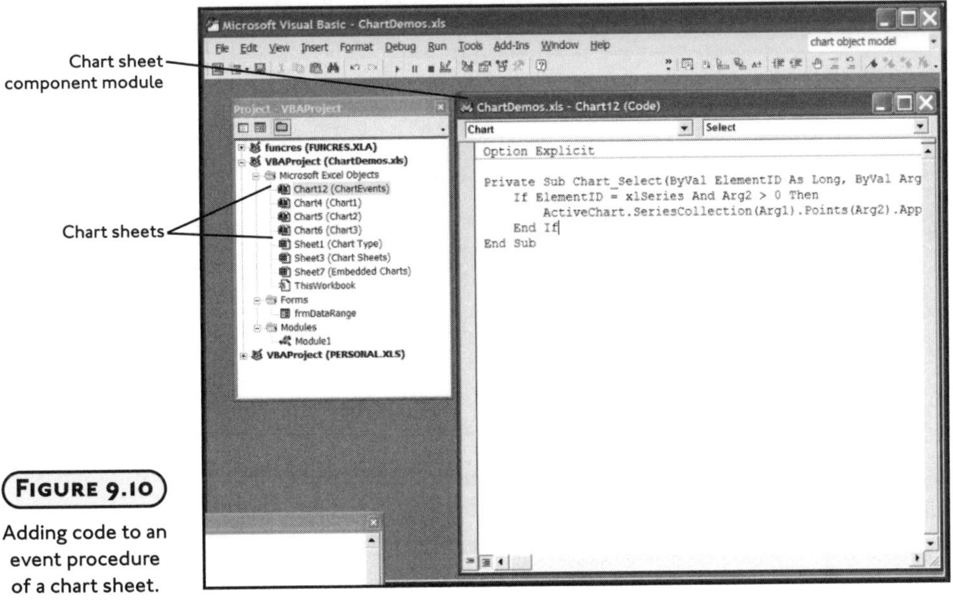

Figure 9.10

Adding code to an event procedure of a chart sheet.

Unfortunately, some of the events unique to the `Chart` object cannot be used with a chart sheet because there is no manner in which the user can trigger them. For example, the user cannot drag and drop a range of cells over the chart when the data is in another worksheet; however, the other chart events work as expected, and an example using the `Select()` event procedure of the `Chart` object is listed here.

```
Private Sub Chart_Select(ByVal ElementID As Long, ByVal Arg1 As Long, ByVal Arg2 As Long)
    If ElementID = xlSeries And Arg2 > 0 Then
        ActiveChart.SeriesCollection(Arg1).Points(Arg2).ApplyDataLabels _
Type:=xlShowValue
    End If
End Sub
```

The `Select()` event procedure of the `Chart` object accepts three parameters: `ElementID` is a long integer that refers to the component object selected by the user (`ChartArea`, `PlotArea`, `Series`, and so on), and `Arg1` and `Arg2` are long integers that refer to specific components of the selected object; thus, the meaning of `Arg1` and `Arg2` depends on the object selected by the user. The definitions of `Arg1` and `Arg2` for some of the more common chart components are listed in Table 9.4.

TABLE 9.4 ARGUMENT DEFINITIONS FOR THE SELECT() EVENT OF THE CHART OBJECT

ElementID	Arg1	Arg2
`xlAxis, xlAxisTitle, xlDisplayUnitLabel, xlMajorGridlines, xlMinorGridlines`	Axis Index	Axis Type
`xlChartArea, xlChartTitle, xlCorners, xlDataTable, xlLegend, xlPlotArea`	None	None
`xlDataLabel, xlSeries`	Series Index	Point Index
`xlErrorBars, xlLegendEntry, xlLegendKey`	Series Index	None
`xlTrendline`	Series Index	TrendLine Index
`xlXErrorBars, xlYErrorBars`	Series Index	None

The preceding `Select()` event procedure is triggered when the user selects a chart component. If that component is a single data point on the chart then `Arg1` holds the index value of the selected `Series` object (representing a series of values) and `Arg2` holds the index value of the selected `Point` object (representing the individual values in the series).

The purpose of the code entered in the `Select()` event procedure is to add a label to any point in a data series selected by the user. To accomplish this, the parameter `ElementID` is tested for equivalence to three (VBA-defined constant `xlSeries`, see online help for additional constants) because that's the value that represents a `Series` object. If the user has selected a single point in a data series, the selected point is labeled with its value by using the `ApplyDataLabels()` method of the `Point` object and setting the `Type` argument to the constant `xlShowValue`. In this example, `Arg2` holds the value `-1` if the entire series is selected and will not hold a meaningful value until the user selects an individual point from the data series. When the user does select an individual data point, the value of `Arg2` is passed to the `Points()` method, which returns a `Point` object from the `Points` collection object. In this case, the `Points()` method returns the specific data point selected by the user.

Consider the chart shown in Figure 9.11 where two data series are plotted in a scatter chart.

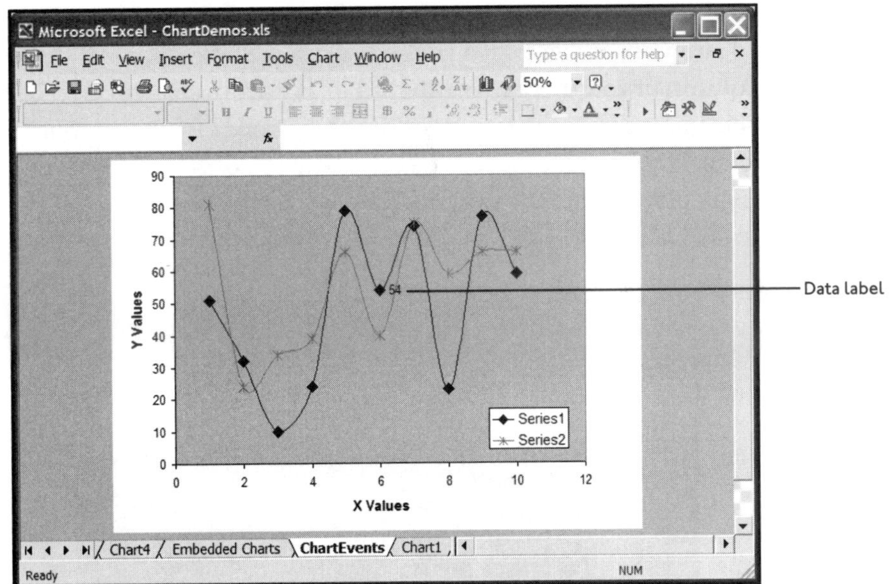

FIGURE 9.11

Detecting a user selection with the `Select()` event of the `Chart` object.

The chart is contained in a chart sheet and the `Select()` event procedure of the `Chart` object contains the previously listed code. If the user selects Series 1 with a single click of the mouse, the `Select()` event procedure is triggered but the parameters passed to the procedure are `ElementID=3`, `Arg1=1`, and `Arg2=-1`; so the conditional expression in the `If/Then` statement is false; therefore, no label is added to the chart. With Series 1 selected, the user then clicks on the 6th data point in Series 1. Again, the `Select()` event procedure is triggered, but this time the parameters passed to it are `ElementID=3`, `Arg1=1`, and `Arg2=6`. This time, the conditional in the `If/Then` statement is true and the label `54` is added to the chart.

Arg is data point
(10) 6th point in Series

Before writing the code for the `Select()` event procedure, I recorded a macro while adding a label to a charted point. This reminded me how to add the label to individual data points using VBA.

To learn how to use the `Select()` event procedure of the `Chart` object, I added the statement `Debug.Print ElementID; Arg1; Arg2` to the procedure and watched the Immediate window while I clicked on various components of the `Chart` object.

Chapter Project: The Alienated Game

The *Alienated Game* uses a chart sheet for the user interface (see Figure 9.12) and illustrates the use of several VBA objects subordinate to the `Chart` object. The program uses the less common bubble chart type because the data markers (represented by `Point` objects in VBA) in a regular scatter chart cannot hold images. A total of ten data series with ten values each are charted and their markers are randomly filled with one of seven images. The object of the game is to swap two images such that it will create a sequence of three or more identical images in a column or row (hereafter referred to as a score sequence). When a score sequence is created, their images are removed from the chart and the images above the score sequence are moved down. Finally, the empty markers at the top of the chart are randomly filled with new images. The player scores ten points for each image removed and the game ends when all possible moves are exhausted.

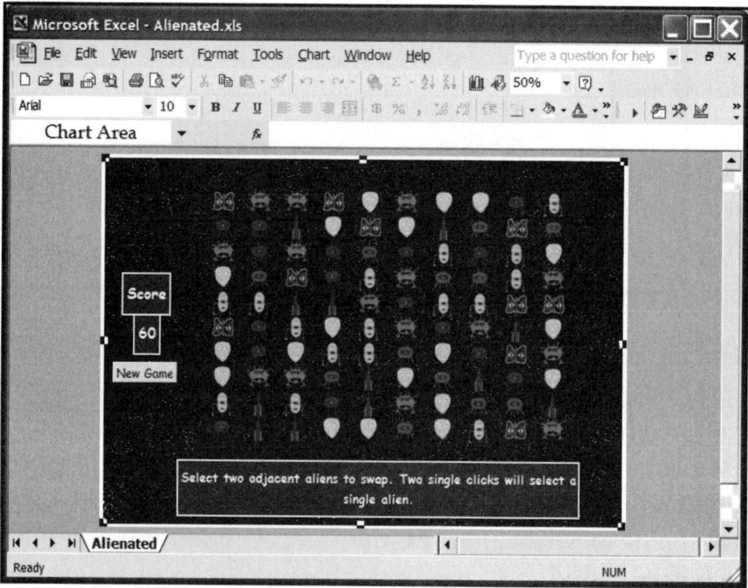

Figure 9.12

The Alienated Game.

Requirements for the Alienated Game

From the user's point of view, the *Alienated Game* is quite simple because all they have to do is select data markers on a chart. From your point of view, I'm betting the game is more of a challenge; especially if you're not that comfortable with charts. If your comfort level is low, that provides all the more reason to spend ample time planning the program.

The following list contains my requirements for the *Alienated Game*.

1. The game interface shall consist of a bubble chart created on a chart sheet.
2. The chart's data point markers shall display 100 images in a 10 by 10 grid.
3. Each image displayed in a data marker shall be randomly chosen from one of seven images.
4. The program shall be initiated from a form button placed on the chart.
5. The program shall track the user's score and display it via a chart title.
6. The program shall display help messages to the user via a chart title.
7. When a new game begins, all data markers in the chart shall be updated with new images.
8. Any time new images are added to the chart, the program shall scan the chart for a score sequence.
9. When a score sequence is found, the program shall record the score (10 pts per image), remove the images, move images above the score sequence down to fill the vacancies, and add new images to the top of the chart.
10. When the user selects two images for swapping, the program shall validate the selection before swapping the images. Selections are valid if they are adjacent and non-diagonal and they must generate at least one score sequence. Valid selections are swapped and the chart is scanned in order to process the score sequence.
11. The source data for the chart shall be added programmatically when a new game begins and the chart is initialized. The source data shall remain static.
12. The images displayed in the chart's data markers shall be mapped to the values in a range of 100 cells in a hidden worksheet. Changes made to the chart during the course of a game shall be a result of changes made to these mapped values.

Designing the Alienated Game

My goal for this project is to illustrate how to program with Excel's `Chart` object model, so its interface must take advantage of an Excel chart. This makes the project unusual with respect to everything you've seen thus far because the game's interface will not involve a worksheet or VBA form. Nevertheless, charts are constructed in order to display data that is typically stored in a worksheet; so the game will still require many of the common Excel objects you have seen in other projects.

The Chart Sheet Interface

This chapter teaches you how to program Excel's `Chart` object so the interface for the project is built from a chart. Specifically, a chart sheet consisting of a bubble chart will serve to display the images.

The requirements state that the game must involve a 10 by 10 grid of 100 images. To satisfy this requirement I will create the chart from ten data sets consisting of ten *x,y*-value pairs. The data is charted as ten different series in the chart. Each data set must use the same set of values for the *x*-axis variable to ensure vertical alignment of the images (for example, if *x*=2 for one element in each series, then their corresponding data markers are vertically aligned across the *y*-axis). In addition, the values for the *x*-axis variable must have a uniform increment for homogeneous spacing of the images. To ensure the images are aligned horizontally the *y*-values must be equivalent within a data series (for example, if *y*=2 for every element in a series, then the corresponding data markers are aligned horizontally across the *x*-axis), and the difference in the *y*-values between data series must also be uniform. The magnitude of the numbers doesn't really matter since the data is static, but I will keep it simple and use 0-9 for the *x*-axis variable, and 0-9 for the *y*-axis series (that is, the first *y*-axis data series is all 0's, the second is all 1's, and so on). The third variable in a bubble chart is expressed by the size of the data marker. I don't need this variable, but I need it to be identical for all data points such that the images are uniform in size. Figure 9.13 shows the chart sheet interface for the *Alienated Game* and how the chart sheet appears before any images are added to the data markers. Note that I formatted the chart to include a background image simulating a starry night sky.

As can be seen in Figure 9.13 a new game is started from the click of a button. The button must come from the Forms toolbar because you cannot place ActiveX controls on a chart sheet. The button is assigned to a public VBA procedure that initializes the chart with new images and clears the score so a new game can begin.

Displaying the score and help messages to the user is a bit more difficult than usual. In previous projects, I have used merged cells or Label controls to display text, but neither of these options is available with a chart sheet. The best way to display text on a chart is to use the axis and chart titles—that's what you see in Figure 9.13.

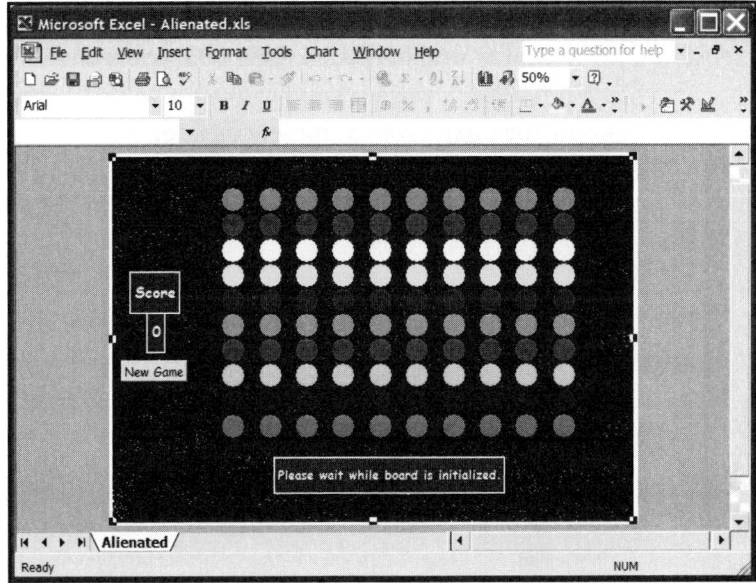

FIGURE 9.13

The *Alienated Game* chart sheet interface prior to filling the markers with images.

For a more advanced version of the *Alienated Game,* check out the Alienated_Embedded.xls project on the Book's CD-ROM. This version of the game uses an embedded chart for the user interface; so a class module is required to enable the event procedures of the `Chart` object.

Capturing User Selections

In order to know what image the user has selected, the program must identify the specific data series and data point whose marker displays the selected image. As discussed previously, selecting a chart component triggers the `Select()` event of the `Chart` object. To identify specific components requires testing the `ElementID`, `Arg1`, and `Arg2` arguments that Excel passes to the `Select()` event. The *Alienated Game* will take advantage of the `Select()` event procedure for identifying user-selected images.

Mapping the Images

Keeping track of the images and their locations in the chart is critical if the game is going to work properly. Keep in mind that the chart's images are actually data markers; it is natural to think of deleting or changing the data values to simulate image swaps or deletions. You could probably even design the program to function by altering the charted values, but that seems too complicated. Since the bubble chart will constantly have to display 100 images in a 10 by 10 grid, it will be a lot easier if the data remains static and all the program changes are the images contained in the data markers.

There are a number of methods you could use to track the chart's images including the use of a multi-dimensional array that is updated with each alteration of a data marker on the chart. This also seems like a lot of extra work when I can use a worksheet range to map each image type and its location in the chart. For example, consider the images shown in Figure 9.14 and their associated file names.

Alien2.png	
Alien3.png	
Alien4.png	
Alien5.png	
Alien6.png	
Alien7.png	

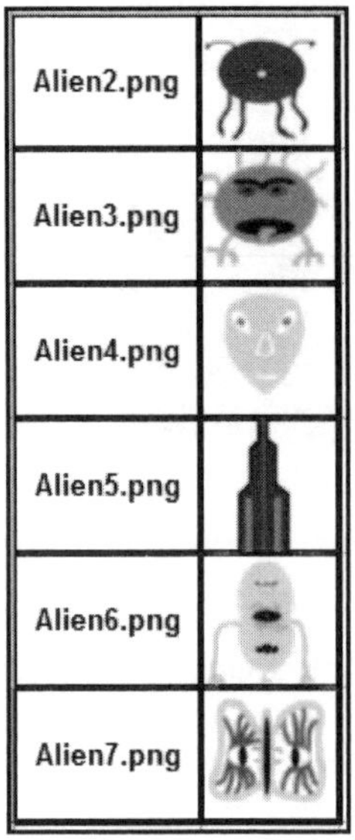

FIGURE 9.14

The images of the aliens and their associated file names used in the *Alienated Game*. Alien l.png is the same as Alien2.png in a different color.

I purposely used integers in each file name to identify the specific alien. To add images to the chart, the program must first create a 10 by 10 map of integers between 1 and 7 in a worksheet range consisting of 10 rows and 10 columns as shown in Figure 9.15. The values in this range (hereafter referred to as the image map) correspond directly to the integer values in the file names of the alien images.

The chart's data markers are then loaded using the values from the image map contained in the `ImageMap` worksheet. Generating the integers randomly ensures that the image markers are filled randomly with one of the seven images shown in Figure 9.14. The chart sheet created from the image map shown in Figure 9.15 is shown in Figure 9.16.

Since the image map identifies each image in the chart, any change to the images required during the course of a game must be mirrored in the image map. In fact, it will be easiest to first update the image map and use it to update the images displayed in the chart.

Microsoft Excel - Alienated.xls

	A	B	C	D	E	F	G	H	I	J	K
1	0	Point1	Point2	Point3	Point4	Point5	Point6	Point7	Point8	Point9	Point10
2	Series1	1	3	7	7	3	4	3	3	4	1
3	Series2	4	7	7	3	5	1	2	5	7	5
4	Series3	2	4	4	2	3	6	7	7	6	3
5	Series4	1	5	7	2	6	6	1	4	1	7
6	Series5	1	1	6	4	5	1	7	1	2	3
7	Series6	6	1	2	5	4	4	1	3	6	1
8	Series7	5	3	6	6	7	3	6	7	5	2
9	Series8	2	4	7	6	5	1	1	7	7	1
10	Series9	7	3	3	2	1	2	7	5	2	3
11	Series10	4	2	5	2	6	5	7	7	1	1

ImageMap / Alienated

FIGURE 9.15

The sample map of image identifiers used by the *Alienated Game* to track image markers in the chart sheet interface.

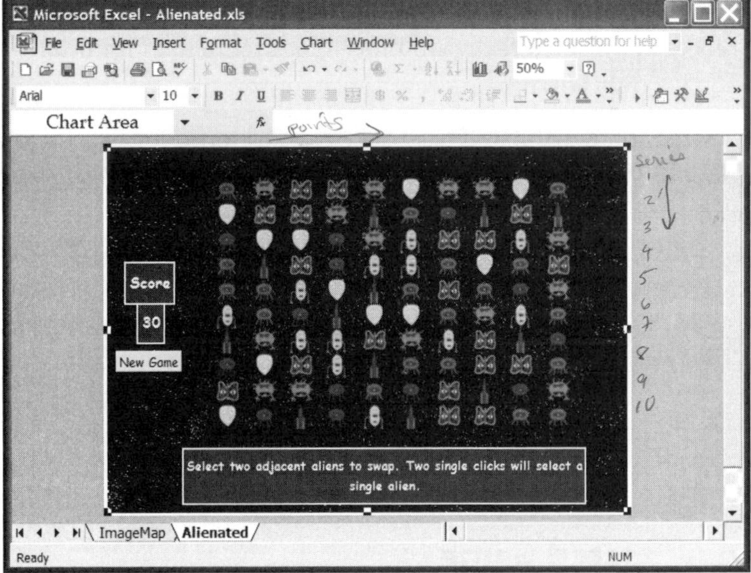

FIGURE 9.16

The chart sheet with data markers filled with images using the integer map shown in Figure 9.15.

Program Outline

When playing a game, the *Alienated Game* should proceed as outlined in the following:

1. The user initiates a new game with a click of the form button drawn on the chart sheet interface.
2. The chart sheet and `ImageMap` worksheet containing the image map are initialized for a new game.
3. The data is added to the chart as ten distinct series.
4. Data markers are filled with images using the image map contained in the `ImageMap` worksheet.
5. The image map is scanned for score sequences. If score sequences are found, the score is updated and their corresponding values and images are deleted from the image map and chart, respectively.
6. Vacancies in the image map are filled by moving values down columns and randomly adding new values to the vacated cells at the top of the columns.
7. The images displayed in the data markers in the chart are updated by reading the image map.

Steps 5–7 are repeated until there are no more score sequences found.

8. The user begins play by selecting two images in the chart for swapping.
9. The user's selection is validated to ensure the swap produces a score sequence. In addition, the swap must involve adjacent data markers (same row or column, no diagonals).
10. If the player's selection is invalid, a message is output to the chart sheet explaining the problem.

Steps 5–7 are repeated until there are no more score sequences found.

11. The game continues until there are no more possible swaps that can create a score sequence or the user decides to start a new game. Creating a sub procedure that scans the chart for potential moves is left as an exercise for the reader.

Coding the Alienated Game

Since the program interface consists of a single chart sheet and the program requires the `Select()` event of the `Chart` object, I have entered all of the program code in the module for the chart sheet.

Module level declarations include a string for holding the path to the image files, integers for holding the series and point numbers for the two images selected by the user, and a custom data type defining the type `DataPoints`. I will use variables declared as `DataPoints` to hold the last cell in the range of cells mapped to score sequences in the chart. A `DataPoints` variable will also hold the number of cells in the score sequence.

```
Option Explicit
Private Type DataPoints
    cellRange As Range
    numCells As Integer
End Type
Private filePath As String
Private pt1Series As Integer
Private pt2Series As Integer
Private pt1Point As Integer
Private pt2Point As Integer
```

Initializing the Chart Sheet

The public sub procedure `Main()` is triggered from the form button on the chart sheet and contains calls to the initialization procedures for the chart sheet, then scans the chart for score sequences. Screen updating is initially turned off otherwise Excel will update the screen as images are added or removed from the chart. Screen updating is turned back on so that the user can see the chart before it is scanned for score sequences. Note that the `ChartTitle` object is used to display help messages to the user telling them how to play the game. The `ChartTitle` object is accessed via the `ChartTitle` property of the `Chart` object, which in turn is returned from the `Sheets` property of the `Application` object. I added the title to the bottom of the chart when initially formatting it.

```
Public Sub Main()
    Dim msg As ChartTitle

    Set msg = Sheets("Alienated").ChartTitle
    '-----------------
    'Call initialization procedures.
    '-----------------
    Application.ScreenUpdating = False
    InitData
    AddSeries
    InitSeriesImages
    Application.ScreenUpdating = True
    Delay 1
```

```
    '------------------------------
    'Scan the chart, remove and score consecutive images,
    'then update the chart with new images...repeat.
    '------------------------------
    ProcessChart

    '----------------------------
    'Update messages and initialize chart for player
    'selection of two images.
    '----------------------------
    msg.Text = "Select two adjacent aliens to swap. " & _
        "Two single clicks will select a single alien."
End Sub
```

The `InitData()` sub procedure is called from `Main()` and serves to reset the score, outputs an informational message, and fills the image maps range in the `ImageMap` worksheet with random integer values between 1 and 7. I named the range `B2:K11` `ImageMap` when formatting the `ImageMap` worksheet.

```
Private Sub InitData()
    Dim msg As ChartTitle, score As AxisTitle
    Dim wsAlien As Chart, wsMap As Worksheet
    Dim c As Range

    '-------------------
    'Initialize Alienated chart sheet.
    '-------------------
    Set wsAlien = Sheets("Alienated")
    Set wsMap = Worksheets("ImageMap")
    Set msg = wsAlien.ChartTitle
    Set score = wsAlien.Axes(xlCategory).AxisTitle
    score.Text = "0"
    filePath = ActiveWorkbook.Path & "\AlienImages\alien"
    msg.Text = "Please wait while board is initialized."

    '----------------------
    'Initialize data on the Hidden worksheet.
    '----------------------
    Randomize
    With wsMap
```

```
        For Each c In .Range("ImageMap")
            c.Value = Int(Rnd * 7) + 1
        Next
    End With
End Sub
```

The AddSeries() sub procedure is also called from Main() and its purpose is to add the data to the chart. Since the data remains static, I can add it programmatically using variant arrays. You can add a data series to a chart via the SeriesCollection object that is returned using the SeriesCollection property of the Chart object. I first delete any existing series before adding ten new series in a For/Next loop. I set all three variables (*x*, *y*, and point size) for each series within the loop. Since each data series requires the same set of *x*-values and marker sizes, I can use variant arrays (xArray and ptSize) with the XValues and BubbleSizes properties of the SeriesCollection object to set the *x*-axis and marker size values. Values for the *y*-axis variable are constant for a given set of *x*-values and are set using the Values property of the SeriesCollection object.

Prior to setting the data values for each series, I set the BubbleScale property of a ChartGroup object. A ChartGroup object represents all the data series charted with the same format (line, bar, bubble, and so on). In this example, all ten series are charted with the same format (bubble) so the ChartGroups property with an index value of 1 returns all ten series as a ChartGroup object. The BubbleScale property only applies to bubble charts and sets a scale factor for the bubbles on the chart. I have to set this property because the images I created are too large to fit in a reasonably sized chart; thus, I scaled them down to 35 percent of their original size.

```
Private Sub AddSeries()
    Dim I As Integer
    Dim chAlien As Chart
    Dim xArray As Variant, ptSize As Variant

    On Error GoTo ErrorHandler

    xArray = Array(0, 1, 2, 3, 4, 5, 6, 7, 8, 9)
    ptSize = Array(1, 1, 1, 1, 1, 1, 1, 1, 1, 1)
    '----------------------
    'Add 10 data series to the bubble chart.
    '----------------------
    Set chAlien = Sheets("Alienated")
    chAlien.ChartGroups(1).BubbleScale = 35
    With chAlien
```

```
        If .SeriesCollection.Count > 0 Then
            For I = .SeriesCollection.Count To 1 Step -1
                .SeriesCollection(I).Delete
            Next I
        End If
        For I = 1 To 10
            .SeriesCollection.NewSeries
            .SeriesCollection(I).XValues = xArray
            .SeriesCollection(I).Values = Array(10 - I, 10 - I, 10 - I, _
                    10 - I, 10 - I, 10 - I, 10 - I, 10 - I, 10 - I, 10 - I)
            .SeriesCollection(I).BubbleSizes = ptSize
        Next I
    End With
    Exit Sub
ErrorHandler:
    MsgBox Err.Description, vbCritical, "Error"
    End
End Sub
```

At this point in the program, the image map in the ImageMap worksheet has been randomly filled with numbers and the chart has been initialized by resetting the score to zero and adding ten new series of data. All that remains is to fill the chart markers with the images of the aliens. This is accomplished in the InitSeriesImages() sub procedure. In this procedure, nested For/Each loops iterate through each Points collection object associated with the Series object for the chart. Recall that there are ten data series in the chart; therefore, the SeriesCollection object contains ten Series objects. Furthermore, each Series object contains a Points collection containing ten Point objects making for a grand total of 100 data points. The nested For/Each loops effectively iterate through each Point object in the chart and use the UserPicture() method of the ChartFillFormat object to load an image of an alien into the data marker. The ChartFillFormat object is returned by the Fill property of the Point object. The specific image is selected using the value of the cell in the ImageMap worksheet mapped to the specific Point object in the chart (recall how the file names for the alien images were named, see Figure 9.14). If the image map does not contain a value, then the ColorIndex property of the Interior object associated with the Point object is set to xlNone. This effectively removes an image from a data marker and leaves the marker without a background color so it cannot be seen. This is included in the InitSeriesImages() procedure because this procedure will be called again when sequential images need to be removed from the chart.

```
Private Sub InitSeriesImages()
    Dim chAlien As Chart
    Dim chSeries As Series, chPoint As Point
    Dim imageIndex As Integer
    Dim wsMap As Worksheet
    Dim I As Integer, J As Integer

    On Error GoTo InitSeriesError

    '----------------------------------
    'Use inital image map to fill data points in chart with images.
    '----------------------------------
    Set chAlien = Sheets("Alienated")
    Set wsMap = Worksheets("ImageMap")
    I = 1: J = 1
    With chAlien
        For Each chSeries In .SeriesCollection
            For Each chPoint In chSeries.Points
                imageIndex = wsMap.Range("ImageMap").Cells(I, J).Value
                If imageIndex <> 0 Then
                    chPoint.Fill.UserPicture PictureFile:=filePath & _
                                imageIndex & ".png"
                Else
                    chPoint.Interior.ColorIndex = xlNone  'Erase image
                End If
                J = J + 1   'Increment column index
            Next
            I = I + 1   'Increment row index
            J = 1       'Reset column index
        Next
    End With
    Exit Sub

InitSeriesError:
    MsgBox "An error was encountered while loading images into the chart. " _
        & vbCrLf & Err.Description, vbOKOnly, "Chart Initialization Error: " _
        & Err.Number
    End
End Sub
```

Scanning the Chart

Scanning the chart sheet is required immediately after images are added to the bubble chart. A chart scan must be triggered when a new game begins and when the player swaps two images. Since a chart scan may ultimately result in the removal of images and subsequent addition of new images, this may trigger more scans.

The last procedure called from sub Main() is ProcessChart(). The ProcessChart() sub procedure essentially outlines the process of scanning a chart for score sequences, updating the score, removing score sequences, moving images down columns in the chart, and adding new images. Since new images are added randomly to replace scored sequences, it is always possible that more score sequences will be created; thus, the whole process is repeated in a Do Loop until there are no more score sequences found. Most of these tasks are accomplished with calls to the ScanImages() function procedure, and the CalcScore(), RemoveImages(), and MoveImages() sub procedures.

The most interesting statement in this procedure is the conditional used with the If/Then code block If (Not MapRanges) <> -1. On occasion, you may need to test if a dynamic array variable has been dimensioned with a ReDim statement. (The variable MapRanges is declared as a dynamic array and its value is returned from the ScanImages() function procedure.) Unfortunately, VBA does not provide a function that will test this condition (the IsArray() function only tests if the variable was originally declared as an array). To work around this deficiency, you can test the numerical value returned by the statement Not ArrayVariableName, where ArrayVariableName is the name of the array variable. If the expression Not ArrayVariableName returns -1, then the variable has not been dimensioned with a ReDim statement. It's a bit cryptic, but in the ProcessChart() sub procedure, it works well in the decision structure to identify whether or not the ScanImages() function procedure found any score sequences and thus dimensioned the array.

```
Private Sub ProcessChart()
    Dim MapRanges() As Range
    Dim scanAgain As Boolean

    '-------------------------------
    'Scan the chart, remove and score consecutive images,
    'then update the chart with new images...repeat.
    '-------------------------------
    Do
        MapRanges = ScanImages
        If (Not MapRanges) <> -1 Then
            scanAgain = True
```

```
            CalcScore MapRanges
            Application.ScreenUpdating = False
            RemoveImages MapRanges
            Application.ScreenUpdating = True
            Delay 1
            Application.ScreenUpdating = False
            MoveImages MapRanges
        Else
            scanAgain = False
        End If
    Loop While scanAgain
End Sub
```

The function procedure `ScanImages()` is called from `ProcessChart()` and serves to search the image types in the chart for score sequences by scanning the values in the image map in the `ImageMap` worksheet. There is a lot happening in this procedure, so examine it closely. First, note that the function procedure returns an array of `Range` objects. This is the first example of a function procedure I've shown you that returns an array of any type. All you have to do to denote an array for the return type is add empty parentheses to the data type in the opening statement for the function.

You cannot create function procedures that return arrays in versions of Excel prior to Excel 2000.

Since the function returns an array of objects (specifically `Range` Objects), each element of the array will have to be referenced with a `Set` statement, but the return value will be assigned without using the `Set` keyword. As always, the data type of the return variable must match the function's data type.

Next, please note that the variables `endPointsRow` and `endPointsCol` are declared as dynamic arrays of the custom data type `DataPoints` defined in the general declarations section of the module. These two variables are assigned the return value from calls to the `ScanRowOrCol()` function procedure (listed later) and end up storing the score sequences. The range component of the `endPointsRow` and `endPointsCol` variables actually hold a reference to just the last cell in a range that must be scored. This is why the second component `numCells` is required in the `DataPoints` defined type. The first call to `ScanRowOrCol()` scans the rows in the mapped range and the second call scans the columns. As an example, consider the map shown in Figure 9.17 where I have emphasized the ranges that the program must score.

Microsoft Excel - Alienated.xls

	A	B	C	D	E	F	G	H	I	J	K
1	0	Point1	Point2	Point3	Point4	Point5	Point6	Point7	Point8	Point9	Point10
2	Series1	4	1	3	1	1	3	7	4	5	1
3	Series2	5	1	1	7	5	5	1	2	1	3
4	Series3	4	4	4	5	3	3	1	5	3	5
5	Series4	2	7	4	7	4	6	2	1	4	1
6	Series5	3	7	2	5	7	7	7	4	2	1
7	Series6	5	5	5	5	2	6	2	3	1	1
8	Series7	1	1	2	7	6	5	4	6	4	1
9	Series8	4	5	4	1	7	4	1	3	7	7
10	Series9	2	5	4	3	5	3	1	2	4	7
11	Series10	7	3	5	3	7	3	5	6	2	3

ImageMap / Alienated

FIGURE 9.17

A sample map showing the image types contained in the bubble chart for the *Alienated Game.*

When this image map is scanned, the array variable `endPointsRow` will be dimensioned with three elements. The `cellRange` components of each element will represent the ranges `D4`, `H6`, and `E7` and their corresponding `numCells` components will hold `3`, `3`, and `4`, respectively. The array variable `endPointsCol` will be dimensioned with only one element whose components are `K8` and `4`.

If a score sequence is found, then the ranges are converted to represent all cells whose values and corresponding images must be removed. This is done with the `ConvertToRange()` sub procedure that is passed the empty array variable `retRange` (among others) that serves as the return value of the `ScanImages()` function procedure. The array variable `retRange` is dimensioned according to how many different ranges containing score sequences have been found in the image map on the `ImageMap` worksheet. The elements of the `retRange` variable are carefully filled depending on whether all elements are in rows, columns, or both. Using the example from Figure 9.17, the array variable `retRange` will be dimensioned with four elements containing references to the ranges `B4:D4`, `F6:H6`, `B7:E7`, and `K5:K8`.

As you will see, scanning the rows and columns in the mapped range is not a trivial task so you will have to follow this code carefully.

```
Private Function ScanImages() As Range()
    Dim wsMap As Worksheet
    Dim mapRange As Range
```

```
    Dim endPointsRow() As DataPoints, endPointsCol() As DataPoints
    Dim retRange() As Range
    Dim endIndex As Integer
    Dim rowsExist As Boolean, colsExist As Boolean

    Set wsMap = Worksheets("ImageMap")
    Set mapRange = wsMap.Range("ImageMap")
    '-------------
    'Scan rows and columns.
    '-------------
    endPointsRow = ScanRowOrCol(mapRange.Rows)
    endPointsCol = ScanRowOrCol(mapRange.Columns)
    If (Not endPointsRow) <> -1 Then rowsExist = True
    If (Not endPointsCol) <> -1 Then colsExist = True

    '-------------------------
    'Convert mapped points to ranges for removal.
    '-------------------------
    If rowsExist And colsExist Then
        ReDim retRange(UBound(endPointsRow) + UBound(endPointsCol) + 1)
        ConvertToRange endPointsRow, 0, True, retRange, endIndex
        ConvertToRange endPointsCol, endIndex, False, retRange
    End If
    If rowsExist And Not colsExist Then
        ReDim retRange(UBound(endPointsRow))
        ConvertToRange endPointsRow, 0, True, retRange
    End If
    If Not rowsExist And colsExist Then
        ReDim retRange(UBound(endPointsCol))
        ConvertToRange endPointsCol, 0, False, retRange
    End If

    ScanImages = retRange
End Function
```

The function procedure `ScanRowOrCol()` is called from `ScanImages()` and returns a variable array of type `DataPoints`. The argument passed to this function is a range variable of the columns or rows (see `ScanImages()` function procedure) in the image map. Nested `For/Each` loops iterate through the rows or columns in the image map searching for score sequences.

When a sequence is found, the last cell in the range is assigned to the `cellRange` component of the variable array `endPts` and the number of cells in the sequence is assigned to the `numCells` component. The variable array `endPts` is returned to the calling procedure after the image map has been scanned.

You will notice that I have to set a reference to a row or column range immediately inside the outer `For/Each` loop. This seems unnecessary since the range variable `r` should return an entire row or column from the image map, and the range variable `c` should subsequently return individual cells from `r` without having to set a reference to the range variable `curRowOrCol`; however, without setting the reference to the variable `curRowOrCol`, the range variable `c` will end up representing the exact same range as the variable `r`. This seems counter-intuitive to me and may be a bug in the VBA language, but at least it has an easy fix.

```
Private Function ScanRowOrCol(rangeToScan As Range) As DataPoints()
    Dim wsMap As Worksheet
    Dim c As Range
    Dim r As Range, curRowOrCol As Range
    Dim prevVal As Integer, consecVals As Integer
    Dim endPts() As DataPoints
    Dim numPts As Integer

    Set wsMap = Worksheets("ImageMap")
    consecVals = 1

    '-------------------------------------
    'Loop through individual cells in input range and determine
    'number of consecutive cells with the same value.
    '-------------------------------------
    For Each r In rangeToScan
        Set curRowOrCol = wsMap.Range(r.Address)
        For Each c In curRowOrCol
            If prevVal = c.Value Then
                consecVals = consecVals + 1
                If (consecVals >= 3) Then
                    If consecVals >= 4 Then numPts = numPts - 1
                    ReDim Preserve endPts(numPts)
                    Set endPts(numPts).cellRange = c
                    endPts(numPts).numCells = consecVals
                    numPts = numPts + 1
                End If
```

```
                Else
                    prevVal = c.Value
                    consecVals = 1
                End If
            Next
            prevVal = 0
            consecVals = 1
        Next
        ScanRowOrCol = endPts
End Function
```

The purpose of the sub procedure `ConverToRange()` is to convert the values of a `DataPoints` variable representing score sequences to their full range; that is, it takes the `cellRange` and `numCells` components of the variable and converts them to a range expressing all cells. For example, the values `H6` and `3` stored in the `cellRange` and `numCells` components of a `DataPoints` variable are converted to `H4:H6` or `F6:H6` depending on whether the variable represents a row or column. The `DataPoints` variable is passed in as the `endPts` array. The argument `start` represents the starting index that must be used to specify the elements assigned to the array variable `retRange` (passed by reference). The argument `isRow` specifies whether or not to convert the values in the array variable `endPts` to a row range or column range, and the argument `endIndex` is used to specify the last index used in the variable array `retRange` (required if this procedure is immediately called a second time when there are both row and column ranges to be scored).

```
Private Sub ConvertToRange(endPts() As DataPoints, start As Integer, _
            isRow As Boolean, retRange() As Range, Optional endIndex As _
            Integer)
    Dim I As Integer
    Dim rIndex As Integer, cIndex As Integer

    '-----------------------------------
    'Convert ranges passed in as single cells to continuous
    'ranges representing consecutive cells with same image map.
    '-----------------------------------
    For I = start To UBound(endPts) + start
        If isRow Then
            rIndex = endPts(I - start).cellRange.Row
            cIndex = endPts(I - start).cellRange.Column - _
                                endPts(I - start).numCells + 1
        Else
```

```
            rIndex = endPts(I - start).cellRange.Row - _
                         endPts(I - start).numCells + 1
            cIndex = endPts(I - start).cellRange.Column
        End If
        Set retRange(I) = Worksheets("ImageMap").Range(Chr(cIndex + 64) & _
            rIndex & ":" & endPts(I - start).cellRange.Address)
    Next I
    endIndex = I
End Sub
```

The sub procedure `CalcScore()` is called from `ProcessChart()` and serves to update the score displayed in an `AxisTitle` object on the bubble chart. The argument `MapRanges` contains references to all score sequences found from the latest scan of the image map. Counting the number of cells in these ranges is easy and ten points are assigned to each cell. The point total is updated by setting the `Text` property of the `AxisTitle` object for the *x*-axis.

```
Private Sub CalcScore(MapRanges() As Range)
    Dim I As Integer
    Dim totPts As Integer
    Dim score As AxisTitle
    Const PTSPERIMAGE = 10

    '-------------------------------
    'Calculates the player's score. 10 pts per removed image.
    '-------------------------------
    Set score = Sheets("Alienated").Axes(xlCategory).AxisTitle
    For I = 0 To UBound(MapRanges)
        totPts = totPts + MapRanges(I).Rows.Count
        totPts = totPts + MapRanges(I).Columns.Count
        totPts = totPts - 1
    Next I
    score.Text = Val(score.Text) + totPts * PTSPERIMAGE
End Sub
```

That gets you through the toughest part of the program. What remains are some procedures that handle removing, moving, and swapping images in the chart and updating the corresponding map in the `ImageMap` worksheet.

The RemoveImages() sub procedure is called from ProcessChart() and its function is to remove images from chart markers that have been scored. The procedure takes advantage of the near one-to-one correspondence between the row and column indices of the image map, and the series and point indices of the chart (there is an offset of 1 because the image map starts with row 2 and column 2 in the ImageMap worksheet, and series and point indices start with 1). A For/Each loop nested inside a For/Next loop handles the image removal. The outer For/Next loop iterates through each Range object referenced in the argument mapRange (variable array) that references the cells in the image map that have been scored. The inner For/Each loop iterates through each cell in a scored range in order to use the cell's row and column indices as indicators for the series, and point indices with the Item() method of the Series Collection object and the Points() method of the Series object. The Item() method returns a specific Series object using the index value passed to the method and the Points() method returns a specific Point object using the index value passed to this method. The ColorIndex property of the Interior object associated with a specific Point object is then used to remove the image by setting its value to xlNone.

```
Private Sub RemoveImages(mapRange() As Range)
    Dim chAlien As Chart
    Dim chSeriesCol As SeriesCollection
    Dim c As Range
    Dim I As Integer

    '----------------------
    'Remove images that have been scored.
    '----------------------
    Set chAlien = Sheets("Alienated")
    Set chSeriesCol = chAlien.SeriesCollection
    For I = 0 To UBound(mapRange)
        For Each c In mapRange(I)
            chSeriesCol.Item(c.Row - 1).Points(c.Column - 1). _
                        Interior.ColorIndex = xlNone
        Next
    Next I
End Sub
```

Figure 9.18 shows the bubble chart after the ranges shown in Figure 9.17 have been used to remove scored images.

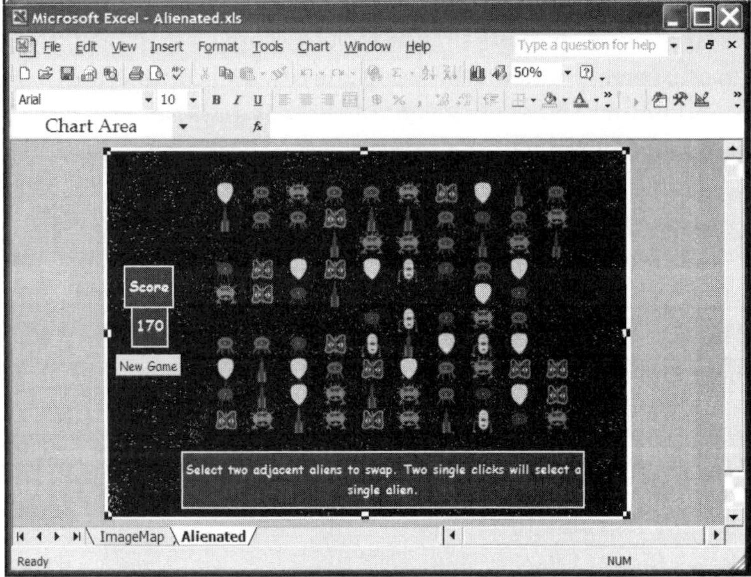

FIGURE 9.18

The bubble chart in the *Alienated Game* after the removal of scored images.

After scored images are removed from the chart, the images lying above an empty set of markers must be moved down. The `MoveImages()` sub procedure is called from `ProcessChart()` to handle this task. Before images can be moved down the chart, the values in the image map in the `ImageMap` worksheet must be moved. The `MoveMap()` sub procedure moves the values in the image map down in order to fill vacancies left by removing these values when scoring a range. Updating the chart is easy—just call the `InitSeriesImages()` sub procedure listed earlier that uses the image map to identify which data markers in the chart receive what alien image.

After a one second delay, the vacancies in the top rows of the mapped range are randomly filled with a call to the `FillMap()` sub procedure before the new images are added to the chart with another call to `InitSeriesImages()`.

Figure 9.19 shows the bubble chart and image map after the images in Figure 9.18 have been moved down, but before new images have been added.

```
Private Sub MoveImages(mapRange() As Range)

    '------------------------
    'Move mapped values down after deletions.
    '------------------------
    MoveMap mapRange
```

```
    '----------------
    'Move images down on chart.
    '----------------
    InitSeriesImages
    Application.ScreenUpdating = True
    Delay 1
    Application.ScreenUpdating = False
    FillMap
    InitSeriesImages
End Sub
```

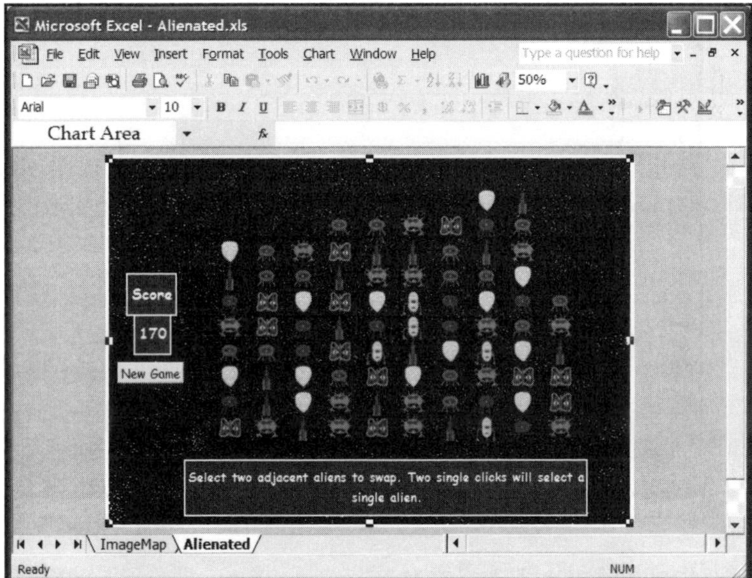

FIGURE 9.19

The bubble chart after moving the images down.

There are probably numerous algorithms that could be developed for quickly and efficiently moving values down in the image map; unfortunately, I couldn't think of any. My algorithm for moving values down is not particularly efficient, but that's okay; the image map only contains 100 cells and it won't take too long to iterate through them all. After clearing the scored ranges (the easy part), the `MoveMap()` sub procedure iterates through the columns in the image map with a `For/Each` loop. With each column returned to the range variable `mapCol`, I first test for an empty cell within this range using the `Find()` method of the `Range` object. If there is no empty cell in the column then the loop iterates to the next column range; so in some cases, this procedure may not have to iterate through all 100 cells in the range.

When an empty cell is discovered, a nested `For/Each` loop iterates through all cells in the column, collecting values from non-empty cells. For example, if a column contains two empty cells, then the array variable `colVals` will end up with eight elements. Immediately following the `For/Each` loop a `For/Next` loop writes the values in the array variable `colVals` back to the column starting with a row index that ensures the values are written in continuous cells, and that the loop finishes in row 11. This process is repeated for each column with an empty cell or cells (see Figure 9.20 to see the result).

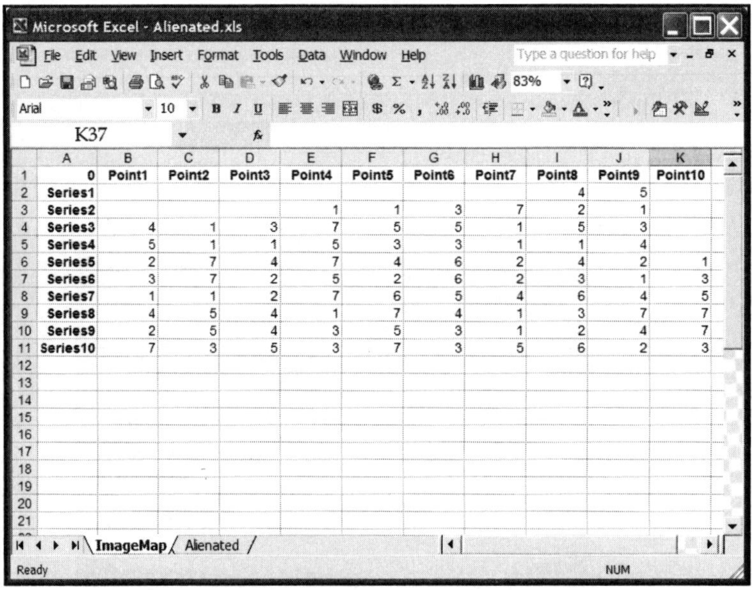

	A	B	C	D	E	F	G	H	I	J	K
1	0	Point1	Point2	Point3	Point4	Point5	Point6	Point7	Point8	Point9	Point10
2	Series1								4	5	
3	Series2				1	1	3	7	2	1	
4	Series3	4	1	3	7	5	5	1	5	3	
5	Series4	5	1	1	5	3	3	1	1	4	
6	Series5	2	7	4	7	4	6	2	4	2	1
7	Series6	3	7	2	5	2	6	2	3	1	3
8	Series7	1	1	2	7	6	5	4	6	4	5
9	Series8	4	5	4	1	7	4	1	3	7	7
10	Series9	2	5	4	3	5	3	1	2	4	7
11	Series10	7	3	5	3	7	3	5	6	2	3

FIGURE 9.20

The `ImageMap` worksheet after vacancies are filled by moving values down.

```
Private Sub MoveMap(mapRange() As Range)
    Dim I As Integer
    Dim wsMap As Worksheet
    Dim mapCol As Range, firstEmptyCell As Range
    Dim colVals() As Integer
    Dim rngDel As Range, c As Range

    '--------------
    'Clear scored ranges.
    '--------------
    Set wsMap = Worksheets("ImageMap")
    For I = 0 To UBound(mapRange)
```

```
        Set rngDel = wsMap.Range(mapRange(I).Address)
        rngDel.ClearContents
    Next I
    I = 0

    '-------------------------------
    'Loop through columns and collect all non-zero values
    'in each column then clear column and write values back
    'in consecutive cells.
    '-------------------------------
    For Each mapCol In wsMap.Range("ImageMap").Columns
        Set firstEmptyCell = mapCol.Find(What:="")
        If Not firstEmptyCell Is Nothing Then
            For Each c In wsMap.Range(mapCol.Address)
                If c.Value <> "" Then
                    ReDim Preserve colVals(I)
                    colVals(I) = c.Value
                    I = I + 1
                End If
            Next
            mapCol.ClearContents
            For I = 11 - UBound(colVals) To 11
                mapCol.Cells(I - 1, 1).Value = colVals(I - _
                                              (11 - UBound(colVals)))

            Next I
            I = 0
        End If
    Next
End Sub
```

Empty cells at the top of the image map are filled with a call to the `FillMap()` sub procedure. Integer values between 1 and 7 are randomly added to any empty cells found in the image map.

```
Private Sub FillMap()
    Dim mapRange As Range
    Dim c As Range

    Randomize
```

```
    '-------------------------------
    'Fill empty cells in image map with random integer
    'between 1 and 7.
    '-------------------------------
    Set mapRange = Worksheets("ImageMap").Range("ImageMap")
    For Each c In mapRange
        If c.Value = "" Then
            c.Value = Int(Rnd * 7) + 1
        End If
    Next
End Sub

Private Sub Delay(pauseTime As Single)
    Dim curTime As Single

    curTime = Timer
    Do
        DoEvents
    Loop While (curTime + pauseTime) > Timer
End Sub
```

Playing the Game

The game is played by searching the chart for two adjacent images in a single row or column that can be swapped in order to create a score sequence. The user selects an image by first selecting a series and then selecting a specific point within that series; that is, it takes two single clicks to select a single point if a series has not already been selected. When the user selects an image (or any chart component), it triggers the `Select()` event of the `Chart` object. This is where I have entered the code that collects the specific `Point` objects representing the chart markers selected by the user.

For the purposes of the *Alienated Game*, I am interested in selections that result in values for all three arguments (`ElementID`, `Arg1`, and `Arg2`) Excel passes to the `Select()` event. Specifically, I am looking for `ElementID=3` (VBA-defined constant `xlSeries`), and values of `Arg1` and `Arg2` that are between 1 and 10. When these conditions are satisfied, the function procedure `AssignSelection()` is called to assign the index values of the `Series` and `Point` objects selected by the user to the module-level variables `pt1Series`, `pt1Point`, `pt2Series`, and `pt2Point`. If the selection is valid (the user selected adjacent, non-diagonal images), then the procedure continues with a call to the `ImageSwap()` function procedure (listed later). The `ImageSwap()` procedure returns a Boolean value indicating whether or not a successful swap occurred (it fails if it doesn't produce a score sequence). If the swap is successful, the `ProcessChart()` sub procedure is called to start the whole process of scoring, removing, and updating the chart. If the swap is unsuccessful, the user must choose two new images.

```
Private Sub Chart_Select(ByVal ElementID As Long, ByVal Arg1 As Long, ByVal Arg2 As Long)
'Catch player's selection of individual points
    Dim msg As ChartTitle
    Dim swapSuccessful As Boolean
    Static selection As Integer

    '------------------------
    'If the first selection only selects a series
    'then exit the sub.
    '------------------------
    If Arg2 < 0 Then
        Exit Sub
    End If

    '---------------------------------
    'Collect points selected by the player. Validate 2nd point.
    'Exit the sub if point 2 is not validated.
    '---------------------------------
    Set msg = Sheets("Alienated").ChartTitle
    If ElementID = xlSeries And Arg2 > 0 Then
        If Not AssignSelection(selection, Arg1, Arg2) Then Exit Sub
    End If

    '-------------------
    'Swap, score, and replace images.
    '-------------------
    swapSuccessful = ImageSwap
    If swapSuccessful Then
        ProcessChart
    Else
        selection = 0
        Exit Sub
    End If

    msg.Text = "Select Two More Aliens"
End Sub
```

The AssignSelection() function procedure assigns the index values of the Series and Point objects selected by the user to the module-level variables pt1Series, pt1Point, pt2Series, and pt2Point. These variables are needed by other procedures that help swap the images selected by the user. The procedure is divided into two parts in an If/ElseIf decision structure. The If block assigns the first image selected by the user and the ElseIf block assigns the second image after it is validated.

```
Private Function AssignSelection(selection As Integer, seriesNum As Long, _
    ptNum As Long) As Boolean
    Dim msg As ChartTitle

    Set msg = Sheets("Alienated").ChartTitle
    '------------
    'Collect first point.
    '------------
    If selection = 0 Then
        pt1Series = seriesNum
        pt1Point = ptNum
        msg.Text = "One Alien Selected"
        selection = selection + 1
        AssignSelection = False
        Exit Function

        '---------------
        'Collect 2nd point if valid.
        '---------------
    ElseIf selection = 1 Then
        If Not ValidatePt2(seriesNum, ptNum) Then
            AssignSelection = False
            selection = 0
        Else
            pt2Series = seriesNum
            pt2Point = ptNum
            msg.Text = "Two Aliens Selected"
            AssignSelection = True
            selection = 0
        End If
    End If
End Function
```

The function procedure `ValidatePt()` validates the second image selected by the user only in that the selections must be adjacent images within the same row or column. If the second image selected by the user is not valid then the user must start over and select two new images.

```
Private Function ValidatePt2(Arg1 As Long, Arg2 As Long) As Boolean
    Dim msg As ChartTitle

    Set msg = Sheets("Alienated").ChartTitle
    '------------------------------
    'Test value of point 2 to ensure its in adjacent row or
    'column cannot be diagonal to point 1.
    '------------------------------
    ValidatePt2 = True
    If (Abs(pt1Series - Arg1) > 1 Or Abs(pt1Point - Arg2) > 1) Or _
            (Abs(pt1Series - Arg1) = 1 And (pt1Point <> Arg2)) Or _
            ((pt1Series = Arg1) And (pt1Point = Arg2)) Then
        msg.Text = "You must select adjacent cells."
        ValidatePt2 = False
    End If
End Function
```

The function procedure `ImageSwap()` is called from the `Select()` event and serves to swap the images selected by the user. First, the values in the image map are swapped with a call to the `ImageMapSwap()` sub procedure. Next, the image map is scanned with a call to the `ScanImages()` function procedure in order to check if the swap is valid. Recall that the `ScanImages()` function procedure returns a variable array whose elements are `Range` objects from the image map that represent score sequences. If the call to `ScanImages()` returns a value, then the user's selection is valid and the whole process of swapping, scoring, and removing images continues with a call to the `ProcessChart()` sub procedure in the `Select()` event. If the swap does not result in any score sequences, then the image map is returned to its original state with another call to `ImageMapSwap()`, a message is displayed to the user, and the `ImageSwap()` function returns false to the calling procedure.

```
Private Function ImageSwap() As Boolean
    Dim msg As ChartTitle
    Dim MapRanges() As Range

    Set msg = Sheets("Alienated").ChartTitle
```

```
    ImageMapSwap
    MapRanges = ScanImages
    If (Not MapRanges) <> -1 Then   'Swapped images should result in score.
        TwoImageSwap
        ImageSwap = True
    Else
        ImageMapSwap        'First swap did not result in scored ranges.
        msg.Text = "Selection must create 3 or more sequential aliens."
        ImageSwap = False
    End If
End Function
```

The last two procedures listed for the *Alienated Game* are `ImageMapSwap()` and `TwoImageSwap()` which swap the two values in the image map and the two images in the chart that correspond to the user's selection. These are both straightforward swapping procedures.

```
Private Sub TwoImageSwap()
    Dim series1Pts As Points, series2Pts As Points
    Dim wsMap As Worksheet

    '-------------
    'Initialize variables.
    '-------------
    On Error GoTo SwapError
    Set series1Pts = Sheets("Alienated").SeriesCollection(pt1Series).Points
    Set series2Pts = Sheets("Alienated").SeriesCollection(pt2Series).Points
    Set wsMap = Worksheets("ImageMap")

    '--------
    'Swap images.
    '--------
    series1Pts(pt1Point).Fill.UserPicture PictureFile:=filePath & _
            wsMap.Cells(pt1Series + 1, pt1Point + 1).Value & ".png"
    series2Pts(pt2Point).Fill.UserPicture PictureFile:=filePath & _
            wsMap.Cells(pt2Series + 1, pt2Point + 1).Value & ".png"
    Exit Sub

SwapError:
    MsgBox "An error occurred while swapping images. The game must end." _
        & vbCrLf & Err.Description, vbOKOnly, "Error: " & Err.Number
    End
```

```
End Sub
Private Sub ImageMapSwap()
    Dim tempInt As Integer
    Dim wsMap As Worksheet

    Set wsMap = Worksheets("ImageMap")
    '--------------------
    'Swap numbers mapped to selected images.
    '--------------------
    tempInt = wsMap.Cells(pt1Series + 1, pt1Point + 1)
    wsMap.Cells(pt1Series + 1, pt1Point + 1) = _
                    wsMap.Cells(pt2Series + 1, pt2Point + 1)
    wsMap.Cells(pt2Series + 1, pt2Point + 1) = tempInt
End Sub
```

That concludes the *Alienated Game*. I had a lot of fun writing it and hope you enjoy playing it and adding your own features.

Chapter Summary

In this chapter, you took a close look at Excel's `Chart` object and many of its related or subordinate objects. You learned how to use specific objects to access charts existing as chart sheets or embedded charts. You also saw several examples of manipulating existing charts through the use of the properties and methods of the `Chart` object and its subordinate objects. You also learned how to create charts (chart sheets or embedded charts) using a VBA procedure. Finally, you learned how to use some of the unique event procedures associated with the `Chart` object.

CHALLENGES

1. **With Excel's macro recorder turned on, create a column chart (chart sheet or embedded) in Excel and format the chart to a desired appearance. Stop the macro recorder and examine the recorded code. Remove any unnecessary code in the macro and change the structure of the procedure to make it more readable. Now run the code from the Excel application.**
2. **Add an embedded chart to a worksheet along with a Scroll Bar control. Attach code to the `Change()` event procedure of the Scroll Bar control that changes the maximum value *y*-axis scale.**
3. **Add a scatter chart to a worksheet from x- and *y*-data points entered in two columns of the worksheet. Create a VBA procedure that animates one of the charted points by changing its x- and *y*-values in a looping structure. Include a delay in the loop as discussed in previous chapters.**
4. **Write a VBA procedure that adds a chart to a worksheet and formats it to a desired appearance. The chart should be added after the user selects the data and clicks on a Command Button control.**
5. **Create a chart sheet with a scatter chart. Using the `Select()` event procedure of the scatter chart, create a procedure that outputs the values of the `ElementID`, `Arg1`, and `Arg2` parameters to the worksheet as the user clicks on various elements of the chart.**
6. **Spice up the *Alienated Game* by adding different levels of difficulty. For example, after the player reaches a certain score, start adding new images to the chart with new identification numbers. This reduces the number of potential moves the player can make.**
7. **Add sound to the *Alienated Game*, such as a small ding or knock that plays once for each image that is scored.**
8. **Add a procedure to the *Alienated Game* that scans the image map and notifies the player if there are no more possible moves.**

Chapter 10 VBA Shapes

VBA shapes refer to those objects added to a document or worksheet from the Drawing toolbar in the application. This includes AutoShapes, freeforms, images, and text. The Drawing toolbar is common to most Microsoft Office applications, so programming its components only differs in terms of the document to which its shapes are added (for example, an Excel worksheet, Word document, or a PowerPoint slide).

These topics are specifically discussed in this chapter:

- The `Shapes` collection and `Shape` objects
- Manipulating a `Shape` object
- The `ShapeRange` collection object
- Activating `Shape` objects
- The `OLEObjects` collection

Project: Excetris

Excetris is modeled after the classic *Tetris* computer game. The object of the game is to fill a predefined region on an Excel worksheet with five basic shapes so that gaps between the shapes are avoided. The player is continuously given one shape to add to the game board within a limited time period. When an entire row across the game board is filled with shapes, the row is removed and the shapes above moved down. Play continues until the player runs out of room for adding more shapes. You will find *Excetris* on the accompanying CD-ROM, stored as Excetris.xls. Figure 10.1 shows the Excel version of *Excetris*.

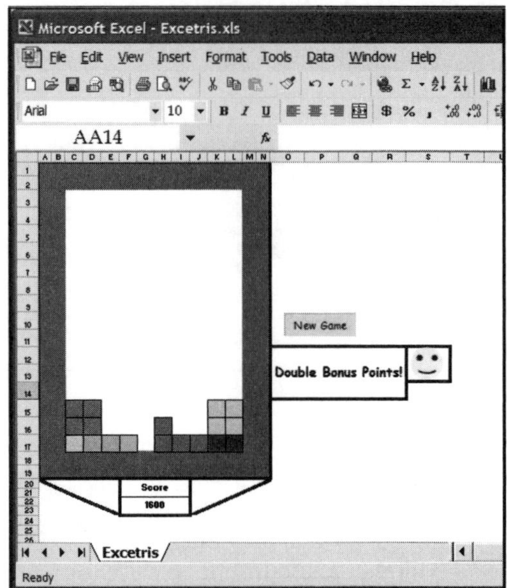

FIGURE 10.1

The *Excetris* game.

THE SHAPES COLLECTION AND SHAPE OBJECTS

The `Shapes` collection object represents all `Shape` objects in the drawing layer of the worksheet. The `Shapes` property of the `Worksheet` object is used to return the entire collection of `Shape` objects in the drawing layer. The following line of code uses the `Count` property of the `Shapes` collection object to return the total number of shapes in the drawing layer of the active worksheet:

```
ActiveSheet.Shapes.Count
```

You can think of the drawing layer as a sheet of clear plastic cellophane draped over the top of the worksheet; therefore, shapes added to the drawing layer are positioned on top of the worksheet and mask the cells underneath. The masked cells can still be used to hold data.

Like other collection objects, an index or name can be specified to return a single `Shape` object from the collection. To return a `Shape` object by index, specify a number.

```
ActiveSheet.Shapes(1).Select
```

Or, to return a `Shape` object by name, include the name in quotes.

```
ActiveSheet.Shapes("Oval 1").Select
```

To add a shape to a worksheet, use one of several `Add()` methods of the `Shapes` collection object. For example, to add a line, use the `AddLine()` method.

```
ActiveSheet.Shapes.AddLine(10, 100, 250, 500).Select
```

The `AddLine()` method accepts four parameters for the starting and ending *x*- and *y*-values representing the *x*, *y*-coordinate pairs of the two points used to define the line. The coordinates are specified in points relative to the upper-left corner of the worksheet. In the preceding example, a line is drawn on the active worksheet from point *x* = `10`, *y* = `100` to the point *x* = `250`, *y* = `500`.

The `Add()` methods of the `Shapes` collection object also return a reference to the newly added `Shape` object, so it is possible to immediately apply a property or method to the shape in the same statement. It is often convenient to select the object then use a `With/End With` structure to manipulate several properties of the object. You'll see an example of this in the section "Manipulating a `Shape` Object."

Other `Add()` methods of the `Shapes` collection object include `AddShape()`, `AddPicture()`, `AddOLEObject()`, and `AddPolyline()`, to name just a few. The `AddShape()` method refers to the AutoShapes found on the Drawing toolbar (see Figure 10.2). The example that follows adds a triangle to the active worksheet and selects it:

```
ActiveSheet.Shapes.AddShape(msoShapeIsoscelesTriangle, 230, 220, 25, 20).Select
```

The `AddShape()` method requires five parameters representing, in order, the shape type (a VBA defined constant, `msoShapeIsoscelesTriangle` in the example), and the `Left`, `Top`, `Width`, and `Height` properties of the object.

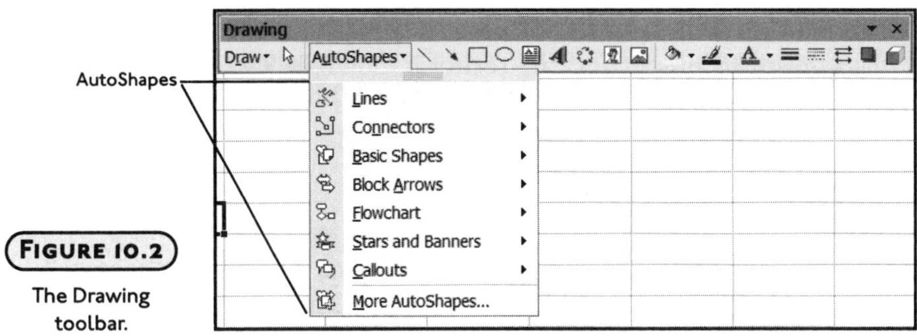

FIGURE 10.2

The Drawing toolbar.

All of the `Add()` methods are implemented in a manner similar to that of the `AddShape()` method, but the required parameters are specific to the shape type. You will see more examples of different shape types in the remainder of the chapter. For details about each method and the parameters it requires, consult the online help or the members of the `Shapes` collection in the Object Browser (see Figure 10.3).

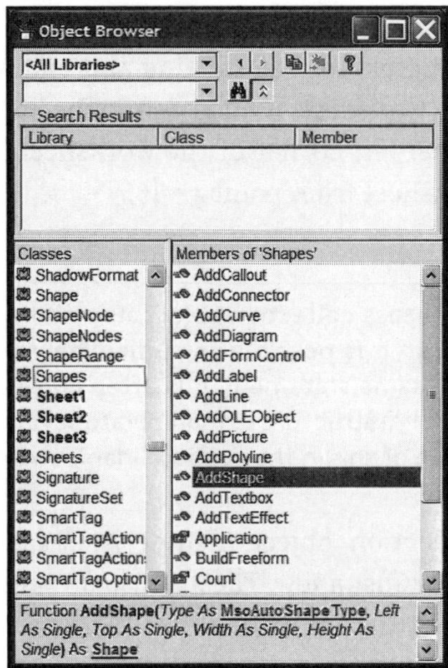

FIGURE 10.3

The Object Browser showing members of the `Shapes` collection object.

Manipulating a Shape Object

After a `Shape` object is selected from the `Shapes` collection object, you can edit the shape through its properties and methods. As always, the properties and methods available are specific to the type of `Shape` object. Also, there may be properties and methods of subordinate objects available for editing. The following example adds a rectangle to the active worksheet and manipulates a few of its properties; the result is shown in Figure 10.4.

```
ActiveSheet.Shapes.AddShape(msoShapeRectangle, 100, 100, 50, 50).Select
With Selection
        .Name = "Red Square"
        .Left = 10
        .Top = 10
End With
With ActiveSheet.Shapes("Red Square")
        .Fill.ForeColor.RGB = RGB(255, 0, 0)
        .ZOrder msoBringToFront
End With
```

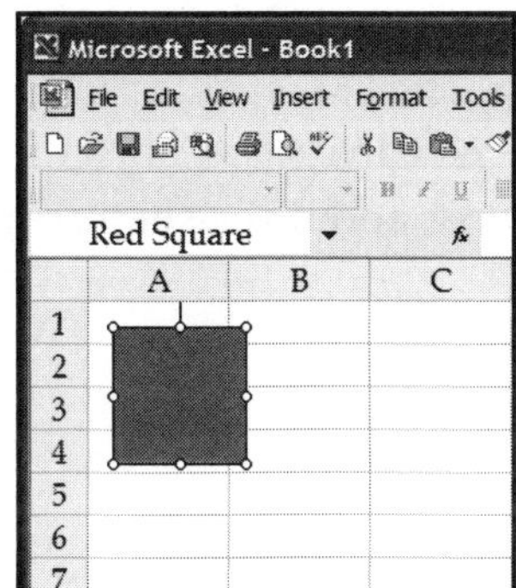

FIGURE 10.4

Adding a Shape object to a worksheet.

The AddShape() method of the Shapes collection object is used to add a rectangle to the drawing layer. In the preceding example, the constant msoShapeRectangle sets the shape type. The shape type is followed by four parameters that represent the Left, Top, Width, and Height properties of the AutoShape, respectively. After the shape is added to the drawing layer, its Name, Left, and Top properties are edited. The color of the shape is set as red (using the RGB() function) by returning a FillFormat object via the Fill property. Finally, the ZOrder() method of the Shape object is used to bring the shape to the front of the drawing layer.

Not all properties and subordinate objects are immediately available from an object selected using the Select() method. In the previous example, the Fill property and ZOrder() method are not available for the Shape object when it has been selected using the Select() method. Instead, another With/End With structure is needed to return the Shape object without selecting it before the Fill property and ZOrder() method can be applied.

The previous example illustrates some of the properties and methods common to most shapes. As is the case with the Chart object discussed in Chapter 9, some shapes and their subordinate objects have unique properties and methods that cannot be applied to all Shape objects. For example, the TextEffect property of the Shape object cannot be applied to shapes that do not contain text; therefore, when manipulating a shape through a VBA program, be careful to use the properties and methods that apply to that specific shape to avoid Run time errors.

Looping through a Collection of Shapes

Looping through a collection of Shape objects is essentially the same as looping through any other collection object. The code listed here loops through the Shapes collection object of the active worksheet. This is comparable to the methods discussed in earlier chapters for looping through worksheet cells contained within a range. An object variable is declared and used as the looping variable in a For/Each loop. The Shape collection object is returned using the Shapes property of the Worksheet object. As each Shape object is returned in the For/Each loop, it is tested for type via the Type property, and if the shape represents a line its name is copied to the worksheet.

```
Public Sub LoopThruShapes()
    Dim sh As Shape
    Dim I As Integer
    I = 1
    For Each sh In ActiveSheet.Shapes
        If sh.Type = msoLine Then
            Cells(I, 1).Value = sh.Name
            I = I + 1
        End If
    Next
End Sub
```

The preceding example represents one possible method for selecting and manipulating specific shapes from a collection. Next, you'll see a method for selecting a subset of Shape objects from a Shape collection using the ShapeRange collection object.

Sample code listed in this chapter and a couple of additional examples illustrating the use of various Shape objects can be found in the ShapeDemos.xls Excel file on the CD-ROM that accompanies this book. Select different worksheets in the workbook to view the different demonstrations. The worksheet labeled Misc Shapes is shown in Figure 10.5.

The ShapeRange Collection Object

The ShapeRange collection object represents a collection of Shape objects that may contain all, some, or just one of the Shape objects in the drawing layer of a worksheet. A ShapeRange collection object can be constructed from the current shapes using any of several criteria defined in decision structures (If/Then). For example, a ShapeRange collection object could be constructed out of just those shapes that are of type AutoShape, or perhaps only those Shape objects that are lines.

If you want to return all selected Shape objects to a ShapeRange collection object, use the ShapeRange property of the Selection object when it represents a group of selected Shape objects.

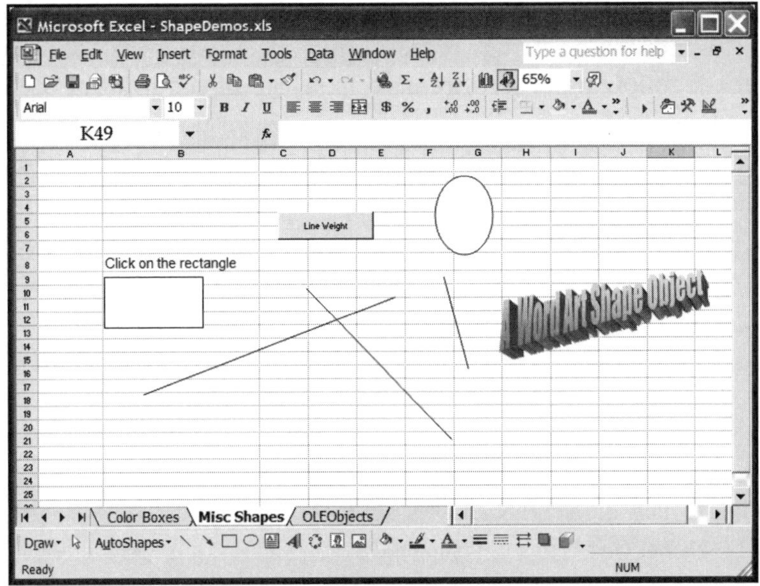

FIGURE 10.5

The Misc Shapes worksheet from the ShapeDemos.xls workbook.

```
ActiveSheet.Shapes.SelectAll
Selection.ShapeRange.Rotation = 30
Selection.ShapeRange(1).Rotation = 60
```

The first line selects all Shape objects in the active worksheet. The second line sets the angle of rotation to 30 degrees for all selected Shape objects. The third line sets the angle of rotation to 60 degrees for the first Shape object that was added to the collection (out of those objects currently selected).

To return a subset of the Shape objects as a ShapeRange collection object, use the Range property of the Shapes collection object.

```
ActiveSheet.Shapes.Range(1).Select
ActiveSheet.Shapes.Range("Line 1").Select
ActiveSheet.Shapes.Range(Array(1, 2, 3, 4)).Select
ActiveSheet.Shapes.Range(Array("Line 1", "WordArt 2")).Select
```

The Range property of the Shapes collection object accepts an integer, string, or parameter array as arguments. A parameter array specified with the Array() function is more practical because the Range property is not needed to select a single shape from the Shapes collection object. The parameter array may contain a list of integers representing the index values of the

Shape objects or strings representing their names. Alternatively, you can build a parameter array holding the integers or strings representing specific objects based on various conditions. Consider the following procedure used to select all the lines in the drawing layer of the active worksheet:

```
Public Sub SelectLines()
    Dim sh As Shape
    Dim lineNames() As Variant
    Dim numLines As Integer
    Dim ws As Worksheet

    Set ws = ActiveSheet
    For Each sh In ws.Shapes
        If sh.Type = msoLine Then
            ReDim Preserve lineNames(numLines)
            lineNames(numLines) = sh.Name
            numLines = numLines + 1
        End If
    Next

    ws.Shapes.Range(lineNames).Select
    Selection.ShapeRange.Line.Weight = 4.5
End Sub
```

The SelectLines() procedure uses a For/Each loop to iterate through the Shapes collection object for the active worksheet and build a parameter array (lineNames declared as variant) containing the names of the Shape objects of type msoLine. The name of each object of type msoLine is copied to the lineNames array for later use.

Next, the parameter array is passed to the Range property of the Shapes collection object, and objects of type msoLine are returned and selected. Additional code can now be added to modify the selected shapes. In this example, the ShapeRange property is used to return all the selected shapes and set the thickness of the lines via the Weight property.

Figure 10.6 shows the result of applying the preceding procedure to the shapes contained in the worksheet displayed in Figure 10.5.

The preceding procedure represents a useful method for selecting a range of Shape objects of a particular type when you don't know the proper names or index values at Design time.

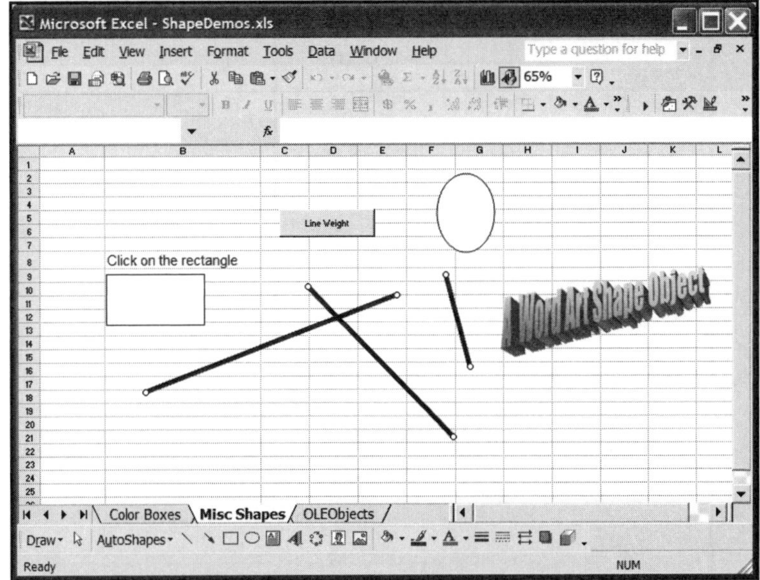

FIGURE 10.6

The Misc Shapes worksheet after execution of the SelectLines() sub procedure.

ACTIVATING SHAPE OBJECTS

Since most Shape objects (with the exception of OLEObjects) do not have any associated event procedures, you can use the OnAction property of the Shape object to simulate a Click() event. After the following code is executed, a Shape object named MyRectangle will activate a VBA procedure called LoopThruShapes() when clicked. Technically, this is not the action of a Click() event procedure, but practically it serves the same purpose.

```
ActiveSheet.Shapes.AddShape(msoShapeRectangle, 100, 100, 50, 50).Select
Selection.Name = "MyRectangle"
ActiveSheet.Shapes("MyRectangle").OnAction = "LoopThruShapes"
```

The OnAction property of the Shape object must be executed before a user's click will activate the specified procedure (LoopThruShapes()). This can be done anywhere in the program, but including it in the procedure that adds the shape used to simulate the Click() event is a good place for the code. Once the OnAction property has assigned a procedure to the Shape object, the connection between the shape and the macro is saved with the workbook and can be viewed from the application by showing the Assign Macro dialog box (right-click on the shape and select Assign Macro) as shown in Figure 10.7.

The LoopThruShapes() sub procedure is listed earlier in this chapter. The result of the LoopThruShapes() sub procedure after application to the Misc Shapes worksheet is shown in Figure 10.8.

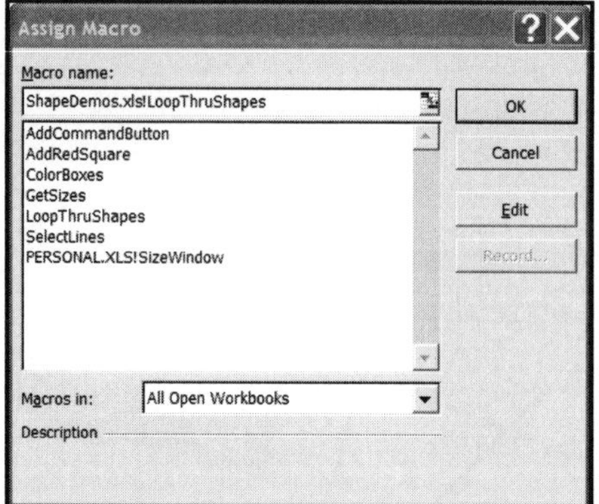

FIGURE 10.7

The Assign Macro dialog box.

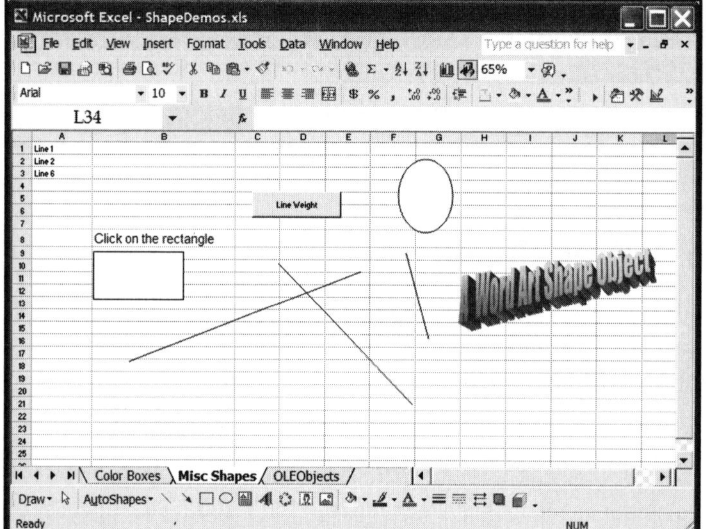

FIGURE 10.8

The `Misc Shapes` worksheet after execution of the `LoopThruShapes()` sub procedure.

THE OLEOBJECTS COLLECTION

The `OLEObjects` collection object represents all of the ActiveX controls on a document or worksheet and can be accessed from the `Worksheet` object or the `Shapes` collection object. Existing ActiveX controls can be accessed and new controls added to a worksheet. For example, a Command Button can be added to a worksheet with either the `Add()` method of the `OLEObjects()` collection object, or the `AddOLEObject()` method of the `Shapes` collection object.

```
ActiveSheet.OLEObjects.Add(ClassType:="Forms.CommandButton.1").Select
```

Or

```
ActiveSheet.Shapes.AddOLEObject(ClassType:="Forms.CommandButton.1").Select
```

Other ActiveX controls are added using very similar code to that which adds a Command Button by including the type of control in the assignment of the `ClassType` argument (for example, `Forms.Label.1` and `Forms.TextBox.1`).

Properties of the newly added `OLEObject` object are manipulated in one of two ways. First, if the property is listed in the Object Browser under the class `OLEObject`, then it can be assigned a new value in the usual way by returning the `OLEObject` from the `OLEObjects` collection object. If the property is not listed under the `OLEObject` class in the Object Browser, then you must return the actual control object by using the `Object` property before setting the new value of the control's property.

The sub procedure `AddCommandButton()` adds a Command Button control to the active worksheet using the `AddOLEObject()` method of the `Shapes` collection object. Returning the object from the `OLEObjects` collection object sets the `Name`, `Left`, and `Top` properties of the `OLEObject`; however, to set the `Caption` property, you must first return the control using the `Object` property of the `OLEObject` object.

```
Public Sub AddCommandButton()
    ActiveSheet.Shapes.AddOLEObject( _
              ClassType:="Forms.CommandButton.1").Name = "cmdTest"
    With ActiveSheet.OLEObjects("cmdTest")
        .Left = Range("C1").Left
        .Top = Range("C4").Top
    End With
    ActiveSheet.OLEObjects("cmdTest").Object.Caption = "Click Me"
End Sub
```

Event procedures for an `OLEObject` object can be written prior to their addition to a worksheet. You must name the event procedure as VBA would name it when adding the control at Design time. For example, if you intend to add a Command Button control at Run time using the `AddCommandButton()` sub procedure and you need its `Click()` event procedure, then you must name the procedure `cmdTest_Click()`. Furthermore, the event procedure must be added to the object module of the worksheet to which the Command Button control will be added. The `Click()` event procedure listed here will trigger when the user clicks on the Command Button control `cmdTest` (previously created by running the `AddCommandButton()` sub procedure) provided the `Click()` event procedure is added to the object module of the same worksheet to which the Command Button was added.

```
Private Sub cmdTest_Click()
    MsgBox ("Hello")
End Sub
```

To execute this code, select the worksheet named `OLEObjects` in the `ShapeDemos.xls` workbook and click on the button labeled `Add Command Button`. A Command Button control will immediately appear on the worksheet with the caption `Click Me`. With a click on the newly added Command Button control a message box appears with the message `Hello`. The final product of this sequence of events is shown in Figure 10.9.

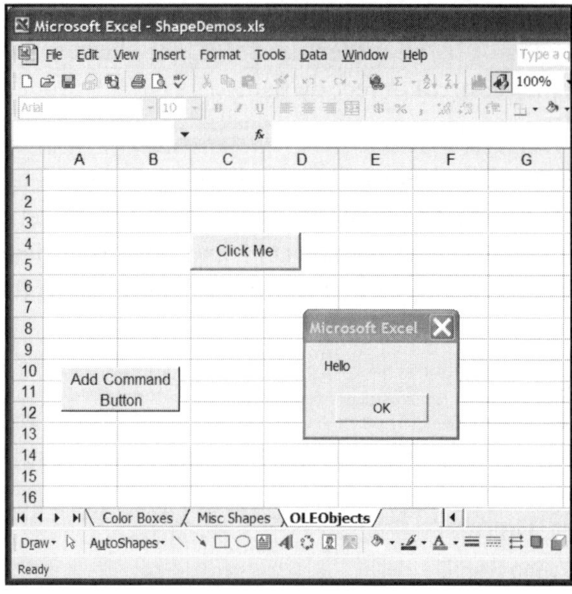

FIGURE 10.9

Adding an `OLEObject` object to a worksheet and activating its pre-defined `Click()` event.

It is sometimes desirable to create programs that are completely independent of a worksheet or even a workbook. For example, you may want to store programs in your personal macro workbook so they can be executed from the Excel application without having to load a specific workbook file. This is a relatively simple task when your program does not require ActiveX controls, because all the worksheet formatting can be handled with code.

Considering the sub procedures listed previously, it may seem tempting to try and create programs that add ActiveX controls to a worksheet at Run time in order to avoid the requirements of a specific worksheet. Unfortunately, this task cannot be completed because the event procedures of the control added at Run time must still be added to the object module of a specific worksheet; therefore, adding ActiveX controls from a VBA program has limited utility and might just as well be added at Design time when the event procedures are written.

Chapter Project: Excetris

How to play the *Excetris* game was described at the beginning of the chapter and the worksheet containing the game is shown again in Figure 10.10. My objective for this program is to demonstrate the use of the `Shapes` collection object and some of its component objects while creating a fun program.

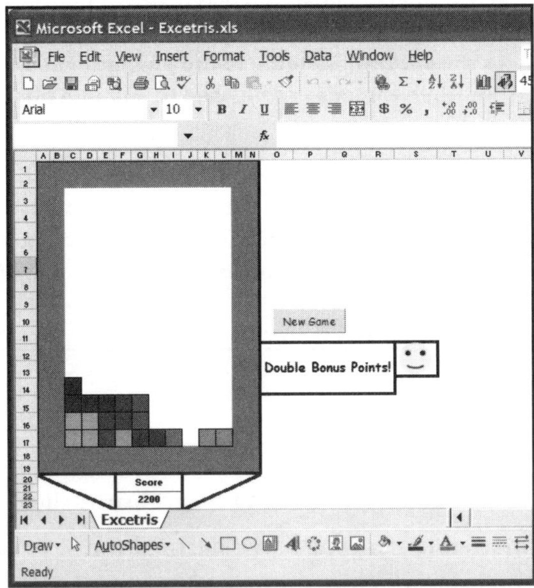

FIGURE 10.10

The *Excetris* worksheet.

Excetris involves a minimal amount of animation involving a small group of `Shape` objects as they move down the area of the worksheet defined as the game board (cells `C3:L17` in Figure 10.10). VBA is somewhat limited with regard to animation. The easiest tool available for use in animating an object is the `OnTime()` method of the `Application` object; however, its minimum one-second interval (see Chapter 4) will prevent *Excetris* from reaching a high level of difficulty for the player.

Requirements for Excetris

My idea is to create a game modeled after the original *Tetris* with an emphasis on programming `Shape` objects in Excel. The game's interface will once again be constructed from a worksheet. A specific range on a worksheet provides the game board and the game pieces are constructed out of `Shape` objects (AutoShapes of type `msoShapeRectangle`). The program tallies a score based on the number of shapes removed from the game board and assigns bonus points when multiple rows are removed as a result of placing a single shape.

In the Real World

***Multitasking* refers to a computer's ability to manage multiple processes with a single central processing unit (CPU). For example, it is common to have more than one application (such as Microsoft Word and Excel) open at the same time. For each application that is open and running, the operating system creates a separate execution path, called a *thread*. In many programming languages it is also possible to create a single application that involves multiple threads. Your program can carry out more than one task at the same time. The ability to create a multi-threaded program greatly enhances the options available to the programmer for extending the power of a program. For example, multiple threads can be used to animate multiple objects in a gaming type application.**

VBA does not fully support the creation of threads; however, multiple threads can be created in a somewhat limited fashion using either the Windows API or ActiveX controls. An ActiveX control that operates in a similar fashion to that of the `OnTime()` method (except with milli-second time resolution) is the easiest method, but unfortunately it is not included with VBA.

The requirements for *Excetris* are listed in the following:

1. The user interface shall be constructed from a single Excel worksheet.
2. The worksheet shall be formatted to contain a well-defined range of cells to serve as the game board. The game board shall consist of 15 rows and 10 columns and the cells shall be sized to identical widths and heights.
3. The worksheet shall be formatted to contain cell ranges for displaying the score and outputting messages to the player.
4. The worksheet shall contain a button for starting a new game.
5. When the user clicks the button to start a new game the program shall clear the game board of all `Shape` objects (excluding the button), reset the score, clear the message area, and initialize program variables.
6. After the game board is initialized, the program shall add one *Excetris* game shape to the top of the game board and begin moving it down in one second intervals.
7. Each game shape shall be constructed from four `Shape` objects with identical properties. Each `Shape` object in a game shape shall be constructed as a square and exactly match the size of a single cell in the game board.
8. A game shape shall continuously move down the game board until it reaches the bottom of the board or another shape, at which point it comes to a rest.

9. After a game shape comes to a rest another shape is added to the top of the game board and the process of moving down is repeated.
10. The user shall be able to direct a game shape's movement by rotating it, moving it to the left or right, or moving it down the game board as far as possible.
11. The user shall direct a shape's movement left, right, or down with different key strokes.
12. After a shape comes to a rest, the program shall scan the game board for rows that are completely filled with shapes. The program shall remove all filled rows, move all shapes above the now vacant row down one row, and update the score.
13. The user shall be awarded 100 pts per row removed unless multiple rows are removed as the result of the placement of a single game shape in which case the point total for a row is multiplied by the number of rows removed.
14. When multiple rows are removed the program shall display a message and image indicating the user received bonus points.
15. The game shall end when a new shape added to the game board overlaps (at least partially) with an existing shape.

Designing Excetris

I constructed *Excetris* from an Excel worksheet and added the code to a standard module, but the program could just as easily be entered into the code module for the worksheet—take your choice. The worksheet cells that define the game board must be square and will match the size of the individual squares in a game shape. The game can easily be initiated from a form button or Command Button control by attaching the form button to a public procedure, or calling the same procedure from the `Click()` event of the Command Button control. I could also initiate the program with a `Shape` object and assign a procedure with the Assign Macro dialog shown in Figure 10.7.

While considering the game's design I focused on three major problems unique to *Excetris*.

- Creating and adding the different shapes to the game board.
- Rotating and moving the shapes left, right, and down.
- Tracking the location of each shape on the game board so they can easily be removed when required.

Creating Excetris Shapes

The program will use just the five shapes shown in Figure 10.11, but the program should be written to make it relatively easy to add more shapes later.

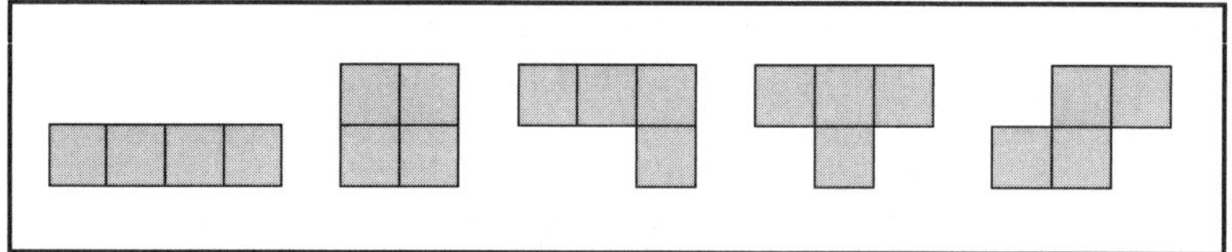

FIGURE 10.11

The five shapes used in the *Excetris* game.

Each of the five shapes used in *Excetris* are built from four distinct `Shape` objects (`msoShapeRectangle`) that are positioned as shown in Figure 10.11. To make it easier to manipulate the four `Shape` objects as if they were a single shape, the program will include a custom data type that defines the properties of an *Excetris* game shape. The elements of the custom type will include the following:

- An integer between 1 and 5 that defines one of five shape types shown in Figure 10.11. The value of this element will be randomly generated making it easy to choose the next shape that is added to the top of the game board.
- A decimal value that defines the line weight of each `Shape` object. The value of this element sets the border thickness around each square in the shape.
- A long integer that defines the fill color of each `Shape` object. Colors will make the shapes more interesting. All four squares in a shape will have the same color, but that color will be randomly selected.
- A `Range` object that defines the location of the active shape relative to the worksheet cells it masks. This range maps the shape to the worksheet and is critical for tracking the shape's location as it moves down the game board.
- A decimal value that defines the size of each `Shape` object. Each of the four `Shape` objects is square so its size will be set to either the width or height of a cell in the game board. The size of each square exactly matches the size of the cells in the game board to make it easier to keep all of the shapes aligned.
- A Boolean that defines whether or not a newly added shape overlaps with an existing shape on the game board. The value of this element will be used to decide when the game is over.

Moving Excetris Shapes

You will notice from Figure 10.11 that each shape is built from four identical squares. As stated earlier, each square is a separate `Shape` object, but the program will have to manipulate these four squares as if it were just one shape. One option is to group the objects using the `Group()` method of the `ShapeRange` object. I decided against this option because of how

VBA sets the axis of rotation for some of the shapes shown in Figure 10.11. For example, consider the shape shown in Figure 10.12 and what happens if the four squares are grouped and rotated counterclockwise 90 degrees.

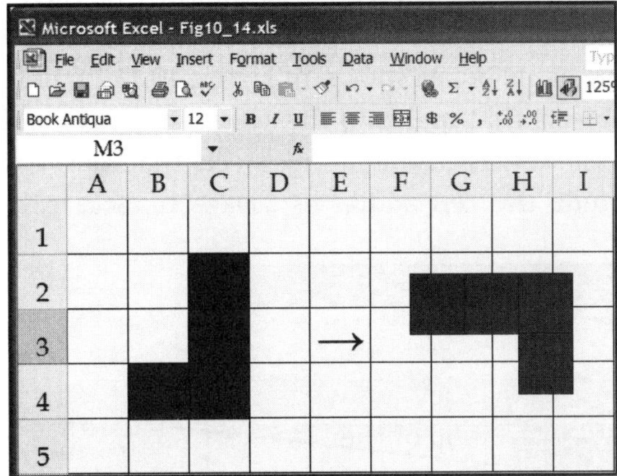

FIGURE 10.12

Rotating a grouped shape 90 degrees.

You will notice that the shape on the left starts with all of its squares directly above a worksheet cell; but after it's rotated counterclockwise 90 degrees (resulting in the shape on the right), each square is offset from the cells below it. This offset causes a problem because the shapes must maintain vertical and horizontal alignment with all other shapes on the game board. Even though it would be relatively easy to programmatically group shapes and move them, it is not as easy to compensate for the offset that results from rotating the shapes with less symmetry. I will, therefore, leave all four squares as separate `Shape` objects, but move them in a way that gives the illusion of one shape.

To preserve the shapes' vertical and horizontal alignment, I am going to use the `Left`, `Top`, `Width`, and `Height` properties of the worksheet cells below the squares. The active shape is moved by incrementing or decrementing the `Left` and/or `Top` properties of each of the four `Shape` objects depending on the required direction.

The new position of the active shape must be validated before moving the shape. To be valid, the new position must be entirely contained within the game board and there must not be any other squares occupying any part of it.

The downward movement of a shape is controlled by repeated calls to the same procedure set up with the `OnTime()` method of the `Application` object. This procedure must move the shape down one row each time it is called. Moving the shape to the left, right, and all the way down the game board is controlled by the player. The `OnKey()` method of the `Application` object can be used to assign a procedure to a keystroke. This allows the player to direct the movement of the active shape using the keyboard.

Removing Shapes

As shapes are added to the game board they will have to be assigned unique identifiers so they can be removed at a later time. The four `Shape` objects that make up the active shape will always be assigned the same name. These `Name` properties of each `Shape` object are changed to include the address of the worksheet cell they mask when the active shape comes to a rest. For example, the game board shown in Figure 10.13 includes a total of eight `Shape` objects. The four `Shape` objects that make up the active shape are assigned the names `Square1`, `Square2`, `Square3`, and `Square4`. The four `Shape` objects that have come to a rest have been assigned names that include the cell addresses `SquareE16`, `SquareE17`, `SquareF16`, and `SquareF17`.

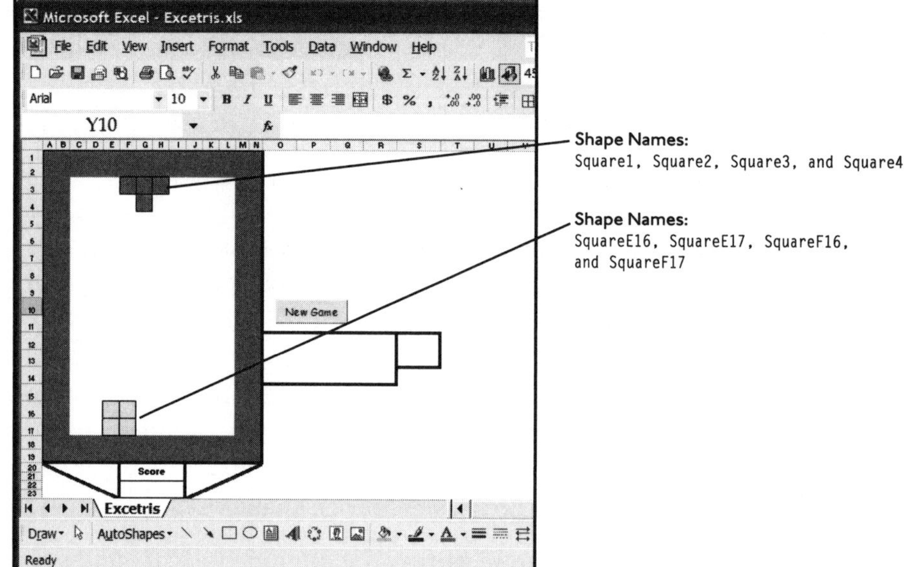

FIGURE 10.13

Using names to track the `Shape` objects added to the game board.

In addition to using the cell addresses in the `Shape` object's name, each cell masked by a `Shape` object will be assigned an `x` to its `Value` property; thus, when the game board is scanned, any row whose cells all contain an `x` are known to be completely masked by `Shape` objects. Furthermore, the location of each `Shape` object is easily identified because their name contains the address of the cell they mask—making it easier to delete them from the game board when required.

Program Outline

When playing a game, the *Excetris* program should proceed as outlined in the following:

1. A randomly generated shape appears at the top of the game board.
2. The shape moves down one row on the game board every second.

3. The player moves the shape to the left right or as far down the game board as possible using various keystrokes. The player can also rotate the shape counterclockwise 90 degrees with another keystroke.
4. When the shape can no longer move down the game board, it stops and another shape appears at the top of the game board.
5. If the player successfully positions the shapes such that a row or rows in the game board are completely masked by shapes, then the shapes are removed from the game board, the score is updated, and the other shapes above the deleted row(s) are moved down.
6. The game continues until a new shape added to the game board overlaps with an existing shape.

Coding Excetris

The entire program is entered into a single standard module. The general declarations section of the program contains just two module-level variable declarations and the definition of a custom data type (`ExcetrisShape`). The variable `gameShape` is declared as type `ExcetrisShape` and will be used to define the properties of the active shape—the shape that moves down the game board. The other module-level variable, `numRotations` tracks the number of 90 degree rotations the player selected for the active shape.

```
Option Explicit

Private Type ExcetrisShape
    esType As Integer
    esWeight As Single
    esColor As Long
    esRange As Range
    esSquareSize As Single
    esRangeOverlap As Boolean
End Type

Private gameShape As ExcetrisShape
Private numRotations As Integer
```

Starting the Game and Initializing the Worksheet

The main sub procedure `Excetris()` is called from the `Click()` event of the Command Button control on the worksheet. The `Excetris()` sub procedure initializes the `numRotations` variable, the game board, and the keyboard before adding a new shape to the game board and starting its movement downward. The short delay (half a second) ensures that the player sees the new shape before it starts moving.

```
Public Sub Excetris()
    '--------------------
    'Initialize worksheet and variables.
    '--------------------
    NewGame
    numRotations = 0
    SetKeys

    '-----------------------
    'Add the first shape and start it moving.
    '-----------------------
    AddShape
    Range("Score").Select
    Delay (0.5)
    MoveShape
End Sub
```

The sub procedure `NewGame()` is called from `Excetris()` and removes all `Shape` objects from the worksheet and clears the cells representing the game board, the player's score, and the message range.

```
Private Sub NewGame()
    Dim sh As Shape

    '-----------------------------
    'Clear the worksheet for a new game. Delete all shapes
    'except the button and clear x's, score, and message.
    '-----------------------------
    For Each sh In ActiveSheet.Shapes
        If sh.Type = msoAutoShape Then
            sh.Delete
        End If
    Next

    Range("GameBoard").ClearContents
    Range("Score").Value = ""
    Range("Message").Value = ""
End Sub
```

The sub procedure SetKeys() is called from Excetris() and serves to initialize the keyboard interface required for the game. The OnKey() method of the Application object sets the procedures that will be called when either the Tab key; or the left, right, or up arrow keys are pressed by the player. If you don't like playing the game with this set of keys, then you can just change the code entered for the OnKey() method. For example, to use the down arrow instead of the Tab key to call the sub procedure DropShapes(), change the appropriate statement to Application.OnKey "{DOWN}", "DropShapes". Available keys and their codes can be found by looking up the OnKey() method in the online help.

```
Private Sub SetKeys()
    '----------------------------
    'Sets procedure calls when these keys are selected
    'by the player.
    '----------------------------
    Application.OnKey "{TAB}", "DropShapes"
    Application.OnKey "{LEFT}", "MoveLeft"
    Application.OnKey "{RIGHT}", "MoveRight"
    Application.OnKey "{UP}", "RotateCC"
End Sub
```

When a game ends, it is important to reset the default action of the keys, otherwise Excel will continue to activate the procedures listed in the SetKeys() sub procedure.

```
Private Sub ResetKeys()
    '----------------------------
    'Resets keys to default action after the game is over.
    '----------------------------
    Application.OnKey "{TAB}"
    Application.OnKey "{LEFT}"
    Application.OnKey "{RIGHT}"
    Application.OnKey "{UP}"
End Sub
```

Adding New Shapes

New shapes are added to the top of the game board as a set of four VBA AutoShapes. This set of shapes represents the active shape for the game that continuously moves down the game board until it comes to a rest at its final location. There is never more than one active shape present on the game board.

The AddShape() sub procedure initializes the elements of the module-level variable gameShape before calling the procedures that initialize the shape's range (range of cells masked by the shape), and builds the shape by adding the four squares to the game board. The type of shape is randomly selected from one of the five possible choices shown in Figure 10.11. The fill color is also randomly generated with three values passed to the RGB() function. The size of each square in the active shape is set to the width of a cell on the game board (I used cell F3, but any would do). After the shape is built and added to the game board an If/Then decision structure tests if it overlaps with another shape on the game board. If it does, then the game ends with a call to the GameOver() sub procedure.

```
Private Sub AddShape()
    Dim ranRed As Integer, ranGreen As Integer, ranBlue As Integer

    '------------------------------
    'Randomly adds one of 5 possible shapes to game board.
    '------------------------------
    Randomize

    ranRed = Int(Rnd * 256)
    ranGreen = Int(Rnd * 256)
    ranBlue = Int(Rnd * 256)

    '------------------------
    'Initialize common properties of the squares
    'that make up every shape.
    '------------------------
    gameShape.esType = Int(5 * Rnd) + 1
    gameShape.esWeight = 0.5
    gameShape.esColor = RGB(ranRed, ranGreen, ranBlue)
    gameShape.esSquareSize = Range("F3").Width

    '------------------------------
    'Initialize the location of the shape, then build it.
    '------------------------------
    InitShape
    BuildShape

    If gameShape.esRangeOverlap Then GameOver
End Sub
```

The InitShape() sub procedure is called from AddShape() and serves to initialize the esRange element of the gameShape variable. This element stores the current location of the active shape, or more specifically, the range of cells masked by the shape. A Select/Case structure testing against the esType element (this value was randomly generated in the AddShape() procedure) of the gameRange variable determines the initial assignment to the esRange element. Note that for shapes 3, 4, and 5, the location is specified using two distinct range values. The active shape is added to the area of the game board specified by the initial value of the esRange element.

```
Private Sub InitShape()
    '-------------------------
    'Initializes location element of the shapes that
    'drop down the game board.
    '-------------------------
    Select Case gameShape.esType
        Case Is = 1
            Set gameShape.esRange = Range("F3:I3")
        Case Is = 2
            Set gameShape.esRange = Range("G3:H4")
        Case Is = 3
            Set gameShape.esRange = Range("F3:H3,H4")
        Case Is = 4
            Set gameShape.esRange = Range("F3:H3,G4")
        Case Is = 5
            Set gameShape.esRange = Range("G3:H3, F4:G4")
    End Select
End Sub
```

The sub procedure BuildShape() is also called from AddShape() and serves to add the four AutoShapes (type msoShapeRectangle) to the game board. Using the range stored in the esRange element of the gameShape variable, four Shape objects are added to the game board using the AddShape() method of the Shapes collection object. A For/Each loop iterates through the range stored in the esRange element and sets the position and size of each Shape object with the Left, Top, Width, and Height properties of the looping range variable representing a single cell. Each Shape object is assigned a line weight and fill color using the esWeight and esColor elements of the gameShape variable that were initialized in the AddShapes() sub procedure. Each Shape object in the active shape is assigned a name by concatenating the string "Square" with a unique index value between 1 and 4. The four Shape objects that make up the active shape will always have these names.

After the active shape has been added to the game board, a decision structure nested inside a `For/Each` loop tests if the new shape overlaps any existing `Shape` objects on the game board. As you will see, when an active shape comes to a rest, the names of each `Shape` object are changed and the cells they overlap are assigned the value `x`.

```
Private Sub BuildShape()
    Dim I As Integer
    Dim newShapes As Shapes
    Dim c As Range

    '----------------------
    'Builds a game shape from four squares.
    '----------------------
    I = 1
    Set newShapes = ActiveSheet.Shapes
    For Each c In gameShape.esRange
        newShapes.AddShape(msoShapeRectangle, c.Left, c.Top, _
                        c.Width, c.Height).Select
        Selection.ShapeRange.Line.Weight = gameShape.esWeight
        Selection.ShapeRange.Fill.ForeColor.RGB = gameShape.esColor
        Selection.ShapeRange.Name = "Square" & I
        I = I + 1
    Next

    '---------------------------------
    'Test if added shape overlaps existing shape on game board.
    '---------------------------------
    For Each c In gameShape.esRange
        If c.Value = "x" Then
            gameShape.esRangeOverlap = True
            Exit For
        End If
    Next
End Sub
```

Moving the Shapes

After a new shape is added to the game board, it must start its trek downward. When the active shape moves, it jumps one row down, or one column to the left or right, or rotates counterclockwise. The program will have to validate each potential move in any direction to ensure there is no overlap with an existing shape and that the result of a move keeps the shape entirely within the defined area of the game board (see Figure 10.14). After the active shape moves, the program must update its location stored in the `esRange` element of the `gameShape` variable. When the movement of the active shape down the game board is blocked by an existing `Shape` object, the program must stop the movement, rename each `Shape` object in the active shape to include the cell ranges they mask, test for filled rows, and then start the whole process over again by adding another shape to the game board. All these tasks require several procedures in order to keep the code organized and readable.

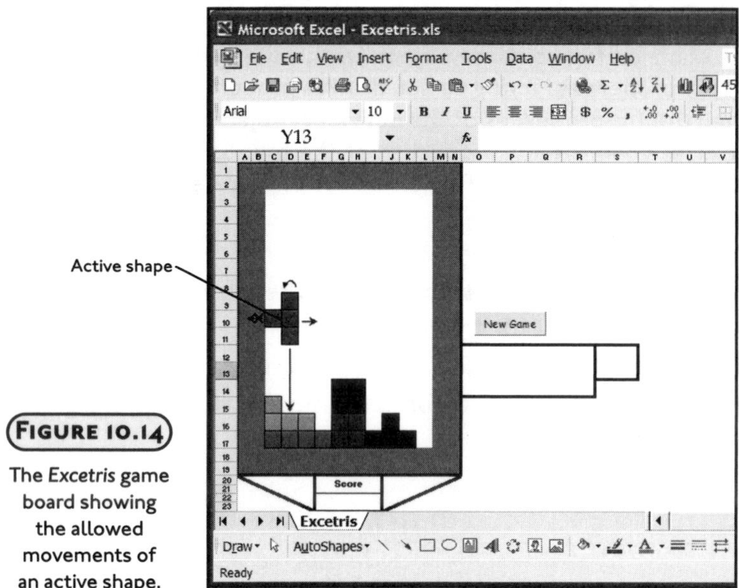

FIGURE 10.14

The *Excetris* game board showing the allowed movements of an active shape.

The `MoveShape()` sub procedure is responsible for moving the active shape down the game board one row at a time. The move is validated first with a call to the `NewActiveRange()` function procedure in the conditional expression of an `If/Else` decision structure. If the move is validated, then a `For/Each` loop iterating through each `Shape` object in a `ShapeRange` collection object moves the active shape down one row, one shape at a time (this happens so fast that it appears as though all four `Shape` objects move simultaneously). Next, the `OnTime()` method of the `Application` object is invoked in order to set up the next call to the `MoveShape()` procedure. I use the minimum time interval of one second so it will not be possible to move the active shape any faster unless you increase the number of rows it moves with each procedure call. Note that the next call to the `MoveShape()` procedure is only set if the current move was validated; therefore, there is never a need to cancel a call previously set with the `OnTime()` method.

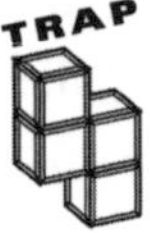

You may wonder why I didn't move all four Shape objects in the active shape simultaneously by returning a ShapeRange object and setting its Top property as shown in the following code:

```
Dim shRange As ShapeRange

Set shRange = ActiveSheet.Shapes.Range(Array("Square4", _
                              "Square3", "Square2", "Square1"))
shRange.Top = shRange.Top + yInc
```

Although this is perfectly acceptable VBA code, it will generate a Run time error in our program because a ShapeRange object is a collection object; therefore the variable shRange contains four distinct objects with potentially four different values for their Top properties. Trying to set the Top property of a ShapeRange variable fails when the Top properties of the individual objects are not identical. In fact, the only case when the Top properties of the four Shape objects in the active shape are identical is when the first shape type in Figure 10.11 is in a horizontal position.

If a move down the game board is invalid (as determined by the return value of the NewActiveRange() function procedure), then a call to the SetActiveRange() sub procedure will rename the Shape objects in the active shape, set the Value properties of the cells it masks to x, and scan the game board for filled rows before starting the whole process over again by adding and moving a new shape.

```
Public Sub MoveShape()
    Dim sh As Shape
    Dim yInc As Single

    '------------------------------
    'Move the shape down one row in worksheet-after validating.
    'Cancel OnTime method when shape must be stopped and set new
    'worksheet range for the stopped shapes.
    '------------------------------
    yInc = gameShape.esSquareSize
    If NewActiveRange("Down") Then
        For Each sh In ActiveSheet.Shapes.Range(Array("Square4", _
                              "Square3", "Square2", "Square1"))
            sh.Top = sh.Top + yInc
        Next
        '------------------------------
        'Set repeated calls (one per second) to this procedure.
        '------------------------------
```

```
        Application.OnTime EarliestTime:=Now + TimeValue("00:00:01"), _
            Procedure:="MoveShape", Schedule:=True
    Else
        SetActiveRange
    End If
End Sub
```

The DropShapes() sub procedure is triggered when the player presses the Tab key and serves to move the active shape as far down the game board as possible. A Do-Loop repeatedly calls the NewActiveRange() function procedure in order to count how many rows the active shape can move down the game board. For example, the active shape shown in Figure 10.14 can drop another four rows. The number of rows the active shape can move is stored in the variable rowCount. The NewActiveRange() function procedure resets the esRange element of the gameShape variable if the move is valid, but does not move the active shape.

After the maximum number of rows the active shape can move down the game board has been determined, each Shape object in the active shape is moved the requisite number of rows using a For/Each loop as was done in the MoveShape() sub procedure.

```
Private Sub DropShapes()
    Dim rowCount As Integer
    Dim sh As Shape
    Dim canMoveDown As Boolean

    '---------------------------
    'Count the number of rows the shapes can be moved.
    '---------------------------
    Do
        rowCount = rowCount + 1
        canMoveDown = NewActiveRange("Down")
    Loop While canMoveDown

    '------------------------------------
    'Drop the shapes as far as possible when player hits the Tab key.
    '------------------------------------
    For Each sh In ActiveSheet.Shapes.Range(Array("Square4", "Square3", _
                                                  "Square2", "Square1"))
        sh.Top = sh.Top + (rowCount - 1) * sh.Height
    Next
End Sub
```

The MoveLeft() and MoveRight() sub procedures are triggered from the left and right arrow keys and serve to move the active shape one column to the left or right. These procedures are essentially identical except for the direction the active shape is moved. If the new location for the active shape is valid, then a For/Each loop iterates through each Shape object in the active shape and moves it to the left or right via the Left property of the Shape object.

```
Private Sub MoveLeft()
    Dim sh As Shape

    '-----------------------------------------
    'Move shape left after validation when player hits left arrow key.
    '-----------------------------------------
    If NewActiveRange("Left") Then
        For Each sh In ActiveSheet.Shapes.Range(Array("Square4", "Square3", _
                                                      "Square2", "Square1"))
            sh.Left = sh.Left - sh.Width
        Next
    End If
End Sub

Private Sub MoveRight()
    Dim sh As Shape

    '-----------------------------------------
    'Move shape right after validation when player hits right arrow key.
    '-----------------------------------------
    If NewActiveRange("Right") Then
        For Each sh In ActiveSheet.Shapes.Range(Array("Square4", "Square3", _
                                                      "Square2", "Square1"))
            sh.Left = sh.Left + sh.Width
        Next
    End If
End Sub
```

The sub procedure RotateCC() rotates the active shape counterclockwise 90 degrees. Most of the work is done in the NewActiveRange() sub procedure, which sets the target range for the active shape and stores it in the esRange element of the gameShape variable. I then use a For/Each loop to iterate through each cell referenced in the esRange element of the gameShape variable and set the Left and Top properties of each Shape object in the active shape to the

Left and Top properties of the corresponding cell. The number of rotations is tracked because setting the target range for the next rotation of the active shape depends not only on the shape type, but also on how many times it has been previously rotated.

```
Private Sub RotateCC()
    Dim c As Range
    Dim I As Integer

    '------------------------------
    'Simulate a counter clockwise rotation (after validation)
    'when player hits up arrow key. Move shape by mapping it to
    'the new range.
    '------------------------------
    I = 1
    If NewActiveRange("CC") Then
        For Each c In gameShape.esRange
            ActiveSheet.Shapes("Square" & I).Left = c.Left
            ActiveSheet.Shapes("Square" & I).Top = c.Top
            I = I + 1
        Next
        numRotations = numRotations + 1
        If numRotations = 4 Then numRotations = 0
        ActiveSheet.Range("Score").Select
    End If
End Sub
```

The NewActiveRange() sub procedure serves two purposes. First, it validates the target range of the active shape before it is moved. Second, if the target range is valid, it updates the esRange element of the gameShape variable that is used by the program to track the location of the active shape. The procedure accepts one string argument named direction that specifies the direction the program has requested the shapes be moved (left, right, down, or counterclockwise rotation). A Select/Case structure uses the value of the direction to set the values in a variant array called changes. The variable array changes contains eight values that are used in the ChangeAllIndices() function procedure to increment or decrement the row and column indices of all four cells represented in the esRange element of the gameShape variable. For example, when the value of the direction argument is "Down" only the row indices should change; thus, the changes array contains alternating values of 0 and 1 (column indices are first). The changes array is passed to the ChangeAllIndices() function procedure which returns a Range object to the variable tmpRng representing the target range for the active shape. The variable tmpRng is then tested to see if its address is contained within the game board and no existing shapes mask these cells. If the value of tmpRng is validated, then its value is assigned to NewActiveRange() and returned to the calling procedure.

```
Private Function NewActiveRange(direction As String) As Boolean
    Dim tempRng As Range, c As Range
    Dim changes As Variant

    '----------------------------
    'Create a new range based on direction the game shape
    'is supposed to move.
    '----------------------------
    Select Case direction
        Case Is = "Down"
            changes = Array(0, 1, 0, 1, 0, 1, 0, 1)
        Case Is = "Left"
            changes = Array(-1, 0, -1, 0, -1, 0, -1, 0)
        Case Is = "Right"
            changes = Array(1, 0, 1, 0, 1, 0, 1, 0)
        Case Is = "CC"
            changes = GetCCArray    'Too long to leave in here.
    End Select
    Set tempRng = ChangeAllIndices(gameShape.esRange, changes)

    '------------------------------
    'Loop through each cell in new range to validate location.
    '------------------------------
    For Each c In tempRng
        If c.Value = "x" Or c.Column < 3 Or c.Column > 12 _
                                Or c.Row < 3 Or c.Row > 17 Then
            NewActiveRange = False
            Exit Function
        End If
    Next
    Set gameShape.esRange = tempRng
    NewActiveRange = True
End Function
```

The `GetCCArray()` function procedure is called from `NewActiveRange()` to return the values for the variable array `changes` for the case of a counterclockwise rotation. I wrote a separate function procedure for this because it requires a rather lengthy block of code. Setting the values for this array is complicated by the fact that the required changes depend on the shape type and the number of previous rotations. To determine the values required for the array, I drew figures of each shape as they would appear when rotated 90 degrees counterclockwise and mapped a range to each shape as shown in Figure 10.15. I obtained the values for the array from the differences in the row and columns indices for the ranges mapped to each shape.

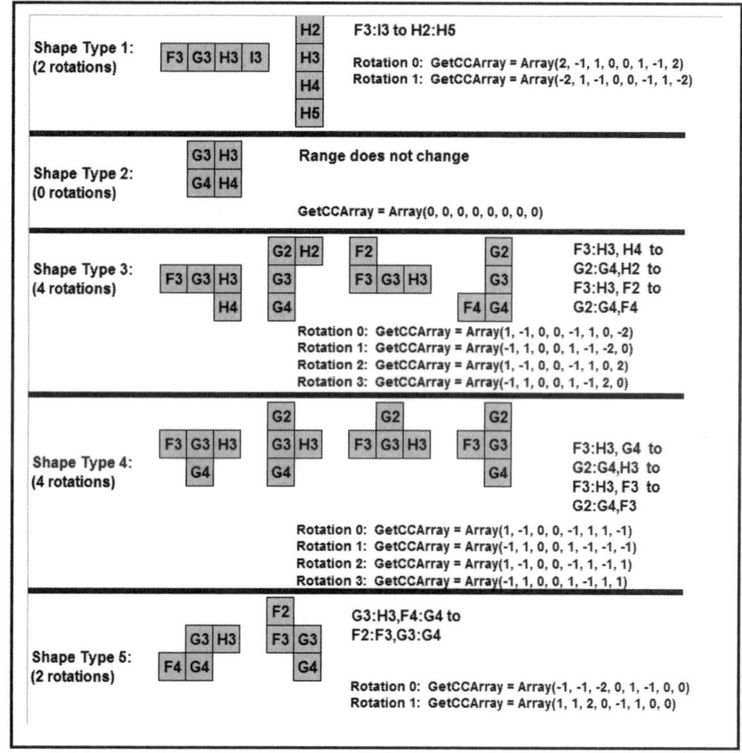

FIGURE 10.15

Mapping shape rotations to cell ranges.

```
Private Function GetCCArray() As Variant()

    '-------------------------------
    'The parameters for rotating the shapes are dependent
    'on the shape type. The parameter array specifies the
    'increment/decrement on the row and column indices for
    'each of the four squares in a game shape.
    '-------------------------------
```

```
    Select Case gameShape.esType
        Case Is = 1
            If numRotations = 0 Or numRotations = 2 Then
                GetCCArray = Array(2, -1, 1, 0, 0, 1, -1, 2)
            Else
                GetCCArray = Array(-2, 1, -1, 0, 0, -1, 1, -2)
            End If
        Case Is = 2
            GetCCArray = Array(0, 0, 0, 0, 0, 0, 0, 0)
        Case Is = 3
            If numRotations = 0 Then
                GetCCArray = Array(1, -1, 0, 0, -1, 1, 0, -2)
            ElseIf numRotations = 1 Then
                GetCCArray = Array(-1, 1, 0, 0, 1, -1, -2, 0)
            ElseIf numRotations = 2 Then
                GetCCArray = Array(1, -1, 0, 0, -1, 1, 0, 2)
            ElseIf numRotations = 3 Then
                GetCCArray = Array(-1, 1, 0, 0, 1, -1, 2, 0)
            End If
        Case Is = 4
            If numRotations = 0 Then
                GetCCArray = Array(1, -1, 0, 0, -1, 1, 1, -1)
            ElseIf numRotations = 1 Then
                GetCCArray = Array(-1, 1, 0, 0, 1, -1, -1, -1)
            ElseIf numRotations = 2 Then
                GetCCArray = Array(1, -1, 0, 0, -1, 1, -1, 1)
            ElseIf numRotations = 3 Then
                GetCCArray = Array(-1, 1, 0, 0, 1, -1, 1, 1)
            End If
        Case Is = 5
            If numRotations = 0 Or numRotations = 2 Then
                GetCCArray = Array(-1, -1, -2, 0, 1, -1, 0, 0)
            Else
                GetCCArray = Array(1, 1, 2, 0, -1, 1, 0, 0)
            End If
    End Select
End Function
```

The function procedure `ChangeAllIndices()` is called from `NewActiveRange()` and uses the variable array argument `rcInc` (passed in as the `changes` array) to change the row and column indices of the `Range` object stored in the `esRange` element of the `gameShape` variable. Recall that the `Range` object returned by this function is assigned to a temporary variable that becomes the new range for the active shape (`esRange` element of the `gameShape`) after validation. The `ChangeAllIndices()` procedure first collects all four cell ranges mapped to the active shape before altering the row and column indices of each range using the values passed in to the `rcInc` array. The new active range is then reconstructed using the four new range addresses.

```
Private Function ChangeAllIndices(inputRange As Range, rcInc As Variant) As Range
    Dim cellRng(3) As Range, cellStr(3) As String
    Dim c As Range, I As Integer
    Dim tempStr As String

    '--------------------
    'Get all individual cells in the range.
    '--------------------
    For Each c In inputRange
        Set cellRng(I) = c
        I = I + 1
    Next

    '---------------------------
    'Alter the row and column indices of all four cells.
    '---------------------------
    cellStr(0) = Chr(64 + cellRng(0).Column + rcInc(0)) & _
                cellRng(0).Row + rcInc(1)
    cellStr(1) = Chr(64 + cellRng(1).Column + rcInc(2)) & _
                cellRng(1).Row + rcInc(3)
    cellStr(2) = Chr(64 + cellRng(2).Column + rcInc(4)) & _
                cellRng(2).Row + rcInc(5)
    cellStr(3) = Chr(64 + cellRng(3).Column + rcInc(6)) & _
                cellRng(3).Row + rcInc(7)

    '----------
    'Rebuild the range.
    '----------
    Select Case gameShape.esType
```

```
        Case Is = 1
            tempStr = cellStr(0) & ":" & cellStr(3)
        Case Is = 2
            tempStr = cellStr(0) & ":" & cellStr(3)
        Case Is = 3
            tempStr = cellStr(0) & ":" & cellStr(2) & "," & cellStr(3)
        Case Is = 4
            tempStr = cellStr(0) & ":" & cellStr(2) & "," & cellStr(3)
        Case Is = 5
            tempStr = cellStr(0) & ":" & cellStr(1) & "," & cellStr(2) & _
                    ":" & cellStr(3)
    End Select

    Set ChangeAllIndices = Range(tempStr)
End Function
```

Before running the *Excetris* program, it is vital that the `Width` and `Height` properties of the cells in the game board are identical. These properties may be difficult to set from the application window because Excel uses different units for the row `Height` and column `Width` (How much sense does that make?). To ensure perfectly square cells, I first adjusted the cell heights to a desired value in the application window, and then executed the `SetColumnWidth()` macro listed next in order to adjust the column widths.

```
Sub SetColumnWidth()
    Dim c As Range

    For Each c In Range("GameBoard").Columns
        c.ColumnWidth = 3.78
    Next

    For Each c In Range("GameBoard")
        Debug.Print "Width: " & c.Width & "  Height: " & c.Height
    Next
End Sub
```

Column widths must be adjusted using the `ColumnWidth` property because the `Width` and `Height` properties of the `Range` object are read-only. I executed the `SetColumnWidth()` procedure until the Immediate window displayed identical values for the `Width` and `Height` properties of the cells in the game board—adjusting the value assigned to the `ColumnWidth` property between executions.

When the active shape can no longer move down the game board, the SetActiveRange() sub procedure is called from MoveShape(). The purpose of this procedure is to mark the cells on the game board masked by the active shape, and change the Name properties of the four Shape objects that make up the active shape. The names of the Shape objects are changed to include the address of the cells they mask. Masked cells are marked by assigning an x to their Value property.

```
Private Sub SetActiveRange()
'Shape is set to the worksheet cell range it is above
    Dim c As Range
    Dim I As Integer

    I = 1
    For Each c In gameShape.esRange
        c.Value = "x"
        ActiveSheet.Shapes("Square" & I).name = "Square" & _
                    Chr(c.Column + 64) & c.Row
        I = I + 1
    Next

    '--------------------------------
    'Scan board to test for a filled row. Once the shape is
    'set and renamed...add another shape...repeat process.
    '--------------------------------
    ScanRange
    numRotations = 0
    AddShape
    Range("Score").Select
    Delay (0.5)
    MoveShape
End Sub
```

After the masked cells are marked and the names of the Shape objects altered, the SetActiveRange() sub procedure calls the ScanRange() sub procedure to look for filled rows before staring the process of adding a new shape to the top of the game board and start it on its way down.

Removing Shapes and Scoring Filled Rows

The remaining procedures handle the process of scanning the game board for rows filled with shapes, scoring the filled rows, and removing their shapes; then moving the shapes above a scored row down one row.

Consider the *Excetris* game board, shown in Figure 10.16, where the player has just dropped an active shape that fills two non-consecutive rows with `Shape` objects.

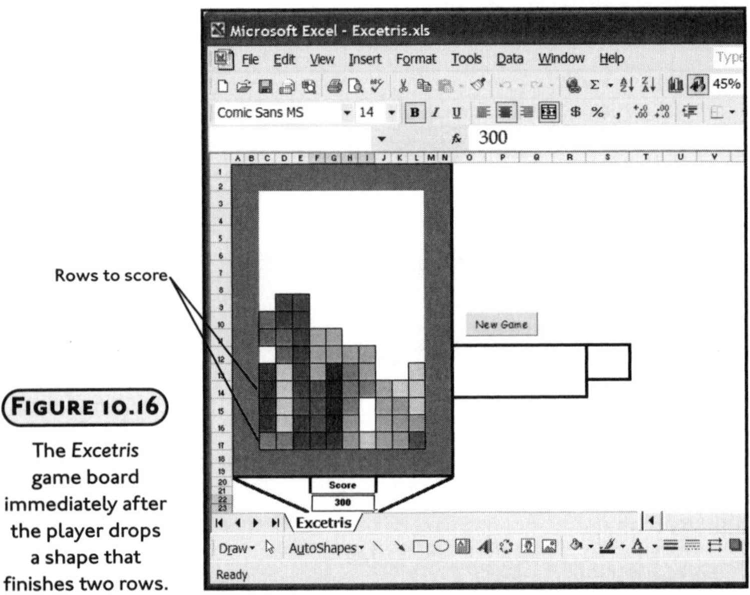

FIGURE 10.16

The Excetris game board immediately after the player drops a shape that finishes two rows.

The `ScanRange()` sub procedure is called from `SetActiveRange()` after the active shape can no longer move down the game board. This procedure uses a `For/Next` loop to iterate through all rows in the game board starting from the bottom. First, the function procedure `TestRow()` is called in order to test if all the cells in the current row contain an `x`. If `TestRow()` returns true, then the row is processed with a call to the `ProcessRow()` sub procedure which removes the `x`'s and shapes from the filled row and updates the score. This results in the game board shown in Figure 10.17.

Next, the game board is updated with a call to the `ProcessBoard()` sub procedure which handles the task of moving the shapes and `x`'s lying above a scored row down one row. The `ProcessBoard()` sub procedure must also update the names of all `Shape` objects it moves to correspond to the new addresses of the cells they mask. After the `ProcessBoard()` sub procedure executes, the game board shown in Figure 10.17 will appear as shown in Figure 10.18.

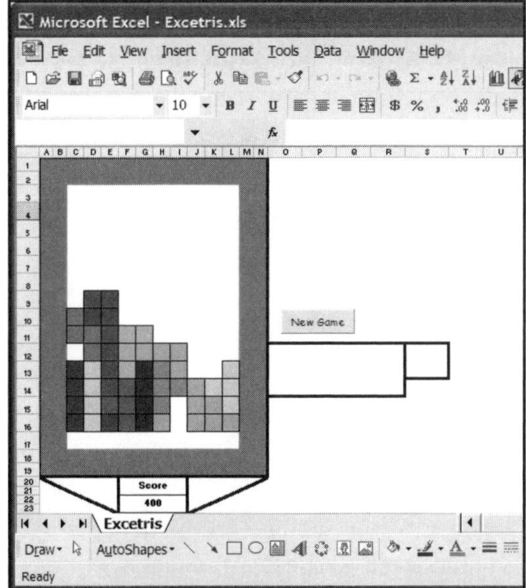

FIGURE 10.17

The *Excetris* game board from Figure 10.16 after one row is scored.

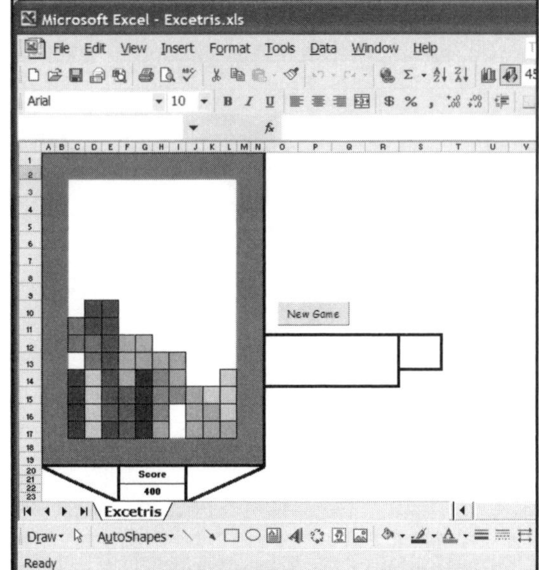

FIGURE 10.18

The *Excetris* game board from Figure 10.17 after the `ProcessBoard()` sub procedure has moved shapes down.

I also added a simple embellishment to the program that assigns bonus points if multiple rows are removed as a result of the placement of a single *Excetris* shape. The `BonusCall()` sub procedure simply displays a message and smiley face to the player (see Figure 10.19). Bonus points are calculated using the number of scored rows multiplied by the number of points per row (100).

When a row is removed and scored, the looping variable I is incremented by one so it retains its value in the next iteration. Although unusual, I did this because the ProcessBoard() sub procedure has already moved the shapes down a row so the program has to continue the scan with the same row index. Rows are removed and scored one at a time, rather than all at once because I found it easier to handle non-consecutive filled rows using this algorithm. Alternatively, I am sure you can work out an algorithm that removes all filled rows and then scores them before moving any shapes down the game board.

```
Private Sub ScanRange()
    Dim c As Range, r As Range
    Dim scoreRow As Boolean
    Dim numRows As Integer
    Dim I As Integer

    '-------------------------------
    'Scan game board for a row filled with shapes. If such a
    'row is found, then remove the row and move others down.
    '-------------------------------
    For I = 17 To 4 Step -1
        Set r = Range("C" & I & ":L" & I)
        scoreRow = TestRow(r)

        '--------------------
        'Score the row and remove shapes and x's.
        '--------------------
        If scoreRow Then
            I = I + 1
            numRows = numRows + 1
            If numRows > 1 Then BonusCall (numRows)   'Display bonus image
            ProcessRow r, numRows

            '---------------
            'Move shapes and x's down one row
            '---------------
            ProcessBoard r.Row

            If numRows > 1 Then DeleteBonus
        End If
    Next I
End Sub
```

```
Private Function TestRow(r As Range) As Boolean
    Dim c As Range

    '---------------------
    'If even one cell does not have an "x"
    'then the row is not scored.
    '---------------------
    For Each c In Range(r.Address)
        If c.Value <> "x" Then
            TestRow = False
            Exit Function
        End If
    Next
    TestRow = True
End Function
```

In order to remove the `Shape` objects representing a filled row on the game board, I create a `ShapeRange` object referenced by the variable `shRange` using the names of the shapes assigned in the `SetActiveRange()` sub procedure. Recall that a shape's name contains the string `"Square"` concatenated with the cell address it masks. The shapes are easily removed from the game board by invoking the `Delete()` method of the `ShapeRange` collection object (see Figure 10.17 or 10.19).

```
Private Sub ProcessRow(r As Range, numRows As Integer)
    Dim c As Range
    Dim shRange As ShapeRange
    Const POINTSPERROW = 100

    '---------------------
    'Clear the x's and shapes from a row.
    'Score the row.
    '---------------------
    Set shRange = ActiveSheet.Shapes.Range(Array("SquareC" & r.Row, _
                 "SquareD" & r.Row, "SquareE" & r.Row, "SquareF" & r.Row, _
                 "SquareG" & r.Row, "SquareH" & r.Row, "SquareI" & r.Row, _
                 "SquareJ" & r.Row, "SquareK" & r.Row, "SquareL" & r.Row))
    r.ClearContents
    shRange.Delete
    Range("Score").Value = Val(Range("Score").Value) + POINTSPERROW * numRows
End Sub
```

The function of the ProcessBoard() sub procedure is to move all shapes above a scored row down one row along with the x's in the cells they mask. In addition, the procedure must rename the Shape objects to update the row index in their names—which turned out to be the most difficult task required of this procedure.

Moving the Shape objects and the x's is easy. I just cut and paste the range on the game board above a scored row down one row. I also have to redefine the named range to its original reference because a cut and paste operation alters the value of the range referenced by a name. Figure 10.19 shows the Shape objects that must be moved and renamed after a filled row has been removed and scored.

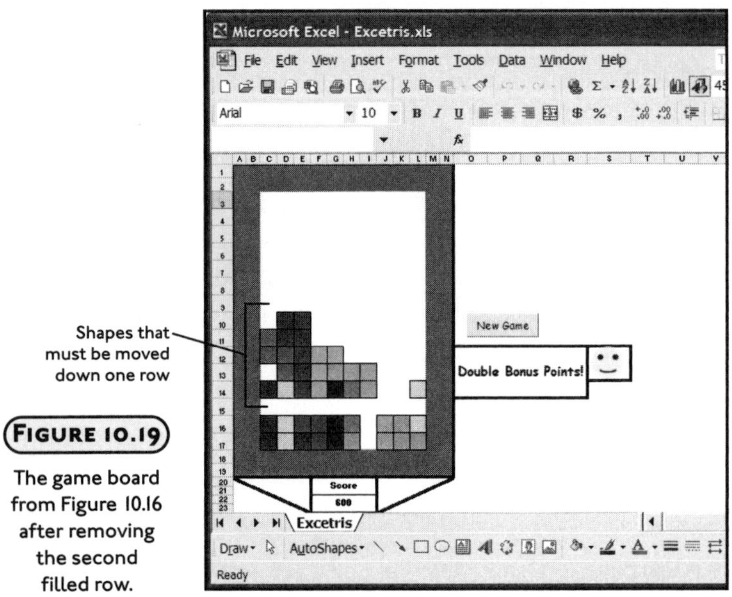

FIGURE 10.19

The game board from Figure 10.16 after removing the second filled row.

Changing the names of the Shape objects requires two steps. First, I collect the numbers at the end of the Name property of each Shape object that represents the row index of the cell the Shape object masks. These row indices are stored in the integer array shNum. Decision structures are required because the Command Button control is part of the Shapes collection object and I don't want to include it here. I also have to be careful to store only the numbers associated with shapes that were moved; therefore, another decision structure tests the row index of the scored row passed in as the argument rIndex. After collecting a shape's row index, its new name is stored in another variable array (shNames) after incrementing the row index by one. The shape is assigned a temporary name beginning with the string "tempName" and a unique index value. After the appropriate shapes have been temporarily renamed, another loop renames them using the values in the shNames array. This seems like a lot of work and I am sure you are wondering why I didn't just rename the shapes to their final string values in the first For/Each loop. The problem I encountered was assigning the same name to two different Shape objects. Consider the Shape objects above cells I13 and I14 in Figure 10.19. If I try to change the row index for the Shape object name "SquareI13" in the first For/Each loop, I will duplicate the name of the Shape object directly below it and this generates a Run time error. Figure 10.20 shows the game board after the shapes shown in Figure 10.19 have been moved down one row.

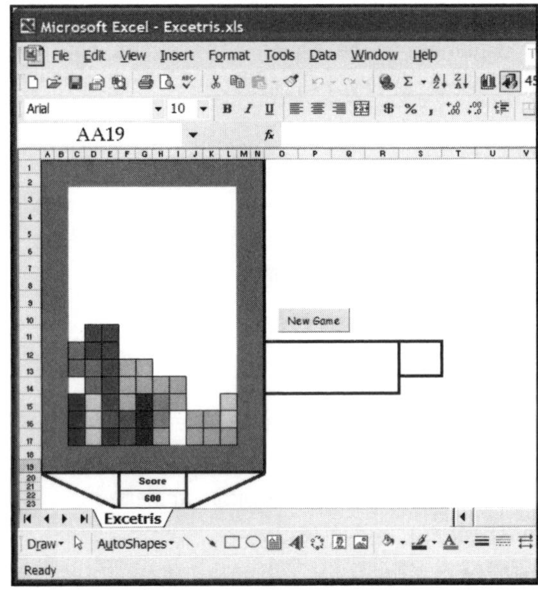

FIGURE 10.20

The *Excetris* game board after the appropriate shapes shown in Figure 10.19 have been moved down one row.

```
Private Sub ProcessBoard(rIndex As Integer)
    Dim cutRange As Range, pasteRange As Range
    Dim allSquares As Shapes
    Dim sh As Shape
    Dim shNum As Integer
    Dim shNames() As String
    Dim I As Integer

    Set cutRange = Range("C4:L" & rIndex - 1)
    Set pasteRange = Range("C5:L" & rIndex)
```

```
    '-------------------------------
    'Copy x's and shapes down one row. Re-define the altered
    'named range that results from the cut and paste.
    '-------------------------------
    cutRange.Cut Destination:=pasteRange
    ActiveWorkbook.Names("GameBoard").Delete
    ActiveWorkbook.Names.Add Name:="GameBoard", RefersTo:= _
        "=Excetris!$C$3:$L$17"

    '----------------------------------
    'Collect existing names of squares to be moved (increment row
    'index in name by 1) before temporarily renaming.
    '----------------------------------
    Set allSquares = ActiveSheet.Shapes
    For Each sh In allSquares
        If sh.name Like "Square*" Then
            shNum = Val(Right(sh.name, Len(sh.name) - 7))
        Else
            shNum = 999
        End If
        If sh.Type = msoAutoShape And shNum < rIndex Then
            ReDim Preserve shNames(I)
            shNames(I) = left(sh.name, 7) & Val(Right(sh.name, _
                        Len(sh.name) - 7)) + 1
            sh.name = "tempName" & I
            I = I + 1
        End If
    Next

    '------------------
    'Rename shapes using stored names.
    '------------------
    I = 0
    For Each sh In allSquares
        If (sh.Type = msoAutoShape) And (sh.name Like "tempName*") Then
            sh.name = shNames(I)
            I = I + 1
        End If
    Next
End Sub
```

The `BonusCall()` sub procedure is called when the player earns a bonus by filling more than one row as a result of placing a single *Excetris* shape. The procedure displays one of three smiley faces on the worksheet using the `AddPicture()` method of the `Shapes` collection object.

Images can also be represented as `Shape` objects and are part of the `Shapes` collection when they are directly added to a worksheet. The `AddPicture()` method requires a path to the image file along with a location (left, top) and size (width, height) specified in points. The VBA-defined constant `msoCTrue` is used with the `LinkToFile` and `SaveWithDocument` arguments that specify that the image is linked to the file from which it was created, and that the image will be saved with the document. After a one second delay, the image is deleted with a call to the `DeleteBonus()` sub procedure in the `ScanBoard()` procedure.

```
Private Sub BonusCall(factor As Integer)
    Dim filePath As String
    Dim wsShapes As Shapes
    Dim picLeft As Single, picTop As Single
    Const PICSIZE = 50    'Units are points

    On Error GoTo BonusError

    '-------------------------
    'Display an image when bonus points are awarded.
    '-------------------------
    filePath = ActiveWorkbook.Path & "\Images\"
    Set wsShapes = ActiveSheet.Shapes
    picLeft = Range("picLeft").left + 5
    picTop = Range("picTop").top
    Select Case factor
        Case Is = 2
            Range("Message") = "Double Bonus Points!"
            wsShapes.AddPicture(filePath & "Smile1.png", msoCTrue, msoCTrue, _
                    picLeft, picTop, PICSIZE, PICSIZE).Select
        Case Is = 3
            Range("Message") = "Triple Bonus Points!"
            wsShapes.AddPicture(filePath & "Smile2.png", msoCTrue, msoCTrue, _
                    picLeft, picTop, PICSIZE, PICSIZE).Select
        Case Is = 4
            Range("Message") = "Quadruple Bonus Points!"
            wsShapes.AddPicture(filePath & "Smile3.png", msoCTrue, msoCTrue, _
                    picLeft, picTop, PICSIZE, PICSIZE).Select
```

```
    End Select
    Selection.name = "BonusPic"
    Range("R9").Select

    Exit Sub
BonusError:
    Range("Message").Value = Err.Description

End Sub

Private Sub DeleteBonus()
    '-------------------
    'Delete the bonus image and message.
    '-------------------
    Delay (1)
    Range("Message").Value = ""
    ActiveSheet.Shapes("BonusPic").Delete
End Sub
```

The `GameOver()` sub procedure is called from `AddShape()` when a new shape has been added on top of an existing shape on the game board. The procedure serves to reset the tab and arrow keys with a call to `ResetKeys()` and outputs the string `"Game Over!"` to the worksheet before ending the program.

```
Private Sub GameOver()
    ResetKeys
    Range("O12").Value = "Game Over!"
    Range("P9").Select
    End
End Sub

Private Sub Delay(pauseTime As Single)
    Dim begin As Single

    begin = Timer
    Do While Timer < begin + pauseTime
        DoEvents
    Loop
End Sub
```

This concludes the construction of the *Excetris* program. The next step in the development of *Excetris* would be to add multiple levels of difficulty to the game. In the original version of *Tetris*, the game is made more challenging by increasing the speed of the shapes as they move down the game board. Unfortunately, the shapes cannot be moved any faster using the `OnTime()` method of the `Application` object because the program already uses its minimum time interval of one second. The shapes could be incremented down two rows instead of one, which would simulate a faster downward motion of the shapes. Other possibilities include creating additional shape types that make it harder for the player to find a fit or include an occasional "Hot" shape that automatically drops to the bottom of the game board as soon as it's added (make its color a bright red-orange!). Use your imagination and you'll think of methods for making the game more challenging and exciting to play.

Chapter Summary

Chapter 10 discussed the `Shape` object and the tools available in Excel for adding shapes to a worksheet and manipulating existing shapes. I discussed the `Shapes` collection object and some of its properties and methods used to add and manipulate `Shape` objects and demonstrated the use of the `ShapeRange` collection object for selecting and manipulating a specific set of `Shape` objects from a collection. You saw the `OLEObjects` collection object and how to add an ActiveX control to a worksheet using a VBA program.

A Final Word

Congratulations on finishing this book. You are now ready to tackle your own VBA projects in Excel. You will find that even with the relatively basic programming skills taught in this book, you will be able to create robust and helpful projects for the home and business. If you are interested in learning more about programming in VBA with Excel, I suggest looking into the .Net languages and how you can use them to create Office applications. You may also want to increase your use of the Windows API for extending the abilities of your VBA programs. Whatever you decide, the most important thing to remember is that you should have fun! Good luck and thank you.

—Duane Birnbaum

Challenges

1. Create a program in VBA that adds several lines, rectangles, ovals, and triangles to a worksheet. Use a looping code structure.
2. Create a VBA program that creates a `ShapeRange` collection object from just the ovals in the drawing layer of a worksheet. Then alter the appearance of the ovals by adding a fill color.
3. Using a `For/Each` loop in a VBA procedure, select just the rectangles created in the first challenge and align them to column C in the worksheet. Use the `Left` property of the `Range` and `Shape` objects.
4. Add several `Shape` objects to the drawing layer of an Excel worksheet, then use the `Group()` method of the `ShapeRange` collection object to group the range of shapes into a single shape. Rotate the grouped `Shape` object using its `Rotation` property.
5. Edit the *Excetris* program to include sound. Find sound files that play when an active shape moves down the game board, when the tab key is pressed in order to drop a shape, and when a filled row is removed and scored.
6. Edit the *Excetris* program to include an additional shape type, bringing the total number of shape types to six. Build the new shape type out of four rectangular shapes as was done with the other five shape types. Edit all procedures necessary for adding, setting, moving, and keeping track of the location of the new shape type.

INDEX

A

B

D

E

F

G

H

M

P

Q

R

S

T

U

V

W

X

Y

Z

License Agreement/Notice of Limited Warranty

By opening the sealed disc container in this book, you agree to the following terms and conditions. If, upon reading the following license agreement and notice of limited warranty, you cannot agree to the terms and conditions set forth, return the unused book with unopened disc to the place where you purchased it for a refund.

License:

The enclosed software is copyrighted by the copyright holder(s) indicated on the software disc. You are licensed to copy the software onto a single computer for use by a single user and to a backup disc. You may not reproduce, make copies, or distribute copies or rent or lease the software in whole or in part, except with written permission of the copyright holder(s). You may transfer the enclosed disc only together with this license, and only if you destroy all other copies of the software and the transferee agrees to the terms of the license. You may not decompile, reverse assemble, or reverse engineer the software.

Notice of Limited Warranty:

The enclosed disc is warranted by Thomson Course Technology PTR to be free of physical defects in materials and workmanship for a period of sixty (60) days from end user's purchase of the book/disc combination. During the sixty-day term of the limited warranty, Thomson Course Technology PTR will provide a replacement disc upon the return of a defective disc.

Limited Liability:

THE SOLE REMEDY FOR BREACH OF THIS LIMITED WARRANTY SHALL CONSIST ENTIRELY OF REPLACEMENT OF THE DEFECTIVE DISC. IN NO EVENT SHALL THOMSON COURSE TECHNOLOGY PTR OR THE AUTHOR BE LIABLE FOR ANY OTHER DAMAGES, INCLUDING LOSS OR CORRUPTION OF DATA, CHANGES IN THE FUNCTIONAL CHARACTERISTICS OF THE HARDWARE OR OPERATING SYSTEM, DELETERIOUS INTERACTION WITH OTHER SOFTWARE, OR ANY OTHER SPECIAL, INCIDENTAL, OR CONSEQUENTIAL DAMAGES THAT MAY ARISE, EVEN IF THOMSON COURSE TECHNOLOGY PTR AND/OR THE AUTHOR HAS PREVIOUSLY BEEN NOTIFIED THAT THE POSSIBILITY OF SUCH DAMAGES EXISTS.

Disclaimer of Warranties:

THOMSON COURSE TECHNOLOGY PTR AND THE AUTHORS SPECIFICALLY DISCLAIM ANY AND ALL OTHER WARRANTIES, EITHER EXPRESS OR IMPLIED, INCLUDING WARRANTIES OF MERCHANTABILITY, SUITABILITY TO A PARTICULAR TASK OR PURPOSE, OR FREEDOM FROM ERRORS. SOME STATES DO NOT ALLOW FOR EXCLUSION OF IMPLIED WARRANTIES OR LIMITATION OF INCIDENTAL OR CONSEQUENTIAL DAMAGES, SO THESE LIMITATIONS MIGHT NOT APPLY TO YOU.

Other:

This Agreement is governed by the laws of the State of Massachusetts without regard to choice of law principles. The United Convention of Contracts for the International Sale of Goods is specifically disclaimed. This Agreement constitutes the entire agreement between you and Thomson Course Technology PTR regarding use of the software.